Politics of the Female Body

Politics of the Female Body

POSTCOLONIAL WOMEN WRITERS OF THE THIRD WORLD

KETU H. KATRAK

Rutgers University Press
New Brunswick, New Jersey, and London

Library of Congress Cataloging-in-Publication Data

Katrak, Ketu H.
   Politics of the female body : postcolonial women writers of the Third World/
Ketu H. Katrak.
   p. cm.
   Includes bibliographical references and index.
   ISBN-13: 978-0-8135-3714-6 (hardcover : alk. paper)
   ISBN-13: 978-0-8135-3715-3 (pbk. : alk. paper)
   1. Commonwealth literature (English)—Women authors—History and criticism.
2. Women—Commonwealth countries—Intellectual life. 3. Women—Developing
countries—Intellectual life. 4. Feminism and literature—Commonwealth countries.
5. Feminism and literature—Developing countries. 6. Women and literature—
Commonwealth countries. 7. Women and literature—Developing countries.
8. Postcolonialism in literature. 9. Body, Human, in literature. 10. Women in literature.
I. Title.

   PR9080.5.K38   2006
   820.9'9287'09171241—dc22

2005011646

A British Cataloging-in-Publication record for this book is available from the British Library.

Copyright © 2006 by Ketu H. Katrak

All rights reserved
No part of this book may be reproduced or utilized in any form or by any means, electronic or mechanical, or by any information storage and retrieval system, without written permission from the publisher. Please contact Rutgers University Press, 100 Joyce Kilmer Avenue, Piscataway, NJ 08854–8099. The only exception to this prohibition is "fair use" as defined by U.S. copyright law.

Manufactured in the United States of America

For my daughter Roshni, the light (as her name translates) that renews my life everyday, and in memory of my mother whose creativity continues to inspire me.

CONTENTS

Preface ix
Acknowledgments xxvii

1 *Theorizing a Politics of the Female Body: Language and Resistance* 1

2 *Indigenous Third World Female Traditions of Resistance: A Recuperation of Herstories* 56

3 *English Education Socializing the Female Body: Cultural Alienations within the Parameters of Race, Class, and Color* 92

4 *Cultural "Traditions" Exiling the Female Body* 156

5 *Motherhood Demystified* 209

   Conclusion 244

Notes *251*
Index *279*

Preface

BODIES OF IMAGINATION IN POSTCOLONIAL CULTURES

I am Indian, very brown, born in
Malabar, I speak three languages, write in
Two, dream in one. Don't write in English, they said,
English is not your mother-tongue. Why not leave
Me alone, critics, friends. . . . The language I speak
Becomes mine.
—Kamala Das, "An Introduction,"
The Old Playhouse and Other Poems

Women with faces full of hope and life crowd on dusty benches in the auditorium of St. Joseph's College, near Calicut, Kerala. They are gathered from all over India, from villages, small towns and cities, some traveling for two nights on the train to reach this place in southern India for the Fourth National Conference of Women's Movements in India, December 1990. I have arrived by plane from my native home in Bombay (via Amherst, Massachusetts, where I lived and worked at that time), flying Air Asiatic, a fledgling new carrier recently established by an enterprising Kerala native, now wealthy in the Middle East. The airline had only two planes at that time, and the entire ground staff arrived onto the Calicut air-strip to welcome us, quite a contrast to landing on one of several runways in Los Angeles, or New York, taxi-ing, and parking at gates leading directly into jetways and plush terminals.

Here in Calicut, we step down the ladder and onto the ground. I am as much, even more, a stranger here than I am in unfamiliar cities in the United States. Here, I must negotiate taxi-fare, without really knowing how far we have to go. I show the written address to the driver, and give myself over to the possibility of a circuitous route and a high fare! Finally, we pull into the St. Joseph's College compound, and as I join the nearly two thousand women at this activist conference, I enter a unique learning experience for the next four days. Faces and dress codes tell the rural from the more sophisticated urban women, and our body language as well as the varieties of English that tumble out of our mouths mark our regional origins, and for some of us, our current multiple locations and identities. The way to the auditorium takes me through the registration area, where I immediately notice the difficult material conditions under which extremely important work is accomplished in third world regions. A woman approaches me and asks, "What language/s do you speak?" "Gujarati and Hindi," I respond. And I am immediately assigned to Gujarati-script writing on placards being prepared for the rally on the final day of the meeting when we will march through town. Language defines so much of one's sense of inclusion and exclusion.

The auditorium is buzzing with the sounds of various Indian languages (ten represented at this meeting)—a challenge in itself, in terms of communicating and sharing activist strategies of organizing. I meet women from Tamil Nadu, Karnataka, Kerala, speaking Tamil, Telugu, Malayalam, and English, women from Rajasthan and Delhi speaking Punjabi and Hindi, and others from Jamshedpur, Baroda, Bombay, and Bangalore speaking Gujarati and Kannada.

My own insider/outsider status floats in and out of my consciousness as I am swept up in the positive energy that permeates the atmosphere. As the welcoming remarks unfold, I hear passionate words in languages that I do not understand, waiting for translations that some women like the highly accomplished scholar and activist Vibhuti Patel undertake—simultaneous translations into Hindi, Gujarati, English. Some two hundred autonomous women's groups participate at this meeting—Stree Jagruti Samiti of Bangalore; Sasvika from Ajmer; Chingari, Sewa of Ahmedabad; Sabla Mahila Sangh from Delhi; and the Forum Against the Oppression of Women from Bombay, among others.[1]

The conference is organized around a number of workshops covering themes such as Women and Media, Feminism and Women's Studies Programs, National Planning and Development, Women and Politics, Women and Violence, and Women and Health. Each session revolves around richly textured personal testimony wherein women of different classes and regional backgrounds speak in their own voices and languages (later getting translated), and share certain tactics and modes of organizing that they have used in their own women's groups. There are no academic papers.[2] This conference confirms many of the premises for this book. My belief that literary and other cultural products play a significant role in issues of social change is strongly reinforced by the activist energies and the remarkable stories of courage that ordinary women display in the face of varying oppressions. Further, my focus on sexuality and the female body evolves from this conference where—paradoxically—there is no specific session on sexuality; instead sexuality is smuggled in, typically for the third world context, under the more socially acceptable categories of women's health, family planning, or violence.

As I participate in conference workshops, I note the silence around the issue of sexuality. Or, when it is mentioned, sexuality in third world societies is equated often rather narrowly with lesbianism. My own interpretation of sexuality acknowledges that it is constituted and influenced by sociocultural, educational, and political elements. All these dimensions are rooted in our colonial and postcolonial history. A politics of the female body must include the constructions and controls of female sexuality, its acceptable and censored expressions, its location socioculturally, even materially, in postcolonial regions. My project attempts to name sexuality as the arena where patriarchal control is exerted most distinctively over the female body—whether in overt domination as rape, or in a variety of controls of the female body through "traditions" of the obedient wife, self-sacrificing mother, and in discrimination against girl children in terms of malnourishment, or, as in the last twenty-five years, technological deployment of amniocentesis being used as an instrument of female feticide. All these have a direct impact on women's bodies.

It is precisely the loud silence around issues of sexuality at the conference that convinces me how important this subject is. One striking incident is extremely instructive: since there is no session titled "Women and Sexuality," a group of mostly urban middle-class, educated women decide to include it unofficially in the program under the generalized title, "Single Women." Contrary to most of our middle-class expectations, the most heart-rending stories pour out of the mouths of young women who are widows, rendered "single," and socially censured and enjoined to adhere to drab dress codes, no jewelry (a deprivation especially significant in the Indian context), strict dietary abstinence, rigid limits upon who they are able to associate with. These women are generally expected to accept a kind of living death. Remarkably, although their stories communicate pain and injustice, the women do not convey total victimization. Several of them talk about fighting back, and one woman even planned to remarry despite the danger of being ostracized by her family.[3]

Naming

This book proposes a politics of the female body in postcolonial women's texts. In the same spirit with which I acknowledge the power of naming forms of women's oppression, such as sexual harassment or marital rape, I consider it important to name this field of study postcolonial, or third world. While noting the inadequacy of both terms, I still perceive a political need to name this geographical terrain for ourselves, using a term that asserts solidarity even as it recognizes commonalities and differences.[4] Critical debates around the terminology of this field, such as in essays by Ella Shohat and Anne McLintock, and by writers such as Ama Ata Aidoo, are very useful and provocative in cautioning against the generalizing, ahistoricizing impulses behind the terms, and therefore I would like to use the terms with some amount of vigilance. Aidoo regards the terms "third world" and "postcolonial" as part of dominant societies' deliberate "misnaming" of reality.[5] "Third" to Aidoo indicates a step close to failure, and she believes that acquiescing in these terms does not make them "legitimate." Aidoo finds "many grotesqueries and absurdities in the term Third World." As Aidoo notes, the "post" in postcolonial implies that colonization is over and this is not true. It is truer that these regions are in the process of decolonizing today, whether in economic, political, or cultural arenas, even if what Neil Lazarus calls "flag independence" has been achieved, poignantly followed by "the mourning after."[6] Forms of economic dependencies and other forms of cultural imperialism are rampant in third world societies.[7] Aidoo recommends a precision in demarcating who is included in "third world," and advocates not to group disparate societies under one heading. She proposes the terms "bourgeois nations" for first world countries, and "proletarian nations" for third world ones. I use a working delineation of the postcolonial world as geopolitical regions that share a past—a colonial history of occupation and domination (and in my study, specifically British colonization)—and a present of continuing neocolonialism that necessitates active decolonizing strategies. Neither the colonial nor the postcolonial world is a given historically and geographically; these regions were deliberately named as such through histories of conquest and domination, of nations and national boundaries drawn often arbitrarily by colonizers.

To adopt Edward Said's analytic paradigm in *Orientalism*, namely that "because of Orientalism the Orient was not (and is not) a free subject of thought or action," a similar reality is perceivable, namely, given a colonial history and continuing imperialist domination (experienced in the functioning of multinational corporations, of free trade zones, of controls and devaluation of local currencies under pressure from the International Monetary Fund), the postcolonial world is not "a free subject of thought or action."[8] I recognize that there is perhaps, right now, no ex-colony that is genuinely postcolonial. Further, postcolonialisms, like feminisms, vary in terms of specific historical and geographical contexts, although all ex-colonies are involved in decolonizing, in freeing themselves from what Paul Gilroy has called "the over-developed world." Writers and other culture producers in their imaginative explorations of decolonizing strategies provide unique illuminations of a colonial history that will always be a part of our social, linguistic, and gender formations—especially for speakers and writers in English, those analyzed in this study. As Aidoo remarks, "Literature and other forms of artistic expression have an unruly way of not only reflecting but also actively spilling into reality" (152).

The recently fashionable discourses on "postcoloniality" are often problematically divorced from primary texts, and from the material realities that face writers in the third world. The actual lived reality of postcolonial economic hardships is very different from its frequent intellectualization in "western" spaces. Let me concretize this issue with an anecdote. On a recent visit to New Delhi, I was strolling along the Janpath pavement market, taking in a feast of colorful fabrics, hand-woven carpets, brass and wood items, silver jewelry, and picturesque handicrafts. Buying anything here required bargaining skills and mine emerged from the depths of years of disuse in the United States. I picked up a carved wooden bowl, and as I bargained about the price, the seller, an elderly man remarked: "Years ago, it was the British Raj, and we struggled for freedom. Now, it is George Bush's Raj, and how are we to struggle against that?" His comment shocked me out of my bargaining skills into recognizing my own insider/outsider status, as well as the unfairness and injustice that ordinary people like the street-seller have to undergo, the grinding poverty and hardships that are invisible to the economic planners making policies in air-conditioned offices in New York, Washington, Tokyo, and elsewhere. His comment also pointed to that awful powerlessness through which third world economies are held hostage to the dictates of multinational corporations, of faceless capitalism for which no one is held accountable. In India, as in other postcolonial regions, the International Monetary Fund forces devaluations of local currencies that become increasingly worthless so that basic survival is difficult.

Personal Journey to Postcolonial Feminist Theory

Before exploring the theoretical implications for a politics of the female body in postcolonial women's texts, let me note how my own background has inspired this study. I grew up in independent India of the 1950s, in urban Bombay, and in a middle-class household that typically amalgamated a traditional family structure with a western-oriented education. I grew up bilingual, speaking both my mother tongue Gujarati and English. At school, English words, English literature, history, and geography came to us from the lips of Indian teachers with our own Indian-English accents. I too had the all too familiar experiences of having to rhapsodize with my female classmates over Wordsworth's daffodils, or Keats' nightingale without ever having seen or heard either one. The curriculum, canonic and male-centered, did not speak to our experience, culture, or femininity. However, we were fortunate enough to also study Indian languages in school—Gujarati and Hindi—that did speak to our cultural fabric, though rarely if ever about our female bodies or sexuality.[9]

At home, the kaleidoscope shifted somewhat in an ongoing mediation of languages and cultures. I belong to the Zoroastrian (also called Parsi) community, which migrated from Iran to India in the fourteenth century and assimilated into Indian culture, adopting Indian social customs, dress, and the Gujarati language, while retaining religious practices. During British colonialism, Zoroastrians, always keenly involved in education, were socialized effectively in European values.[10] So I learned to play the piano though never enjoyed it. Even as I practiced scales on the piano, striking up a cacophony of sounds, I could hear in the background, wafting in from adjoining rooms and from the neighborhood bazaar, the familiar sounds of the Vividh Bharati Hindi radio programs, alive with Hindi film songs, familiar advertising jingles for Vajradanti toothpaste, or Hamam soap. The sounds became all of a piece, floating in and out of C# major tunes, Carnatic music (a south Indian classical tradition), and Hindi *bhajans* (devotional songs).

As Zoroastrians, we have had insider/outsider status in Indian society. We adapted several of the Gujarati Hindu community's customs and rituals to our own. We spoke Gujarati as our mother tongue and wore sarees in the Gujarati style. Politically, prominent Zoroastrians made a name in the nationalist struggle and were reputed as highly educated industrialists and philanthropists. So I grew up in the midst of a throbbing cosmopolitan metropolis that was formed by Anglophone colonial culture along with retaining the aromas, sensitivities, and the complex linguistic and ethnic fabric of being "Indian."

My father had lived through India's independence struggle and as a staunch Gandhian, had run a *sarvodaya* (locally made goods) store. He was enamored of Gandhian ideals, of the value of the simple life, the importance of *khadi* (hand-woven cloth) within the Indian economy. Born in 1902, he lived through the height of the anti-colonial struggle, then celebrated independence (1947), and imbibed the cultural politics of khadi so integrally and sincerely that all his life until his death at the age of eighty-nine, he wore only khadi, often to the chagrin of family members and relatives who would revel in "phoren" polyester and terylene shirts and trousers. Thinking about it now, I grew up quite in the shadow of my father's formidable personality—as a Gandhian, as a man who espoused the Victorian ideals of Tennyson and Ruskin, as well as the views of Indian nationalists like Nehru. Contemporary writers like T. S. Eliot and their unrhyming work whom I studied in college never appealed to my father who pronounced that such writing was not "poetry" including my own attempts at non-rhyming poems. I did not question his position or the almost exclusive male-authored syllabi (excepting Jane Austen and George Eliot) that we followed in our academic study of English literature. My mother's quiet creativity, her ability to run a household and to stay up with me late at night as I studied for those awful comprehensive exams all through school and college infused me with her strength.

My awareness of feminism came late in life. Growing up within a traditional household, I recall many occasions of sadness, often of rage, against my father's normative authoritarianism and my mother's mostly silent acceptance of her female role. But I did not have the language or the intellectual know-how to articulate those sexist inequalities, so I silenced my own rage. But my father was also ahead of his time in his keen commitment to higher education not only for his sons but also his daughters. So, I came to the United States to study for a Ph.D. I was away for the first time, from the structured, protective (though confining) boundaries of my family. Here was a totally different scene where male-female contact was socially accepted in ways quite different from India. I did not quite know what it meant to go on a date with a man. And I brought my own stereotypes about sexual promiscuity in the United States. Paradoxically, it was in this foreign environment that I began to study texts by third world writers and found new ways of returning "home," of creating what Salman Rushdie calls "imaginary homelands."

Along with a burgeoning personal feminist awareness, I felt inspired to delve into academic feminism in my professional work. Curiously enough, during my doctoral studies, I skirted any work on India or on women's texts. I had an unconscious need to prove myself in the educational system in the United States by staying within the academically validated area of English literature. So initially I retained my interest in twentieth century English authors. Later, in my doctoral work, I began to long for a field of study to which I could relate from my own experience rather than always studying foreign works. Through a close friend at the University of California, Los Angeles, I began to read African literature avidly and found connections with the Indian pantheon in African mythology and cosmology. My work in African literature then led me to discover cross-cultural commonalities and differences among peoples who have shared a British colonial history. I recognized the value of fluency in the English language—if I met a fellow Indian from Calcutta who spoke Bengali, I realized that English was indeed the link language for communication. Or, at conferences, when I met people from Nigeria, or from Trinidad, we connected on the basis of similar memories of a colonial education—reciting nursery rhymes by rote (though often as children we had not understood their racist meanings), having read the Enid Blyton series, and having cricket teams that regularly defeat the British!

Although there are several social science and literary studies on Indian, African, or Caribbean women as separate regional studies, there is no comparative study that connects these postcolonial regions as I attempt to do in this book.[11] Second, among existing studies, female sexuality and the body are studied from sociological and anthropological perspectives, but they are not primary arenas of concern in analyzing third world women's literary texts. My study attempts to fill significant gaps in recognizing and analyzing the female body as a site of women's oppression and resistance as represented by a variety of women writers.

There are several reasons why the arena of female sexuality is often mystified in third world societies. Sexuality is not named as such although many concerns clearly involve matters of sexual control over female bodies and fertility. Female sexuality is often represented in elevated terms in terms of glorification of motherhood, or it is demoted to objectifying the female body. My study demonstrates that in fact every aspect of female identity and struggle for autonomy is affected by the controls of female sexuality as defined by different patriarchal structures. I also situate my analysis of gender within socioeconomic, political, and cultural frameworks that support patriarchy within the home and outside. Contrary to rigid binary dichotomies of private and public definitions of womanhood, I attempt multilayered discussions of female sexuality as defined, controlled, and expressed within confining patriarchal parameters: from the moment of birth, among certain traditional Indian communities, a girl-child is regarded as unwelcome and inauspicious; as adolescents with burgeoning sexuality, young women face controls over female bodies; as adults, they live within strict definitions of wife and mother.[12] Other parameters of female sexuality come in for other kinds of prejudice, for instance, widows, single women. I analyze female roles at different ages and stages of a woman's life not simply, as is usually done, as social roles (daughter, wife, mother), but in fact as bodily-sexual roles controlled by husbands, fathers, and sons. For example, I ask how a wife's sexuality is sanctioned and restricted in certain cultures, such as the carefully codified behavior/roles defined in *The Laws of Manu*, part of Hindu scripture with its attendant patriarchal authority. The sexual dimensions of a female role such as that of a wife are mystified often into a purely social dimension because doing so suits a patriarchal authority that under the guise of protection controls and defines female sexuality.

Two broad parameters of my study include the impacts on female bodies of English education (in chapter 3), and of cultural tradition (in chapter 4). Motherhood, often the most highly valorized "tradition" in postcolonial societies, and one that excludes infertile women, or those who may elect not to have children, is discussed in chapter 5. Cultural tradition and social custom often mystify controls of the female body—an example is the horrors of dowry murders escalating in India, ironically among the upper middle classes and the wealthy. What else but the woman's body is on the line in these brutal incidents when "kitchen fires" are staged in order to cover up acts of cold-blooded murders? The woman's body is burnt often beyond recognition. The victim of dowry murder, killed by a staged "kitchen fire" is often an abused wife, hardly regarded by her murderers as a human body of flesh and blood. Indian patriarchal norms rigidly situate a wife only beside her husband, hence even if she recognizes that her life is threatened, she has hardly any options given social conditioning and censure. Women's groups attempt to provide shelters though these are hardly adequate. Parents often refuse to take in a married daughter. Only after she becomes a victim and dies, do the same parents take up a crusade against dowry (testimonies discussed in chapter 4).

Comparative Scope

In this book, my focus is on selected English-language writers from areas of Africa, India, and the Caribbean that have experienced British colonization. The primary emphasis is on contemporary literary texts written in the periods after independence.[13] The particular comparative method that I propose here is rooted not in literal and simple similarities among texts but in a shared British colonial history and the consequent postcolonial material reality out of which these texts emerge. The writers share a common British colonial culture—similarities that result from an English educational system, patriarchal norms, and post-independence decolonizing struggles within a world that continues to function under imperialist domination, resulting in re-colonizations of supposedly "post" colonial spaces. This study also recognizes crucial differences among cultural milieus, local patriarchies, uses of the English language, and varying paces of change and modernization among different areas of the colonized world. The interconnections evoked by this cross-cultural method, organized along thematic concerns rather than geographical boundaries, correspond to feminist strategies for strengthening ties among women from, say, Zimbabwe and Trinidad, as well as India. I have left out geographical areas like the Middle East and Latin America because of important cultural and linguistic variances from the English-language writers that I analyze. A focus only on English language writers is both a strength and limitation of this study. The strength lies in cohesiveness among writers who share a common language; limitations are apparent in my exclusion of writers in indigenous languages from Africa and India.[14]

Rather than attempting an exhaustive study of the large and vastly diverse geographical arena of ex-British colonies in Africa, the Caribbean, and India, I have selected writers whose work illuminates what I term a politics of the female body (discussed in chapter 1). My choice of writers has been determined as much by the availability of texts (given material conditions of cultural production in third world areas and the struggles of local publishers) as by work that is socially and politically engaged. I select cultural products that engage with or leave spaces for explorations of modes of female resistance to oppression. I draw upon texts which, for instance, name and thus validate resistance to what was not traditionally accepted in these cultures as oppressive for women; texts which enable a rethinking of the dialectic relations between culture and power (cultural forms which are sustaining and empowering for women, and others which are disempowering and fatal); and texts which challenge unequal gender relations by evoking specific kinds of feminisms, which empower writers and readers to imagine a better future for their children and their communities.

Within Gayatri Chakravorty Spivak's vast and seminal work as a postcolonial theorist, I find her remarks in the Afterword to *Imaginary Maps* very useful.[15] She cautions against "the reading and teaching (of) so-called 'Third World' literature (as) an uninstructed cultural relativism" (197). She argues for the importance of the specificity of different languages, cultures, histories. I relate one of my goals in this study to Spivak's (even though she is more skeptical than I am), namely, to reach social justice through chance encounters with exceptional people and events. With Spivak's intellectual gifts, she does render these into useful theoretical and practical tools in the struggle for social justice. I agree with Spivak's caution against "an uninstructed cultural relativism" in the broad study of third world literature. Specificity and difference are key components along with a wholeness that allows for solidarity in common struggles of decolonization and anti-imperialism whether in the form of ecological dominance that often renders thousands homeless, or the "complicity of local developers with the forces of global capital" (198). Spivak, via Mahasweta asserts the need for "a vision of inter-nationality that is not only impossible but necessary" (198). "Global devastation" has resulted from ecological failures promoted by globalization. For Spivak, "the lesson of Mahasweta, activist/journalist, and writer" presents a kind of "witnessing love and a supplementing collective struggle, the relationship between her 'literary' writing and her activism" (201). Although Spivak's further invoking of Mahasweta's example "as the silent gift of the subaltern and the thunderous imperative of the Enlightenment to 'the public use of Reason'"(201) renders silent Mahasweta's powerful activist and literary voice that Spivak has indeed so far celebrated, nonetheless, Spivak's contribution here is remarkable—in her learning from Mahasweta, in recognizing the importance of the writer/activist, and "interventionist journalist," that Mahasweta is. Spivak's always carefully crafted and particularized theorizing here benefits from somewhat broad strokes such as "learning from below," and being open to new modes of learning via indigenous knowledge, not romanticized but recognized as valuable, and to be judged by criteria different from hegemonic Eurocentric norms of reason or literacy.

The issues of female sexuality addressed in this book and the positions from which they are addressed are dictated as much by the academic state and status of colonial and postcolonial literary studies as they are by my own background and professional context, and by the directions of women's movements within postcolonial societies. Geography has re-written history for ex-colonial peoples, who, caught in the historical process of decolonization, find themselves relocating from their spaces of origin into western spaces. Location and relocation, home, exile, and displacement are part of a contemporary historical geography for ex-colonial peoples. In the twenty-first century, the postcolonial writer's and critic's geographical location is a particularly complex one. She may or may not live in her birthplace, which may be Trinidad or London. This is, as Salman Rushdie puts it, "the century of the migrant . . . there have never been so many people who ended up elsewhere than where they began, whether by choice or by necessity."[16] Locations for writers and critics are mediated by geography as well as by choices of language, audience, and constituency. I am a part of this contemporary cartography, which draws geographical boundaries not only along nationalist lines but according to criteria such as language, ethnicity, education, religion. One criterion that demarcates the postcolonial world is geography based on language. This study focuses on English-language writers because English is part of a colonial heritage, and because it links ex-colonial peoples who speak different languages.

I share the goals of "participatory research" with the kinds of activist researchers whom I encountered in India—Vibhuti Patel, Sonal Shukla, Nandita Gandhi, among others. At one of the workshop sessions, Patel asserted the importance of dialogue between researchers and activists and of listening to the needs of both sides. A researcher can undertake a project that an activist women's group *needs* rather than yet another research project on a topic that does not have much usefulness to activist groups. How can scholars and activists facilitate one another's efforts rather than living in separate camps, often using ready-made arguments that exacerbate disparities in material resources and arise from institutional privilege rather than common goals? Patel also spoke about the importance of ethics and personal integrity in sharing resources—it is hardly productive to see every researcher as suspect. Activists claim that their voices are appropriated without credit, rendered anonymous as statistical material, or marginalized in appendices; activist work is looked down upon as "data collection" that the researcher can simply take without giving anything back.[17] It is so important to foster events that enable dialogue among activists, scholars, and artists.

A more concerted sharing is called for—accessible postcolonial theorizing that illuminates, even enhances work on the ground. At the same time, researchers, rather than fetishizing "grassroots" activities, need to acknowledge that there might be alternative theories than those they encounter in libraries, and that research paradigms can be challenged and rethought. As Achola Pala remarks in an essay about development issues in African societies, researchers often arrive into the field with preconceived questions, and refuse to listen to on-the-ground concerns expressed by women.[18] For instance, the latter may be more concerned about getting clean drinking water than answering the researcher's queries about kinship patterns. In India, scholar-activists such as Vibhuti Patel have combined research with important social change issues. Patel and other research-activists were successful in challenging census data that previously reported only 14 percent of women "workers." The bias against non-wage women's work, its treatment as being totally invisible, was taken up in an intense lobbying effort, and after research documentation and activist efforts lasting several years, the Indian census-makers had to acknowledge that for rural women, for instance, collecting firewood, walking to the village well or river, and carrying water for their families constitutes work.

It is instructive to note Spivak's warning against "migrant academic's desire to museumize a culture left behind gaining thus an alibi for the profound Eurocentrism of academic migrancy" (xxiv). She remarks that "to be human is to be always and already inserted into a structure of responsibility.... The possibility of learning from below can only be earned by the slow effort at ethical responding—a two-way tread—with the compromised other as teacher." Spivak demonstrates that "Mahasweta's fiction resonates with the possibility of constructing a new type of responsibility for the cultural worker" (xxvi). Spivak is inspired by Mahasweta's work to declare that "when the subaltern 'speaks' in order to be heard and gets into the structure of responsible (responding and being responded to) resistance, he or she is or is on the way to becoming an organic intellectual" (xxvi). Although Mahasweta's work celebrates many organic intellectuals, Spivak notes that her work remains largely unknown among cultural studies and multicultural studies scholars—a good instance of how primary work from third world women is ignored in the west. Spivak looks for "postcolonial women writers cognizant of the aporias or ethico-historical dilemmas in women's decolonization" (xxvi). Mahasweta's writing and activism "reflect one another"; they are a "re-flection in the root sense." In a characteristically brilliant turn of phrase, Spivak, through Mahasweta's work points out "the difference between the literary text and the textile of activism" (xxvi). The two are related and different. "Mahasweta's fiction resonates with the possibility of constructing a new type of responsibility for the cultural worker" (xxvi).

Even as Spivak confesses to her "double-edged feeling about the type and area of effectiveness of testimonial work," she claims a different status for Mahasweta whose writing "amounts to political interventionist and informative testimonials" (xxvii). Mahasweta has the unique ability to move in between the worlds of the literary and the political via her creative voice and provides the space and inspiration for Spivak's theorizing. One key insight that Spivak gleans from Mahasweta's character "Douloti" is most useful for my work on the politics of the female body, namely, facing "a severe truth: that one of the bases in women's subalternity (and indeed in unequal gendering on other levels of society) is internalized constraints seen as responsibility . . . the very basis of gender-ethics. Here women's separation from organic intellectuality is a complicity with gendering that cannot be perceived by many as sweetness, virtue, innocence, simplicity" (xvii). Although Doulati "is not a subject of resistance," Spivak notes most usefully that "internalized gendering perceived as ethical choice is the hardest roadblock for women the world over. The recognition of male exploitation must be supplemented with this acknowledgement. And the only way to break it is by establishing an ethical singularity with the woman in question, itself a necessary supplement to a collective action to which the woman might offer resistance, passive or active" (xviii).

I take Spivak's insights into my analysis of postcolonial women writers in their representations of complicity and consent as internalized oppressions that may even be embodied as "female responsibility" as in putting up with oppressive marriages, complying to dominant spouses, even making the body available for the other's pleasure. The texts that I analyze demonstrate women resisting these internalized oppressions such as when Esi in Ama Ata Aidoo's novel, *Changes*, decides to leave her husband after her encounter with what she names as a "marital rape."[19] Although in traditional patriarchy this is hardly objectionable, Esi decides to exert her "ethical singularity" by making this unacceptable as an act perpetrated on her female body. The novel depicts Esi's other encounters with her body, becoming a "second wife," and by the end, realizing that a certain aloneness with her body is all that is possible in the patriarchal structure of the time and space that she inhabits.

Spivak's prolific and useful work in postcolonial theory has had a wide-ranging impact. Along with her path-breaking scholarship, I also rely on progressive feminist scholars like Barbara Harlow, Michele Barrett,

Hazel Carby, among others. Edward Said's seminal work in *Orientalism*, *Culture and Imperialism*, and other texts provides extremely enabling illuminations for my study even as I add gender considerations into Said's otherwise astute analyses of cultural imperialism and literary representations.

The Importance of a Postcolonial Female Literary Tradition

A postcolonial female literary tradition is in the making—dynamic, changing, growing. A study of this field is therefore quite different from studying "established" literary areas in say, English or American literature. Canon-forming tendencies are to some extent inevitable, especially because the Nobel Prize in Literature has been awarded in recent years to Nigerian Wole Soyinka (1986), South African Nadine Gordimer (1990), and to St. Lucian Derek Walcott (1992), but they need to be challenged by undertaking a serious study of women writers and culture producers. Women's participation in culture and politics enables a redefinition of both of these arenas of action.

Although this book primarily covers literary culture, I attempt to broaden the parameters of "literary criticism," to use, as Barbara Harlow suggests, theory as strategy, to make academic theorizing relevant for social change issues in third world areas. "Is there, in [third world] theorizing," asks Harlow, "a different agenda, different priorities, a different sense of urgency from those which impel theoretical developments in the West?"[20] I also attempt to use literary texts and other cultural productions as the bases for theorizing. In my selection of primary materials, I include published novels, poems, stories, essays by third world women writers, and also activist materials, pamphlets, street theater materials—forms that enable me to push against the boundaries of what is considered strictly "literary." In this mutually illuminating juxtaposition of third world women's cultural productions, I include various forms of cultural expression—written and oral, expressive, and activist.[21] Street theater, oral story-telling, song, among other oral forms used by activists, explore issues facing women on the ground. My interest in this work has a pointed political agenda—to share strategies of social change, to discuss avenues of female resistance across linguistic and cultural boundaries, to recognize the common onslaughts of multinational corporations and the varieties of cultural imperialism that seep into the daily lives of people in third world societies. As with literary expression that can speak to peoples across national boundaries, it is increasingly important to share activist strategies across different regions of the postcolonial world.[22]

The use of *natak* and *gana* (drama and song) for serious issues confronting women, such as the rising tide of communalism and religious fundamentalism, was both valorized and criticized during the opening festivities at the Fourth National Conference of Women's Movements in India that I attended. Sonal Shukla who runs a women's library called Vacha, has done important work in "Alternate Media"—the production of two cassette tapes of songs that use feminist lyrics over the music of popular *bhajan*s (religious songs), *garba* (female folk-dance form from Gujarat), even film melodies that have a popular resonance.[23] Sonal speaks about the "effectiveness" of these efforts, especially when a feminist consciousness is usually absent from commercial cinema songs. She acknowledges the problem in using film song melodies with patriarchal biases. Similarly, the religious context of bhajans takes over; the new feminist lyrics do not prevent listeners from lapsing back into the known and familiar. An audience, already conditioned, tends to sing the original words. In using alternate media, these pioneers of women's groups realistically face what they can accomplish given the enormous popularity of commercial media and their own modest material resources. They also acknowledge that when they need a melody for a written poem or song, they go to the songs that already exist since there are very few feminist composers or music directors. Nonetheless, they recognize the joy of creating feminist poems and songs that provide an outlet for women's self-expression and performance. Women as authors of such creative expression find it invigorating. Such alternate media may have limited distribution, but these productions are extremely effective when used as training material for building awareness and solidarity by women's groups. As one popular women's movement song in Hindi puts it, "*Tod, tod ke bandhano ko, dekho behne ayi hai. Naya jamana layegi*" (Look, women have arrived in great numbers. Thousands have come by breaking many shackles, and they are determined to create a new society).

Goals of Study

I have multiple aims in this study, given my comparative scope and selection of cultural products. I incorporate written, and where available, oral, expressive, and activist forms of cultural production that enable me to push the parameters of what is considered "literary." I attempt to conceptualize and create critical practices from literary texts. I regard cultural productions, and literary/theoretical analyses as active agents of social change. I wish to make a broad-based audience aware of this literature, and to enhance the development of postcolonial women's literary tradition. Overall, this study aims to discover areas of solidarity by analyzing a shared colonial history, and by probing and sharing resistance strategies in ongoing struggles of decolonization.

This study makes the literary and cultural work of various women known both within and outside their geographical regions. Often, given our neocolonial legacies, it is only after third world writers have been published in metropolitan areas that they are recognized in their home territories. One of the most striking examples from the body of literature that I study is Zimbabwean Tsitsi Dangarembga's case, which reveals the negative impacts on women's creativity of sexist double standards, and of material conditions of book production, especially fiction in third world regions. Her incredibly rich and complex first novel, *Nervous Conditions*, completed in 1984, was rejected repeatedly in her local Zimbabwe, to the point that Dangarembga's self-confidence as a writer was shaken deeply.[24] In a poignant autobiographical article in *The Women's Review of Books* she remarks, "My own experiences as a young writer illuminate grotesquely the energy-depleting toll on Zimbabwean women who grapple with their country's version of the usual sexist codes."[25] Her desire to be a writer "was a difficult proposition.... The sheer scope and complexity of the mental processes required to effect the feat of composition were still believed to be beyond the capacity of the female brain. The stuff of art—war and peace, the torment of the soul and the like—were considered the essential raw materials of men" (43).

Even as Dangarembga, "determined to ignore any obstacles," started work on her novel, she was aware of the risks: "The sentiments I was expressing were dangerous: they were untempered, conceding nothing to the tastes of the society about which I was writing.... Part of my problem getting published in my own country was certainly commercial. Fiction, no matter by whom, hasn't a wide market in Zimbabwe: textbooks do" (43). Further, her novel's portrayal of "unsafe issues" also deterred its publication. After completing the novel in 1984, Dangarembga faced rejections that she describes as "manifestations of a conspiracy of silence.... I told myself, 'I cannot write.' ... I began to get ill.... I'm not the kind of writer who writes humanely under conditions of agony" (43).

Had it not been for a friend, Julia Odaka, who loved the manuscript and insisted on sending it to The Women's Press in London, the novel might never have been published. Then of course, a stamp of approval from the heart of the m/other country ensured that Dangarembga received recognition from her own people. "*Nervous Conditions* has subsequently been published in Zimbabwe," remarks the author, "where it has proved extremely popular." One Zimbabwean reviewer gives her credit for "treading where angels fear to tread." Dangarembga ends this personal story with hope: "As I take up the sequel to *Nervous Conditions*, the smothering gags I have described are beginning to fall away, and liveliness, vivacity and resilience are once more moving in to determine my creative self" (44). Her story about the difficult conditions of artistic production for women writers in third world regions is sobering even as readers and teachers eagerly await her "sequel."[26]

The case of *Nervous Conditions*, "rescued" by The Women's Press, raises serious questions about the politics of publishing and distribution of third world writers. The struggles of local publishing houses include small attempts, such as Flora Nwapa's, to start her own publishing house, Tana Press in her native Nigeria. On the other side, publishers based in the west such as Heinemann develop "lists" that monopolize local and foreign markets, for instance, "African Writers Series," "Caribbean Writers Series," and most recently, an "Asian Writers Series."

Among local publishing, Kali for Women is a unique feminist publisher in India. Under the leadership of Urvashi Butalia and Ritu Menon, Kali has published such important texts as Kumkum Sangari and Sudesh Vaid's edited volume of essays, *Recasting Women: Essays in Colonial History*; Nandita Gandhi and Nandita Shah's text, *The Issues at Stake: Indian Women's Movement*; and Radha Kumar's *The History of Doing: Indian Women's Movement*.[27]

This study of a politics of the female body is rooted in my personal experience as a postcolonial female subject who grew up in independent India of the 1950s, and who is educated in English-medium schools as they are termed, in postcolonial India, and later in the United States. Colonization as a powerful historical reality was present in the fabric of growing up bilingual; colonization in its many metaphoric ramifications became real to me when as an adult, I developed a feminist consciousness. Colonizations of the land, of physical territories, and of colonized female bodies are part of the concerns of this study. Much of the enterprise of women writers involves imaginative explorations of deterritorializing—not simply to gain freedom from an external colonizer, but to clear a space—physical, psychological, and emotional—for female autonomy. Postcolonial women writers do not advocate a separatist female utopia without men; rather, they undertake a much more difficult struggle to forge frameworks (even if fluctuating) of equality and solidarity. They attempt to create structures of support for cultural work, and to work toward building a better future for their societies.

Acknowledgments

This book has traveled with me for many years and traversed many spaces that I have inhabited in the United States, my professional location, and in India, my home of origin. My research and writing have been facilitated by The Bunting Fellowship (Radcliffe-Harvard), and Faculty Research and Travel Grants from the University of Massachusetts, Amherst where I taught in the English department for ten years. Institutionally, this was my first "home" in finding the space to teach and write about postcolonial literature in the 1980s when the field was relatively new. In keeping with its progressive reputation, the University of Massachusetts welcomed this new field of study, somewhat taking a risk in hiring me as a junior colleague. Among my colleagues at the university who provided a stimulating and supportive environment in which I grew as a scholar, I thank Jules Chametzky, R. Radhakrishnan (now at the University of California, Irvine and who has read and commented on sections of this book), Arlyn Diamond, Lee Edwards, Margo Culley, Stephen Clingman, Sara Lennox, and Deborah Carlin, and the late Agha Shahid Ali. Arlene Avakian and Martha Ayers provided personal and intellectual support over the years. I also wish to thank my colleagues at the University of California, Irvine where I have relocated since 1996. June Kurata has been a source of strength and support. Moving from the present to the past, I thank my teacher and friend, Eunice de Souza in Bombay, India who has remained a source of inspiration to me over the years since my undergraduate student days at St. Xavier's College.

My friend, Professor Esha De of the University of California, Los Angeles, has provided invaluable feedback on my drafts, having gone way beyond the call of friendship in making time to wade through reams of paper. I owe a debt of gratitude to Esha for believing in this project. I am deeply grateful to Beheroze Shroff for her emotional support and undying faith in my abilities over the years. I am most grateful to Melanie Halkias, my editor at Rutgers who recognized the significance of this project. Her discerning editorial contribution has made this a readable and exciting book and I thank her for dealing deftly with my wordiness!

I thank the many admirable activists and scholars in India who shared their time, expertise, and resources with me. Sonal Shukla of Vacha Library in Bombay, for her intellectual guidance, for sharing her research findings, and making me aware of nineteenth-century women's texts such as *Anandi Gopal*. Librarian Sandra's assistance at Vacha was most useful. I also thank the household helper, whose smiling presence and willingness to prepare tea and coffee helped to wash down the dust from a bumpy rickshaw ride to Vacha from Vile Parle railway station in suburban Bombay. Vacha provided me a quiet space for contemplation and intellectual work that is a challenge to produce in the midst of family demands, part of a communal life style.

At SNDT Women's University, Bombay, I learnt a tremendous amount from Vibhuti Patel (who has since left this academic position), an incredible scholar-activist, extremely productive and generous. I had several productive conversations with Vibhuti about the predicament of women and the women's movement in India. I also thank other staff members at SNDT who helped in locating library materials and photocopying them, for screening documentaries on issues of dowry and *sati*. It is noteworthy that Vibhuti and I often had no research space (faculty members in universities in India often share a common staff room with not much privacy) to conduct interviews. So we used to meet in noisy little Udipi restaurants (coffee/snack shops) while I tried to record her voice over the clanging of stainless steel plates and waiters shouting out food orders to the kitchen staff.

Also, in Bombay, I thank Nandita Gandhi and other members of The Forum Against the Oppression of Women, the members of Stree Mukti Sangathana, members of Majlis, and Madhushree Dutta for sharing reviews of her work with the Women's Cultural Program, "Expression," and for enabling me to screen "Anuradha," a twelve-part TV serial dealing with the abuses of amniocentesis. I am grateful to the members of women's groups Saheli, and Jagori in Delhi for conversations about their groups' activities and the state of the women's movement in India.

My thanks to the many students in classes on postcolonial literature and theory who shared their passion in discovering the work of writers whom they were often reading for the first time, and who provided challenges to linking theory and practice. I am also grateful to librarians for their research assistance, and to very capable research assistants Lisa Estreich, Hedy Chang, and Susan English. For technical and computer assistance, I thank Doris Newton of the English Department at the University of Massachusetts, Amherst, and Stan Woo-Sam at the University of California, Irvine.

This book is for my eight-year old daughter Roshni, the light (as her name translates) that renews my life on a daily basis. I hope that my many hours at the computer will make sense to her when she is grown up enough to read this book. This book is also in memory of my mother who passed away recently in May 2004 at the age of ninety-three. Her remarkable dignity, and struggles as a woman in the early twentieth century when feminism was hardly a concept that could help her, but who always retained a fierce independence and autonomy, have infused me with her quiet strength and creativity. This book is inspired by and honors her spirit, even as it looks forward to my daughter's life and her generation's realities of multiple diasporic languages, cultures, and belongings in the twenty-first century.

Politics of the Female Body

CHAPTER 1

Theorizing a Politics of the Female Body
LANGUAGE AND RESISTANCE

I am convinced that they have other reasons for disapproving of me. They do not like my language, my English, because it is authentic and my Shona, because it is not! They think that I am a snob, that I think I am superior to them because I do not think that I am inferior to men. . . . I very much would like to belong, Tambu, but I find I do not.
—Nyasha, in Tsitsi Dangarembga, *Nervous Conditions*

This book creates a theoretical framework for a study of postcolonial women writers by giving primary attention to literary and cultural productions that participate in the process of decolonizing from indigenous and colonial patriarchy and other forms of domination. Nyasha's words in the opening epigraph from Zimbabwean Tsitsi Dangarembga's novel, *Nervous Conditions* evoke two of the most significant concerns for postcolonial women writers: the uses of English (over indigenous languages, in this case, Shona) imposed by colonialism and how linguistic choices encode cultural belonging or alienation, and second, the female body and gendered inequities in patriarchal postcolonial society. Dangarembga among other women writers discussed in this book gives readers particular "insight into" what Francoise Lionnet describes as "the mediated process of reading and decoding which is central to most of our cultural activities."[1] In line with Francoise Lionnet, I regard literature as "open(ing) us up to a more complex understanding of difference and 'marginality'. . . . The challenge is more than ever, to build bridges between the academy and the 'real world' without replicating the divisions and debilitating dogmas that can become cultural currency in both arenas" (11).

My primary argument, derived from reading literary and non-literary texts by postcolonial women writers and culture producers is that the female body is in a state of exile including self-exile and self-censorship, outsiderness, and un-belonging to itself within indigenous patriarchy (historicized within different cultures and histories) strengthened by British racialized colonial practices in the regions of India, Africa, and the Caribbean that this study covers. I include literal and metaphoric connotations of exile, as well as the concept of internal exile of the female body from patriarchy, and external exile as manifest in migration and geographical relocation necessitated by political persecution, material conditions of poverty, and forms of intellectual silencing in third world societies. Female protagonists undergo what I term "internalized exile" where the body feels disconnected from itself, as though it does not belong to it and has no agency. The complex experience of colonialism provides a significant frame within which I analyze female exile, for instance, British colonial(ist) education accompanied by racial superiority leading to linguistic and cultural alienations (explored in chapter 3); the traps of cultural tradition, both colonial and local, prejudice against lesbians who endure invisibility for fear of violence (discussed in chapter 4), and pressures of motherhood (chapter 5). Several texts demonstrate female bodily exile resulting from "forgetting" one's native language and cultural ways supplanted by English language and mores; or from breaking "tradition"; or for resisting the patriarchal authority of fathers and husbands.

The experience of internalized exile unfolds as a process that includes the female protagonists' complicated levels of consent and collusion to domination. The unfolding, indeed the process of the body being exiled, brings female protagonists to a "liminal" state of consciousness, to use Victor Turner's evocative concept. I interpret liminality as a space for the female protagonist to cope with, and at times, to transcend exile. They resist domination and attempt to reconnect with their bodies and communities. In resisting exile they often use their female bodies via speech, silence, starvation, or illness. At times, resistances fail and fatal outcomes result in murder or suicide.

Among different forms of resistances to bodily exile, it is necessary to demystify "resistance." Rather than glorify any and all resistance, I ask, resistance to what end? How does a resistant action or non-action enable a protagonist to grow, change, learn, or be destroyed? What is the complicated interplay between a female protagonist taking autonomy over her own body (for instance, refusal of marriage to fight the dowry system in India, or a widow's decision to defy social custom and to remarry), and sociocultural controls of female bodies (patriarchal strictures on female dress codes, levels of education, choices of life partners)? Bodily responses by female protagonists vary from successful verbal and physical challenges to patriarchal authority such as Lucia standing up to Babamukuru in *Nervous Conditions*, to the sadly more common self-destructive responses such as Nyasha's bulimia in the same text, or Anowa's suicide in Aidoo's drama, *Anowa,* or Bim's professional success and personal isolation in Indian Anita Desai's novel, *Clear Light of Day*.[2] Despite tragic and negative conclusions—madness, death, suicide, other forms of social exclusion and un-belonging—in women's texts, it is important to recognize the strategic use of those same female bodies, often the only available avenue for resistance. Women writers portray how their protagonists resist patriarchy or colonial oppression covertly from within the system rather than overt political resistance or imprisonment depicted more commonly by male postcolonial writers. Female covert resistances are undertaken with self- consciousness and remarkable creativity that decides to take risks and confront domination selectively and strategically in the interest of self-preservation.

My scope in this book encompasses a vast geographic area—India, parts of Africa, and the Caribbean that were colonized by Britain. I connect these distant areas by the common experience of the imposition of the English language on peoples with many other indigenous languages, and I study works originally written in English (not translations). Certainly, there are significant literatures in many Indian and African languages. However, there is a whole body of literature in the English language that demands study, especially that by women writers which is my focus. Postcolonial writers' remarkable uses of English have earned some of them the honor of the Nobel Prize. English in its many forms (Jamaican patwah, Ghanaian pidgin, Indian English) is the link language in my study of women writers from India, Jamaica, Ghana among other nations. However, I recognize significant differences of local cultures, sexual mores, and tradition. One of my goals in including this vast scope is to connect postcolonial women writers and support their common resistances against sexual inequities and domination, and to strengthen ties in their imaginative strategies for social change. I link writers like Botswanan Bessie Head (her relocated home after she left the "stench of apartheid," as she puts it, in South Africa), Indian Eunice de Souza, Ghanaian Ama Ata Aidoo, and Trinidadian Merle Hodge among others. I create critical practices that analyze their representations in fiction, drama, and poems, of the exilic conditions of the female body, resistances to exile, and resolutions in reintegrating with the body and community, or ending in death.

My comparativist and cross-cultural methodology resonates with Chandra Mohanty's, namely, to "reorient transnational feminist practice toward anticapitalist struggles," and to highlight common decolonizing efforts in postcolonial areas.[3] My critical practice is also in conversation with Francoise Lionnet's method of linking women writers from areas as distant as Guadaloupe, African Americans in the United States, and South Africa in an assertion of a kind of feminist universalizing of the representations of female domination. Lionnet describes the linking of "geographies of pain" and argues convincingly for the critical importance of this universalizing, one that is not essentialist, and that pays attention to regional differences of cultures, gender roles, and histories.

Critical Practices

Critical practices that I derive from primary literary texts are placed in dialogue with third world writers' own critical-imaginative statements in essays and interviews, as well as feminist theory on third world women (Kumari Jaywardena, Chandra Mohanty, Lucille Mathurin Mair), the work of scholar-activists (Vibhuti Patel, Nandita Gandhi), and selected activist materials in letters and essays generated from struggles on the ground by women's groups such as Saheli (India), and Sistren (Jamaica). I am particularly indebted and inspired by the work of scholar-activists who challenge strict divisions between theory and praxis, and who pay serious attention to the material realities of women's daily lives. My critical method gives primary space to writers' essays that are often dismissed as not theoretical enough. I challenge the theorizing from above, so to speak, a tendency common in postcolonial theory. I do not take an anti-theoretical stance; rather I demonstrate that as scholars, our reading and critical practices, when derived from the literary works can echo the writers' goals of a progressive future for their communities. I do not want to essentialize the "postcolonial" or "third world" woman writer but I rely on Spivak's useful phrase, "strategic essentialism" and use the broad rubrics even as I recognize their limitations.

Politics of the Female Body includes a varied canvas of literary, cultural, theoretical, and activist registers as inspired by the ways in which women's bodies are exiled, and by their resistances to indigenous and colonial domination. As Maithreyi Krishnaraj notes in an occasional publication on "Advances in Feminist Scholarship," "All feminist research is not done in academic institutions. . . . Feminists question the notion that so-called scientific knowledge is indeed objective. . . . The way a society selects, classifies, distributes, transmits and evaluates knowledge . . . reflects both the distribution of power and principles of social control. It is not just a coincidence that women have remained outside the production of knowledge. Invisibility of women is not a problem of individual cussedness of males but a structural problem built into the production of knowledge."[4]

I attempt to expand the parameters of "theory" by including a variety of decolonizing strategies deployed for social change. My stance is not opposed to theory as such; rather, it is to expand the boundaries of what is usually accepted as theory. My challenge is not so much to any particular theory or theorist, but an attempt to derive theoretical insights from literary works and from other cultural productions such as feminist work in occasional publications, pamphlets, and magazines such as *Manushi*, *The Lawyer's Collective* (both from India), or *Sistren* (Jamaica). Such creative and conceptual work is more germane and useful in theorizing third world feminism than relying solely on academic postcolonial theory.

I redefine the critic's role by returning the critical/theoretical task "to the source," to use Amilcar Cabral's phrase.[5] This "source" is as much the literary texts as it is the history and culture (colonial and postcolonial) from which the texts emerge. It is useful within a postcolonial context to think of theory itself, as Barbara Harlow suggests, as strategy, as one among several means aiming at social change; to consider integral links between theory and practice.[6] In this study, I aim 1) to challenge theoretical productions as ends in themselves wherein the literary texts themselves are often abstracted out of existence; 2) to use a language lucid enough to inspire writers and readers to struggle for social change; 3) to forge creative alliances among writers and critics working toward the common goal of a better future for postcolonial societies; and 4) to bring the critic of postcolonial literature from the periphery to an active participation in creating equitable societies. Within a postcolonial context, there are more serious challenges than in the first world between academic feminism and women's movements because often, women face literally life and death issues, such as dowry murders in India, and the resurgence of sati (widow-immolation). I attempt to lessen the gap between feminist theory and activism and to make postcolonial feminist criticism respond to and recognize the issues that women's movements in the third world deal with. I attempt to demystify the concept that semiotics can easily be identified with politics and to challenge mystified and obscure language that can deter a progressive political agenda.

Literary and Non-Literary: Written and Oral Forms

In line with my goals, I expand the boundaries of what is considered "literary" by including the "non-literary" (especially oral and expressive materials) in my study. These include activist pamphlets on personal laws that have direct bearing on women's bodies such as rape, feminist revisions of traditional songs, and magazine articles that analyze and suggest alternatives to women's domination. This inclusion enables my analyses to resonate within the material realities of many third world women. Oral forms such as educational workshops conducted by Sistren, or street theater such as *Nari Itihas Ki Khoj Mei* (Women in Search of Their History) mounted by women's activist groups in India—are more involved in struggles for social change than, say, the more easily available novels of Anita Desai. Orality expressed in testimony, song, and ritual challenge our "literary" dichotomies between art and politics, gender and class, and means of production and marketability (determined often by literary and cultural fashions). For large non-literate populations in postcolonial societies, these oral forms are important. Here, a "dialogic" and "multi-vocal" exchange, to use Mikhail Bakhtin's provocative concepts, among the literary, non-literary, and activist, the written and oral, visual and performative provide rich tools for resistance. And for colonized peoples, dialogic interaction and the inclusion of multiple viewpoints are especially enabling since they challenge colonial versions of history, and combat the denigration of native cultures and civilizations. A dialogic interplay among different genres and languages enables female protagonists to resist bodily exile.

Written forms, on the other hand, in terms of who makes it into print, and what themes are profitable are governed often by a profit-oriented publishing industry that produces third world texts for mainly western consumption. Hence, ironically enough, even literate people in postcolonial societies cannot find, or afford books by their own writers as was seen when Wole Soyinka received the Nobel Prize for Literature in 1986; his books were difficult to find in his native Nigeria.[7]

Within oral traditions, folk tales retained in memory by women provide ways of sustaining the exiled female body. In oral testimonies the body speaks, and women find voice in narrating their lives. Along with voice, women's knowledge gathering and experience are conveyed via the female body in movement, dance, and other non-verbal, visual, and aural forms. Women's oral testimony in stories, or street theater operates outside the norms of writing, and the knowledge generated through these media challenges a usual reliance on print-media and the privileging of printed fiction. These oral forms provide alternative ways of thinking even about women's position in third world societies, and about non-dominant ways of meaning-making. The first step is to put the story out there, to externalize the pain of bodily exile and marginality. Speaking orally and writing or performing the stories, as well as cultural and activist work as in street theater, are significant acts of resistance. They serve as models for other women in the larger project of social change. In a useful volume of essays entitled, *Feminist Genealogies*, editors Chandra Mohanty and Jacqui Alexander specifically link story-telling to "democratic futures."[8] Among the texts I analyze, the short stories of Botswanan Bessie Head, and Ghanaian Ama Ata Aidoo illustrate these contemporary writers' creative uses of oral traditions in their modern-day written stories. Several of Bessie Head's short stories are based on village gossip and small-talk, especially important avenues for women, and Head as a griot (one who remembers and orally relates and passes on a community's history from one generation to the next) faithfully captures the community's memories. As a writer, she recreates ordinary and unusual events of village life with considerable imagination and artistry, using local folklore, historical records, myth, and her considerable imagination and artistry. I use one of Head's short stories below to illustrate my critical method.

In this bodily journey of exile and recuperation, I analyze postcolonial women writers' representation of two significant and related factors, namely, language (English and other indigenous languages, oral, written, expressive as in performance), and location (internal migrations from village to city, and external relocation from native lands to western metropolitan areas). The English language was imposed upon peoples with other languages in the colonized world; hence, in the postcolonial era, the "empire writes back" in a variety of English-es. As Nyasha notes in the epigraph to this chapter: "They do not like my English."

In terms of location, women exiled from their body are looking for a space to re-belong to their bodies. And the communities in which they are placed, or to which they relocate provide sustaining or un-nurturing environments for the bodies to inhabit. A search for home and belonging involves the politics of location. My own location, as a native of India who teaches postcolonial, Asian American, and diasporic literatures in the

United States reveals some aspects of loss and gain embedded within a colonial history and geography. *What* one can say *where* requires mechanisms of self-censorship, often dictated by self-preservation. When I did my B.A. and M.A. in India, we followed a tradition-bound syllabus of English literature (even American writers were considered too recent). It was not until I came to the United States to work on a doctorate that I explored writers from third world areas whose cultures and experiences were closer to mine than those of the English male canonic tradition. Now, nearly thirty years after I was a student in Bombay, there have been curricular changes. However, I would not have the freedom (I use it un-ironically here) that I do here, to design a course, to select and even pair texts subversively. My geographic location has serious repercussions in terms of my intellectual production, my uses of particular languages, theories, and the addressing of certain audiences. Echoing Mohanty, I also "write from my own particular political, historical, and intellectual location, as a third world feminist trained in the United States, interested in questions of culture, knowledge production, and activism in an international context."[9] This situation is not only a trajectory of colonial and postcolonial history and educational systems, but equally significantly of "human geographies" to use Edward Soja's phrase.[10]

What is a Politics of the Female Body?

A politics of the female body includes the constructions and controls of female sexuality, its acceptable and censored expressions, its location socioculturally, even materially, in postcolonial regions. Third world women writers represent the complex ways in which women's bodies are colonized. Similar to anti-colonial struggles for independence on the macro political arena, women resist bodily oppressions by using strategies and tactics that are often part of women's ways of knowing and acting. A geographical deterritorializing that forces colonizers to depart parallels how women attempt reclaiming their bodies from patriarchal domination. "Flag independences" and neocolonialisms continue in arenas of education, and government by the Fanonian "black skin white masks" class of natives. Continuing decolonizations include the reality of decolonizing female bodies occupied by colonial education and local tradition that perpetuate women's subordinate status while ensuring male privilege. The narrator Tambu in *Nervous Conditions* arrives at this epiphany after a harrowing incident when her uncle, the family patriarch Babamukuru, unfairly calls his daughter Nyasha a whore, "making her a victim of her femaleness." Tambu reflects: "The victimization, I saw, was universal. It didn't depend on poverty, on lack of education or on tradition. It didn't depend on any of the things I had thought it depended on. Men took it everywhere with them. Even heroes like Babamukuru did it . . . what I didn't like was the way all the conflicts came back to this question of femaleness. Femaleness as opposed and inferior to maleness" (115–116). Tambu and Nyasha, as adolescents undergoing an English education struggle against varieties of sexism and colonialism (the novel is set in 1960s colonial Rhodesia) that are different from what their mothers' generation had faced.

Both sexist inequities and other cultural differences are at play in dominating and exiling women, indeed in rendering Nyasha a foreigner in her own culture. Out of this state, she may bring new insights into her community. I find Mikhail Bakhtin's comments on how human beings understand other cultures to be provocative in my analysis. Bakhtin's distinctive use of the "body," as "material bearer of meaning" in terms of "bodies of meaning," and "outsidedness" are analyzed usefully in *Speech Genres and Other Late Essays*.[11] Bakhtin remarks, "In order to understand, it is immensely important for the person who understands to be located outside the object of his or her creative understanding—in time, in space, in culture" (Introduction, xiii). Nyasha, when named "a whore" is rendered an outsider to her culture; she is not behaving as a "proper daughter." Although Nyasha's exilic state leads to bulimia and near-death, she serves as a warning model to her cousin Tambu and gives her the tools to fight domination and survive.

A politics of the body involves *socialization* involving layers and levels of ideological influences, sociocultural and religious, that impose knowledge or ignorance of female bodies and construct woman as gendered subject or object. Women writers present the struggles of protagonists to resist patriarchal objectification and definition as daughter, wife, mother, grandmother, mother-in-law. Sociocultural parameters of womanhood—wifehood, mothers of sons valued more than mothers of daughters, infertility, widowhood—are grounded within economic, political, and cultural norms that consciously and unconsciously constitute an ideological framework that controls women's bodies.

For female subjects, experiences of colonial domination are gender-specific and rooted in the control of female sexuality throughout a woman's life. In most postcolonial cultures, a traditional, pre-colonial patriarchy is reinforced by colonial Victorian morality. Socialization patterns combine to have a hold on women even after education, migration, re-location out of the original family and coded structures of morality and behavior. There are documented cases in India of educated women's inability to step out of dangerous marriages where dowry demands lead to women's murders. Even when women see imminent deaths, they do not leave. In Indian society, there is a grave dearth of options for a woman who leaves her husband's home; however, apart from such objective factors are the psychological and subconscious holds of female conditioning through mythological stories and cultural norms that define a woman as not only belonging to her husband but as not having an autonomous self that can make a life outside of a marital sphere. The consequences for stepping outside the boundaries established by the cultural code of *pativrata* (literally translated: husband as god), can be severe as in the woman's ostracization in overt and subtle ways. Often, her parents, her only refuge, encourage a married daughter to put up with physical and emotional abuse, until sadly, she might pay the ultimate price of her life. In the text, *In Search of Answers: Indian Women's Voices from Manushi*, several heart-rending cases are recorded. In "A Mother's Crusade," Neena Vyas records the case of Satyarani Chadha who had the misfortune of seeing "the gruesome sight of her 24-year old daughter Sashi Bala, big with child, lying burnt out like a pile of garbage . . . there were no eyes, no mouth . . . one could not tell whether the body was that of a man or a woman; it was just a twisted black bundle lying in a corner."[12] Satyarani takes up the struggle with police who were not too concerned since this case "was just another among a string of similar suicide-murders. . . . It suits them to register a suicide as then no follow-up is needed." In relating this case, Vyas questions whether this mother will now refuse dowry for her younger daughter. But Satyarani hesitates; she cannot step out of her own tenacious social conditioning: "It is accepted that man and woman are unequal and that something must be thrown in with a bride to make up the difference." In spite of woman's productive and reproductive labor, she is considered less worthy than a man and hence a dowry is needed "to make up the difference."

A politics of the body involves a study of acceptable versus censored expressions of sexuality such as motherhood, only within heterosexual marriage, at one end as validated, glorified, romanticized; other manifestations that pertain to female sexuality are disrespected or pitied such as childless women who may be single by choice, or infertile women, or widows. Women who remain single or childless by choice have marginal networks of support. Lesbian partnership and love are often mystified as sisterhood for fear of violence. Although lesbianism is often dismissed as part of westernization, there are recent studies that trace the indigenous historical roots of this same-sex love. The condition of widows in traditional Indian societies enforces cruel sexual and social abstinence that in fact mask economic reasons sanctioned by religion. Widows, reduced to the level of domestic slaves, must remain in the deceased husband's household and not remarry. Widows do resist these unfair strictures and at times remarry in defiance of tradition. In certain African cultures where the woman as reproductive unit is paramount, a widow is sometimes remarried (with or without her choice) to the deceased husband's brother so that she may continue to reproduce and augment the family's property in the form of children. A politics of the female body involves the demystification of these several roles that reinforce control over women's bodies.

In traditional societies, mystifications of sexuality work at times to women's advantage and at others to their detriment—for instance, when sexuality is mystified as spirituality and religion and ritual provide rationales for women's domination. Or, when motherhood is mystified as the only desirable state for a woman to arrive at, even if that occurs without discussion of desire, or knowledge about the facts of reproduction. The latter are left for infertile and childless women. Sexuality is also mystified in other arenas of "cultural tradition," for instance, the Indian tradition of *kanyadan*, that is, a virgin daughter (*kanya*) is given as a gift (*dan*) along with a dowry to a husband. This "gift" must fulfill its reproductive purpose or face prejudice for being infertile. Rarely is the husband made accountable for impotency or infertility. When Anowa in Aidoo's play finally realizes that her husband is sterile she is still made to carry the full burden of being childless. But once the husband's reality is known socially he is humiliated enough to take his own life, and Anowa drowns herself.

Key controls of female sexuality are located in the arena of "cultural tradition" particularly when women are expected to be the "guardians of tradition" in anti-colonial struggles. Further, "traditions" most oppressive to women are located within the arena of female sexuality—not only the glaringly violent ones such as sati, but other more normative forms of objectification in customs like dowry, multiple childbearing, as well as in fulfilling traditionally expected roles as daughter, wife, mother. This analysis of how women are colonized within their very bodies, and of how they try to transmute the controls of their female bodily spaces from patriarchal hands into their own hands, offers significant knowledge to work toward broader changes in society.

Female resistance to oppression and the uses of female agency are important in this study of a politics of the female body. Esha De and Sonita Sarkar's edited volume of essays entitled *Trans-Status Subjects*, particularly their Introduction presents a nuanced discussion of resistance and agency through their discussion of the interplay between space and place and how issues of gendered mobility within and across national boundaries mark new ways of "marking time and territories."[13] Movement across historical time (as in memories of the past in the present relocations) and across geographic boundaries are common in our globalized world. However, the particular gender implications and the negotiations of female agency in both "traditional" and diasporic spaces is illuminated by many essays in the volume including mine dealing with "alien-homes" De and Sarkar bring new insights on interpretations of mobility, so when women are regarded as "static" in one space, it is significant to acknowledge "their active adaptations to new circumstances." They also argue convincingly that "resistance and social change arise only from an entanglement with regimes of dominant knowledge/power, not outside them" (2). Often women are regarded as "fixed" in a temporal trajectory as they are required to perform traditionalist values more than men are. But De and Sarkar demystify an often glib valorization of spatial mobility as part of the modern and progressive. They pay attention to the small acts of subversion and resistance that women undertake from within circumscribed spatial boundaries. They also challenge the notion that only mobility across and outside traditional nation-states spells progress. They recognize that "we are unequally mobile on the routes to knowledge and capital—between 'backward' Asian peripheries and centers in the 'West'—but we all appear to mark time (synchronize) with masculinist notions of socioeconomic progress" (3). They explore how women and men strategize from within the structures "created by globalization" to challenge "dominant histories but also re-author them."

De and Sarkar's distinction between "place" as indicating "the dimensions of lived experience and 'space' as grounds that are emptied" is extremely enabling in theorizing colonial occupations of supposedly "empty spaces," and in recuperating concrete "places" where peoples, cultures, languages, artistic expressions unfold dynamically. Their analysis is usefully complicated as they include gender, and class, into this paradigm. They demonstrate how history and geography become intertwined especially in the "spatial image of the woman at home assaulted, or nurtured, by urban-industrial modernism. A feminist geography is imprinted by a masculinist history" (7). They come up with their "trans-status" phrase to describe "individuals ... caught in transition from one (economic, social, political) status to another, at the same time as they try to redefine their places-turned into-spaces." In highly original theorizing, they demonstrate how "subjects recast their status by assembling familiar and new practices to survive attempted erasures of known, geo-histories into space, and reassert place."

Different geographic regions are regarded as "relational and contextual" with "links inside and across these geopolitical spaces." And if regions seem to relate in terms of cultural practices that oppose the west, there are also other forms of "convergences and divergences (that) subjects enact, modify, and resist 'ideas' of their nations." Also, intraregional flows within globalization control discourses of economic "development" even as spaces are "feminized and sexualized" in the interest of capital accumulation. Even as there is an overt narrative of "progress" in the movements from rural to urban economies, for instance, there is equally the state's arm of disciplining and regularizing lives such as in immigration/citizenship policies. The state not only maintains national borders, but as De and Sarkar indicate, the state controls a host of lived experiences and mobility such as migrancy of domestic labor, mail-order brides, and formal quotas in education and employment for minoritized populations such as the tribals in India.

De and Sarkar create a word, "placetime" to bring together history and geography and to demonstrate how "trans-status subjects re-member how individuals and groups survive in and resist imposed definitions of place. . . . Placetimes also extends Soja's observation about the radical potential of geography in that it defines the production of new histories from these geographies" (21). They argue forcefully against the postmodern tendency to "evade the question of history in the production of spaces," but rather emphasize how important it is for the subaltern classes to deploy the past to remake the present and the future in working toward social change.

Reconfigurations of space and place, of mobility (not always evoking modernization), of resistance have received theoretical attention in third world women's studies. My study contributes to literary and cultural studies work on third world women. However, my analysis of female sexuality through the lens of the female body as exiled within patriarchy brings significant new insights into this field.[14] I explore why the arena of sexuality is mystified and not named as such within third world contexts, even by women's groups who are involved in issues that have a direct impact on women's bodies, such as rape, and other forms of violence. There are many barriers to articulating this knowledge and obstacles to information different from discussions of sexuality within Euro-American feminist discourse. Further, is it always and necessarily liberating to articulate this knowledge, or are there strategic and positive uses of the silences around sexuality in third world contexts?

Most third world cultures, rather than naming sexuality as such, displace this category onto a variety of other forms of control over women's bodies. Traditions such as dowry, polygamy, that in fact control the uses of the female body are mystified as social custom with the weight of ancient, at times, scriptural authority. And social custom is regarded as distinct from anything to do with sexuality although that is often its major arena of control in terms of regulating marriage arrangements, childbearing, socialization of daughters and sons. To borrow from Eve Sedgwick's provocative text, *Between Men*, the uses of "traditions" to mystify controls of the body are precisely examples of " 'sexualizing' social or political relationships."[15] " 'What difference does the inclusion of sex make,' " she asks, "to a social or political relationship" (6)? I would take Sedgwick further and add the categories of spirituality and religion as explanatory indices for controls of female bodies. Often, what is "sexual" is presented as "religious ecstasy," the longing for union between the physical and the divine, where the body is sublimated into the godly, where sexual abstinence, fasting and starving the body become acts that will lead to that union. A demystification of sexuality mystified as spirituality is an important element in my study of a politics of the body.

In cultures where any talk about female sexuality is repressed and silenced, we need to look more carefully for the relations between "sexual desire" and "political power." I would again add to Sedgwick's delineation of "power asymmetries, such as those of class and race, as well as gender," access to education in the former colonies. Within the category of "race," I would include the highly complicated mediation of race with caste (Brahmins in India), and race with color hierarchies (the privileges accorded to the light-skinned middle class in the Caribbean). "Only the model of representation," as Sedgwick puts it, "will let us do justice to the (broad but not infinite or random) range of ways in which sexuality functions as a signifier for power relations. The importance of the rhetorical model in this case is not to make the problems of sexuality or of violence or oppression sound less immediate and urgent; it is to help us analyze and use the really very disparate intuitions of political immediacy that come to us from the sexual realm" (7). My approach, historical and material, shares Sedgwick's focus on "the ways in which the shapes of sexuality, and what counts as sexuality, both depend on and affect historical power relationships. A corollary is that in a society where men and women differ in their access to power, there will be important gender differences, as well, in the structure and constitution of sexuality" (2).

Sedgwick's recent text, *Touching, Feeling: Affect, Pedagogy, Performativity* deals with sexuality along with the feelings of shame and mourning.[16] Sedgwick, with characteristic brilliance, critiques dualistic theories though she admits that it is much harder to put this theory into practice. She notes that often what is most useful in such non-dualistic work "occurs near the boundary of what a writer can't figure out how to say readily . . . that confounds agency with passivity" (2). This evocative phrase, namely, that agency can be figured as passive rather than its usual active stance, is very useful in my analysis of women writers who have to resist gender oppressions in traditional societies by highly creative uses of agency, sometimes even by exerting a passive agency, as in using illness in order to resist an oppressive situation, or slave women using breastfeeding for prolonged periods in order to avoid inhuman demands on their labor.

The dialectic interconnections between the sexual and political are vivified in the ideological baggage that British colonizers imposed, for instance, a gendered English education that conflicted with indigenous cultural norms, resulting in forms of cultural alienations for female subjects. Further, colonial educational policies collude effectively with indigenous patriarchal norms to control female sexuality. Education as an important aspect of socialization is mediated, complicated and complex, often paradoxically empowering and disempowering for women. Women's texts explore female resistances to a contradictory empowerment through education whereby protagonists face ostracization from family, community, and at times, from their own bodies. Education does not lead necessarily to women's personal liberation.

An analysis of education as a key arsenal in colonial weaponry recognizes both the macro level of how power is exercised through institutions, as well as its multifarious impacts in female personal lives and bodies. A feminist politics of the body both as it is controlled and as it resists such powerful repositories of power such as an educational system pays attention to both the individual female situation as well as locating that power within other power relations (language, class, color, education) within society. Such theorizing of the body politics is located within the larger body politic which, after all, sustains systems of power.

Third world writers' statements in essays and interviews provide significant materials on issues of language, culture, and feminism. In postcolonial studies, it is common to include essays by established male writers like Chinua Achebe, Wole Soyinka, and Ngugi wa Thiong'o. Collections such as Achebe's *Hopes and Impediments*, Soyinka's *Art, Dialogue and Outrage: Essays on Literature and Culture*, Ngugi's *Decolonizing the Mind: The Politics of Language in African Literature* are extremely important in the field.[17] However, one needs to pay more attention than is given commonly to the voices of women like Ama Ata Aidoo, Bessie Head, Olive Senior, Erna Brodber among others. The critical/activist work appearing in local publications, often unavailable in the west, needs to be read here or else postcolonial theory fall into similar racist traps as the colonizers who assumed that when something is unavailable in the form that they are familiar with such as written versus oral texts, such materials did not exist. A few such local and activist publications that need to be included in discussions of postcolonial theory are Jamaican Erna Brodber's *Yards in the City of Kingston*, the Indian SNDT Women's University and its faculty's occasional mimeographed essays, local publications by activist women's groups such as Saheli and The Forum Against the Oppression of Women.[18] The unavailability of such materials, given the unequal material resources among first and third world regions and publishing constraints that do not foster the distribution of local publications are issues for serious discussion by postcolonial theorists.

It is regrettable when any discussion of women's issues is dismissed as "feminism equals westernism equals not relevant for third world women." Even as feminism in western locales must contend with attacks to its perceived power, it has a vocabulary and a system of ideas to contend with that.[19] This academic engagement is more recent in postcolonial societies, not to imply that indigenous women whom we would describe as feminists are also a recent phenomenon. Naming is important, whether one defines feminism for African, or Indian, or Caribbean women. Without a name, it is that much more difficult to contend with attacks and as the following discussion reveals, when the "feminist flag" is raised, it can be shot down since feminism is regarded as "western" and irrelevant for third world contexts. The need then is highly significant for postcolonial women writers to define feminism for their own purposes, and to identify issues that demonstrate how relevant feminism is for their societies.

At a symposium of African writers, male writers like Taban Lo Liyong spoke about feminism as a declared war by African women against African men: "I think I should appeal to us to keep the African household intact at the end of the day otherwise we may have our younger sisters going off and joining in dances in Lapland which concern the people of Lapland only."[20] To this remark, Aidoo makes an impassioned response:

> Please don't let us oversentimentalize anything. Anytime it is suggested that somehow one is important we hear that feminism is something that has been imported into Africa to ruin nice relationships between African women and African men. To try to remind ourselves and our brothers and lovers and husbands and colleagues that we also exist should not be taken as something foreign, as something bad. African women struggling both on behalf of themselves and on behalf of the wider community is very much part of our heritage. It is not new and I really refuse to be told I am learning feminism from abroad, from Lapland. Africa has produced a much more concrete tradition of strong women fighters than most other societies, So, when we say that, we are refusing to be overlooked. We are only acting today as daughters and grand-daughters of women who always refused to keep quiet. We haven't learnt this from anybody abroad. (183)

Other women writers, Lauretta Ngcobo and Buchi Emecheta, present at this meeting supported Aidoo. Ngcobo notes that "the movement in the West enlivens our own consciousness" at the same time that certain re-definitions are crucial for African women. She notes that by and large, the feminist movement in the west has "restrict(ed) itself to a certain class," and often, has excluded working-class women, and in certain cases, men. Miriam Tlali remarked that "there is a definite fear of feminism in the African man, especially in South Africa. . . . Anytime you ask him to do something, to go and fetch the child today, or something like that he says, 'Look, you are already a feminist. You are a white woman and a feminist.' It is thrown into your face in the same way in which Communist is thrown into the face of the blacks in South Africa" (185).

Buchi Emecheta in an essay, "Feminism with a small 'f'!" outlines what is important to her, as someone who since 1972 has written sixteen novels:

> Being a woman, and Africa born, I see things through an African woman's eyes. I chronicle the little happenings in the lives of the

African women I know. I did not know that by doing so I was going to be called a feminist. But if I am now a feminist then I am an African feminist with a small f. In my books I write about families because I still believe in families. I write about women who try very hard to hold their family together until it becomes absolutely impossible. I have no sympathy for a woman who deserts her children, neither do I have sympathy for a woman who insists on staying in a marriage with a brute of a man, simply to be respectable. I want very much to further the education of women in Africa. . . . It is true that if one educates a woman, one educates a community, whereas if one educates a man, one educates a man. I do occasionally write about wars and the nuclear holocaust but again in such books I turn to write about the life and experiences of women living under such conditions."[21]

It is commonly accepted that feminisms are historically, culturally, and geographically specific. This does not eliminate hegemonic tendencies in certain schools of feminism that continue to be universalist, perhaps not overtly, but subtly, and hence more dangerously, and even with the challenges of black and third world feminist theorists.

Criticism participates in the construction and development of a literary field of study. In her essay, "To Be an African Woman—an Overview and a Detail," Aidoo makes a plea for African women writers to be taken seriously by critics, publishers, and editors. She acknowledges that although males and females had to "suffer the varied wickednesses of colonialism, apartheid, neo-colonialism and global imperialists and fascism," she identifies a particular issue facing the female cultural worker: "It is especially pathetic to keep on writing without having any consistent, active, critical intelligence that is interested in you as an artist" (158). African male writers have received this attention. Aidoo cites incidents at scholarly meetings where it was assumed as "natural" to marginalize or render women writers invisible. "Why should it be 'natural' to forget that some African women had been writing and publishing for as long as some African men writers?" she asks, naming Efua Sutherland, Bessie Head, Flora Nwapa, and herself. As Lloyd Brown notes in his *Women Writers in Black Africa*, it has become almost a tradition to ignore women writers "in the repetitive anthologies and predictably male-oriented studies in the field."[22] Aidoo notes that even as late as 1985, Emmanuel Ngara's *Art and Ideology in the African Novel*, neglects to note a single woman writer "even in passing because he did not think anything African women are writing is of any relevance to the ideological debate" (162).[23] According to Aidoo, this lack of critical attention is "tragic," especially since it is "one factor that has definitely damaged the career of so many women writers." Aidoo does not wish to compete with male writers, or to debate whether what women write "in the face of the greatest odds (is) literature." She cites Virginia Woolf: "what so many women write explains much and tells much and that is certain" (163).

When women writers do receive critical attention, it is often on the level of "insults and naked slander" remarks Aidoo, "veiled ridicule and resentment . . . or condescension." She cites Oladele Taiwo's text, *Female Novelists of Modern Africa* as an example.[24] Taiwo asserts sexist value judgments regarding women's roles, and goes the full range from "self-righteousness" to "insensitivity" in his readings of women's texts. Here are some samples of Taiwo's "critical" comments: "A happy and stable family life is essential for the child's ultimate success. . . . It is only then that the mother can claim she has successfully carried out the more important obligation of parenthood which is the proper upbringing of children. . . . It may be the intention of the author [referring to Aidoo] to prove that women can do without men in their private relationship. . . . But it is an error to think that they can live a full life without men. If such a situation is tenable in Europe, it has no chance of succeeding in Africa" (166–167). Aidoo argues that women writers are not "looking for approbation. What we have a right to expect though, is that critics try harder to give our work some of their best in time and attention, as well as the full weight of their intelligence, just like they do for the work of our male counterparts" (168). Aidoo herself has been "the victim of a rather vicious and consistent campaign of defamation which (she has) never known how to handle." She has been accused wrongly of borrowing the phrase "no sweetness here" from the male Ghanaian writer Ayi Kwei Armah. In fact, Aidoo's short story, "No Sweetness Here" was published first in 1962, before Ayi Kwei Armah's novel, *The Beautyful Ones Are Not Yet Born*, published in 1968. He uses the phrase "no sweetness here" and as a male writer he gets the credit for Aidoo's phrase that she is then accused of plagiarizing from him!

Aidoo's plea for serious critical attention is particularly poignant given the neocolonial intellectual forces that women writers confront when not recognized within their own environment, they sometimes get validated from outside, from metropolitan European spaces in order then to be acknowledged by their own critics. Tsitsi Dangarembga gives a heart-rending account of the rejections she endured within Zimbabwe for *Nervous Conditions* that is now hailed as one of the most important novels in contemporary literature.[25] My study takes Aidoo's plea seriously, namely, to devote serious critical attention to women writers.

Critical Practice Derived from Literary Text

I illustrate my critical practice of theorizing from within the literary text by using Bessie Head's title story in her collection, *The Collector of Treasures*.[26] I draw upon multiple materials—autobiographical and biographical, scholarly analysis, colonial history, feminist theory, and Head's use of orality as a literary historian. The female body, both internally and externally exiled, is perhaps best represented among the writers whom I study by South African/Botswanan Bessie Head. Head left apartheid South Africa on an exit-permit (which meant that she could never return) and lived in self-exile in Botswana until her premature death at age forty-eight. In her life and work one discovers, most powerfully, various conditions of internal exile—as woman, colored, non-native of Botswana, not speaking the local language. At a time when most South African writers migrated out of the continent, Head stayed in a sort of geographical margin of South Africa. She chose this "drought-stricken, semi-desert land" to be her "home," a place "where a bit of ancient Africa was left almost intact to dream along in its own way."[27] Head's own personal struggles to create a home, to make "new worlds out of nothing" inspired all her texts.

This search for belonging also led her to undertake, as griot, a history of Botswana in her book, *A Bewitched Crossroad*.[28] In her own painful search for home and a country to call home, she found sympathetic echoes in the migratory history of the Bamangwato people. Head contests the marginal, or unrecorded, or mis-represented histories of colonized peoples by becoming a modern-day griot herself, a scribe, a historian who undertakes oral history projects, conducts interviews, and rewrites a history of African peoples. The historian's eye is visible in all of Head's creative work, "a mingling," as Craig MacKenzie puts it, "of journalistic reportage and narrative commentary."[29] Head's *The Collector of Treasures* is based on community gossip, tales she has heard; eight of the thirteen stories "have close links with interviews." In an interview with the BBC, Head remarks, "We had in operation a kind of village newspaper."

Head believed that a story-teller, in the act of telling stories and suggesting alternative visions particular to the violence that women face, has the potential "to shape the future." As in the Jamaican Sistren's text, *Lionheart Gal*, where modern-day oral testimony was the base for written stories that could simultaneously reach back into the empowering potential of the tale-telling tradition and de-code suppressed knowledge locked into working-class women's bodies and minds, in her role as modern-day griot, Bessie Head takes what George Lamming terms "a backward glance," and reveals strengths within suppressed histories.[30]

In *Serowe: Village of the Rain Wind*, Head captures what she terms a "precarious orality." Here, Head experiments with oral history—she selects stories that illustrate the issues she deals with, like self-help, education, social reform. She lets her subjects tell their stories without apparent authorial intervention, although such "intervention" is throughout embodied in the very selection of the tales and of the tellers. Her motivation is also to give something concrete and useful back, in terms of a written record, "the Botswana of [her] own making" to the community of Serowe that has taken her in as an exile. Head's creative use of this geographic space flows into the imaginative locale that she builds in her own "decisively female way"—in the epilogue to *Serowe*, she acknowledges the need for her as an intellectual, as a woman to be in touch with "the friendly motherliness" of "the very old women of the village who know so well how to plough with a hoe ... [and their] insistent greetings as they pass [her] fence with loads of firewood or water buckets on their heads" (179).

Head's remarks, in the same autobiographical piece, on her own location are resonant for this discussion of resisting internal and external exile and creating home within the female body. "I like a repetition of everyday events—the weather, the sunrise, or going to the same spot everyday, depending on whether that spot is hallowed ground. I am most unhappy in unholy places. So, while knowing my ideal and the simplicity of my own needs, I have continually lived with a shattering sense of anxiety—that human beings are unfortunately set down in unholy places, and Southern Africa may be the unholiest place on earth" (72). In her relocation, Head chose an extremely simple life, almost spartan in its hardships, but a place where she could live her own truth in the best sense of the word "simple." Head's life as a refugee in Botswana was harsh. After Botswana became independent in 1966, it "turned out to have an extremely hostile policy toward South African refugees. In 1966 they put us on a police roll, and from then to this day [1975] I have been reporting to the police every week. . . . Nothing can take away the fact that I have never had a country; not in South Africa or in Botswana where I now live as a stateless person" (73). Head did receive Botswanan citizenship in 1975 and ironically, is posthumously valorized as a national writer whose papers are in Botswana's national archives.

In her personal life and her work, Head was able to reconfigure both literal and metaphoric forms of exile into enabling materials for her creative productions. Head's work also provides a transformative feminist politics that is grounded in the material realities of survival. Her texts show how issues of exteriority (material survival) and interiority (psychological feelings, subalterity as psychological and political) are rooted in systems of political domination and silencing of female subjectivities. Head subtly makes us aware of a feminist politics that recognizes the personal need of negotiation and belonging within communities and within human hearts that must somehow struggle to make good win over evil.

Head's work also enables a *re-conceptualization of politics* in women's stories—a politics that is integrally personal, and often not named or acknowledged as political. This feminist exploration is very different from obvious political issues such as neocolonial leaderships or the role of the intellectual in liberation struggles, themes explored commonly by postcolonial male writers like Chinua Achebe, George Lamming, and Wole Soyinka. Postcolonial women writers redefine what is politically relevant for their female protagonists. Their work allows a reconstruction of what colonialism meant for women versus men—sexual politics and colonization of female bodies. In their literary representations, race does not subsume gender as is found often in the work of anti-colonial male thinkers. For instance, in Head's story, "The Collector of Treasures," the female characters themselves claim that "politics" belongs to the male realm, and is outside their female lives. But the struggle over school fees, Dikeledi's material struggles as a mother of three children abandoned by their father, her painstaking efforts to raise their school fees are deeply and integrally political. Dikeledi struggles with these political issues even as she is marginalized from a publicly political involvement, and even as she states her own erasure from any part in issues of social change. With the help of women writers like Head, readers can rewrite women like Dikeledi into that historical narrative.

Head represents Dikeledi's internal exile within patriarchy, growing up from a young age as an orphan, married off to an irresponsible man, Garesego, who after fathering three sons abandons her, and when he returns demanding sex, she kills him. This remarkably creative woman who raised her children alone, using the skills of knitting, weaving, sewing, and weaving baskets, ends up in prison for life. "She had soft, caressing, almost boneless hands of strange power," (90) notes the narrator, and it is "with the precision and skill of her hard-working hands [that] she grasped hold of his [Garesego's] genitals and cut them off with one stroke" (103). Her weapon significantly enough is a kitchen knife that she had sharpened "slowly and methodically" at a grinding stone that afternoon. Dikeledi is rightly apprehensive that Garesego will pollute "her life [which] had become holy to her during those years that she had struggled to maintain herself and the children. She had filled her life with treasures of kindness and love she had gathered from others and it was all this that she wanted to protect from defilement by an evil man" (101). Dikeledi's act is spurred by a desire to preserve her "holy" space. This is not a religious concept in Head's work, but rather an animist, even social idea grounded in racial, sexual, class inequities. Dikeledi echoes Head's sentiments in protecting her "holy" space: "I like," remarks Head, "going to the same spot everyday, depending on whether that spot is hallowed ground. I am most unhappy in unholy places . . . and Southern Africa may be the unholiest place on earth" (72). Head is concerned with the "unholy" life that Dikeledi must face if she were to allow Garesego to literally re-enter her body, and her life.

The crisis occurred when Dikeledi runs short by R.20 for their son Bonabothe's fees. After eight years of being ignored by Garesego as "a lower form of human life," she decides to "remind (him) that he is the father of the children." Her plea is immediately desecrated by Garesego who not only refuses to take his responsibility, but who tells her to ask her neighbor Paul, described in the story as "a poem of tenderness," for the money since "Everyone knows that he is keeping two homes, and that you are his spare" (99). The issue of school fees with which the story ends—Paul promises to "give them all (the three children) a secondary school education"—is the catalyst for Dikeledi's decision to murder Garesego.

Head mythifies the reality of women killing their abusive spouses by having Dikeledi meet four women in prison, all of whom have murdered their husbands by "cutting off their special parts." The sexual and psychological abuse that lead to these drastic acts of murder are of no interest to a sexist justice system that condemns these women to life-imprisonment, and that gives only five years to a husband who murders his wife named Life in another of Head's stories. This murder committed by the husband is excused as "an act of passion."

"The Collector of Treasures" weaves in South African history in Head's disarmingly simple representation of destructive men like Garesego analyzed over three different historical time-periods: pre-colonial, colonial, and postcolonial. Head delineates the sexist inequalities enshrined in local pre-colonial custom, followed by the colonial exploitation of male labor, and dislocation from family in order to work in the mines. Finally, post-independence time in Botswana is described as "one more affliction" visited upon males who found themselves with "no inner resources" to deal with external changes. As money assumes supreme value, many men became more socially and sexually irresponsible than before. As the narrator notes ironically, "Independence produced marvels indeed." Money and sex become linked in a near-fatal union as exchange values. Men like Garesego do not take responsibility for the children they father or for the women they impregnate.

In prison, where "The Collector of Treasures" begins, there is an immediate rapport among the women:

> "We are all here for the same crime," Kebonye said, then with her cynical smile asked: "Do you feel any sorrow about the crime?" . . .
>
> "Our men do not think that we need tenderness and care. You know, my husband used to kick me between the legs when he wanted that. I once aborted with a child, due to this treatment. . . . Well, he was an education-officer and each year he used to suspend about seventeen male teachers for making school girls pregnant, but he used to do the same. The last time it happened the parents of the girl were very angry and came to report the matter to me. I told them: "You leave it to me. I have seen enough." And so I killed him. (89–90)

Although life in prison is hardly the most constructive alternative for women, Head implies that even the confined prison space is "holier" than the space that these women have had to share with their men. Moreover, their imprisonment, although a literal exiling from the community, is not a totally negative experience. They create a unique, nurturing female solidarity based on acts of kindness, caring, and support, a kind that would be difficult to establish outside prison walls. Rather than a calamity, this is a remarkably liberating space for Dikeledi who "*began* phase three of a life that had been ashen in its loneliness and unhappiness. And yet she had always found gold amidst the ash, deep loves that had joined her heart to the hearts of others. She smiled tenderly at Kebonye because she already had found another such love. She was the collector of such treasures" (emphasis added, 91).

Language and Literary Form as Resistance

The various linguistic and formal choices in the work of postcolonial women writers are historically specific and strategic. When is it tactical to use standard English, or to use pidgin, patois (radically re-spelt as "patwah")? What purposes does a certain kind of English serve? Most postcolonial societies use standard English for state, legal machinery; other forms of English are often considered "bad" though they help to build pride and self-worth among a people. Historically specific time inspires the linguistic and formal choices of Louise Bennett in Jamaica (dialect poems), Ama Ata Aidoo in Ghana (short story, drama), Kamala Das (poet, autobiographer) in India, and so on. At a certain time, oral street theater rather than a published drama inspires social change; at other times, a pamphlet on rape such as the one which was circulated by the Lawyer's Collective in Bombay, in response to the outcry surrounding sixteen-year-old Mathura's rape in police custody is an effective political intervention; at yet another time, literacy and educational workshops, such as those conducted by Sistren (Jamaica), aim at raising women's consciousness about discriminations that they experience within the home and workplace.

The type of English one is equipped to use often shapes one's position in postcolonial society. English language/s exist in standard, Creole, and other manifestations—what Edward Kamau Brathwaite calls "nation language," an English that can imitate "the sound of the hurricane, wind, howl, waves"; or, what Honor Ford-Smith in *Lionheart Gal* re-names "patwah," to be distinguished from the French word, "patois."[31] Issues of cultural domination, educational policies, the status of English studies and the role that "English literature" played in a liberal colonial enterprise are of concern in postcolonial scholarship today. Even as colonies such as India, Kenya, Barbados absorbed the imposition and institutionalization of English literature into curricula, there were counter-movements, for instance, Ngugi wa Thiong'o's dramatic call for the abolition of the English Department from the University of Nairobi and its replacement by a Department of Literatures and Languages. In her essay, "Currying Favor: The Politics of British Educational and Cultural Policy in India," Gauri Viswanathan argues how "under the guise of liberal education," British educational policy located in English literature "a perfect synthesis to ease different tensions—religious and secular."[32] Western literary knowledge assumed the qualities of "objectivity, rationality, universality." Viswanathan gives examples of an educational policy that worded exam topics in such a way as to predetermine student response, for instance, "On the Disadvantages of Caste and the Benefits of its Abolition," "On the Internal Marks of Falsehood in the Hindu Shastras."

Educational policies that trained male and female "natives" differently, that made knowledge of the English language mandatory for work in colonial administration, are factors that seriously disadvantaged women over men. Kumkum Sangari and Sudesh Vaid in their very useful edited collection of essays entitled, *Recasting Women: Essays in Colonial History* present a feminist historiography that demonstrates how "each aspect of reality is gendered" (2) and re-writes the "legitimizing ideologies" of colonial rule that pretended to be "gender-neutral."[33] They remark, "The workings of an impersonal bureaucratic 'rule of law' . . . marginalized women from the 'public' sphere [legal, judicial machinery conducted in English] even while it subjected them to its control. Such marginalization intensified their dependence on men" (6).

Particular kinds of English are determined by one's class and context—in school, at home, at work, at job interviews. In postcolonial societies, standard English is the language of power, status, and privilege. It is the language of government and law courts. Not having the ability to read and write standard English is a serious disadvantage, and renders one marginal in various ways. When I started going to college in Bombay, I recognized, not without some shock, that having gone to an English-medium school (that is, English was the medium of instruction, although we learnt other languages such as Gujarati, Hindi, French), I was at a tremendous advantage over students who came from "vernacular-medium" schools, derogatorily called "the vernacs." Those students had to make an impossible, almost overnight transition to studies conducted at the college level entirely in English.

In postcolonial India, there is the other side of the problem, as Eunice de Souza points out in her essay, "The Language We Use."[34] De Souza records her own experience of an educational system that taught her "Irish jigs, Irish songs, and Gregorian chant." Indian languages "such as Hindi and Marathi were so ineffectually taught," she adds, "that we did not learn a thing." This reveals a different kind of alienation for a writer like de Souza who as an Indo-Anglican writing in English is less integrated into the literary scene of India as a whole where literary traditions in several languages exist. In India there are twenty-two officially recognized languages (this figure is debated, as is the figure of some 300 dialects to be distinguished from the "official" languages). Ironically though, de Souza's

English-language position also gives the kind of power that only English-language users have in postcolonial society.

For colonized peoples, a key question every time one holds a pen is, which language to use? English or one's mother tongue? Colonization imposed a severe linguistic violence in disrupting integral links between language and culture. The denigration, at times, erasures of native languages, had severe cultural and psychological impacts on people's self-respect, identities, and values. The loss of mother tongues is recognized and bemoaned by many writers, most of whom are multilingual. They have been to colonial schools and mastered English as a necessary tool to succeed in a world where it is a world language; they also inhabit different emotional and mental spaces when they speak their own languages. The loss and recovery of one's own tongue juggling new words and new worlds is a constant negotiation for these writers. As Aidoo states in an essay, "There is no denying the pathos and the wonder in being an African (and a woman) with sensibilities that are struggling ceaselessly to give expression to themselves in a language that is not just alien but was part of the colonizers' weaponry. . . . There is pathos in writing about people, the majority of whom will never be in a position to enjoy you or judge you. And there is some wonder in not letting that or anything else stop you from writing. Indeed, it is almost a miracle in trying and succeeding somewhat to create in an aesthetic vacuum" (157).[35]

A version of the cultural and economic violence perpetrated by the colonizers is now appropriated by writers' "violation" of the English language in its standard usage, and of literary form as defined by the western tradition—a sort of linguistic revenge. As with nearly every aspect of the history of colonization, violence, and this includes linguistic violence, is initiated by the colonizer against the native. This linguistic violence takes different forms in different parts of the postcolonial world; it is crucially tied to British educational policies, the imposition, institution of the English language, and of "English literature" as promoting a "civilizing" mission. Although the British assumed a stance of racial superiority in their attempt to educate natives in all the colonies, the level of linguistic and cultural repression in African and Caribbean communities was certainly more devastating than in India. African cultures were primarily oral; and since African languages were not written and could not be seen, they were rendered invisible by a print-oriented and limited western perspective. Along with the denial of African languages went several leaps of illogic (by the proud possessors of "reason," with their hegemonic claim to rationality as a

European possession, versus "native intuition")—racist claims, such as the non-existence of African culture and civilization. The "dark continent" was supposedly brought into history, and given a culture and civilization by Europeans. In India, the evidence of several written languages, of scriptural texts, made the racist enterprise of cultural alienation somewhat subtler than in African colonies. This linguistic scenario partly accounts for the most radical revisions of the English language coming not from postcolonial Indian, but from African and Caribbean writers. Yet, ironically, in India, given the written authority of ancient texts, particularly those that have encoded women's inferior status, a struggle against those notions is harder than in postcolonial cultures where such evidence is absent. For instance, in the outcry against the case of Roop Kanvar's sati in 1987, the Indian government's efforts to rewrite the legislation prohibiting sati had to contend with religious scripture and other written historical documents on sati. The issues of selection and interpretation of these materials is of course, wide open. Ironically, a postcolonial administration in its legislative and linguistic formulations on a "tradition" such as sati draws upon tactics similar to those of the colonizers over a century ago.

The use of the English language itself is an issue often debated with anger and bitterness. Since language is tied crucially to a sense of identity, it is bound to be an emotional issue. Moreover, writers must reconcile themselves to using the oppressor's tongue, although it has so effectively denigrated indigenous cultures and languages. Chinua Achebe's early essay, "The African Writer and the English Language" (1964), presents a conciliatory position that he still holds today: his goal is to transform the English language from its standard use, to re-shape it in order that it may "carry the weight of (his) African experience. It will have to be a new English, still in full communion with its ancestral home but altered to suit its new African surroundings."[36] Aidoo agrees with Achebe although she is more wary of the negative impacts on colonized peoples' identities when they are brain-washed into an English education. "None of us writers," remarks Aidoo in her essay "To be an African Woman," "in our formative years was involved in any formal process, through which we could have systematically absorbed from our environment, the aesthetics that govern artistic production in general, and writing in particular. Some of us were lucky enough to have mothers and grandmothers who could sing traditional lyrics. Some of us grew up around griots and other traditional poets" (158).

Ngugi wa Thiong'o's position on using the English language is radically different from Achebe's. Ngugi bids farewell to the English language for his creative work in his highly influential essays in *Decolonising the Mind*. Ngugi regards African writers' use of English as part of a continuing cultural imperialism that began over a century ago when the continent itself was divided up at the 1884 Berlin meeting of European powers. Geographical areas set up as English-speaking, French-speaking, Portuguese-speaking have continued to define African identity even today. In contrast to Achebe, Ngugi would have African writers expend their creative energies not in vitalizing the English language, but in rejuvenating their own languages and literatures. "We African writers," remarks Ngugi, "are bound by our calling to do for our languages what Spenser, Milton, Shakespeare did for English; what Pushkin and Tolstoy did for Russian; indeed what all writers in world history have done for their languages by meeting the challenge of creating a literature in them" (10). Recently, Ngugi re-conceptualizes the place of English as one among other languages, and advocates the use of English as "enabling," even as a tool of translation, without "disabling other languages."[37]

Ngugi evokes the Prospero/Caliban power relationship in Shakespeare's *Tempest*, which has at its root the teaching of the English language by the master to the slave. Prospero "took pains to make (Caliban) speak . . . when thou didst not, savage,/Know thine own meaning." Among Caliban's own responses to this generous distinction of learning English is the ironic, though well-reasoned comment: "Thou hast taught me language/ And my profit on't is that I have learnt how to curse." Postcolonial writers' uses of the English language explore the many ways of "cursing" the colonizer in English.[38]

The language debate in the Caribbean takes on somewhat different overtones, mainly because in contrast to the pre-colonial, linguistic situation in Africa and in India, Caribbean writers do not have any particular language to return to. The multiracial populations of the Caribbean, some of whom were part of the slave trade, and others who came in as indentured labor from India and China, also brought in varied linguistic legacies. The latter were subordinated under the dominant language of the particular colonizer, often multiple colonizers in different Caribbean islands. Trinidad, for instance, underwent Spanish and French occupation before the British took over and prevailed from 1797 to 1962. All these linguistic echoes can be heard in contemporary Trinidadian Creole-English. The effective decimation of native Caribs and Amerindians in the Caribbean makes it nearly impossible to recover any linguistic heritage from those groups.[39] Perhaps for these historical reasons, Caribbean writers in English have been the most successful in radically changing standard English, and in creating a Creole, "patwah" language that is vitally part of Caribbean cultural identity.

When women writers enter the language debate, they do not explicitly connect the use of English to cultural imperialism as Ngugi might. They evoke a route that goes via the female body, the repercussions, even reprisals of an English educational and missionary system. In her long prose-poem, *She Tries Her Tongue, Her Silence Softly Breaks*, Marlene Nourbese Philip laments the loss of a mother tongue and the attendant grief and loss.[40] In contemporary times, in a common enough phrase, the empire writes back, and in a variety of Englishes, pidgins, and patois. Along with innovations in language, postcolonial women writers transform literary forms. The novel as a favored form is due in some part to conditions of marketing and publishing.[41] Also, to borrow Bakhtin's concept of dialogism that gives primacy to dialogue and multiple voices as the hallmarks of the novel genre, are particularly suited to postcolonial writers' rewriting history from the points of view of indigenous peoples that challenge colonial records from the British standpoint.

Another very important form for women is the short story, used particularly by Aidoo and Head because it is rooted in *oral story-telling traditions*. Women writers also use different forms of personal narrative that combine oral and written forms, such as songs that are sung and at times recorded, oral testimony that is heard, first, then recorded in writing either by the teller or by a sympathetic listener. Buchi Emecheta traces her novelistic productions directly to the heritage of oral story-telling, and to what she heard as a child on her visits from Lagos to Ibuza from her aunt, called "Big Mother." The impact of both the stories as well as the manner of telling them left indelible impressions on her consciousness:

> We would sit for hours at her feet mesmerized by her trance like voice. Through stories she could tell the heroic deeds of our ancestors, all our mores and all our customs. She used to tell them in such a sing-song way that until I was about fourteen I used to think that these women were inspired by some spirits. It was a result of those visits to Ibuza, coupled with the enjoyment and information those stories used to give us, that I determined when I grew older that I was going to be a story teller, like my Big Mother.
>
> I learned to my dismay at school in Lagos that if I wanted to tell stories to people from many places I would have to use a language that was not my first—neither was it my second, or third, but my

fourth language. This made my stories lose a great deal of colour, but I learned to get by. My English must have been very bad because when I first told my English teacher, who came from the Lake District, and who was crazy about Wordsworth that I was going to write like her favourite poet, she ordered me to go to the school chapel and pray for forgiveness, because she said: "Pride goeth before a fall."[42]

Emecheta took to writing as part of her own cultural heritage, not as something "clever or unusual," and despite racist prejudice from colonial teachers. She also notes in an interview that when African men realized that there was money to be made in transcribing oral stories into written ones, "what had once been the province of women was taken over by men."

Oral story-telling and dialogue are significant forms used by women. Mikhail Bakhtin's path-breaking concepts of the dialogic, multivocality, and heteroglossia are useful in theorizing third world women's uses of these expressive forms. Although feminists evoke Bakhtin, one recognizes that in his most cited "Discourse on the Novel" (hereafter DN) he does not mention a single nineteenth-century female novelist such as Jane Austen, or Charlotte and Emily Bronte.[43] It is equally important to recognize that Bakhtin's writings are part of ongoing conversations and intellectual debates among his contemporaries on language and literary form. Bakhtin favored a kind of "open unity" as indicated by the subtitles of his essays with phrases such as, "Notes toward..."

Bakhtin's paradigm-shifting work gives enormous importance to dialogue, to the open-endedness of speech and orality, of discussion rather than closure. These are enabling concepts in theorizing female agency especially in creating different forms of resistance via speech, silence, and the female body. Bakhtin was not concerned with colonial domination and the literary work that emerges from that historical reality; nonetheless, dialogue is a crucial aspect, perhaps a first step toward overcoming racist and sexist oppression.

Bakhtin favors dialogic open-endedness, "the impossibility of closure" over dialectic thinking that aims at synthesis.[44] He notes that "within language there is always at work a centripetal force which aims at centralizing and unifying meaning (necessary for social interaction) and used by any dominant social group" (15). I interpret this dominant group to be the colonizer who imposes his own "monologic, unitary perceptions of truth." However, in histories of anti-colonial struggle, one discovers what Bakhtin terms "the force of heteroglossia" that militates against unitary meanings and that recognizes "language as ideologically saturated and stratified." Heteroglossia also "includes multiple social discourses" whereby speakers can recognize different ideological configurations (DN, 369). This is liberating for colonized people since it disrupts any hegemonic truth-claims upheld by any one language, such as the colonizer's English, and the ideological baggage of racist superiority conveyed in English.

For Bakhtin, the dialogic is most effectively at play in the novel, "a supergenre whose power consists in its ability to engulf and ingest all other genres" (Introduction, *The Dialogic Imagination*). Indeed he privileges the novel over the epic and other genres and postulates that other forms become "novelized" when they come into contact with this genre ("Epic & Novel," in *The Dialogic Imagination*, 39). I apply Bakhtin's privileging of the novel over other forms to non-European traditions of story-telling, folklore, and oral traditions as used by African, Indian, and Caribbean women writers, and women's ways of knowing that engage a politics of the female body from the female point of view.

Similarly, Bakhtin's concept of "carnival" introduced in his text, *Rabelais and His World* makes room for the "informal" that draws from folk culture and notes how such usage works toward undermining hegemonic officialdom.[45] "Carnival is a syncretic pageantry of a ritualistic sort," he remarks, hence it is not "anachronistic." Rather, carnival is "a symbolic network of concretely sensuous forms accumulating over a centuries-long tradition of popular festivals, carnivals, celebratory and seasonal rituals, market-place spectacles."[46] I extend Bakhtin's discussion of the body at play in a carnival setting into female protagonists' uses of their bodies to resist patriarchal domination via the use of silence, illness, voice, and so on. Similar to the Bakhtinian carnivalesque, such deployments of the body to assert female agency are deeply ambivalent—subject to ridicule and celebration (as in a carnival), to be both elevated and debased. Bakhtin extends how the body operates in carnivalesque situations from a single body to a "communal body of the people" that brings together "in one sensuous image life and death as a continually renewing process of generation." And finally, Bakhtin's linking of such bodily expression as "an important means of liberating human consciousness from a verbal, hierarchical perception of the work [to] opening up the possibility for a horizontal understanding of change" (40) richly supports women's, if I may call them "carnivalesque" resistances, located in their bodies, often their only means of asserting agency.

In my attempt to expand the boundaries of the literary and to include women's oral life stories, Bakhtin's emphasis on "the speech aspect of language, utterance" explains elements of orality in drama where multi-vocality is evident in dialogue among human bodies on stage. Of course, language itself, even if it means communicating with one's own inner voice, embodies that interaction in order to make meaning. Bakhtin is useful in my study of women writing in various genres. Although Bakhtin is partial to the novel, his insights into language itself, and "literary language itself [as] just one of these languages of heteroglossia" is useful in analyzing different literary forms.

Another important literary form transformed by women writers is the autobiographical narrative where the oral, heard story, and the vivid elements of orality are brought into a written story. *Lionheart Gal: Lifestories of Jamaican Women* began as oral testimony recounted orally and then edited and written down by Honor Ford-Smith. The written stories represent feminist politics that take into account the complex social history, economic facts, and political ideology that govern working-class women's lives. This unique cultural text brings together the oral and written and creates a new mode of expression that retains the vibrancy of heard speech and spoken idiom of Jamaican patwah. The Sistren Collective also uses oral story-telling and personal testimony for their dramatic productions. Verbal articulation and gestural language constitute bodily steps toward changing social realities such as ignorance leading to teenage pregnancy, trading sex for food, and the exploiting of female labor. Similarly, in India, street theater, performed by women's activist groups, uses dramatic form, gesture, song, to discuss issues of women's health, history, and violence.

While these oral and written forms convey a deeply personal, even confessional tone, they simultaneously draw upon traditions of female resistance—when overt struggle is not possible, resistance is couched in covert language, proverbs, riddles, games so that the actual lived reality of oppression is presented imaginatively, hence less threateningly.

The transposition from oral to written provides a crucial way to challenge marginality of women's voices, especially working-class women who often do not have the benefits of English education available to middle-class women. *Lionheart Gal* provides one of the finest examples of transforming orality into a written form that retains elements of a speaking voice and an articulate human being behind the printed page. Oral testimony material is gathered around particular questions and later edited. The stories, shaped with considerable artistry, retain the spirit and refrains of the oral narration of a "lifestory." These stories use interview as a creative literary form, a new type of editorship in a progressive feminist politics (for instance, the types of leading questions asked by the interviewer of the *Lionheart Gal* stories are: "What are your experiences of oppression? What have you done to change that?"). The interviewer's selection from oral testimony, the process of transcribing tapes, or relying on memory, all play a part in recording life stories. The final product evokes a multi-vocal register, heteroglossic even as it is the story of an individual woman that has ripple effects on several others in similar class and racial backgrounds. Feminist scholarship has already charted critical methodologies for the use of personal testimony.[47] Hence, although this is not a new critical move that I'm proposing, it is a necessary and under-studied area in postcolonial scholarship.

In the Caribbean, class and color often pave the way for educational and hence economic privilege. The ability to speak "proper English" is required for most jobs. Working-class speakers of "patwah" are marginalized from economic privileges largely because they lack education in formal English. The remarkable achievement of a text like *Lionheart Gal* is that it combines oral and written forms: thirteen of the fifteen stories are based on oral testimonies/interviews that record working-class women's daily language.

The Sistren Collective came together in May 1977 when a group of twelve working-class women employed as street cleaners under the Michael Manly government "special make-work program called Impact" presented a drama entitled *Downpression Get A Blow*. They were assisted by Honor Ford-Smith (who also became a part of Sistren) of the Jamaica School of Drama. She served as artistic director for the group from 1977 to 1988 when Sistren grew from a drama collective to a multi-faceted organization that uses its drama methodology based on personal testimony to organize groups of women around particular social issues, and has led to Sistren Research, a silk-screen printing project, a quarterly magazine, etc.

Ford-Smith created the interviews and edited the stories in *Lionheart Gal*. The project started out along the same method as Sistren's theater work, that is, "taking in from women through testimony and shaping into a final product." Each interview was constructed around three questions: "How did you first become aware of the fact that you were oppressed as a woman? How did that experience affect your life? How have you tried to change it?" The oral testimony was transcribed and as editor, Ford-Smith consciously transformed the oral material into a written story with a structure, remaining faithful to the richness of the oral transmission in elements such as imagery, repetition, and above all, the women's use of patwah. "However, the stage of development of the written language constantly undercuts the richness of the oral version," notes Ford-Smith. "There is, for example, as yet no accepted spelling of Patwah. . . . The syntax has been retained as purely as possible . . . the definitive tone, rhythm, and whole way of thinking of a language."[48]

Lionheart Gal's use of patwah is a radical choice that "expresses the refusal of a people to imitate a coloniser, their insistence on creation, their movement from obedience towards revolution," notes Ford-Smith. "Not to nurture such a language is to retard the imagination and power of the people who created it." She continues:

> Writing in dialect, with its improvised spelling and immediate flavor, the women learned to write a form of English that had previously been considered "bad, coarse and vulgar." In fact, Jamaican Creole is a variation of English with its own strict rules of grammar, a language which retains much of the Twi construction of its creators. By writing a language that had hitherto been that of a nonliterate people, the women broke silence. By translating their work into English (standard English remains for Sistren, as for many other women, a second language) the women create an equal relationship between their idiom and the language of the powerful—one they mostly understand but do not speak. It is the official language of the country, and they must learn it . . . if they are to communicate their needs and demands to the powerful.[49]

The use of "patwah" for serious writing and reflection confronts the notion that patwah is purely for entertainment purposes. Since working-class people who speak patwah often cannot write it, the rift between the oral and the literate cultures and classes gets deeper. In its linguistic choice of patwah where standard English is effectively marginalized (since only two of the fifteen stories are in standard English) and in its formal choice of written stories based on oral personal testimony, *Lionheart Gal* challenges the neocolonial linguistic prejudices still rampant in postcolonial societies. There is, of course, a long way to go in redressing color-class-language prejudices so embedded in colonial histories, but a text like *Lionheart Gal* by taking "patwah" seriously, and making it available in printed form to a wide readership takes a significant step toward that social change.

This text, combining orality and literacy, voices the experience, even wisdom of working-class women who have often "facilitated the preservation of African traditions." Ford-Smith notes that since "much of this legacy has been denied by the wider society and has been submerged beneath the official character of the country, its emergence into the open requires different methods of communication than those that survived in the past. It demands a reexamination of the past, with all its taboos and restrictions, in the language of the *present*. It requires that women, hitherto the preservers, become the authors." Sistren has also made a film entitled *Sweet Sugar Rage* that records the use of drama-in-education workshops that were used to organize women in the Jamaican sugar belt.

There is vast potential for cultural resistance within what Kamau Brathwaite calls "a submerged language" in his important text, *History of the Voice*. When expressed, this language is empoweringly subversive, particularly within Caribbean society where middle-class attitudes about "proper speech" prevail. Brathwaite provides the useful concept of "nation language" which is "English in a new sense . . . English in an ancient sense. English in a very traditional sense. And sometimes not English at all, but language" (5). Brathwaite discusses how African languages were "submerged" because the conquerors' official languages prevailed—English, French, Dutch, Spanish. However, "that underground language" survived, and "was itself constantly transforming itself into new forms."

Brathwaite distinguishes "nation language" from "dialect." The latter is used pejoratively. He describes "nation language" as "the submerged area of that dialect which is much more closely allied to the African aspect of experience in the Caribbean. It may be in English: but often it is in an English which is like a howl, or a shout or a machine-gun or the wind or a wave. It is also like the blues. And sometimes it is English and African at the same time" (13). Nation language works as a "strategy," for instance, when "the slave is forced to use a certain kind of language in order to disguise himself, to distinguish his personality and to retain his culture" (16); Brathwaite also stresses the importance of noise in nation language, of sound, song, calypso, and the basis of nation language in orality, a condition which makes the audience much more important than in written forms of expression.

The historical reasons behind the "invention," evolution of languages such as nation language are many, and varied. One reason is certainly rooted in the kind of education that was propagated through English. Brathwaite uses a calypso by Sparrow: "Dan is the Man in the Van" which states that "the education (they) got from England has really made (them) idiots because all of those things that (they) had to read about—Robin Hood, King Alfred and the Cakes, King Arthur and the Knights of the Round Table—all of these things really didn't give (them) anything but empty words" (25). And Sparrow made this statement in the calypso form in which he creates "a counterpoint between voice and orchestra, between individual and community": "THE THINGS THEY TEACH ME A SHOULD A BEEN A BLOCK-HEADED MULE." Literary models such as *The Royal Reader* provided models such as, "the cow jumped over the moon," "Ding Dong Bell." "The problem of transcending this," notes Brathwaite, "is what I am talking about" (25). As Bob Marley puts it in one of his songs, "Don't let them fool ya/ Or even try to school ya/ Oh no/ We've got a mind of our own."

The story of women's significant role in preserving oral traditions, and in contemporary times, of revising these traditions for their written creative work is told again and again. Emecheta remarks, "Women are born story-tellers. We keep the history . . . we conserve things and we never forget. What I do is not clever or unusual. It is what my aunt and my grandmother did, and their mothers before them."[50] Aidoo consciously uses oral tradition in her short stories, and in her drama. In an interview she remarks, "One doesn't have to really assume that all literature has to be written. I mean one doesn't have to be so patronizing about oral literature. There is a present validity to oral literary communication. I totally disagree with people who feel that oral literature is one stage in the development of man's artistic genius. To me it's an end in itself. . . . We don't always have to write for readers, we can write for listeners. . . . All the art of the speaking voice could be brought back so easily. We are not that far away from our traditions."[51]

Just as Aidoo emulates elements of oral tradition in her short stories, she also relies on "the traditional narration of a folktale" for her modern drama in the English language. She remarks, "In order for African drama to be valid, it has to derive its impetus, its strength from traditional African dramatic forms, however one conceives these forms, they exist. What we must do is find out what they are, and how we can use them" (23). Accordingly, her drama *Anowa* is "more or less my own rendering of a kind of legend," she remarks, "because, according to my mother who told me the story, it is supposed to have happened. . . . The original story I heard . . . was in the form of a song." Aidoo uses the legend, though significantly, "the ending is [her] own, and the interpretation that she gives to the events that happen" (23). The story, set in the 1870s, significantly includes the historical situation of slavery, and Aidoo evokes provocative connections between the economic drain through slavery and the psychic damage to the slave-trader; between the physical bondage of slavery and the mental/psychic bondage of the female protagonist Anowa as wife.

Choice of Language and the Politics of Location

The female body, internally exiled, is located in the geographic space of a native land, a postcolonial nation whose boundaries are drawn with colonial influence. For women in patriarchal cultures, nation and geography are experienced in terms of internal belonging to the body. In contemporary times, whether at home or outside, female culture producers mediate the particular conjuncture, or to use Arjun Appadurai's word, "disjuncture" of colonial history within new geographies where maps need to be redrawn as ex-colonial peoples re-territorialize.[52] As they migrate and create new homes, this spatial reality fundamentally affects their cultural productions and their choice of writing in English. Language and literary form are transformed in new locations. Colonized peoples have a history of dealing with dominance and they are adept at using and transforming the master's tools, such as the English language, which has been made to evoke different cultural milieu, as well as to talk back to the colonizer. Now, this history is extremely enabling within new alien-homes and new geographies that inspire writers to experiment with literary forms.

Within the complex and troubling historical times that we live in, a new geography permeates the globe. Displacement of large numbers of people, by "choice" or by necessity continues apace in a world where the category of "home" has derived new parameters. Home is not a uni-dimensional category; where home is, that is, the location itself, geography, is determined partly by historical factors. Homes are created within margins, as borderlands become homes. Gloria Anzaldua provides a useful formulation of "borderlands" as "physically present wherever two or more cultures edge each other, where people of different races occupy the same territory, where lower, middle and upper classes touch, where the space between two people shrinks with intimacy."[53] Anzaldua includes in borderlands not only physical territory, but also "psychological . . . sexual . . . and spiritual borderlands."

Soja's discussion of "the spatialization of history, the making of history entwined with the social production of space, the structuring of a historical geography" is enabling for my study of postcolonial women's spaces, especially since there are always a set of social relations within any external lived space, and that "space is fundamental in any exercise of power."[54] Henri Lefebre's concept (quoted by Soja) of "l'éspace vécu" illuminates the gaps and silences especially resonant in women's texts, voices that are heard or silenced in between "actual lived and socially created spatiality, concrete and abstract at the same time, the habitus of social practices."

Geography and space are related to the female body in analyzing power inequities. Who has the space to speak, which knowledges are given academic space, and women's need for public space come into play. Foucault explores the place for *geography* in his "archaeology of knowledge," and his ideas are relevant for colonized peoples' mastery of the English language (from various locations), its grammatical transformations, its displacement (de-centered from the Queen's and King's English to what Marlene Nourbese Philip calls Kinglish). English is transposed geographically from the mother country to the colonies, and now "returns" in new idioms of postcolonial writers often "speaking back" from within metropolitan areas to which they have migrated. Foucault remarks that through "spatial obsessions" he was able to probe the "relations between power and knowledge". Once knowledge can be analyzed in terms of region, domain, implantation, displacement, transposition, one is able to capture the process by which knowledge functions as a form of power and disseminates the effects of power.[55]

Foucault's provocative connections between knowledge and location as in domain and territory, and further, the displacement and transposition of knowledge are enabling for theorizing colonized peoples' uses of English. Although English was imposed upon them via colonial(ist) educational policies that created a civil servant class, colonized peoples transformed English from a foreign "domain" into one with local idiom, landscape, and culture. They take over the "field" of English so to speak, and make that their own "territory." Foucault notes that "the politico-strategic term is an indication of how the military and the administration actually come to inscribe themselves both on a material soil and within forms of discourse" (69). The very relocation of knowledge (such as English literature in colonial schools) endows it with power. Gauri Viswanathan in her useful study, *Masks of Conquest* demonstrates how English literature was used as a key colonizing tool in nineteenth-century India, long before it was used in British schools where "high culture" was embodied in Greek and Latin.[56] When the colonizer brings English into the colonies, it gains power often embodied in theories of racial superiority, and in its denial and denigration of other languages and cultures. Knowledge and territoriality, the need and recognition for de-territorializing say the "canon," and how a particular literary field is defined, are ongoing matters of concern in postcolonial studies. And issues of territoriality that include who learns what language, where one lives, the education one has access to are part of colonial history.

Within this colonial educational infusion, the mediations of identity and geography, of naming and location, of the intersections of history and geography became, and still are, extremely complex. A fine discussion of these concepts is undertaken by Jamaican-American Michelle Cliff in an essay, "If I Could Write This in Fire, I Would Write This in Fire": "The red empire of geography lessons. 'The sun never sets on the British Empire and you can't trust it in the dark'. Or with the dark peoples. . . . Another geography, or was it history lesson?"[57]

The temporal trajectory of history, of events unfolding in time, places necessary boundaries around the past, present, future. When one adds a spatial dimension, for instance, migrations, into this temporal unfolding, the intersection of geography with history opens up new areas of imaginative exploration—returning home through the imagination, recreating home in narrative, creating a simultaneous present, of being here and there, of being in the past and the present. As Jamaica Kincaid remarked in an interview, "I don't know how to be there [Antigua], but I don't know how to be without there."[58]

In contemporary times, "the spatiality of history" underlies the creation of new literary forms. The spatial realities of travel and migration, of fragmentation, of several "homes" illuminate choices of literary and cultural forms of expression. Such fragmentation is at times a daily reality for populations such as black people who until recently in apartheid South Africa had to travel from black townships to white cities, from single-sex male hostels to the misnoma of black "homelands." Non-linear narrative structures recreate the simultaneities of spaces. The presence of ethnicities and languages pervade texts that record how minorities express themselves within majority populations versus within their own groups. These categories of ethnicities and languages are not fixed but fluid and metamorphosing. Literary forms negotiate these fluidities of homes and migrations and reflect the simultaneities of time and space, of historical and geographical movements for ex-colonial peoples.

Today the question of location and the geographic intellectual is crucial for postcolonial writer and critic. The intellectual site of both culture producer and theorist is already always politicized, whether it be a position which validates the status quo (Naipaulicity), or whether it is in line with struggles for social change.

Feminisms for the Third World

Interlocking forces of racial, economic, and national divisions and inequalities are important factors in third world feminism. For third world peoples with histories of colonial domination, race is extremely important, and it is important to deal with that without reifying or subsuming it into the category of ethnicity. Race and ethnicity are to be distinguished and both are important especially in societies that if not overtly racialized (as the United States is), are definitely color-coded where the lighter-skinned class is more privileged than the darker one, most overtly in play in the Caribbean, though India and African societies have their own versions of color prejudices. Racism and colorism both among local peoples and in their interactions with colonizers, sexism, and class divisions are interlinked analytic categories within third world feminisms. We live "in a world with powerful histories of resistance and revolution in daily life," notes Chandra Mohanty in her Introduction to *Third World Women and the Politics of Feminism*, "and organized liberation movements. And it is these contours which define the complex ground for the emergence and consolidation of third world women's feminist politics."[59]

Mohanty draws "links among the histories and struggles of third world women against racism, sexism, colonialism, imperialism, and monopoly capital" (4). Mohanty's suggestion of "an 'imagined community' of third world oppositional struggles" is useful in forging "potential alliances and collaborations across divisive boundaries" that enable imaginative links among common struggles of third world women "in spite of internal hierarchies within third world contexts" (4). These "imagined communities of women with divergent histories and social locations," notes Mohanty, can be "woven together by political threads of opposition to forms of domination that are not only pervasive but also systemic" (4). Mohanty takes these concerns further in her recent text, *Feminism without Borders: Decolonizing Theory, Practising Solidarity*, in asserting the importance of "internationalist commitment ... in the best feminist praxis." She notes that if women are punished severely for stepping outside "safe" boundaries of traditions, then, "Our most expansive and inclusive vision of feminism, needs to be attentive to borders as well as learning to transcend them." She posits feminist solidarity "as the most principled way to cross borders—to decolonize knowledge and practice anticapitalist critique" (7). In asserting a sense of solidarity, evoking "the deeply collective nature of feminist thought" (5), Mohanty is not glibly asserting universal sisterhood. In fact, she is as cognizant of the historical moment when a text like *Sisterhood is Global: The International Women's Movement Anthology* is published, as she is critical of its broad sweep and essentializing categories.[60] Mohanty provides a more complex vision of solidarity that is aware of every step of difference (race, class, education, sexual preference), but that holds on courageously to some notion of unity. This kind of feminist work is deeply resonant with my own that also draws a broad canvass across geographical regions with the aim of creating solidarity among women with a shared history of British colonization and vastly varying languages and mores. My work is in tandem with Mohanty's twin goals outlined in *Feminism without Borders*: namely, to "decolonize feminism, and demystify capitalism" in the interest of producing "transnational feminist praxis" (9–10).

Productive theoretical models for a study of postcolonial women writers foster *dialogue* and cross-fertilization among feminist thought from different parts of the world despite unequal power hierarchies and material resources. Nonetheless, in the spirit of sharing and learning, I bring insights from different geographical locations to benefit intellectual growth. Even with the many differences among women's concerns in different parts of the world, there is much to teach one another. As Bina Agarwal points out in her essay, "Positioning the Western Feminist Agenda," as an educated and privileged third world woman she finds many commonalities with western feminists in terms of "challenging patriarchy." And even as she questions "the often ethnocentric preoccupations of First world feminist academia with its economic and intellectual privilege," Agarwal recognizes the gap between her own privileged class and educational status in comparison to the majority of less privileged women in India. However, she "seeks to build bridges with them."[61] It is important to be honest and have integrity about one's privilege, to recognize the contradictions that face progressive intellectuals, and to keep the door open for dialogues across class, caste, race, educational privilege, and increasingly across national and linguistic boundaries. If the feminist movement in India emphasizes, in Radha Kumar's phrase, "the history of doing" along with abstract thinking, then that history of women involved in campaigns such as anti-price rise, anti-sati and other anti-patriarchal campaigns in arenas of law, education, popular culture, have much to teach women in the first world. For instance, in cases of dowry murders, women's groups in India successfully use strategies of humiliating and shaming the male perpetrators of violence by public denunciation.

The women's movement in India has grown around various key events on the ground, such as the gang-rape of fourteen-year-old tribal girl Mathura in March 1978, or the Chipko movement when women challenged the authorities against deforestation by hugging the trees and singing songs. Over the past decade, popular resistance to mega dam projects such as on the Narmada river have gained recognition by outspoken women activists like Medha Patkar and writer-activist Arundhati Roy.[62] Women's groups have compelled the state and popular media to recognize that women's issues are a crucial part of social change. Vibhuti Patel's very useful essay, "Women's Liberation in India" elaborates on the mobilization of women's groups around key events. Patel also discusses the uses of cultural forms such as song, folk-dance, and street theater as means to fight against sexual oppression and discrimination.[63] Similarly, the concerns of Euro-American women and also of third world women living within the belly of the first world have much to impart to postcolonial women about issues of gender discrimination, Affirmative Action and race politics, backlashes against feminist and ethnic studies.

Krishnaraj, in "Evolving New Methodologies" indicates how the fields of history, sociology, psychology, political science, anthropology have all been transformed by inclusion of gender; economics has been most resistant to feminist agendas, in particular in recognizing women's work within the home as productive rather than unquantifiable and invisible. Feminist economists work toward creating "new categories of analysis: market work (self-employed in household production/wage work, family labor in household production, housework proper . . . Disaggregating housework reveals the degree of economic contributions by women and yet they are labeled 'dependent' " (20).

Such recognition is part of acknowledging women in general as "creators and subjects of knowledge" not simply in terms of making women visible but in "challenging the prevailing notion of knowledge, methodology, source of data, etc. It presumes a different perspective in analyzing participation, it calls for a need to look at non-conventional sources of data, it considers woman not merely as an object of study but as an actor articulating her feelings from inner recesses" (6).

Krishnaraj argues that in the third world context, women's struggles are not divorced from men's, that rather than being confrontational, women's movements work in solidarity with other progressive organizations. "Power in women's studies," she remarks "is conceptualized as reduction of helplessness or vulnerability. (If women are beaten up, build shelter homes; inequality in education for girls is sought to be erased by reducing fees, not by addressing the problem of parental preference for boy's education and the sexual division of labor.) Power as power to change, power as autonomy are outside our model.... Much of the empowerment today is in the form of elbow room."[64] She points out various contradictory spaces where women are supposedly given "power," for instance, in religious ritual, or, in a tightly knit familial kin situation, women acquire self-esteem by being self-sacrificing, even suffering in ways that ultimately deny their own autonomy. Krishnaraj advocates study of such contradictory power scenarios. I attempt such analyses in my discussion of the contradictory empowerments of English education and cultural alienation (chapter 3), of valuing constructive and rejecting destructive cultural traditions (chapter 4), and the paradox of motherhood, the most valorized tradition along with the damaging stigma against infertile women or those who reject biological motherhood (chapter 5).

Nandita Gandhi and Nandita Shah in their text, *The Issues at Stake: Theory and Practice in the Contemporary Women's Movement in India*, note that there is no formal "beginning" of the women's movement in India but that struggles against oppression are deeply embedded in the cultural and social fabric of mythology, folk tales, and songs. Such sources also encode how women have resisted whenever possible. Their work provides a useful overview of how the contemporary women's movement formed around "three main issues: violence, health and work as political, emotional and intellectual experiences" (16). They also provide a good historical overview of "the woman question" by male social reformers as part of the anti-colonial struggle in nineteenth-century India. Later, in the mid- to late twentieth century, women's autonomous groups were formed. They undertake scholarly and activist projects, are attentive to issues on the ground, regionally oriented, and linguistically different across the Indian subcontinent. Shah and Gandhi's text is a fine compendium of local activists' work along with documentation and analysis. It offers a good example of theorizing that includes local publications, police reports, individual women's testimonies, discussion of laws, and feminist resistances, statistics on dowry deaths; the role of advertising and the media in validating violence against women, school textbooks, beauty contests, data on sex ratios and female discriminations in access to nutritious food, medical care; female feticide;

theorizing violence via published scholarship, and occasional documents put together by women's groups.

Even as one acknowledges the necessity of solidarity among third world men and women, and does not uphold a separatist radical feminist movement that might work for certain classes of women within western economies, it is crucial not to romanticize this solidarity. Third world feminism's goal is to work toward the full participation and dignity of women along with men. Filomena Steady's articulation that "African feminism combines racial, sexual, class, and cultural dimensions of oppression to produce a more inclusive brand of feminism through which women are viewed first and foremost as human, rather than sexual, beings" mystifies and contains the specifically sexual aspects of women's oppressions.[65]

Oyeronke Oyewumi's text, *The Invention of Women: Making African Sense of Western Gender Discourses*, sets up a theoretical dichotomy between Africa and the west that is limiting.[66] Although Oyewumi argues convincingly of the dominance of western knowledge and modes of knowing on African societies, her further assertion that the category of "woman" also enters with western influence is not as useful. Nor the claim that "western concepts of gender [work] on the assumption that gender is a timeless and universal category" (31). Oyewumi does not want to recognize that feminist theorizing of gender as a social category, wherever that took place, in different parts of the world, and not only in the west, remains a most useful category in formulating a politics of third world women. A retreat into "biology is destiny" as part of the entire western theorizing on women is not sustainable. Oyewumi relies on the problematic tendency that she identifies as part of Yoruba studies, namely, "the manifestation of this preoccupation with finding African equivalents of European things" and this also applies to feminism (21). Oyewumi argues that the concept of "gender" comes in with westernization and that prior to that, in Yoruba society "the social categories of men and women were nonexistent . . . Rather, the primary principle of social organization was seniority, defined by relative age" (31). Even an acknowledgment of this as a different system of categorization does not erase the issue of male dominance and privilege. Indeed, Oyewumi's labored analysis of Yoruba kinship and nomenclature promotes a kind of ethnocentricity without any concrete manifestation of how such gender distinctions, different from "western" theorizing lead to any different articulations of unequal gender relations.

Another step that makes women's issues secondary is the economistic flag. Since third world women struggle for survival, they cannot be interested in anything as esoteric as sexism, and feminist rebellions are for those who have enough to eat! This dichotomy does immense disservice to women's struggles for social change. Just as one would regard racism and sexism as interlocking and not separate or hierarchized categories of analysis, so also are the economic and sexual. Imperialism, economic and cultural, along with personal exploitations in the family and workplace are connected and not separate categories that overtly and covertly endorse fundamental sexual inequalities. A politics of female sexuality must be analyzed within a framework of imperialism and not separated from it.

Hazel Carby's analysis in "White Woman Listen! Black Feminism and the Boundaries of Sisterhood,"[67] where she argues that within categories like the family, patriarchy may not function equivalently as the site of oppression for black women as for white women, is furthered usefully in Valerie Amos and Pratibha Parmar's essay, "Challenging Imperial Feminism."[68] Amos and Parmar critique the "political limitations of Euro-American feminism" which does not pay adequate attention to race, and when it does make black women visible, it does that in problematic and distorted ways. "What forms of contemporary feminist and socialist theories share is an inability to adequately deal with the contradictions inherent in gender and class relations within the context of a racist society. 'Race and sex are social realities which at particular historical moments structure class relations in as much as class relations structure them' " (5). Amos and Parmar caution against a sentimental "sisterhood" of women on an essentialized biological commonality, and they also warn against "the idealization and culturalism of anthropological works" that regard "others" as "exotic subjects."

Amos and Parmar discuss the troubled arena of "cultural tradition" that is branded by well-meaning feminists as "feudal residues" without a necessary historicizing and contextualizing. They critique "the 'imperial' nature of feminist thought" rooted in Eurocentric historical and philosophic traditions of analysis that brings its own prejudices to bear on the study of third world women. Ironically, in their haste to liberate, say, passive Asian women from their family's oppressive cultural practices like arranged marriages, feminists perpetuate stereotypes. Further, when white feminists unproblematically accept "racist assumptions about the Black family, (their) critical but uninformed approach to 'Black culture' has found root and in fact informs state practice" (11). Amos and Parmar assert the importance of rewriting histories from a community's own perspective that recognizes changing historical conditions.

Similar to the family, the category of "wife" has specific cultural definitions as Niara Sudarkasa points out in her discussion of "The 'Status of Women' in Indigenous African societies."[69] Sudarkasa argues convincingly that the distinctions between public and private as they exist within a European framework do not work within African traditional societies where women worked within the home and outside. There are no strict dichotomies. "Wife" indicated a belonging to one male and often also to the lineage or compound. "Work" needs redefinition too so that if for middle-class white women, feminist gains meant the "freedom" to work outside the home, it meant something quite different for African women who might see the reverse as a feminist gain.

As one redefines feminisms appropriate for third world societies, one needs to be vigilant and sensitive to historical, social, cultural conditions that are different from realities in the first world. This is evoked beautifully in Jamaican Olive Senior's poem, "Letter from the Lesser World." Economic and cultural divisions between the first and third world are depicted in "sickle cell anemia or sleeping on pavements" as part of third world life, and "baseball season or fall" as first world realities. For Senior, this "Friend of the cellophane world" needs to understand that progress for third world societies entails "reducing the distance between hospitals."[70] In another poem, "Reaching my Station," Senior bemoans the fact that "mothers know the starkness/ of these times/ guns easier to obtain than milk" (77).

In further distinguishing feminisms in different parts of the postcolonial world, Carol Boyce Davies provides a useful discussion of "African feminism as a hybrid of sorts, which seeks to combine African concerns with feminist concerns"; a sort of "balancing" act where women's own issues along with a "common struggle with African men" against imperialism is important.[71] Davies acknowledges the "inequities and limits" within traditional, often feudal societies, and she cites Molara Ogundipe Leslie's important point, namely, a struggle against women's own internalized oppressions: "Women are shackled by their own negative self-image, by centuries of the interiorization of the ideologies of patriarchy and gender hierarchy" (15). Boyce Davies, echoing Aidoo, also asserts the need for serious re-evaluations of women writers who have been dismissed casually by a male literary establishment. She cites Flora Nwapa's recuperation in recent critical work by Lloyd Brown, and the work of Naana Banyima-Horne (in Davies' own collection). Constructive criticism, according to Davies, can enable women writers to move beyond the image of woman-as-victim, to transform voicelessness into speech.

Further, African feminist criticism develops the tools of "an African Female Aesthetic" where oral literatures are recuperated and re-evaluated, where the modes and forms of creative expression are constructively criticized. For instance, Boyce Davies cites the inclusion of "small talk" as an important literary tool rather than a weakness in the writing as judged by certain Euro-American standards of narrative excellence. Above all, gender analysis needs to be located historically and socially within the context of power relations in different societies.

Sexuality, the Body, and Feminists "Disciplining Foucault"

Feminist revisions and strategic appropriations of Michel Foucault's theorizing of power illuminates my argument of the internal exile of women's bodies even though he is not concerned specifically with women, or with race. Foucault's analysis of where sexuality belongs, in multiple effects of power relations within a society's institutions is relevant in colonized societies that were forced to deal with new forms of power and knowledge. British colonizers brought their own ideological baggage of sexuality into the colonies through their educational and legal systems, and they transformed, often fundamentally, the ways in which colonized women's (and men's) bodies were regularized. Indigenous patriarchies, in contending with new institutionalized modes of sexuality often colluded with colonial patriarchy thus adding to women's domination. Though these macro levels of power are significant in colonial administrations, Foucault's analysis of the micro levels at which power operates is significant for the internal exile of women's bodies that I trace in postcolonial women writers' texts.

In an interview, Foucault describes "the mechanics of power" as "its capillary form of existence, the extent to which power seeps into the very grain of individuals, reaches right into their bodies, permeates their gestures, their posture, what they say, how they learn to live and work with other people."[72] Jana Sawicki's *Disciplining Foucault: Feminism, Power, and the Body* attempts "to think feminism through Foucault" (15), and to recognize that Foucault offers "a critical method" that is useful to feminists as to other theorists (29).[73]

In *The History of Sexuality*, Foucault traces the discourses on sexuality from models of silence, penance and punishment in medieval times, and in later times to new articulations of sexuality.[74] He describes how the nature of power underwent transformation in the seventeenth century: "One of these poles . . . centered on the body as a machine: its disciplining, the optimization of its capabilities . . . an anatomo-politics of the human body. The second . . . focused on the species body. Their supervision was effected through an entire series of interventions and regulatory controls: a biopolitics of the population" (139).

What is left out of Foucault's articulation of "a biopolitics of the population" is precisely how different bodies, in particular, different races, are controlled, and as Ann Laura Stoler's astute analysis in *Race and the Education of Desire* shows, how race and nation are often elided under Foucault's emphasis on sex. However, sexual control of bodies is also part of controlling racial bodies via laws that prohibit interracial sexual contacts in colonial societies. Colonialism and race were not part of Foucault's project in *The History of Sexuality*, though as Stoler points out, Foucault intended to return to the problem of race later in this six-volume project, but he never did. Later, his concerns focused on the state and governmentality, and race was subsumed as part of that control structure.

Foucault's analysis of discourses on sexuality demonstrates that to speak about sexuality is not necessarily liberating. In its very articulation lie the interstices of containment, even co-optation. Disciplinary discourses led to new controls of bodies through institutional mechanisms operating from within families, schools, medical, legal practices. The growth of scientific knowledge about human bodies gave rise to new, more subtle modes of social control. Foucault argues that discourses on sexuality emerged as part of the "normalizing disciplines of medicine, education, and psychology," remark Irene Diamond and Lee Quinby in their Introduction to a volume of essays, *Feminism and Foucault: Reflections on Resistance*, "and that discourses on sex became part of a mechanism of new ways of organizing knowledge."[75]

Part of my impetus for this study was to create alternate models to postcolonial theory's reliance on poststructuralism. Though there are lessons to be gained from a thinker such as Foucault, such as his seminal analyses of sexuality and power, how power operates at the macro levels (of prisons and hospitals) and at the micro, even capillary levels (resonant for my discussion of women's internal exile in patriarchy), there are aspects of poststructuralism that need to be challenged for their usefulness in postcolonial theory. Spivak's critique of Foucault even as she acknowledges his tremendous importance is useful for postcolonial theory, namely, in Foucault's analysis of the "networks of power/desire/interest that are so heterogenous, he systematically ignor(es) the question of ideology and

[his] own implications in intellectual and economic history ... [which] can help consolidate the international division of labor."[76] Spivak astutely identifies the crux of the problem in Foucault, namely, when "two senses of representation are being run together; representation as 'speaking for', as in politics, and representation as 're-presentation', as in art or philosophy" (42).

Although poststructuralist concepts such as unitary identity of subjects and authority of an author are useful for postcolonial theory, it is important to acknowledge that they emerged out of European historical and social contexts. Hence, they need to be adapted to the intellectual and political realities of decolonizing societies. For colonized peoples of color, it is crucial first to formulate and construct identities before they can be fragmented or "played with." Postcolonial authors need, first to take authority in revisiting colonial versions of history, and in speaking back to the colonizer. It is problematic when the Foucauldian "crisis of the subject" is transposed wholesale into other cultures. Even as one acknowledges the potential of authoritarianism in any system of belief such as religion, or science, these systems are culturally specific as are resistances in particular contexts. A literal adoption of the Foucauldian "death of the subject" is not useful for postcolonial contexts.

Helen Tiffin's essay, "Postcolonialism, Post-Modernism and the Rehabilitation of Post-colonial History" presents a useful critique of certain disconcerting trends in postcolonial discourse.[77] She objects to the label "post-modern" for postcolonial texts as an example of European theory appropriating these texts into its own terms as "a means of control into European post-structuralism [that] invokes a neo-universalism which reinforces the very European hegemony so many of the works from India, the African countries ... and the Caribbean have been undermining. Thus the so-called 'crisis of European authority' continues to reinforce European cultural and political domination, as potential relativisation of its epistemology and ontology acts through such labeling once again to make the rest of the world a peripheral term in Europe's self-questioning" (171).

Tiffin identifies "a number of strategies" that are part of a "postmodern" condition, such as a refusal of closure, or a move away from realist representations. However, even when postcolonial writers use these strategies, they are informed, according to Tiffin "by different theoretical assumptions and by vastly different political motivations" (172). She gives examples of Achebe's use of Igbo cosmology and ontology, of Raja Rao's use of Puranic techniques in their novels, as modes of "escap(ing) historical and textual containment, or engulf(ing) it on behalf of their own metaphysics." Tiffin considers it important "to refuse contemporary critical enclosure by the neo-hegemonic thrusts of post-modernism and post-structuralism whose very nomenclatures, capturing world space for the accidentals of European cultural time, invoke a neo-universalism from which all post-colonial literatures have been deliberately detaching themselves" (179).

Another of Foucault's influential concepts of replacing any totalizing system, explanatory or revolutionary, with genealogy is both useful and problematic for postcolonial theory. While historical and cultural specificity is crucial, the naming of certain large systems of oppression such as patriarchy is necessary in a discussion of women's oppression. Similarly, the category of "woman," though much discredited in recent postmodern feminist analyses, is important to recuperate within the specificity of different women's subjugations and resistances in different contexts.[78] Radhakrishnan usefully locates Foucault in his own historical context, namely after Stalinism and such dominant totalizing systems, when any form of organizing spelt oppression. But the opposite of not having any common cause that works towards solidarity and coalition building is highly problematic for colonized peoples. Spivak and Radhakrishnan agree that Foucault's refusal to include any ideology in his thought makes difference a somewhat idealist trope. Formations via class, gender, nationality are all important, but simply valorizing difference brings us to what Radhakrishnan calls "a near-solipsistic aestheticization of the political."[79] A denial of the unitary self leads us to a dizzying plurality and "the individual as multiple" loses out both as a singular self, and as a unique part of a collective in any kind of political action.

As R. Radhakrishnan indicates, Foucault's theoretical contributions, path-breaking as they are, do not go far enough to suggest a politics where individuals are agents working toward social change. Foucault does not include "the historical realities" of subjugated knowledges that after all, did exist in history but "in the domain of theory they have been written out of effective existence" (32). They exist as "absences" and hence when recuperated such as in the case of colonized peoples' histories, they assume an oppositional tone, vis-à-vis dominant history, and they are regarded as "transgressive and reactive." Radhakrishnan probes the shortcomings in the term "genealogy" which enables Foucault to work against totalizing and globalizing discourses though this entails a disconnection from the real world.

Radhakrishnan analyzes "another contradiction in Foucault's politics," namely, his disavowal of the global in favor of the local, and basing his theories on the local events of regional France that then somehow "speak" for an entire world that Foucault "chooses" not to include in his theorizing. Radhakrishnan articulates his critique in terms of where Foucauldian thought has important shortcomings for postcolonial theory:

> A pure European countermemory is suspect and disingenuous, for it would seem to exonerate Europe's past all too easily and thereby forfeit the lessons to be learned from the past. A contemporary Europe that will not negotiate with the moral authority of its erstwhile 'Other', Africa and Asia, is a Europe that will not pay a price or atone for its colonialism. More generally, any dominant subject position that is in the process of deconstructing or calling itself into question cannot do so in solipsistic isolation, but must do so rather in a participatory dialogue with the subaltern positions. (39)

In my goal of analyzing postcolonial women writers and creating links of solidarity among them, Foucauldian resistance to coalition building is a drawback. For Foucault as for Deleuze the masses are in touch with "reality" as it takes place in "factories, asylums, prisons, houses" and the masses "do not need theory" since they live "theory in practice." Radhakrishnan demonstrates that contemporary intellectual movements in ethnic, feminist, anti-colonial struggles all have had their leaders such as Martin Luther King, Mohandas Gandhi, W.E.B. Dubois and many others who are not "coercive leaders." Foucault neglects to make "crucial distinctions ... between leaders and intellectuals who are organic with the movement and those that are traitors, between forms of power that are repressive and those that are liberating, ameliorative, and emancipatory" (40).

Radhakrishnan turns rather to Gramsci, who prior to Foucault historically, enables intellectuals to recuperate the "political" by acknowledging the individual in relation to the masses, the specific role of intellectuals, and the very real possibilities of effecting social processes toward social change. For Gramsci, "the issue of agency is a valid and live one" (48). The human being as agent acts with intention and in relation to historical events. Gramsci's "organic intellectual" is his way to demystify intellectual activity and at the same time assign it a particular valence. Further, intellectuals, in Gramsci's world, as they have a whole set of relationships to their particular world, are also its "functionaries." Radhakrishnan connects Gramsci's "world" to Edward Said's "wordliness." "Said's complaint is not that people in contemporary Western society do not have a politics, but that these very people seem not to know what it is to be political as intellectuals" (51). At issue "is the very meaning of the term 'political'. Gramsci will not entertain a politics without direction ... without relation to the general. Not having lost the vision of a total (and not totalized) historical bloc collective, it is still meaningful for Gramsci to take into account the imbalances and inequalities within the same society ... His aim is to cure and rectify these imbalances through the critical-theoretical practice of a dialectical relationship between the masses and 'its' intellectuals" (53). Gramsci gives full weight to the importance of intellectuals and organizers in leading movements for social change, and recognizes that "without the theoretical aspect of the theory-practice nexus" there can be no effective organization. Intellectuals and leaders are important for decolonizing societies and as Radhakrishnan notes, there is a need for "organic leaders" from within their midst rather than relying on "metropolitan intelligentsia that is all too easily drained away into a deracinated international continuum" (54). This is not to essentialize ethnic or feminist groups but to be vigilant about the realities of institutionalization and co-optation that are common.

Conclusion: Postcolonial Theory and Social Responsibility

This study brings postcolonial theory into the realm of social responsibility. I use critical practices that give primacy to literary texts, to writers' own statements in essays and interviews, even as I engage with feminist scholarship and activist material. Critical reading practices, as one among other modes of resistance, need to be an integral part of the struggles of postcolonial women writers and their representations in novels, poems, short stories, and dramas. My study gives serious critical attention to writers, a need that many of them have expressed. Ama Ata Aidoo's impassioned response to an interviewer's question, "where are the female Achebes?" recognizes the lack of intellectual and material support structures that underlie the production of art.[80]

A socially responsible postcolonial critic decolonizes several disconcerting trends in the production and consumption of postcolonial theory: 1) Theoretical production as an end in itself, confined to the consumption of other theorists who speak the same privileged language in which obscurity is regularly mistaken for profundity. 2) Very little theoretical production by postcolonial writers which is grounded in a politics geared toward social transformation of their societies is given the serious attention that it deserves, or it is dismissed as not theoretical enough by "western" standards. A new hegemony is being established in contemporary theory which can with impunity ignore or exclude postcolonial writers' essays, interviews, and other cultural productions while endlessly discussing concepts of the "Other," of "difference," and so on. 3) The use of postcolonial texts by theory producers and consumers of western academia as raw material without accounting for their specific histories and cultural contexts is problematic. Such trends inevitably assert an intellectual and political domination. Often, with the best intentions, intellectuals are complicit in an endeavor that ends up validating the dominant power structure, and ironically, even when they ideologically oppose such hegemonic power. Fredric Jameson's controversial essay, "Third World Literature in an Era of Multinational Capitalism" begins with a disturbing arrogance, even a paternalism based on Jameson's own privileged status as a first-world, white, male, highly reputed theorist: "Judging from recent conversations among third-world intellectuals, there is now an obsessive return of the national situation itself, the name of the country that returns again and again like a gong, the collective attention to 'us', and what we have to do and how we do it, to what we can't do and what we do better than this or that nationality, our unique characteristics, in short, to the level of the 'people.' "[81]

Jameson suggests a method of reading third world novels for the western, post-modern, alienated intellectual. He draws familiar distinctions between private/public, poetic/political as located within capitalist, industrialized, first-world societies. The "third world" is not described as part of any particular mode of production. An assertion such as, "the individual story and the individual experience cannot but ultimately involve the whole laborious telling of the experience of the collectivity itself," is reductive and inaccurate. Jameson's analysis is based on what he describes as his "sweeping hypothesis," namely, "What all third world cultural productions seem to have in common and what distinguishes them radically from analogous cultural forms in the first world [is] that all third world texts are necessarily allegorical, and in a very specific way they are to be read as what I will call national allegories" (66).

Jameson, as a western intellectual, can only approach these texts not on the basis of their world-views, but rather on the basis of his—one in which "allegory" serves to explain "all third world cultural productions" notwithstanding that such a category would distort an interpretation of certain works. As Aijaz Ahmed in his response to Jameson points out, only those texts which are "national allegories" by Jameson's definition would be admitted as third-world texts.[82] And, one must also ask whether there are no other useful categories such as gender, class, ethnicity, language, race, region, apart from "the nation" in a discussion of this literature?

I do not suggest that postcolonial texts are best theorized by "insiders," and not by "westerners." These very categories, insider/outsider, are mediated by the complicated location of postcolonial writers and critics in terms of geography, constituency, audience, as well as racial, educational, gender, and class parameters. Whoever the postcolonial theorist may be, there is "the urgent need," to use Chandra Mohanty's words, "to examine the *political* implications of *analytic* strategies (original emphasis)."[83] We need to find critical practices that will challenge what Mohanty aptly calls "a discursive colonization." Critics and theorists are not made as accountable as writers to respond to urgent social issues and to inspire social change. As Wole Soyinka asks astutely in his essay, "The Critic and Society: Barthes, Leftocracy, and Other Mythologies": "What is the critic's society? For whom does the critic write? For Mr. Dele Bus-Stop of Idi-Oro? Or for the Appointments and Promotions Committee and Learned Journals?" He points out that "Unquestionably there is an intellectual cop-out in the career of any critics who cover reams of paper with unceasing lament over the failure of this or that writer to write for the masses of the people, when they see themselves assiduously engage ... only with the incestuous productivity of their own academic, bourgeois-situated literature."[84]

A socially responsible postcolonial critic responds as do the postcolonial women writers analyzed in this study, to material and social conditions, and to sexual inequalities in societies where the long arm of British colonialism shook hands with individual patriarchies in exiling women from their bodies. This study probes literary and non-literary representation of female protagonists who resist internal exile from their bodies and who struggle to reconnect with their bodies and communities in working toward a more just society for their families and communities.

CHAPTER 2

Indigenous Third World Female Traditions of Resistance

A RECUPERATION OF HERSTORIES

*C*ontemporary women writers' representations of female protagonists' exile from their bodies and resistances to such bodily disempowerments are rooted in indigenous female traditions during pre-colonial, colonial, and postcolonial historical times. Such struggles against bodily and mental oppression often have to be recuperated from the margins of history. I excavate selected pre-colonial traditions of resistance that use the female body—via voice, silence, reproductive abilities, and militancy—to counter domination; second, I cite examples of women's opposition to British colonial practices such as taxation. Anti-colonial theorists, usually male, such as Martiniquan Frantz Fanon, or India's Mohandas K. Gandhi, recognize the need to deploy female bodies in nationalist struggles—after all, half the population could not be excluded.[1] But "flag independence" left many gaps between national and female liberation, along with other disillusionment that continues in postcolonial societies, even into the twenty-first century, of the "black skin, white mask" phenomenon. Indeed, as Mohanty and Alexander note in their Introduction to *Feminist Genealogies*, in contemporary decolonizing struggles, one needs to work not only toward national but also transnational democracies in third world societies.[2]

It remains significant for feminists committed to the study of third world women to dig into local herstories and discover *indigenous roots of feminist traditions*, as well as to deploy useful aspects of western feminism such as the theorizing of women's experience, testimony, and agency.[3] It is more productive to redefine feminism for postcolonial social contexts rather than a dismissal of feminism as western, and the confusion, as Kumari

Jayawardena points out, between anti-westernism and anti-imperialism. In a talk entitled "Women and Myths of Colonialism," Jayawardena notes that "alarming allegations [are] made against feminists—that they were inspired by foreign ideology, paid with foreign money and [that they] were following policies which would divide families and split the movements. . . . It was such attitudes that led women in South Asia to examine their own history in order to disprove the allegations that feminism was imposed on Asian women by Western feminists. This meant a re-examining of history in order to restore women's place, literally from the footnotes to the main body of the text."[4] Along with documenting indigenous roots of feminism in postcolonial regions, it is important to demystify history, as Jayawardena puts it, from "both colonial distortions and nationalist exaggerations." In the geographical areas included in this study, there are specific female figures and indigenous traditions of struggle against both native and colonial patriarchal domination, for instance, goddess figures among the Ashanti of Ghana, or a descendant of the Ashanti Oheama, in the figure of the warrior-woman Ni in the Caribbean; Rani of Jhansi in India; and female spirit-mediums like Nehanda in Zimbabwe. Women warriors are historical foremothers of contemporary female protagonists who defy traditional female roles—for instance, Aidoo's protagonist Anowa in the drama *Anowa*, and the Akan tradition of female resistance; Flora Nwapa's or Buchi Emecheta's female protagonists and the Igbo tradition of "sitting on a man." Traditions of female priestesses often provide examples of strategic uses of religion and attempts at transforming situations of oppression.[5] Most of these figures are excluded from official histories that focus on male liberationists in anti-colonial movements.

The fact that women's resistances in pre-colonial times may not have been named as feminist does not mean that they did not exist. This is a misconception similar to the racist claim that since African cultures existed orally, and were invisible to a narrow print-oriented European bias, they did not exist at all! I distinguish between what is identified today as feminist models from what might have been recognized previously as female traditions of courage and resistance. Feminism as a political and academic area of struggle and study belongs after all, to the twentieth century. However, it is important in this study to identify, and derive inspiration from earlier models of female power and strength.

I draw a further distinction between female power and strength. Power is an ideologically conditioned and historically contextualized concept. When exerted in situations of dominance, power has inscribed within it unequal social relations, so for instance, when an oppressed person retaliates to domination, that may or may not shift unequal power relations. As a concept, power is often evoked glibly to describe what would more accurately be regarded as female strength. For instance, for slave women, owned by white slave masters, autonomy over their bodies—such as by aborting children—did not transform, though it did disrupt the economic and sexual power hierarchies of Caribbean plantation societies. However, resistance through strategic uses of their bodies—singing satirical songs, or speaking back even when it meant physical reprisals—required enormous courage. The task of decoding indigenous traditions of female resistance is very important because, when overt defiance of patriarchal structures carried severe penalties such as social exclusion and exile from community, and even death, women creatively invented covert means with which to resist. The goal was survival. Covert resistances are couched in folktales, mythology, religious scripture, popular culture, uses of magic, and obeah (indigenous ritual practices).

Feminist demystifications of mythological figures that have been represented in general by a male gaze are part of this recuperation and reinterpretation of indigenous models of female strength. In the ancient Indian epic, *The Ramayana*, the figure of Sita, contrary to its classical representation as a model of silent suffering and self-sacrifice, also provides, in folk and popular versions, an example of female resistance to patriarchy. In an important essay, "Breaking out of Invisibility: Rewriting the History of Women in Ancient India," Uma Chakravarti and Kum Kum Roy recuperate women who "like other subordinate groups, are among the muted or even silent voices of history."[6] They challenge official records of history "whose function has been to record and document events as seen by those who succeeded in history." Hence, women as "neglected subjects" have been "the unmourned casualties of history." Chakravarty and Roy significantly recognize that "the distinction between mythology and history was never very rigorously maintained in early times" (320). This insight is useful in analyzing the powerful impacts that mythical-historical figures such as Sita and Draupadi exert in contemporary times within a collective subconscious via popular iconography and television representations.

Chakravarty and Roy provide a concrete historicization rather than the timeless and transcendent virtues that Sita carries as a model of Indian womanhood. A historical approach reveals that the classical version of the epic represents the most patriarchal image of Sita as subservient and silent, whereas folk forms of the epic demonstrate an outspoken woman. "An analysis of the Sita legend in a historical context," note Chakravarty and Roy, "reveals that the emphasis on chastity and the assumption that ideal marriage is based on female devotion are aspects which were grafted onto an originally simple story. Over the centuries important details were added to the story and these had a crucial bearing on the shaping of feminine identity" (334).

One important addition in the classical version of the epic attributed to Valmiki was Sita's abduction by the demon Ravana which made her a victim who "had to prove her chastity," note Chakravarty and Roy, "not just once but repeatedly." The abduction also "propagat(ed) the twin notions that women were the property of men and that sexual fidelity was the major virtue for women" (334). Another important historical underpinning is discovered in the fact that "the Valmiki *Ramayana* clearly represented a later stage of marriage aimed at the begetting of children of undisputed paternity to inherit the father's wealth. It was this development that accounted for the emphasis on chastity and fidelity at the core of the Sita legend" (334–35). This classical version contrasts with "hundreds of versions which are part of the oral tradition." Each version served a purpose and the classical one gained dominance. However, feminist historiographers discover that "the Sita of the folk version has much greater contempt for Rama after she is abandoned by him." She repudiates Rama in her own voice, gives her sons a matrilineal heritage and refuses to go back to Rama. The folk versions rescue Sita from the passivity with which she is associated in the classical one.

In fact, the tale of Sita's abduction by Ravana and her subsequent status as the ideal of womanly chastity and virtue is told in different ways, notes Romila Thapar, prominent Indian historian, depending of where "the story traveled" and how it was influenced by "the social structure of that area, the kin relations, ethnic relations, and belief structures of the people there." Thapar presents historical examples on the premise that "the depictions of traditional Indian womanhood ... even when they are handed down, do not remain frozen."[7] Thapar discusses "a floating tradition of stories" that made up the Indian epics. Hence, although Valmiki's classical version of *The Ramayana* has survived as the most widely known version, there are Buddhist, Jain, and other folk renditions of the story. Thapar discusses how "in the Jaina versions, Sita is a much more assertive person" than in Valmiki's rendition. When Sita has to undergo a trial by fire to prove her chastity, and when she ultimately wills her death by asking mother earth to open and receive her, Thapar interprets this as "a woman who finds her own way of release from hardships" (6). Sita is believed to have been born "out of a furrow" in the earth, and hence her appropriate return to her mother provides for Thapar, "a compensatory model" for women.[8]

In most patriarchal cultures, women's elevated status in mythology stands paradoxically alongside their harsh lived realities. Mythology and religion constitute powerful ideological bases that sustain patriarchal controls of women within the family and in daily life. Female uses of religious authority provide instances of patriarchally sanctioned space. From within this space, women function overtly, or they resist the system covertly. As priestesses and goddesses, women gain privilege and authority, though such power is mystified which enables a containment of any form of female authority. As other forms of power, patriarchal power is not absolute; rather, following Foucault, I would argue that "relations of power are not in superstructural positions" that are imposed from above. "Power comes from below, (from) the manifold relationships of force that take shape and come into play in the machinery of production, in families, limited groups, and institutions."[9]

Female uses of religious and cultural modes such as possession and magic are useful weapons of resistance to patriarchal control. In Frantz Fanon's otherwise seminal studies of race and colonial domination, there is a fear and distancing from such supernatural means of resistance. Fanon remarks that "the atmosphere of myth and magic frightens [him],"[10] and since he cannot be certain where these energies lead, often true in cultural work in terms of unquantifiable results, he rejects them. Although Fanon states that "the struggle for liberation is a cultural phenomenon," his analysis is limited by his skepticism about the uses of cultural means and these are especially important for women. In line with his analysis of the tension, repression, both physical and mental, that the native is under during colonization, Fanon interprets the energy released in dance, ritual, or possession, as a channeling of violence into "a permissive circle," rather than being turned against the colonizer. "The circle of the dance," he remarks, "is a permissive circle; it protects and permits," and in the very physical release of tensions, "a community exorcizes itself" (57). Within a ritual arena there is space for "the hampered aggressivity to dissolve as in a volcanic eruption." Fanon, however, inaccurately assumes that within such ritual practices, "there are no limits." Strict codes of conduct and behavior usually protect and guide the ones who go into possession and experience supernatural energies.

Other indigenous female traditions of resistance were often eroded by racist colonial practices. In India, for instance, there were many extraordinary warrior queens whose histories were recuperated by nineteenth-century

Indian social reformers to counteract colonialist assumptions about "the general backwardness of the country." Kumari Jayawardena in *Feminism and Nationalism in the Third World* notes the following: "Sultana Razia who succeeded to the throne of her father, the King of Delhi (in the 13th century), and led her troops into battle; Nur Jehan who exercised real power and led the army in war during the reign (in the early 17th century) of her husband Emperor Jehangir; and Lakshmi Bai, the Rani of Jhansi, who during the war against the British in 1857, led her troops on horseback in fierce battles against the invaders and died in combat."[11] In their essay, "Rewriting the History of Women in Ancient India," Chakravarti and Roy draw significant differences between a figure such as Sultana Razia (named in their essay significantly as "Razia Sultan"—Sultan meaning king) and Lakshmibai. They quote from a thirteenth-century historian who praises Razia as "'a great monarch . . . endowed with all the qualities befitting a king but she was not born of the right sex and so in the estimation of men all these virtues were worthless.'" As a contrast, Lakshmibai has greater appeal in Indian history since she belongs to the respected tradition of "regent queens (who) stepped in to wield power on behalf of their minor sons. Lakshmibai combined heroic valour and uncompromising resistance against a foreign power with spirited action to preserve the throne for her son, exactly the right combination to be approved by nationalist historians" (324). Chakravarti and Roy point out that recuperations of history by male nationalists usually supported "the belief that women did not feature in history. . . . Women remained at best footnotes or punctuation marks in a narrative essentially concerned with the achievements and ideas of men. If anything, occasional references to them in mainstream history led only to the belief that women did not feature in history more often because they had done so little, rather than leading readers to the alternative conclusion: that history itself had neglected women" (325).

In the Caribbean context, Lucille Mathurin's text, *The Rebel Woman in the British West Indies during Slavery*,[12] usefully documents how female slaves strategically used their bodies to resist male oppression and colonial exploitation. Mathurin argues in her Introduction that contrary to historical accounts, "female slaves adopted some of the same techniques as men to defy the system. They frequently ran away from the plantation, on their own, or in mixed groups, and in addition they resisted in ways which were peculiar to them as women. For example they could and did use periods of childbearing to do the minimum of work, and to extract the maximum of concessions from their masters" (8).

Such resistances were rooted in native traditions of the Gold Coast communities in West Africa from where most of the slaves were brought into the Caribbean. Their militancy was based on a demand for self-respect. African societies like the Ashanti gave women an elevated political status embodied in the power and authority of the Queen Mother's Stool. Mathurin notes that since slaves between the ages of fourteen and forty were captured, they arrived into the New World steeped in their own cultures and equipped with traditions of militancy. For women in particular, one must emphasize not only the nightmare history of the slave trade, but worsened conditions after the abolition of the slave trade in 1807, when women's bodies, as reproductive commodities were forced to breed in order to supply hands for labor. Such was the need for labor that "if a pregnant woman were convicted of a crime punishable by execution," notes Mathurin, "her sentence should be suspended until after the birth of her infant" (7).

Mathurin documents varieties of resistances from relatively unthreatening ones such as an unwillingness to work, to scheming against masters, burning property, poisoning, running away ("pulling foot"), and open rebellions. The strategy "to work slowly, to work badly, or not to work at all" was interpreted as "black laziness." Mathurin dispels this stereotype in her discussion of how blacks worked very hard especially when it was on their own small plots of land, or as free human beings. Women especially, often walked miles to sell their products, a legacy carried on by "the higgler woman," an important part of Caribbean domestic economy today. Open refusals to work brought severe reprisals such as hard labor. Hence, Mathurin notes the adoption of "more clever and subtle methods of avoiding work [such as] illness.... One favourite device which planters often described was that of allowing the tiny insect parasite, the chigoe, to lay its eggs in the toes, and so cause sore legs which could lay up the patient for a considerable time" (10–11). Such power plays even to the extent of causing physical pain on oneself unfolded within a situation where slaves and slave owners tried to outsmart one another.

Female bodily processes such as menstruation and breastfeeding became effective times for absenteeism. Mathurin notes that "a number of witnesses testified to the British Parliamentary Committee on slavery in 1789" that black women took up to two years, "an extraordinarily long time to wean their babies." Part of the "low productivity" and the expense of maintaining a chattel system resulted directly from women withholding forced labor through their bodily strategies.

Another powerful bodily weapon used to resist oppression was the tongue, "that powerful instrument of attack and defense" as noted by the Governor of Trinidad in the 1820s. Mathurin relates several historical events of women's deployment of speech, of quarrelling, argument, noisiness, of being unmanageable. "Hot-tempered 'vixens' and 'viragos'" were tried for "their language which was described as 'indecent', 'scandalous', 'outrageous', 'insulting', 'abusive', or 'threatening'" (15). Mathurin points out that one reason for women's fearless defiance was that their owners were often the fathers of their brown children. They also used their speech in satirical songs revealing the hypocrisy of white preachers who "while he palaver and preach him book/At the negro girl he'll wink hum yeye" (16).

Although forced to be illiterate, slaves were remarkably aware of slave laws, especially domestic slave women who heard conversations and often ironically learnt of their rights from conversations in white households. Mathurin documents twenty-one cases in Port Royal in the 1820s of which eighteen were lodged by women: Lizzy, Dido, Rosetta, Augusta, Tuba, Susanna Tucker, Camilla Eping, Mary McBeth, and others. The odds were so heavily against them and most often, in response to their appeals against cruel treatment they received sentences of imprisonment or hard labor. Mathurin notes the remarkable fact that they

> continued to press the courts with their complaints.... In spite of the strong likelihood that rather than receiving justice, they would receive punishments for daring to lodge a complaint, women would not be silenced ... They were obviously prepared to risk being flogged or imprisoned for the satisfaction of knowing that they had taken up the time of the magistrates, they had forced owners and overseers to appear in the court and answer for their actions: while these proceedings took place they themselves were naturally absent from work. Whether they won, or whether they lost, they ... forced their presence on the consciousness of many. (18)

Women also participated in armed rebellion. Mathurin documents the story of Cubah, a female slave who was crowned "Queen of Kingston" and was probably expected to perform the functions of a traditional West African Queen Mother. She was one of the plotters of "one of the major black uprisings of the era of slavery" when six parishes in Jamaica in 1760 were to participate simultaneously. Cubah was captured and shipped off the island. Although she managed to return, she was caught and executed.

Even if they survived as runaway slaves, life in the bush was extremely difficult. Women played a most significant part in the lives of bush rebels, in particular those of Jamaica, the Maroons. These

> Jamaican freedom fighters ... had more women and children than armed men.... The leaders of these Jamaican Maroons ... were Akan people: their place-names, such as Accompong, were Ashanti, so also were the names frequently found among their leaders, for example Cudgoe, Quaco, Kofi. Their village organisation, their strong beliefs in the magical gifts of their religious leaders, as well as a recognised position for the women in their society, were all aspects of their previous African experience which they reproduced in their rebel life. These traditions helped to produce a well structured and disciplined community, which was essential for a life of continuous warfare. (30)

Women played key roles in these communities in providing food and keeping guerilla activities possible. The Maroons managed "to hold the white community in fear, for nearly one hundred years after the English first entered the island" (32).

As a stark contrast to the feminist recuperation of Maroon history by Lucille Mathurin, consider the colonial, racist version in Bryan Edwards's "The History of the West Indies":

> Concerning the Maroons, they are in general ignorant of our language, and all of them attached to the gloomy superstitions of Africa (derived from their ancestors) with such enthusiastick zeal and reverential ardour, as I think can only be eradicated with their lives.... Their language was a barbarous dissonance of the African dialects, with a mixture of Spanish and broken English.... They had no inclination for the pursuits of sober industry.... I could never perceive any vestige of culture.... The Maroons, like all other savage nations, regarded their wives as so many beasts of burden; and felt no more concern at the loss of one of them, than a white planter would have felt at the loss of a bullock.[13]

Though Edwards recounts the prolonged and difficult struggle that the British had in controlling their "desultory foes," he grudgingly admires the Maroons' "great bodily perfection" with "prominent muscles" unhindered by clothing, "acute sight" and "remarkably quick hearing." This follows a typically othering generalization that explains, and thereby contains what is threatening to the colonizer: "These characteristics, however, are common, I believe, to all savage nations, in warm and temperate climates; and like other savages, the Maroons have only those senses perfect which are kept in constant exercise" (244). The fact that the British were forced to negotiate with the Maroons, what they called "pacification" was a result of their inability to control them. Maroon militancy, "frequent robberies, murders, and depredations" in Edwards's account, led to the "diminution of his Majesty's revenue, as well as of the trade, navigation, and consumption of British manufactures" (234). Maroon victory against the British was won in their being given 1,500 acres of land to cultivate, and a detailed peace treaty was signed in order to end "a state of war and hostility." The British of course took full credit for achieving peace as stated in the "Articles of Pacification, 1738": "Peace and friendship among mankind, and the preventing the effusion of blood, is agreeable to God, consonant to reason, and desired by every good man" (237). The Maroons certainly did not belong within the company of such "good men" whose civilizing mission was built on stealing land, subordinating people, their languages and cultures.

The very condition of enslavement evokes opposition. In the British Caribbean, Akan Slave Rebellions, as analyzed by Monica Schuler even as they challenged the slave system, also asserted an "ethnic exclusivism of the Akan and their distrust of the creole slaves" as Goveia points out. Even as the Akan might preserve their own African traditions and rituals, the slave system effectively maintained "ethnic divisions among the Africans themselves."[14] The particular racial hierarchies that were in place in the plantocracy environs effectively kept the various oppressed slaves, of different hues, apart. If the all too well-known British tactic of divide and rule operated along religious lines in India (Hindus against Muslims), the Caribbean policy was helped by color superiorities and class exclusivities. The colonial administration like the slave system was maintained more by tactics playing upon religious and color rivalries than upon force. That is also why "decolonizing the mind" to use Ngugi wa Thiong'o's phrase, is a more complex and longer-lasting process than gaining political independence.

In *The Rebel Woman*, Mathurin's concluding essay, "Nanny: Rebel/Queen/Mother," memorializes the most exceptional of the Maroon women, Nanny or Ni whose spirit inspires contemporary Caribbean feminist consciousness. The few facts about "this remarkable Ashanti chieftainess," notes Mathurin, have survived "largely through the strong oral traditions of her descendants." Official historical accounts attempt to dehistoricize her life and achievements and "reduce" her to mythological status. But as Mathurin states, "Nanny was very much alive, she survived the end of the first Maroon war in 1740," and remarkably was given five hundred acres of land. Though it is not definite if Nanny was born in Jamaica or in Africa, her Ashanti origins are definite. She was never a slave herself, and though it is important to distinguish, as Orlando Patterson points out, between the militancy of Maroons in Jamaica who were not enslaved from the blacks who were slaves, "the very presence of the Maroons contributed to the climate of revolts in that their existence was living proof of the vulnerability of the whites and encouraged the slaves to challenge the system."[15]

Sister of Cudjoe, a famous Maroon leader, Nanny was married to a Maroon who was interestingly non-militant unlike his wife. Nanny had no children "but was revered as the mother of her people." From 1690, Nanny's leadership established a free community where women and children were respected, until the British attempted to capture it in 1730. In this first Maroon war "Nanny's genius," notes Mathurin, "dominated the fighting strategies of the guerillas.... Her role was very much in the tradition of Ashanti priests/priestesses who performed essential functions in African warfare. Such magico-religious leaders customarily advised on the best time for waging war, they gave warriors charms to protect them from injury, they participated with the military commanders in rituals designed to weaken the enemy" (36).

Across the seas, in a different land, the female spirit-medium Nehanda among the Shona people of Southern Africa is comparable to Ni. Like Ni, Nehanda also advised soldiers on warfare strategies, on propitious timings for battle, and gave them protective charms. Both female figures used their supernatural powers for the purpose of protecting their people and land from foreign invaders. Nehanda's story is recaptured vividly in texts by Christine Qunta, David Lan, and Terence Ranger.[16] An important paradox underlies both patriarchal cultures, Ashanti and Shona, where women performed strictly defined roles, where the division of labor was drawn on gender lines, but that also allowed these crucial, spiritual spaces for the exercise of female authority and power.

Nanny became celebrated as a great worker of magic. She could catch bullets and hurl them back; she could keep a huge cauldron boiling without the use of fire. "Maroon history has it," notes Mathurin, "that when curious soldiers and militiamen came close to inspect this freak of nature, they fell into the cauldron and were suffocated" (38). Nanny retained her militancy when other Maroon leaders like Cudjoe compromised with the British.

"She resolved never to come to terms with the English. She infected her followers with this determination, and their aggressiveness became legendary." Although Nanny reluctantly agreed to peace terms for her own people, "it is significant that as the men signed the truce, the women stood by wearing defiantly round their ankles as ornaments the teeth of the white soldiers who had been killed in battle" (38). The evocative power of such stories of defiance and struggle for self-determination and pride as black people cannot be gainsaid, and continue to survive long after Nanny's death in the 1750s. Nanny, or Ni, is embraced as a significant ancestor of the contemporary Caribbean feminist consciousness and her stories inspire many cultural representations such as Lorna Goodison's poem, "Nanny," and Sistren's play, *Nana Yah*. "My womb was sealed/ with molten wax/ of killer bees," begins Goodison's poem. Bodily imagery describes how Nanny made her body fit to be a warrior: "all my weapons within me. . . . When your sorrow obscures the skies/ other women like me will rise."[17] Further, as Honor Ford-Smith notes in her Introduction to *Lionheart Gal*, "behind the figure of the subservient nanny (black domestic) lurks the militant Ni." Perhaps, in times when overt militancy such as Ni's is too dangerous, women can preserve, though hidden, their courage and strength, lurking under the skin and behind the bones, singing a coded tune until the time arrives to strike and be victorious.

Similarly, the evocative power of the events of 1896 in Rhodesia, and the key role played by the female spirit-medium Nehanda, "have become," notes Terence Ranger, "an essential part of the consciousness of the liberation movements. . . . Zimbabwean poets and novelists draw their themes from the risings. . . . In the recent [anthology] *Black Fire*, we hear of guerilla bands being blessed by the Nehanda medium in ecstatic trance."[18] Similar to Bryan Edwards's account (quoted earlier) of the "savagery" of Maroons in Jamaica, "colonial missionary accounts of the Shona incredulously denied that they had any religious system." "As Dr. Kuper tells us," notes Ranger, "the Shona have an elaborate cult, unusual in Southern Africa, centering in the Supreme Being, Mwari" (17). Mwari was to be approached through the system of spirit-mediums or the Mondoro cult. The male or female spirit-medium would be possessed and would act as intermediary between ordinary people and ancestors. To the colonizers, they were "conscious frauds" (19).

When religion is central to community life as among the Shona, divisions between ritual duties and political activities are challenged. Further, ritual powers often kept the political power of chiefs under control. White settlers in the 1890s forcibly evicted Africans from their land, and proceeded to extract mineral wealth often by tricking indigenous chiefs. As Qunta notes, "In 1889 Cecil Rhodes, assisted by a missionary who spoke Ndebele, deceived King Lobengula into signing away the mineral rights of his country" (56), the people consulted their religious leaders before they decided to fight the invaders. Nehanda heard of the settlers' crimes and declared, notes Qunta, "the first 'Chimurenga' (liberation) war in 1896" (56). Like Ni, she was well-versed in military strategy and was regarded by the whites as "the most powerful wizard in Mashonaland" (57). Like Ni, Nehanda advised her people to attack white settlers, their farms, mines, and trading posts, as well as policemen and Africans who collaborated with the invaders. "Besides coordinating and commanding her forces, Nehanda also gathered intelligence.... Her main sources were spies, informers and fire signals.... Looting was forbidden except to replenish their own stocks. Gunpowder was manufactured from local materials. Missiles were made from lengths of telegraph wire, nails and glass balls from soda-water bottles" (59). Although Nehanda required strict discipline, she could effectively boost the morale of her followers by predicting victories. As Ni had magical powers, so did Nehanda who made "ndudzo," war medicine. "It is important to understand the confidence of people," notes Mr. Chivanda quoted in Ranger's *Revolt in Southern Rhodesia*, "if we realize that the presence of the *mhondoro*, who was a warrior himself (sic), was constant and reassuring. People felt safe because the *mhondoro* were believed to be able to prophesy and ward off danger" (392). Along with her military tactics, Nehanda could provide spiritual protection, similar to the beliefs about Ni, even immunity from enemy bullets. Along with her powerful male partner Kagubi, Nehanda could "turn their [enemy's] bullets into water" (217).

As with the Maroons, the British were forced to enter negotiations since this disciplined force proved formidable. When Nehanda was captured, "charged with causing and instigating rebellion and with murdering the Native Commissioner, Pollard, notorious for his cruelty," Qunta recounts that a Catholic priest tried to convert her. She refused, and "remained fearless and defiant to the very last" (58). Apparently, Nehanda resisted the first two attempts to kill her since she had her magical snuff on her person. It was only when the enemy found and removed it that she could be killed. Nehanda demonstrates how a traditional religious authority serves a people's revolutionary movement, a kind of liberation theology that inspires people to struggle by appealing to the woven fabric of a cultural past before it was rent asunder by plundering colonizers.

In more recent times, Ranger recounts other religious authorities that were revered during nationalist movements of the 1950s, such as Mai Chaza regarded as a "messianic liberator" (381), continuing a female legacy that is traced to Nehanda. Even within the modern struggle of evolving a nation state, it was important to involve the rural masses in the liberation struggle and an appeal to traditions such as that of the spirit-mediums was extremely enabling. A popular appeal to religious tradition that had once proven to be successful against powerful outsiders was effective. Such memory as that of the 1896 uprising, often painfully reconstructed from oral sources (that usefully balance colonial records) is critical in inspiring modern day leaders. This was evident when a ninety-year-old survivor of the 1896 events presented "a spirit axe as a symbol of the apostolic succession of resistance" to Joshua Nkomo in 1962 "so that he might 'fight to the bitter end'" (385).[19]

Other similar female spirit-mediums such as "Alice Lenshina Mulenga in Zambia, Marie Lalou in the Ivory coast, and Gaudencia Aoko in Kenya" are recorded by Bennetta Jules-Rosette.[20] Mai Chaza is believed to have healing powers for "women who were barren, those possessed by alien spirits, and the blind." Unfortunately, as Jules-Rosette notes, these women do not have female successions, so Mai Chaza's place was taken after her death by "a male Malawian, Mapaulos, who began to perform extraordinary healings in her name" (102). Women who acquire such "ceremonial leadership," notes Jules-Rosette, "have difficulty maintaining this authority. As prophetesses and symbols of ritual purity, (they) are recipients of positions of symbolic privilege without political power" (115). These indigenous traditions were potentially powerful cultural weapons during periods of domination such as colonization and the particular colonizing of female bodies. Such enslavements provoked resistances.

Pre-colonial Traditions of Women's Strength

Certain pre-colonial traditions of women's groups that protected women's rights within communities, and that ensured power-sharing between the sexes were often misunderstood by British colonizers who brought their own legal systems. Colonialism and capitalism worked together to women's detriment. Gender analysis is not to be reduced only to women's participation in and exclusion from the operation of capital. The task before us, as Michele Barrett puts it, is "to identify the operations of gender relations as and where they may be distinct from or connected with the processes of production and reproduction."[21] The social arrangements of gender within several pre-colonial societies such as the Igbo and Yoruba of Nigeria illustrate that before colonialism women played an active part in the sociopolitical life of their community. Today, despite the external advantages of education and modernization, women's actual participation in the political sphere has been marginalized. Both capitalism and patriarchy, and the multileveled arenas of their operation, within institutions like family, schools, courts, prisons, and into intimate bodily activities, are part of systems that perpetuate women's oppression.

Women's active participation in political life before colonialism did not mean that there was perfect equality between the sexes. However, traditional sexist structures within pre-colonial societies were greatly reinforced by western sexual mores dictated by Victorian morality and Christian missionary zeal, for instance, the Victorian belief that a woman's place was in the home and not in the sphere of business or politics. Moreover, certain inbuilt structures of shared power between men and women on the sociopolitical level were destroyed by colonial administrative policies.

For instance, in traditional Igbo society there were two sorts of women's associations: the *inyemedi* (the wives of a lineage), and the *umuada* (the daughters of a lineage) that protected women's interests as traders, farmers, wives, and mothers. Within a shared power base between the sexes, the British introduced their methods of "native administration" with warrant chiefs and a new hierarchy of law and order fundamentally different from traditional structures of governance and justice. Often, warrant chiefs were appointed by the British only because these men had some knowledge of English and not because they had earned their communities' respect by earning titles and other indigenous forms of gaining status. British judicial practices gradually outlawed all "self-help" procedures used by women to secure their demands, particularly the tradition of "sitting on a man": "To 'sit on', or 'make war on' a man," explains Judith Van Allen, in her useful essay, " 'Aba Riots' or Igbo 'Women's War'? Ideology, Stratification, and the Invisibility of Women," "involved gathering at his compound at a previously agreed upon time, dancing, singing scurrilous songs detailing the women's grievances against him."[22] When Igbo women, through their sophisticated communication networks, used this method to protest British taxation in 1929, and when they organized to "make war on" and to "sit on" the British, the response was police violence and fifty women were killed. The inherent sexism of British attitudes initially led the British to assume that the women had been organized by the men. They lost a key opportunity in history to recognize women's role and participation in civic and political life. To them, women continued to remain invisible in the public domain. The British refused to accept that the women had used their own institutionalized method of protest, a grassroots activity under organized female leadership.

This event in British colonial records is described as "Aba Riots," which according to Van Allen, is a colonialist translation of the Igbo expression, "Ogu Umunwanyi," meaning, "women's war." Van Allen points out that "this is more than a word game. In politics, the control of language means the control of history" (59). Van Allen describes the convergence of thousands of women on native administration centers in "dress and adornment signifying 'war'—all wearing short loin-cloths, all carrying sticks wreathed with palm fronds (used to invoke the power of the female ancestors), and all having their faces smeared with charcoal or ashes and their heads bound with young ferns. What has not been seen by Westerners is that for some African women—and Igbo women are a striking example—actual or potential autonomy, economic independence and political power did not grow out of western influence but existed already in traditional 'tribal' life" (73).

Other traditions of female authority in colonies such as India were also disrupted or destroyed by colonial mechanisms. Talwar Oldenburg's essay, "Lifestyle as Resistance: The Case of the Courtesans of Lucknow, India,"[23] asserts through a study of colonial civic tax ledgers of 1858–1877 that certain women described derogatorily as "'dancing and singing girls' were in the highest tax bracket, with the largest individual incomes of any in the city." As with re-naming the Igbo women's war as a "riot," so again the British colonizers naming these women "dancing and singing girls" represents "one of the many profound cultural misunderstandings of 'exotic' Indian women," notes Oldenburg, a naming that marginalized these women from history. And for what the colonizers called their "rebellion against British rule in 1857" their property was confiscated. The other colonial records in which the courtesans appeared were in medical records and the concern over European soldiers afflicted with venereal disease. "It became clear that the battle to reduce European mortality rates would now be joined on the hygienic front," remarks Oldenburg, "to ensure a healthy European army for the strategic needs of the empire.... The imposition of the contagious diseases regulations and heavy fines and penalties on the courtesans for their role in the rebellion signalled the gradual debasement of an esteemed cultural institution into common prostitution" (260).

Similar to the Igbo women's resistance to British taxation, these courtesans invented ways of resisting "an intrusive civic authority," remarks Oldenburg, "that taxed their incomes and inspected their bodies. Characteristically, they responded by keeping two sets of books on their income, bribing the local *da'i*, or nurse, to avoid bodily inspections . . . publicly refusing to pay taxes when threatened with imprisonment. The tactics were new but the spirit behind them was veteran. These methods were imaginative extensions of the ancient and subtle ways the courtesans had cultivated to contest male authority in their liaisons with men and add up to a spirited defense of their own rights against colonial politics" (261). British propaganda only regarded the women as prostitutes and forcibly relocated them for sexual use, hence "dehumaniz(ing) the profession, stripping it of its cultural function. . . . It also made sex cheap and easy for the men and exposed women to venereal infection from the soldiers" (265). Though Oldenburg usefully explores how these women were adept at "manipulating men and means for their own social and political ends" she romanticizes the institution of courtesanship itself in her claim that "their 'life-style' is *resistance to rather than a perpetuation of patriarchal values*" (original emphasis).

Oldenburg's interviews with contemporary courtesans reveal the painful personal histories of widowhood, desertion, battering, in short how these women chose this option over situations of traditionally sanctioned abuse within families. They challenged the respectability, often hypocritically given to wives enslaved to their family's needs. The courtesans asserted their own autonomy in having control over their bodies and material possessions.

The uses of the female body, trading sex for money, continue in different forms. For instance, an article entitled, "Bar Girls: It's All About Money, Honey," in *The Times of India* (August 23, 2004, 3) records that thousands of women in Bombay "were out in the open to protest 'police harassment'. Although the women wanted to continue their profession 'in peace', stories of economic hardship and exploitation abound." Interviews with some two hundred bar girls revealed that most of them were duped into the trade "with false promises of marriage or jobs in cities." Some were forced into the trade by unemployed fathers or husbands, and "some lower middle-class girls dance in bars to pay for their education." Although employed as bar girls, many are prostitutes earning much more money (approximately Rs. 10,000 a month or more) than they would by doing domestic jobs of cleaning and cooking (around Rs. 3,000 per month). Most of them keep their sexual work a secret, often telling families that "they work in a call center" all night! Surely, an excuse made possible by globalization and the proliferation of jobs in call centers for American Express, Visa, and other companies in urban sites in India.

Colonial Disempowerments: Staying Home

One arena of significant disempowerment that women faced during colonialism is located in a rigid separation between private and public realms fostered especially by the Victorian ideology of women as "good wives and mothers." Christianity further reinforced these female roles within clearly circumscribed spaces. Missionaries set out to educate girls to be good wives and mothers, discouraging them from participating in the world of politics or business outside the home. Notions of domesticity were imposed on colonized women, the majority of whom (except for upper-caste women in India) had had no rigid separations in their participation between the home and the outside world. This rigid bifurcation soon entrenched class and gender stratification that worked to the disadvantage of women. The enforced middle-class privacy of institutions such as wifehood and motherhood tended to isolate women and separate them from traditional practices of collectivity and communication. As "book" knowledge became necessary for participation in political life, women were increasingly marginalized; worst of all, they were excluded from policy making that had a direct bearing on their lives, often their bodies. The control of women's bodies passed more and more into the arena of state policies where women hardly had any say.

I do not wish to romanticize the pre-colonial era as perfect. However, colonization colluded with and reinforced an indigenous patriarchy to worsen women's predicament, mainly in disempowering women from a political process. Some concrete areas of contradictory disempowerments with colonization are those of English education (discussed in chapter 3), and indigenous tradition (discussed in chapter 4). Fewer women than men had access to education and since English language abilities were required for most jobs, women were increasingly marginalized from a public sphere. Urbanization is only one example of contradictory modernizations for women. Consider, for instance, the humiliation of female bodies forced to practice polygamy in city apartments within cramped spaces (portrayed in Buchi Emecheta's novel, *The Joys of Motherhood*); other sexist options required women to objectify their bodies in order to survive in cities.[24] As

Bessie Head's protagonist Life remarks, she had exercised her bodily options as "a beauty queen, prostitute." With capitalist systems being introduced, wage earnings begin to dominate these societies and traditional economies in which women played an integral role, such as the market-women of Nigeria or Ghana, become severely disadvantaged. Further, women more than men fall between the cracks of tradition-modernization pressures. Women are required often to maintain traditions within urban settings and they also need to participate in modern economies to raise children in cities. A different type of economy prevailed in rural and farming communities. Colonial interpretations of local traditions, often racist, necessitated a regressive embracing of native customs, often to the further detriment of women. Not that traditions have to be valorized blindly. However, the colonial interruption to the historical evolution of social customs had particularly negative impacts on women. This history is part of current struggles against traditions such as sati. In their Introduction to *Recasting Women: Essays in Colonial History*, the editors, Kumkum Sangari and Sudesh Vaid undertake a useful discussion of "the implications of the reconstitution of patriarchies in the colonial period [as they] bear significantly upon the present."[25] Their historical analysis of "the inter-relation of patriarchal practices with political economy, religion, law and culture—in sum, questions about the politics of social change" in colonial India sheds light on similar concerns in contemporary times. Their feminist historiography recognizes "that each aspect of reality is gendered," and challenges any gender-neutral methodologies: "The act of understanding our construction as agents and subjects of social processes is itself a kind of intervention in the creation of exclusive knowledge systems. Perhaps the greatest difficulty lies in relating the ideological to the experiential" (3). They acknowledge "the regionally differential intervention of colonialism" and hence no claim is made to be "representative" or to speak for "all Indian women." However, there is a "common concern with the changing position of women both in its material specificity, and in its often inverse representations in the discourses which legitimize their social status." (4).

Sangari and Vaid analyze the interrelationship between patriarchies and classes: "Not only are patriarchal systems class differentiated, open to constant and consistent reformulation, but defining gender seems to be crucial to the formation of classes and dominant ideologies.... The lives of women exist at the interface of caste and class inequality, especially since the description and management of gender and female sexuality is involved in the maintenance and reproduction of social inequality" (5). They argue that colonial rule created its "legitimizing ideologies" that exacerbated already existing unequal gender relations in Indian society. The colonizers' apparently gender-neutral "social restructuring" was in fact, part of "a process of re-constituting patriarchies in every social strata" (6). Sangari and Vaid draw out the gender implications of most of this "unrecorded or hidden history." The introduction of colonial legal systems, as also for Igbo women discussed earlier, "further marginalized women from the 'public' sphere, even while it subjected them to its control. Such marginalization intensified their dependence on men" (6). Similar to colonial enterprises elsewhere, when women were displaced from "traditional village occupations," they found "limited opportunities in the new sector, for instance in the textile and jute mills. . . . Thus many women of the productive classes were pushed into the 'domestic' sphere, replicating to some extent the division between the 'private' and 'public' domain as defined by middle class ideologies" (9).

Sangari and Vaid effectively demystify the role of social reformers, both colonists and Indians, for women's issues. "This is a hidden history," they remark, "swept under the liberal carpet of 'reforms'; though these reforms have been stringently interrogated in terms of their class and caste character, their role in redefining gender and patriarchies has been largely ignored" (9). Other feminist sociologists like Kumari Jayawardena concur with these views in asserting that male social reformers such as Rammohan Roy, Ranade, Vidyasagar were predominantly liberal in their outlook, and even as they campaigned for reforms such as widow remarriage, prevention of sati and child marriage, they did not confront unequal gender relations within the family. Their propagation of female education was regarded as revitalizing the patriarchal family structure since it would "produce more companionate wives and better mothers and therefore have a stabilising impact on society," and not as autonomously important for women themselves. Even advocates of female education like Vivekananda, "a revolutionary on many issues," notes Jayawardena, "believed that a woman should not be educated in the modern sciences but should be trained to achieve fulfillment within the family."[26] In fact, their impulse in advocating social reform was often paradoxically anti-woman when faced with colonialist racist assumptions about native culture. The reformers were at pains to show that women had a very high status in ancient India. They tried to show that Hinduism was not "backward"; in fact, it could be compatible with modernizing ideas and change. Their arguments and the frameworks in which they were located remained within patriarchal boundaries, religious, social, or educational. The sexual status quo was not shaken; in fact, that was not even regarded as an issue that needed change.

Ironically, in Indian reform movements, the issue of women's emancipation was often built on the backs of female populations. The reformers wished to retain and even strengthen a traditional family structure. So, rather than have widows tempted into prostitution which threatened a family's sanctity, reformers encouraged widow remarriage and in this they styled themselves "progressive." Issues of female desire or of women's own agency do not enter their discourses. The irony remains that widows when remarried would be re-inscribed within the heterosexual marital codes of female sexuality. Their sexuality would once again be contained and controlled within parameters determined by males. "Since all the areas of social reform concerned the family," remarks Jayawardena, "the effect of the reforms may have been to increase conservatism and far from liberating women, to merely make conditions within the family structure less deplorable—especially for women of the bourgeoisie" (90). A recently published text, *Anandi Gopal*, provides an important literary documentation of the life of an exceptional nineteenth-century woman who was married as a child-bride to a supposedly progressive man, Gopalrao who initially wanted to marry a widow in order to make a political statement.[27] The story is a fascinating recreation of his attempts and failures at procuring a widow-bride until he settles for the child-bride Anandi. In challenging one regressive tradition (that prevented widow-remarriage) he reinscribes another equally devastating one—child-marriage. Further, he insists in the face of familial and social censure to educate his wife. Although seemingly progressive, Anandi bears the brunt of social censure, beatings, and exilic outcasting from female family members who cannot accept her husband's "eccentric" and aberrant plans to educate his wife.

There were a few notable female social reformers, pioneers like Pandita Ramabai (1858–1922), "a reputed Sanskrit scholar, whose courageous and independent life of activity in women's causes made her, perhaps, the foremost woman agitator of her time" (121) as noted by Jayawardena. Jayawardena records her unusual life that was enabled by her father who educated her in Sanskrit and theology—unusual achievements for her time. Armed with such knowledge, Ramabai could take on "social evils that are disguised as religious orthodoxy." As a widow, she did not conform to traditional restrictions and faced criticism from orthodox priests whom she confronted openly. In 1883 she traveled to Britain and in 1886 to the U.S. and Canada. She converted to Christianity and was involved with various projects in establishing schools, widow's homes, and orphanages. Other remarkable women who were active in the nationalist non-violent struggle were Sarala Devi, and Sarojini Naidu, and Ramabai Ranade who were dedicated social workers among the destitute, visiting hospitals and prisons. Among the militant female advocates, Bhikaji Cama (1861–1936) from a wealthy Parsi family of Bombay, left her husband at the age of twenty-seven and became active in nationalist politics, attending Congress sessions in Bombay. She went to Europe in 1901 and became a revolutionary nationalist advocating the cause of Indian independence in Europe and the U.S. At the 1907 Stuttgart Congress of the Second Communist International, Cama spoke against British imperialism and unfurled the flag which was to become the Indian national flag in 1947. The British regarded Cama and others like Perin Captain as "terrorists and anarchists" who worked for Indian freedom from outside the country. Even within India, there were female militants like Kalpana Dutt "who often put on male attire and was arrested and deported for life for her role in the Chittagong Armoury raid, and Preeti Waddadar who led a raid on a Railway Officers Club . . . Bina Das who fired on the British Governor of Bengal at a college convocation in 1932 and was imprisoned, and Kamala Das Gupta, who used to act as courier, carrying bombs in Calcutta" (130).

National Liberation and Women's Liberation

It is necessary, as Kumari Jayawardena has pointed out, "to demystify history from both colonial distortions and nationalist exaggerations."[28] Women were always involved in resistances to colonial domination. Women's roles within liberation struggles reveal the complex theoretical and practical dissonances between national liberation and women's liberation. I rely on Jayawardena and other feminist reconstructions of women's political participation in nationalist struggles. For instance, in India, recent feminist analyses by Madhu Kishwar, among others, of the involvement of women in Gandhi's *satyagraha* (truth-force) movement reveals that although women's participation in a nationalist cause politicized them in terms of emerging from a domestic sphere, it did not challenge or change the root of female subordination within the family.[29] Hence, after national liberation, women most commonly return to patriarchal controls within their families.

Even as guarding traditions was regarded as women's primary responsibility in a nationalist cause, this exacerbated the dichotomy between private and public that did not exist as rigidly in pre-colonial times where women worked inside and outside the home. The female home sphere increasingly became a middle-class bourgeois ideal with an economic rationale. "The need for a common middle-class culture may have been produced as part of new economic market relations," note Sangari and Vaid. The links, overt or covert, between "middle class cultural production and wider economic and political processes as well as to the anxieties of nationalism," enable us to fathom the new dichotomies between private and public.[30] Victorian and Christian ideals of public and private domains for women gave more power and superiority to the middle class over the lower classes. Class plays a key role in women's work outside the home. Sangari and Vaid also include a linguistic dimension within their class analysis: "The relation between gender, speech and status, and the making of a 'literary' as opposed to a popular language," attracted the middle class "to the morally ennobling texts of English culture" (21). Their embracing of "the 'English literary' model' " is in line with their welcoming a public-private dichotomy in social life.

Women's mobilization in anti-colonial struggles was often specifically directed for a nationalist cause and not to question their unequal status within family structures which continued to dominate all aspects of their lives. As discussed, male social reformers in nineteenth-century colonial India did not challenge a patriarchal family structure. They set a trend whereby women could be included in social reform as in nationalist struggle without threatening male authority or the fulfillment of their family roles. Jayawardena remarks:

> Revolutionary alternative or radical social changes affecting women's lives did not become an essential part of the demands of the nationalist movement at any stage of the long struggle for Independence, and a revolutionary feminist consciousness did not arise within the movement for national liberation. Women in the nationalist struggle did not use the occasion to raise issues that affected them as women. Rather than liberating themselves from traditional constraints and bondage as Mazumdar states, 'the women's roles within the family as wives, daughters and mothers were re-emphasized or extended to be in tune with the requirements of the family in a changing society.'[31]

In liberation struggles, male social reformers often evoked Hindu scripture as embodying cultural tradition. The limitations of male definitions of "national culture" that marginalize or subsume women's culture as secondary to national liberation are decoded in feminist critiques of male nationalists like Fanon and Gandhi.

In India, social reform movements were class-bound and male-initiated. Sangari and Vaid rightly question which classes benefited from the social reform movements against child marriage or sati. When colonial legislation entered the picture, it often made things worse as I discuss in chapter 4 with the issue of sati. The British, in deference to Brahmin authority did not ban sati outright. Rather, they introduced the notion of "legal" and "illegal" satis, voluntary or forced, and this translated often into their tacit approval of the custom. Ironically, as history demonstrates, their position led to increased sati fatalities. The Widow Remarriage Act of 1856, which, according to Sangari and Vaid was "virtually a paper legislation" did more damage than good in terms of the clauses for property inheritance, since "the economic stake which the high castes had in not allowing widows to remarry, was firmly protected by the Act" (16). Sangari and Vaid are rightly skeptical of any kind of reform movement—"colonial, indigenous, nationalist"—since each is framed within patriarchal assumptions. Women as such "tried to do their best but inevitably could not exceed the limits of their age. . . . We think this is more a question of being able to see how the history of feminism in India (and probably elsewhere) is inseparable from a history of anti-feminism . . . nowhere can or have reforms been directed at patriarchies alone, but they have also been involved in re-aligning patriarchy with social stratification . . . and with changing political formations. To be rid of patriarchies altogether then would consist in imagining and effecting a thoroughgoing social change" (19). As they state at the end of the Introduction, "Patriarchies after all are still being reconstituted" (25), hence anti-women practices are not merely remnants of feudal times but are very much part of contemporary "reformulations of patriarchies."[32]

Middle-class women's participation in political nationalist movements in India did not raise feminist consciousness of their domestic roles within the home. In fact, as Sangari and Vaid point out, "Not only do familial ideologies of the middle class mediate in different ways the entry of women into the labour market and the economic sphere, they also become a constricting force which has often ensured that political or economic participation of women will not mean or be equal to a wider emancipation" (14). In fact, women's key participation in most nationalist struggles has resulted in few feminist gains. An analysis of women's roles in two opposing nationalist paradigms, one theorized by Fanon who advocates the use of violence, and the other practiced by Gandhian non-violence in India demonstrates that in both strategies, women's issues are considered secondary to a nationalist agenda. Fanon developed his theories, particularly in *The Wretched of the Earth*, from his work as a psychotherapist and his treatment of torture victims in the Algerian liberation struggle. Both Fanon's and Gandhi's political ideas grew out of their personal involvement in national struggles. Even as their personal experience and testimony[33] provide a base for their political work, both male liberationists problematically deployed women's bodies for nationalist causes.[34]

Different liberation movements and how they politicize women—political parties constituted by the urban elite, armed struggle, interim forms of government leading to self-rule—are significant in analyzing the contemporary socio-economic and political status of women in postcolonial societies. Revolutionary change that promises to transform the economic structure does not always lead to changing gender inequities. The history of revolutionary struggle where women's issues are considered "secondary," or "divisive," are all too common. Moreover, the most regressive aspects of tradition, particularly detrimental to women persist through most anti-colonial strategies.

Fanon's concept that "decolonization is always a violent phenomenon" is accurate even in contemporary postcolonial societies. Problematic and dichotomous as it is, I find his analysis of violence compelling in its ramifications beyond physical violence into the colonial legacies of violating language, culture, and the psyche. Gandhi's non-violent philosophy, ironically mystified economic disparities between Hindus and Muslims and hence repressed the outbreak of violence that erupted tragically in the bloodshed of the partition riots. Muslims were expelled from their homes in India to a newly created Pakistan, and Hindus with homes in Pakistan were forced to relocate within India. This legacy of so-called religious hostility continues to haunt contemporary politics as seen in the disastrous communal riots in the wake of the Babri Masjid destruction (1992), and again, the genocide of Muslims in Gujarat in 2002 fuelled by the Bharatiya Janata Party (BJP) and its fundamentalist Hindu sentiments.[35] Women bear the worst violence in these horrific events in terms of violence on their bodies—rape and dislocation of home, family, and community.[36]

The BJP and the Rashtriya Swayamsewak Sangh (RSS) use religion tactically for political ends that instigate communal tensions. Religious hostilities are often an effective mask for severe economic disparities which was certainly true for the Hindu-Muslim conflicts in India. And, when independence is achieved without a change in the basic "bread and land" issues, as Fanon puts it, there will be continued violence. "Violence (after independence) has all the less reason for disappearing since the reconstruction of the nation continues within the framework of cutthroat competition between capitalism and socialism" (75).

Adopting and Rejecting the Veil: Women's Resistances

Male liberation thinkers such as Fanon and Gandhi do have gender blindspots and these very gaps and silences when scrutinized bring significant illuminations to my discussion of women's resistance. Fanon's most direct articulations of women's involvement in liberation struggles is found in "Algeria Unveiled," part of *Studies in a Dying Colonialism*.[37] Here, Fanon's insights, though sympathetic to women ironically are in line with any male gaze—colonial or native—interpreting women's bodies and the veil as an icon of cultural identification. He also romanticizes women's involvement in revolution as "purifying": "In reality, the effervescence and the revolutionary spirit have been kept alive by the woman in the home. For the revolutionary war is not a war of men. . . . The Algerian woman is at the heart of the combat. Arrested, tortured, raped, shot down, she testifies to the violence of the occupier and to his inhumanity. As a nurse, a liaison agent, a fighter, she bears witness to the depth and density of the struggle" (66).

For Fanon, the veil serves a revolutionary purpose as he observes the Algerian woman who "relearns her body [and] re-establishes it in a totally revolutionary fashion" (59). He traces the stages of wearing or discarding the veil dictated by the liberation struggle rather than by women's choice. In Fanon's discussion, the woman has no autonomy—whether she effaces herself under a veil or reveals a face when unveiled. He interprets her decisions as following the dictates of revolutionary necessity rather than her subjectivity.

Fanon does not overtly recognize that the colonized woman is doubly oppressed, racially and sexually. She has to struggle against local and colonial patriarchal attitudes. While Fanon acknowledges that colonialist racism leads to alienation and inferiority among natives in general, he is much more critical of the native black woman who aimed to raise her social status by "whitening the race" through marriage or co-habitation. Historians of slavery such as Elsa Goveia in *Slave Society in the British Leeward Islands* note that "not only was social status largely conditioned by skin colour, but that epidermal criteria frequently determined one's political, economic and legal status" (10).

As Marie Perinbam astutely points out, Fanon's analysis is limited since he "generalized mainly from the experience of the bourgeois woman, and did not consider the characteristics of the peasant or the working-class urban woman."[38] Perinbam also notes that Fanon idealizes the participation of Algerian women in the liberation struggle, and was generally harsher in his analysis of West Indian women whom he considered to be more interested in "lightening" up the race. However, as Perinbam indicates, Fanon refuses to acknowledge the contradictions faced by Algerian women within their own traditional oppressions—Islam, and male attitudes which at the end of the war "revived the status quo ante." Thus, Perinbam continues that "many Algerian women disappeared into their ashes, donned their haiks, and resumed their pre-war unreciprocal relations with the external world. . . . In 1966, a survey of young men between the ages of sixteen and twenty-two revealed that the majority preferred women excluded from public life" (12).

While I would agree with Perinbam's analysis, I do not agree that "the failure of the Algerian woman to retain her war-time dynamism calls into question Fanon's entire theory about the liberating role of violence." Fanon was certainly caught in his own sexism for as is common with revolutionary ideology, he believed perhaps naively that "at the war's end, the Algerian male, perhaps out of gratitude, would voluntarily relinquish his traditional role." And Fanon's analysis is limited in his refusal to acknowledge the power and authority of Islamic tradition and of religion generally, particularly in how religious principles shackle women more than men. Perinbam does point out, and I agree, that if Fanon were alive today, he "would probably be among the first to modify his position." Fanon, as a man of his time is not able to acknowledge female agency in resistance acts especially those couched in cultural expression such as in songs, folklore, and proverbs.[39]

In a provocative text, *The Colonial Harem*, Malek Alloula, himself an Algerian, undertakes a study of postcards of Arab women and the harem displaying the most obvious exotica and displays of the female body.[40] Barbara Harlow's Introduction discusses its importance "which reveals an intense preoccupation with the veiled female body" (x). Although these postcards belong to the early twentieth century, they "are part of a conflict," remarks Harlow, "whose consequences continue to intersect contemporary global politics and . . . has important ramifications in the intellectual arena as well, . . . [These postcards] represent the Frenchman's phantasm of the Oriental female and her inaccessibility behind the veil in the forbidden harem" (xi–xii), a titillating enterprise. Alloula makes "the necessary connection between phantasm and political agenda" because in these images colonialism has appropriated the orient in images that can be repatriated "to the devouring appetite of the great mother countries, ever hungry for raw materials" (3).

In Alloula's text, the veiled and unveiling female images embody the links between imperialist conquering of lands and male fantasies of invading female bodies. The representations remain voiceless, nameless and perpetuate cliches of the oriental woman. Alloula's material evidence of postcards adds to Edward Said's listing of intellectual and ideological weaponry that created and sustained "orientalism." In *Orientalism*, Said discusses how the production of the orient was "an integral part of European material civilisation, a mode of discourse with supporting institutions, vocabulary, scholarship, imagery . . . a Western style for dominating, restricting and having authority over the Orient" (2). This orientalist exercise of power has a specific gender dimension as Jayawardena points out, a "colonial nostalgia" that continues in "the fantasy of the Oriental woman, deliberately cultivated by the airlines, tour operators and those involved in prostitution . . . a nostalgia for lost power."[41]

Harnessing the Female Body for Anti-Colonial Struggle: Indian Women and Gandhian Satyagraha

Gandhi as a major figure in the Indian nationalist struggle involved women in non-violent action against the British. He has been described as "a political actionist and a practical philosopher,"[42] and as one who made religion integral to politics which according to Nehru (the first prime minister of independent India) "prevented all clear thinking."[43] Gandhi's autobiography entitled *The Story of my Experiments with Truth*, presents a system of ethics and a philosophical politics. Gandhi's "experiments with truth" intersect with Hindu traditions.[44] In fact, his moralism, his insistence on truth, and further on "Truth [as] God," and that there was "no way to find Truth except the way of non-violence,"[45] create an ambience in which religious and cultural traditions lose their specifically historic time and place, and become universalized and ahistoricized. This had particularly negative impacts on his deployment of women in the anti-colonial struggle.

"History [for Gandhi] does not record Truth," remarks Partha Chatterjee, "Truth lies outside history; it is universal, unchanging. Truth has no history of its own." (94). Gandhi was not interested in "the historical underpinnings" of texts such as the *Gita*, or *Mahabharata*: "The persons therein described may be historical, but the author of the *Mahabharata* has used them merely to drive home his religious theme" (94). He regards the epics as "poetic," describing "the eternal duel that goes on between the forces of darkness and light" rather than as "historical documents."

Gandhi displays the same impulse to ahistoricize scriptural authority that denigrates women. He says, as quoted in Chatterjee: "The question arises as to what to do with the *Smritis* that contain texts . . . that are repugnant to the moral sense. . . . The true *dharma* is unchanging, while tradition may change with time. If we were to follow some of the tenets of *Manusmriti*, there would be moral anarchy. We have quietly discarded them altogether" (96). Today, in India, although there is a vibrant women's movement with several triumphs, challenging problems remain, and part of their low status as inscribed in texts such as Manu's persists. Murders of wives rooted in dowry disputes, the disturbing resurgence of sati (in Rajasthan in 1987), the horrors of female infanticide and female feticide (given the abusive uses of amniocentesis), provide distressing evidence of the struggles facing Indian women. Popular media, as in commercial Hindi cinema and state-run television, often reinforce regressive and disempowering gender images.

Gandhi's involvement of women in his satyagraha movement did not challenge men's and women's roles, and patriarchal traditions that oppressed women within the home. Furthermore, his specific representation of women and female sexuality, and his symbolizing from Hindu mythology of selected female figures who embodied a nationalist spirit promoted a "traditional" ideology wherein female sexuality was legitimately embodied only in marriage, wifehood, motherhood, domesticity that can all control women's bodies. Another aspect of non-violence that women optimally embodied, according to Gandhi, was a dual impulse for both "obedience and rebellion against authority" primarily in the family, and when mobilized by someone like Gandhi, against the state. Gandhi himself assumed these "female" strengths of non-violent resistance for a nationalist agenda.

Gandhi's literal uses of women's bodies are mediated throughout by his own personal history, and his interpretations of female figures from Indian epics. His views on female sexuality were part of his own life-long struggle with his own sexuality. He could not reconcile himself to the notion of sexual needs, and records his battle with his own sexuality in letters and articles. In a fascinating study entitled "Gandhi and Women,"

Sudhir Kakar, an Indian psychiatrist analyses how Gandhi's own tortured relationship to his body, his experiments of sleeping with naked women to see if they aroused desire in him, although all part of a sexual battle with his own body, became translated into his political and moral philosophy.[46] Gandhi candidly explored his sexual obsessions as a married adolescent, and as an autocratic husband consumed by jealousy: "I have viewed myself as someone blinded by sexuality. It took me a long time to free myself of lust and I have had to undergo many ordeals before I could attain this freedom" (89).

Kakar analyzes how Gandhi's attempts to push his sexual preoccupations underground resulted in their re-emergence in "two different streams . . . increasing preoccupation with religious and spiritual matters . . . [and] his obsession with food" (91). The connections between his sexual struggles and his spiritual interests and between sexuality and food led him into avenues that are crucial cornerstones of his political mobilization techniques.[47] Kakar discusses how "the transformation of sexual potency into psychic and spiritual power . . . (is part of) Hindu metaphysics and practice" (93). Along with truth and non-violence, celibacy became an important aspect of Gandhian thought, one which he advocated to his followers in national service.

Gandhi regards sex not as a physical act but as learned social behavior, hence his struggle to control it. For Gandhi, the inequalities between the sexes could not be solved by social and legal reform but by a thoroughgoing desexualization of the male-female relationship in which women must take the lead: "If they will only learn to say 'no' to their husbands when they approach them carnally," he notes, wanting "women to learn the primary right of resistance" (125). Gandhi's naive remark assumes that women have complete agency over their bodies and can resist their husband's authority and physical power. Gandhi also "desexed" women through idealization: woman is "the incarnation of *Ahimsa. Ahimsa* means infinite love, which again means infinite capacity for suffering" (126).

Kakar comments on Gandhi's own feminization in the very qualities that he admired in women, the ones that he almost regarded as woman incarnate. He embraced and embodied these female qualities of motherly concern and care for his followers, self-suffering, fasting, mortifying the flesh, all part of a "militant non-violence" that took on many violences on the physical body. His "political campaigns," notes Pat Caplan, echoing Kakar, "were often intimately linked with bodily functions."[48] But ultimately, a Gandhian feminization of self-sacrifice, or motherly love remains male, with male gains rooted in religious authority. Men's exercising or withholding of sexuality can be self-willed and geared to spiritual power. The same is hardly true for women, especially wives whose bodies are owned by their husbands. Ironically, as Kakar points out, Gandhi believed that "by preaching *brahmacharya*, he was freeing women from the yoke of sexual servitude and, at the same time, enabling men to control the 'animal' part of their nature" (292). Gandhi could be regarded as giving women a role "outside sexual relationships," but only through denial and sublimation of bodily desire into national service and spirituality. Surely a male-directed agenda for sexual liberation!

Pat Caplan reveals the striking similarities between Hindu India and Victorian England on notions of sexuality—"the production of semen is highly weakening to males . . . chastity for both men and women was a key ideal in the Victorian value system. . . . The cult of the lady, which reached its apotheosis in the nineteenth century, completely split sex from marriage and domestic life" (287). Upper-class women became desexualized and sexual desire was sublimated in domesticity, duties, and children. Women were to be the "angel in the house." Women had to purify their husbands and their baser natures. Female participation in public life would also "purify" male endeavors in national service. Although such male definitions of female sexuality are problematic, historians like Nancy Cott, quoted in Caplan, point out how women "colluded in the view of themselves as desexualized, and in promoting passionlessness through the temperance and social purity movements, asserted some semblance of control in the sexual arena, even if that control consisted of denial" (289). Gandhi's views echoed Victorians such as Ruskin who regarded women's infinite capacity for suffering as making them "nobler" than men.

It has often been noted that Gandhi lived his personal life most publicly. Further, as Madhu Kishwar argues in her essay "Gandhi on Women," he "is one of those few leaders whose practice was at times far ahead of his theory and his stated ideas." For instance, though he insisted on the sexual division of labor and the home as the major sphere of activity for women, he also "actively created conditions," continues Kishwar, "which could help women break the shackles of domesticity." This too forms part of the contradictory Gandhian legacy.

Gandhi's symbolizing and mythologizing of female sexuality was in line with his assertion of an essentialized "national identity," based on symbols such as the *charkha* (spinning-wheel), and *khadi* (home-spun cloth). These national symbols were also strategically gendered through his evocation of mythological figures like Sita, Draupadi, Savitri as embodying roles for women in the nationalist struggle. His representations of these figures deliberately dehistoricize them. The identification of Sita with *swadeshi* (Sita only wore swadeshi, that is, home-spun cloth) demonstrates how the female body and what it is clothed in becomes a symbol of national liberation. Further, since it is "the mother's duty to look after children, to dress them," comments Gandhi, "it is necessary that women should be fired with the spirit of *Swadeshi*."[49]

Gandhi represented himself as "female," performing "feminine" roles like spinning. His own feminization in this type of political iconography—the image of the "Mahatma" sitting before the charkha patiently spinning khadi—was effective particularly in mobilizing women and men for satyagraha work. Khadi was specifically gendered in Gandhi's following words: "In spinning they [women] have a natural advantage over men . . . spinning is essentially a slow and comparatively silent process. Woman is the embodiment of sacrifice and non-violence."[50] A further contradiction is apparent in Gandhi's response to the charge that he was "wasting the energies of the nation by asking 'able-bodied men to sit for spinning like women' ": "It is contrary to experience to say that any vocation is exclusively reserved for one sex only. . . . Whilst women naturally cook for the household, organized cooking on a large scale is universally done by men throughout the world."[51]

Female sexuality was essentialized through Gandhi's appeal to "female" virtues: chastity, purity, self-sacrifice, suffering. Gandhi's model for female strength was Draupadi, not the militant Rani of Jhansi who, "dressed like a man" and on horseback led her troops in a battle against the British in 1857. Draupadi's is the more appropriate feminine courage that in the face of imminent dishonor calls upon Lord Krishna for help. These "female" virtues were an "investment" in his nationalist non-violent strategy. "To me," Gandhi stated in 1921, "the female sex is not the weaker sex; it is the nobler of the two: for it is even today the embodiment of sacrifice, silent suffering, humility, faith and knowledge."[52]

The notion of female suffering in the Hindu tradition is legitimized, even elevated dangerously through mythological models. The subconscious hold of socialization patterns inculcated in girls through the popular mythological stories of the ever-suffering Sita as virtuous wife, the all-sacrificing Savitri who rescues her husband from death, are all part of the preparation for suffering in the roles of wives and mothers. Further support rather than resistance to such ideological notions is embedded in popular cultural productions such as dance, drama, and in religious ritual. The dominant message is that for women, suffering is purifying, even inevitable.

According to Gandhi, a woman could only be pure and noble if she renounced sex altogether. This problematic denial of female sexuality, equating sexual abstinence with nobility and national service is a projection of Gandhi's personal conflicts between sex and service, between personal passion and public work. As he himself had done, a woman who is "pure and noble" will make the necessary sacrifice—after all, women's "nature" according to Gandhi was supremely suited to sacrifice. Such an analysis could offer only unfair either/or choices to women: be a wife and a sexual being or remain unmarried and sexually abstinent. Gandhi enjoined the educated woman to remain unmarried and to abnegate her sexuality so that she could dedicate herself "to work with her rural sisters."

Even as Gandhi's tactics of mobilizing women in the nationalist cause drew upon indigenous symbols, they were ironically in line with British Victorian attitudes toward gender. Like other Indian social reformers, Gandhi reinforced British liberal and imperial policies since he did not challenge women's subordinate position in patriarchal family structures, and since he evoked Hindu scripture and mythological figures for political ends. Hence Gandhi's satyagraha movement was not perceived as a threat by either Indian or British patriarchy. Gandhi went further than his British counterparts like Mill, Darwin, Ruskin in assuming "female" tasks like spinning and in validating female participation in a national struggle. Yet, British and Indian male thinkers, viewing their "woman questions" from different geographical vantage points, arrived at similar conclusions.[53] A Victorian concern with morality feared that women's honor would be unsafe outside the home. Home and hearth assumed an over-determined reality that women needed to protect and to be protected in. For Gandhi, that sanctity of the domestic sphere was never questioned or jeopardized in his harnessing of female energies for an anti-colonial struggle. Women were stepping out into a public world only for the nationalist cause; after that they would return to their "separate sphere" within the home walls. This was somewhat different from English women leaving their homes to work in factories; their politicizations would have long-term effects and would shake, as Gandhi's agenda did not, unequal sexual arrangements both within the home and outside. Although Gandhi's movement did give women a chance to participate in a public sphere and to build solidarity, they did not organize to transform the root of their oppressions within traditional family structures.

Gandhian Legacy for Indian Women's Movements

Gandhi's legacy for women's movements in India today is a complex, fascinating, and debatable area. Certain feminist gains are specifically attributed to Gandhi in his success in involving vast numbers of women in the satyagraha movement. Both gains and losses of Gandhi's strategies, particularly for contemporary Indian women, need to be acknowledged and problematized. The positive legacies of a non-violent ideology—passive resistance, mass demonstration, appeal to the moral aspects of wrong-doers—are used today to protest against murderers greedy for dowry, or other customs harmful to women. The tactic of public humiliation when women *gherao* (surround) the residences of dowry-related murderers is effective in a culture where it still matters what one's neighbors think of one's private conduct.[54]

In terms of women's formal participation in government, the Gandhian influence set "a trend," as Madhu Kishwar remarks in "Gandhi on Women," "for sponsored, patronised participation of urban, middle class women in the political life of the country." Even today, leadership in women's movements comes from middle-class women.[55] However, at the height of the civil disobedience movement, almost all classes of women participated. This tradition of a kind of male patronage was itself an integral part of the Gandhian legacy. As Suresht Renjen Bald states,

> In India the leadership of the 'women's movement' and the definition of the 'women's question' initially came from Western-educated, urban, upper class/caste *men* whose primary concern was to build a strong 'modern' India fit for self-government. The 'women's question' became defined within the context of the changing goals and strategies of the emerging Indian nation, and the women's movement became an appendage of the nationalist movement. Political independence, therefore also marked the paternalistic 'granting' of gender equality in the Constitution. The patriarchal social system that had remained untouched by the women's movement, however continued to demand and expect gender hierarchy, thus negating the legal equality embodied in the Constitution (original emphasis).[56]

Given this type of political initiation, the women's movement in India is faced today with a central contradiction, namely, a discrepancy between progressive laws and assurances of equality inscribed in the Constitution along with a sociocultural environment that in Bald's words, "systematically denies women such equality in society, the family, and the workplace."

Participation in the satyagraha movement certainly gave women a sense of power, albeit localized and for a historic independence struggle. Women's public involvement in satyagraha enabled them "to rid themselves," as Nehru put it, "of domestic slavery," though this cannot be equated with a transformative politicization that would have challenged familial gender roles. Gandhi went as far as "extending" women's roles as wives and mothers but not in making interventions in patriarchal order or political power. If social customs were challenged at all, they were "in the cause of '*Swaraj*' " (independence from British); and after Swaraj, the gains could easily be repealed. The contradictions in Gandhi's strategies of mobilizing women, the points of convergence and divergence between national liberation and sexual liberation were mystified through typically nationalist appeals—colonialism as the common enemy, and women's "personal" issues as secondary to the national cause. As in other liberation movements, women's roles remained largely supportive rather than central as evident in Gandhi thanking "the many heroines whose mute work the nation will never know."[57] "Women were lauded as good *satyagrahis* (non-violent activists), but the real issues that concerned them as women," remarks Jayawardena, "were regarded by the men as of secondary importance" (99). While acknowledging Gandhi's success in mobilizing women, we also recognize the significant work of women themselves in the nationalist movement, and the continuing struggles undertaken by Indian women's movements today.[58]

It is instructive to glance at the women's rights movements in the west in order to consider whether these movements aided or hindered the struggle for women's rights in India. According to Kishwar, Liddle, and Joshi, for example, Katherine Mayo's controversial book, *Mother India* "attributed India's subjugation and slave-mentality to the organisation of sexuality, and suggested that the abuse of women by Indian men was to blame for India's plight."[59] However, the subordinate position of Indian women is a complex matter and not one solely dictated by male dominance. Kishwar et al. point out in their discussion of Mayo that the women's movement in India did recognize points of convergence and difference between anti-colonial and women's struggle for equality, between sexist and imperialist dominations. But Mayo's orientalizing approach focused on the most drastically visible forms of abuse—child marriage, female infanticide, sati—heaped upon Indian women by Indian men. She completely ignored the colonizer's role in women's oppression. Mayo's book was certainly influential at the time and extends even to a recent writer like Mary Daly who describes Mayo's work as "exceptional."[60] However, as Kishwar et al. argue, neither Mayo nor Daly see themselves to have had any knowledge of the women's movement in India. Daly discusses male atrocities against women, but she, like Mayo "does not address the impact on Indian women of British colonialism." It is as if the abuses suffered by women belong in nativist-culturalist, and essentialized-biologistic realms, free of colonial and imperialist impacts.

As feminists dig deeper into history, we discover many examples of female foremothers whose contributions are "hidden from history." On this journey of discovery, the strength of unnamed slave women who resisted their master's authority, of the Jamaican Ni, the Indian Rani of Jhansi, the Zimbabwean Nehanda provide inspiration to contemporary postcolonial women writers and the many different struggles that women encounter in the continuing process of decolonization.

CHAPTER 3

English Education Socializing the Female Body

CULTURAL ALIENATIONS WITHIN THE PARAMETERS OF RACE, CLASS, AND COLOR

> Borrowed images
> willed our skins pale
> muffled our laughter
> lowered our voices
> let out our hems
> dekinked our hair
> denied our sex in gym tunics and bloomers
> harnessed our voices to madrigals
> and genteel airs
> yoked our minds to declensions in Latin
> and the language of Shakespeare
> Told us nothing about ourselves
> There was nothing about us at all
> —Olive Senior, "Colonial Girls School," *Talking of Trees*

> Education as the exercise of domination stimulates the credulity of students, with the ideological intent ... of indoctrinating them to adapt to the world of oppression.... The unfinished character of men [sic] and the transformational character of reality necessitate that education be an ongoing activity.
> —Paulo Friere, *The Pedagogy of the Oppressed*

Colonial power was consolidated with the chalk and blackboard, more crucial ideological tools than military might. The telling comment in Chiekh Hamidou Kane's novel, *Ambiguous Adventure*, notes: "school fascinates the soul."[1] The inculcation of English language and literature affect mental colonizations through the consent of the colonized. In a colonial structure, there are complex interconnections between the knowledge of English and raising one's social and economic status. The colonized subject acquires a sense of power by learning, even "mimicking," to use Homi Bhabha's evocative analysis of how the colonized assert subjectivity, via knowledge about the colonizers' world—their history, geography, and value-systems in their language.[2] A fascination with school effectively colonizes the mind, and its effects persist into postcolonial times.

Colonialist educational policies were both racialized in terms of asserting the superiority of English language and culture, and gendered in terms of instituting different curricula for male and female students. Racial and gender hierarchies were rooted in Victorian ideologies of domesticity, and its rigid compartmentalizing of public and private spheres, a much more fluid division in most pre-colonial societies. Colonialist curricula and the imbibing of English history and geography often went along with denying and denigrating indigenous cultures. Colonial schools introduced and institutionalized standard English, "Kinglish or Queenglish," as Marlene Nourbese Philip puts it, among colonized peoples who spoke other languages.[3] In the postcolonial world, standard English is transmuted into a variety of indigenous African, Indian, Caribbean pidgin, and Creole forms, for instance, Nigerian pidgin, or Jamaican patois, or in India, "Hinglish/Hindlish," a combination of Hindi (considered, though not without controversy, the national language) and English.[4] Among numerous indigenous languages, some written, others oral, English assumed power since it was used in government and law courts. Colonized peoples studied their "A for Apple" primers, and learned to rhapsodize over daffodils and nightingales, unseen and unheard in tropical climates of Africa, the Caribbean, and India. Today, since standard English has a position of power, speakers of non-standard usages are disadvantaged seriously, such as users of African-English pidgins, or Caribbean-patois, or "vernacular language" students, "vernacs" as they are referred to derogatorily in India.[5] Unfortunately, as postcolonial texts demonstrate, certain legacies of racist and gendered hierarchies persist in postcolonial educational systems.

The promotion of female education in most postcolonial societies raises several questions—the kind of education and its relevance, connections between education and economic betterment, education raising social consciousness and leading to more sexual equality in society, or paradoxically, strengthening male patriarchal privilege and alienating women as anomalous educated outsiders. In her essay, "Women's Education and Class Formation in Africa, 1950–1980," Claire Robertson argues that "rapid educational growth" in the immediate post-independence era in several impoverished African nations led to serious problems particularly for women—increased unemployment, and exacerbated social and gender inequities as the upper classes acquired higher education.[6] Only primary education which most women had access to, was "devalued," hence "more and more education was required to obtain even poorly paid jobs" (108). Simply providing more education to women, notes Robertson, does not "remedy the situation for them or for African economies" (111). This kind of education hardly challenges "sex-stereotyping either in education itself or in the labor market" (112).

Prior to colonial intervention, indigenous societies had their own elaborate forms of knowledge and learning. In pre-colonial African cultures, as discussed by A. Babs Fafunwa, the purpose of education was functionalist, and served as a means to an end, preparing males and females for social, political, spiritual responsibilities to their families and communities.[7] Indigenous education was participatory where "children learnt by doing" (9). They learned community rituals and ceremonies as well as practical skills such as farming, weaving, cooking. "Recreational subjects included wrestling, dancing, drumming ... while intellectual training included the study of local history, legends, the environment (local geography, plants and animals), poetry, reasoning, riddles, proverbs, story-telling and story-relays. Education in Old Africa was an integrated experience. It combined physical training with character-building, and manual activity with intellectual training" (10). This learning, based on "observation, imitation, and participation" inculcates the capacity to reason, and form judgments. Fafunwa's otherwise excellent recapitulation of indigenous learning is nostalgic; there are no patriarchally based inequities or other conflicts in this idyllic system. However, Fafunwa's important point is that indigenous education was geared to the needs of a communally based culture, respectful of age where learning was passed, often orally, from the old to the young. Not that this system is at all simple; on the contrary, it is highly evolved and complex—Fafunwa cites "different formulas for games, dancing, or drumming, for sitting or standing, for tilling the soil, or fishing, for weaving, swimming, walking ... yam-growing ceremonies, the rituals of ancestor-worship" (14). One literary representation of this highly ordered and structured social and communal life is in Chinua Achebe's 1958 novel *Things Fall Apart* where Achebe's aim was "to set the record straight," to counter racist charges of the inferiority or even absence of civilized cultures among Africans.[8]

Colonial adventurism and racist stereotypes about the backwardness of these sophisticated cultures was a rude interruption to local educational methods. Primarily dominated by missionaries, education was simply a way to purchase African souls, not to equip local people with skills that would improve their daily lives. Even when colonial governments brought in "a diluted semi-secular education" their goal remained the furthering of their own interests, what Nyerere calls, as quoted in Fafunwa, the colonial "need for local clerks and junior officials" (237). The colonizers' "conscious and obvious attempts . . . to educate the African away from his culture," as Fafunwa puts it, could be articulated more strongly in terms of racist contempt for most aspects of black civilization. Europeans simply dismissed what they did not understand as unworthy of superior white culture. Hence, African ways of knowing and learning suffered severe denial and obliteration.

There are important differences among policies adopted by different European colonizers.[9] British colonial policies in Africa left education in missionary hands for several years. Not until the pre-independence period when political stability became important, did the British government take responsibility for educating Africans. Colonial Africa was marred by shifts in power among colonial officials and missionaries for the souls and/or minds of Africans. Such religious and secular debates in education marked British policies in other colonies such as India where it had a much longer and more involved confrontation. After independence, African nations had to contend with this historical legacy, and undertake their own religious-secular educational negotiations. A landmark in this history is the 1925 Phelps-Stokes Commission on African Education.[10] Another aspect of British education in African societies was "the principle of racial segregation," notes Fafunwa, perpetuated in Kenya, Tanzania, and South Africa. Kenya, different from Nigeria or Ghana was a settler colony with Europeans "owning" land having appropriated the best coffee-growing region called the Highlands by dispossessing local peoples and forcibly removing them, and then extracting labor from them. Education was one among other social and political disparities endured by Kenyans. European education received the highest financial support from the colonial government; next, the education of Indians, and at the lowest rung, the Africans. The government shifted the responsibility for educating Africans to the missionaries. This pyramid structure—similar to color-coded educational pyramids also encouraged by the British in Caribbean islands—is a disempowering legacy that has to be confronted even in contemporary times.

There were important local movements that promoted education, most strikingly in Kenya where the Kikuyu Independent Schools Association was formed as early as 1929. Also, in Kenya, Tom Mboya "launched the famous Airlift of 1959 in which young Kenyans of African descent" were flown to London and the U.S. for education. In Tanzania, notes Fafunwa, Julius Nyerere's significant leadership advanced an educational system "founded on African values and ideals" (26). For all these efforts, the road to relevant education, and to higher education was long and arduous—for instance, in 1922, Makerere College in Uganda was the only higher learning institution that served the entire East African British colonies of Kenya, Uganda, Tanganyika, and Zanzibar.[11] Only much later, in 1970, was University College, Nairobi established as a national university in Kenya. This is in striking contrast to western Africa where there were three institutions in Ghana alone.

In South Africa, educational policy buttressed the general inequities between whites and blacks. As the Interdepartmental Committee on Native Education of 1935–1936 noted as quoted in Kitchen's *The Educated African*, "The education of the White child prepares him for life in a dominant society and the education of the Black Child for life in a subordinate society" (267). This sentiment, perhaps with more subtle overtones, continued into the apartheid years of the Bantu Education Act of 1953. Here again, as in other parts of colonial Africa, the government was reluctant to take responsibility for educating blacks—this was left to missionaries. Another major area of contention was the issue of language—English, Afrikaans, and African languages. Since the Bantu system's agenda was to clearly disadvantage the black majority, they demanded English education without which they would not be able to compete for higher education and desirable jobs. Post-apartheid is a far cry from the days of the Soweto uprising of 1976 over education reform; however, equality of opportunity in education is yet to be achieved among blacks, whites, and coloreds.[12]

Racially based British colonial policy was accompanied by their "indirect rule system" as practiced in northern Nigeria. This resulted in imbalances between educational development, according to Fafunwa, between Nigeria's north and south.[13] Most colonial educational policies were wrapped up in bureaucracy, in the establishment and maintenance of education boards, directors, and other authority figures. In general, what is sadly important to note, is that the colonial period was marked by "very pronounced illiteracy" (25).

The acquiring of western education in English is both desirable and a liability for educated women in postcolonial societies if they side-step social custom, especially in dress-code, body language, or verbal speech. They face prejudice, located unfairly in their "western education." The educated woman's "physical appearance was viewed," notes C. S. Lakshmi, "as the first outward sign of breaking away from tradition. . . . The poet Bharati had heralded her [as one who] would walk erect with an unfaltering gaze and would be a slave to no man. Many like the poetry but probably did not think it would be a reality."[14] This reality was often interpreted in the outward physical manifestation of "high heels, dark glasses," stylish saris. As Lakshmi points out, the discussion of clothes, whether she wears silk or georgette saris is "in actuality the age-old discussion of the kind of education women must be given. . . . Who is an educated woman? What is her education for?" (276). One stereotype was that educated girls would have to hide their learning if they were to get married; another was that they would not abide by the rules of chastity, and indeed representations of educated women gone "bad" are rife in popular fiction and film. If they become pregnant, they are "appropriately punished" by cruel and violent deaths such as "jumping into wells or [being] run over by military trucks." Lakshmi analyzes how "the notion of punishment and purification" is used against the educated woman as a means to control her. Even working women downplay their involvement in work, and mystify it as essential only for the family income. Her first duty is to her household, and if necessary she would give up her career. The contradictions of women required to be traditional and feminine along with "one who can strike like lightning and burst like a storm when degraded or when she sees injustice," as stated by a women's group discussing a modern woman, only evokes the good wife and mother "willing to serve others," and if crossed, striking out in images that evoke powers "normally attributed to the mother goddess." Goddesses as powerful and as tender evoke positive and troubling aspects of tradition, particularly in the contemporary climate of Hindu fundamentalism that "has not only given a new character to hitherto forgotten temples of mother goddesses and more powerful roles to religious leaders but has also . . . caught the woman at that point where they have understood and perceived oppression outside the home but are as yet powerless to fight oppression both at home and outside. At this moment, calls for utilizing education to strengthen traditional roles can start looking almost attractive. . . . In the name of strengthening the culture, the women may go back to the philosophy of endurance, suffering and power" (280). Lakshmi points out that education rather than challenging exploitation within the family makes the educated woman even more complicit within the system "with all its drawbacks, for the family should be nurtured at whatever cost. It is a peculiar logic that makes the modern girl feel that upholding tradition is the most modern activity of an educated girl" (279).

Such "peculiar logic" pursues female protagonists who discover that knowledge of English is not liberating necessarily. Similar to a Foucauldian analysis where the knowledge of sexuality, and its increasing scientification and discussion increased control over human bodies and behavior, so also, knowledge of English language and culture lead to new boundaries for women within patriarchy, which remains intact through innovations of language and thought. When English education equips women to challenge patriarchal boundaries especially those around their female bodies and acceptable sexual behavior, they struggle against a sexual status quo. Just as speaking about sexuality, rather than liberating, often led to complex institutional controls in the practices of law and medicine, similarly, English education, though important particularly for female subjects who may not have had educational avenues open to them, is not always liberating. Consenting to colonial education is fraught with dangers of colluding and co-optation into the master's values that may lead to alienation and exclusion from one's own community.

Colonial benefits like education for women often come with heavy personal costs, and at times physical reprisals on the body. Socialization through English education has a multiplicity of mental and physical effects. Postcolonial women writers present English education as a double-edged sword, not always and necessarily liberating; in a language-power duel, the colonizer often wields the handle, leaving the blade to the colonized. English education can lead to severe alienation from one's own language, culture, and context. Although my analysis focuses on the impacts of English education on women, the English language in general provides contradictory empowerment for colonized peoples. The power and privilege gained by knowing English may marginalize one from one's un-English educated family. Such linguistic outsiderness is accompanied at times with a fatal "forgetting" of one's mother tongue.

English education provides particularly contradictory empowerments for women—both benefiting them and rendering them outsiders from their bodies, families, and communities. In other words, English education along with providing new skills and knowledge also disempowers women. Female protagonists experience cultural alienation from their own communities.

Such struggles are often marked on their bodies, physically manifested as bulimia, nervous breakdown, illness (real and feigned), and isolation. Resistances are expressed physically and psychologically, at times by women writers and their protagonists quite literally transporting their bodies outside their own communities, taking refuge in migration, temporary or permanent. In such situations when women place their bodies outside their spaces of origin, and become expatriates or exiles, their knowledge of English provides a paradoxical way of belonging within alien cultures that may be more welcoming in alien homes than one's native home.

Education creates autonomous and thinking women who sadly, often un-belong to their communities where they are expected to follow traditional female behavior. Their outsiderness often plays out destructively on the site of their female bodies in exilic expressions—outsiders because they are more proficient in English than in their own languages, outsiders in their newly acquired ways of thought and dress. Writers often locate these struggles around patriarchal desires to control the female body, to make it conform and not resist or change the status quo as inspired by new ideas. Postcolonial women writers provide diverse literary representations of cultural alienation experienced by female protagonists as they are caught between English and their own language and cultural ways.

The benefits of an English education often necessitate crossing indigenous hierarchies of class and color, the latter exacerbated by colonial racism. Female protagonists are forced often to leave their working-class homes, and relocate with middle-class relatives in order to go to school as in novels by Trinidadian Merle Hodge's *Crick Crack, Monkey* and Zimbabwean Tsitsi Dangarembga's *Nervous Conditions*.[15] Along with the colonizers' racism based on superiority of language and culture, texts such as South African/Botswanan Bessie Head's *Maru*, and Jamaican Erna Brodber's *Jane and Louisa will Soon Come Home* explore the internal racism among indigenous communities.[16] Head probes local prejudice against the "outcast" Masarwa group who are looked down upon by the dominant Bamangwato people in Botswana; Brodber portrays the prejudices inflicted by and endured by the light-skinned middle class in the Caribbean. Both the privilege and marginalization of this light-skinned class are also represented in Dominican Jean Rhys's novel *Wide Sargasso Sea*, and in one of the Jamaican Sistren stories, "Grandma's Estate" in *Lionheart Gal*.

When English education exacerbates cultural collisions based in differences of race, class, color, such conflicts place female protagonists in spaces where their bodies become battlegrounds on which English and indigenous tongues and ways of life get inscribed. At times, such conflicts are reconciled uneasily; at other times they drag the female body into outsiderness that is manifested in madness, suicide, or intellectual isolation that can be a kind of death.

Location of Knowledge and Relocating the Female Body

Knowledge goes with territoriality in the broad sense of who learns what language, and who has access to English education in the colonies. English knowledge travels with colonized people when they enter the mother country or other western spaces for higher education. After that, they may or may not return "home." As portrayed in Ama Ata Aidoo's short story, "Everything Counts" (significantly, this is the opening story in her excellent collection, *No Sweetness Here*), Sissie, unlike her male compatriots decides to return home to Ghana after higher studies abroad.[17] The story powerfully illuminates a politics of the female body in Sissie's exilic sense of non-belonging in this home-space that feels ironically like "another country." All her female students brazenly wear a wig, a beauty contest is won by a mulatto who has "natural, luxuriant" hair, and her family expects their foreign-returned scholar to have a car, a refrigerator, and other material goods. As students abroad, Sissie had argued with her compatriots that she had a right to wear the wig if she so desired. It was after all a matter of convenience. Upon her return, the shock of being confronted with her people's wholesale buying into "western" notions of beauty manifested in straight hair and fair skin, brings painful self-recognition that is expressed in bodily "streams of water pouring from the nape of [Sissie's] neck down her spine . . . [After the beauty contest] she hurried home and into the bathroom where she vomited and cried and cried and vomited for what seemed to her to be days" (7).

As an educated woman she had agreed with her male compatriots on the negative impacts of imperialistic greed and irresponsibility that dump technological throw-aways on the third world like "outmoded tractors. Discarded aeroplanes." As a woman though, bodily notions of beauty in terms of skin and hair become vividly and painfully clear when she returns home. Significantly, she cannot discuss these issues with her male compatriots because "nearly all of them were still abroad. In Europe, America, or some place else. They used to tell her that they found the thought of returning home frightening. They would be frustrated. Others were still studying for one or two more degrees. A Master's here. A Doctorate there. . . . That was the other thing about the revolution" (1). Acquiring degrees becomes a career in itself and enables the men in this story to remain abroad and to indulge in armchair criticism, and theories of revolution. As the narrator's appropriately ironic tone conveys, they are cop-outs whereas Sissie is the only courageous one who returns home however frustrating that might be.

Aidoo's story illustrates how knowledge and space are connected, and in specific historical ways for colonized peoples. Space is fundamental for colonizing adventurers, occupying supposedly "empty" lands. Space is also economically and emotionally resonant for colonized peoples whose native lands were occupied. Domination of this space is ensured not only by military might, but also, very importantly, by the weaponry of knowledge. The space of colonial administration can only be occupied when armed with English. So, the colonized aspire to occupy that space (and the attendant status and power) through mastering English. Without that linguistic power, colonized peoples experience various spatial marginalities. They often have no place within colonial and postcolonial walls of power—legal, educational, governmental institutions—and at times even in their personal and intimate relationships, as I discuss in the context of Indian Meenakshi Mukherjee's short story, "Dancing Dogs and Bears."[18]

Linguistic marginality from English heightens the unnamed wife's sociocultural exclusion within her own home in Meenakshi Mukherjee's "Dancing Dogs and Bears." This "mere wife" as she calls herself is caught in a sea of voices speaking English, a language that she has learnt but that sounds incomprehensible when her husband speaks to his foreign guests. This female protagonist could have been a "vernac" student whose authoritarian husband, ironically a professor of English literature, expects her to cook elaborate dinners, to entertain his academic guests from the U.S., and Australia, and to speak "a little English" to them. "You were supposed to have passed your B.A." he complains, implying that that was one of his reasons for marrying her. "Why in heaven's name can't you speak a little English?" The trouble is that she cannot understand "their English"; even her husband's English "seems to change" around these foreigners as he tries perhaps to imitate and impress them with a put-on accent. The wife is marginalized completely from a conversation ironically enough about "the concept of marriage in the Elizabethan age [that] they were all very critical about" (64). So, she keeps quiet, and smilingly hands them chilled tomato juice, or ashtrays. She is marginalized both by lack of fluency in English, and by not being a part of the English literary texts that the guests are discussing.

In her essay, "English in a Literate Society" Gauri Viswanathan notes an important slippage, sometimes an error between "literacy" of English in India, and "literary" study of English classics.[19] The study of the language is conflated often with valorizing English literary texts. "The history of modern Indian education," remarks Viswanathan, "can be said to have evolved between these two poles, the conflation of 'literary' and 'literacy' being one of the ideological achievements of a discipline functioning as the carrier of both secular and religious culture" (36). It is almost impossible, given the colonial enterprise, to separate a study of the English language, as one among other world languages, from the ideological inculcation of the values of superiority in English values and culture. Viswanathan reminds us, via Paulo Freire that "literacy is reducible neither to mastery of language structures nor internalization of institutionalized systems of thought and ways of knowing" (37).

Postcolonial women writers depict how education makes both men and women needlessly arrogant and irresponsible. Aidoo's short stories include scathing remarks about educated men as Adwoa puts it in "Something to Talk About on the Way to the Funeral": "These our educated big men have never been up to much good." As the two women walk to Auntie Araba's funeral, they recall that "after all, was it not a lawyer-or-a-doctor-or-something-like-that who was at the bottom of all Auntie Araba's troubles" (115). These "big men" with their "big cars" incur "big debts." Their education does not go along with morals about sustaining their "high living," ripping off their new fledging nation-states as corrupt politicians, and exploiting women as mistresses. They are not accountable for their casual mating, not "keep[ing] their manhood between their thighs."

Women writers do not romanticize educated women who can also become proud simply because they have "chewed more books" (a phrase used for Babamukuru in *Nervous Conditions*) than their non-literate relatives. Women writers criticize needlessly uppity educated protagonists such as Neo in Bessie Head's short story, "Snapshots of a Wedding."[20] Named symbolically, Neo is the new one in her family to have passed the "O levels." Her superior attitude toward her uneducated relatives is conveyed by her physical bearing and deportment: "She walked around with her nose in the air; illiterate relatives were beneath her greeting—it was done in a clever way, she just turned her head to one side and smiled to herself or when she greeted it was like an insult" (77).

Neo's mother is "bemused" but her relatives are not: "What's the good of education if it goes to someone's head so badly they have no respect for the people?" Neo's "familiar careless disrespect went with her so-called, educated status" (78). Such schooling, notes the narrator ironically, gives her "endless opportunities"—to be a "typist, book-keeper, or secretary." She is to marry Kegoletile who has made both Neo and also the "completely uneducated" Mathata pregnant. He of course proposes to Neo because "they will both get good jobs and be rich in no time." Although Kegoletile preferred Mathata's "natural" ways to Neo's "false postures and acquired, grand-madame ways," his materialistic values get the better of him: "it didn't pay a man these days to look too closely into his heart. They all wanted as wives, women who were big money-earners and they were so ruthless about it!" (79). Head conveys that people get corrupted from the inside, that they lose their inner resources and values for the sake of money.

Women of older generations, as Neo's great-aunts and mother, had no formal English schooling as also the grandmother, Sejosenye, in another of Head's stories in *The Collector of Treasures*, "The Wind and a Boy" who reminisces about being sent to the mission school for only one year because "girls didn't need an education in those days when ploughing and marriage made up their whole world" (72). Fascinatingly, what lingers in old Sejosenye's consciousness from that one school year is the story of Robinson Crusoe that lives on as an "out-of-context memory of her schooldays" (72). She then invents what she does not remember—Crusoe as a great warrior who "killed an elephant all by himself . . . making up a story on the spot" to entertain her grandson. This story is now contextualized and made relevant, even in its entertainment value for her listener, quite different from the hegemonic imposition of a British-oriented interpretation of that novel. Only Crusoe's name, like her grandson Friedman, named after a kind doctor that Sejosenye meets in the hospital where the child is born, is foreign. All other details of her adaptation are Africanized—the village setting, dialogue among the villagers, how the elephant's skin and bones would be used. "There was something for all the people in the great work Robinson Crusoe did" (73).

Quite unlike such creativity demonstrated by women of Sejosenye's generation, Neo remains superficially locked in her new learning whose only worth is measured in cash. Although she is alienated from her rural origins, her marriage takes place in that setting, and even though "this is going to be a modern wedding," Neo's relatives perform the traditional ululating, the ceremonial asking for the bride, dancing with the hoe (which Neo would never use since she has an office job). The enactments of these rituals are merely symbolic for this modern couple who partake of them almost as the outsiders that they have become.

English Language and Colonial(ist) Educational Policies

The English language was imposed and institutionalized through colonial(ist) educational policies that were devised carefully to create a civil servant class that would aid a colonial administration. A discussion of English educational policies in India is instructive, particularly since India served as a trial ground for several issues such as the teaching of English literature, elevating that field to the status of the classics which was first tried out in the Indian colony before being repatriated to Britain.[21] India was also the colonial trial ground for the balancing of religious and secular education and the role of missionaries often inculcating Christian ideology under the veneer of teaching the English language. Colonial methods of pedagogy, and colonial assumptions about race, class, gender persist even today. It is an ongoing political effort to challenge these entrenched cultural assumptions ingrained so formatively within our earliest learning experiences. The domination of English language in daily life in postcolonial societies, and the influence of English studies in postcolonial academic institutions testify to the reality that this is hardly an academic matter and one cannot dismiss it as of curious historical interest, or, in Rajan's words in *The Lie of the Land*, "as another post-colonial 'mimic' activity" (7).[22]

In the colonies the study of the English language was synonymous with studying the English literary "classics." Gauri Viswanathan's book, *Masks of Conquest: Literary Study and British Rule in India* discusses how India provided fertile ground for experimentation of British educational policies, markedly, the deployment of English literature which was canonized in colonial curricula much before its elevation to such status in the mother country still under the burden of classical Greek and Latin education. And as Rajeswari Sunder Rajan's *The Lie of the Land* indicates, such assertion of the hegemony of English literature was resisted by "Britain's own local colonies—Wales, Scotland, Ireland" (9).[23] Even today, Irish writers such as James Joyce and Sameul Beckett are appropriated within English literature.

The ideological implications of English education in the colonies is asserted by Rajan. She notes that the study of English was consolidated "as a recognizable body of knowledge and as a collection of texts in the eighteenth and early nineteenth centuries.... A recognizable 'English' literature—marked by scholarly editions of texts, literary histories, critical works, biographies of writers—took shape in Britain concurrently with the project of imperialism, within a common social and historical configuration" (9). Rajan points out that this education effected "social control (chiefly on the English working class, women, and 'natives')," while Franklin Court (quoted by Rajan) contends that the study of English politicizes people and leads to reform (8). Whether the agendas were social or political, English literature assumed a transcendent position, possessing universal values, and somehow "uncontaminated" as Viswanathan and Rajan indicate "by the material practices of colonialism." Rajan continues, "In other words, English *literature* was not indicted on ideological or historical grounds by association with the English ruler. Rather it became the surrogate—and also the split—presence of the Englishman, or a repository of abstract and universal values freely available to the colonized as much as to the colonizer" (original emphasis, 12). The native intelligentsia certainly participated in this enterprise even as they negotiated maintenance of the sanctity of their religious beliefs. Rajan indicates that this "dissociation of English literature from its national origins has made possible its unproblematic retention and continuance in the post-Independence education syllabus in India" (12). Rajan cites how this is represented in R. K. Narayan's novel *The English Teacher* published on the eve of independence. Even though the hero "rebels at the methods of English teaching ('a whole century of false education'), [he] venerates English literature itself: 'What fool could be insensible to Shakespeare's sonnets or *The Ode to the West Wind*, or 'A thing of beauty is a joy forever!' " (13).

Colonial educational policies were as classist in the mother country as they were racist and classist in the colonies. Language is key in the successful colonial maintenance of law and order. "Law is of vital importance to the good government of the country," as the sanctimonious tone of the *British Parliamentary Papers* declares, and "language is the ground-work upon which all future improvements must materially depend." Law and language, and their functioning together as instruments of power are crucial concerns for colonized peoples facing transformations of indigenous judicial systems conducted in native languages into a British legal system in English. Although the British paid lip service to "the poorer classes" for whom legal proceedings should be conducted "in the vernacular language of the particular zillah or district," English had usurped a dominant position in the conduct of justice. The marginalization of the un-English educated "poorer classes" deepened. As power rested more and more in English language skills, acquiring them carried a clear class bias. "Natives of rank" use English in courts and for political negotiation. Examples of British disruption of indigenous justice systems are rife. For instance, in African societies, the British, contrary to indigenous tradition, assigned authority to local males called warrant chiefs, only because they spoke English. These men were often untitled and hence not highly respected according to native custom. As warrant chiefs they had the colonial master's power to function as intermediaries between their own people and the colonizers. The abuses of power by warrant chiefs taking bribes, and betraying their own people in other ways are recorded in fictional accounts as in Chinua Achebe's *Things Fall Apart*.[24]

As recorded in the *British Parliamentary Papers* (1832), English education would accomplish various goals, and "the dissemination of the English language [would] . . . identify the people with the interests of their rulers." These goals include the moral upliftment of natives, raising their economic status and class aspirations, and supplying colonial administration with trustworthy servants. Sir Thomas Munro asserted that "the first object of improved education should be to prepare a body of individuals for discharging public duties. [Education] will contribute to raise the moral character of those who partake of its advantages, and supply you with servants to whose probity you may, with increased confidence, commit offices of trust" (*Parliamentary Papers*, hereafter *PP*, 1832).

Even as English education in India aimed to train a class of civil service workers, another, not-so-hidden agenda was the propagation of the superiority of European learning in general over indigenous knowledge. Education would accomplish "a familiarity with European literature and science, imbued with the ideas and feelings of civilized Europe . . . [and] principles of morals and general jurisprudence" (*PP*, 1832). Further, there were discussions about giving natives even more incentive to study English by offering them not only service jobs, but key positions. In contemporary times, English retains its domination, even elitism in most middle-class employment opportunities. And, as Rajan indicates, the learning of English proliferates beyond academic sites: "The mushrooming of bazaar institutes offering crash courses in spoken English and for a variety of other 'real life' communication purposes—interviews, exams, business correspondence— is an indication of the marketplace response to this need" (19).

The advantages of training natives, though not allowing them "the highest [offices] in the Revenue and Judicial Departments," were debated. As Charles Lushington, Esq. admits condescendingly—he has "a very high opinion of native talent." Others such as Holt Mackenzie, Esq. propose enticing natives to the benefits of English education, through incentives such as "the distribution of prizes for education, and the making, in some measure, the acquisition of the English language a condition of preferment and employment."

A rather different situation prevailed in the British African colonies where the availability of western education was extremely low (excluding the Southern African region where different factors prevailed). Contrary to British interest in fostering English education in India, ideological agonizing over what *kind* of education to implement, the British did not commit the same material resources or intellectual energy to educational matters for Africans. Robertson notes that "the decade of 1950 to 1960 was atypical of colonial rule as a whole [because] . . . colonial administrators finally expressed concern about providing skilled Africans either to satisfy the demands for reformers or to prepare for independence. . . . After independence the annual growth rates in school enrollment were spectacular given the poverty of many African countries. . . . Nothing indicates more clearly the faith in education as a prime contributor to economic development" (93).

In India, religion was a troubling issue for the colonizers. Initially, the British East India Company advocated an educational policy divorced from religion—a position that was strongly opposed by missionaries who "were led to suspect," remarks Viswanathan, "that the official policy of secularism in India was merely being used as a 'fair and open field for testing the non-religion theory of education'" (8). Christianity came along with English education, despite all the poses of secularism. Missionaries as schoolteachers often proselytized their superior religion along with the English language. Colonized peoples rightly feared religious proselytizing that pretended to veil conversion under the guise of teaching English literature, history, or geography.

Missionaries were extremely skeptical about purely secular education. The fear was that a purely secular training not only turned people away from Christianity but from all religions. These "godless students" believed in western reason and some strong Anglicists regarded "the policy of knowledge without religion as no less pernicious to the stability of British rule than idolatry and superstition" (52). Thanks to missionary efforts that were strongly opposed to giving only language learning to the natives (as though that is divorced from moral values), the increasing importance of English literature was seen as the way to reconcile language learning and moral values.

Very different race politics governed the deployment of religion in educating natives in African and Caribbean colonies. Clear bias is revealed in promoting "religious and moral instruction without literacy" for slave populations (prior to emancipation in 1834) in the Caribbean. "The exception was a small 'slave' school started in 1832 by the Church of England," notes Carl Campbell.[25] Generally, slave owners wanted obedience and servility rather than questioning of their authority, which might be inspired by literacy. Emancipation in 1834 "marked the real beginning not only of popular education, but of public education" (50). Protestant missionary societies began to enter the Caribbean colonies and with the support of the British colonial government, established schools. The purpose of cheap elementary schools was to promote Christian values and literacy, and importantly, "not to encourage upward social mobility" until much later. Education was one among other social institutions governed by the particular color and class hierarchies of plantation society. As Campbell remarks, "The society was shaped like a three-tier color and class pyramid with the black masses at the bottom, the coloureds largely as a middle class, and the whites at the apex" (11). Campbell also points out that this description is "an oversimplification" since there were poor whites, and some affluent coloreds whose wealth enabled transcending racial underprivilege.

Given these color and class divisions in Caribbean societies, the role of religious schools had different ramifications than in Indian society. In Trinidad, as Campbell records, Roman Catholic schools used French and Spanish in the immediate post-emancipation era. (Trinidad had been conquered by the French and Spanish before the British took it over as a colony in 1797.) Even non-denominational schools in the nineteenth and early twentieth centuries were not truly secular. Religion intervened in different ways—as in India, even putative secular education found no contradiction in assigning such essay topics as "On the Falsehoods of the Hindu Shastras!" Similarly, Campbell notes how in Trinidad, "when Governor Lord Harris . . . immortalized himself by establishing a system of secular government schools called ward schools . . . [they] were never completely secular, as the books used a considerable amount of general Christian precepts" (48) and children were expected to attend Church. As in India, English language and learning gradually began to take the place of overt religious learning. The English language would "bring children of various cultural backgrounds together," notes Campbell, "and teach them English values" (13). Of course, there were many twists and turns to this "ideal" of deploying English language as unifying the differently colored Caribbean peoples since the language vouched for "universalizing" effects. However, Campbell notes the increasing tensions between government-run and church-run schools although both propagated socializing techniques that promoted the values of colonial society. Natives would benefit from education "to a limited extent" and as dictated by colonial forces not of their making. Secondary education could lead to upward social mobility for blacks, Indians, and the colored in Trinidad, "but normally it worked to reproduce class relations," notes Campbell, "rather than create new ones" (55). For Indians, land sometimes overrode education as a priority; for blacks, education was paramount as the way up from manual labor. Campbell's analysis is somewhat idealistic: "Over the century after emancipation the society was increasingly becoming more stratified according to economic classes.... The spread of education moved the society appreciably... towards the greater, but imperfect, acceptance of universalist-achievement values in a less unequal, but still racist society. This was a modernizing function of education; it had the effect of modifying the plural society" (57).

During nationalist struggles that gained ground after the Second World War in most British colonies "the transforming potential of education" was harnessed by social reformers and politicians. In Trinidad, a leader like Dr. Eric Williams challenged "denominational schools which he stigmatized as a 'breeding ground of disunity' " (71), and under his leadership, "non-denominational government secondary schools increased from only three in 1957 to twenty-one by 1967" (72). The Indian population of Trinidad (from 5.8 percent in 1851 to 35.1 percent in 1891) resisted since they wished to protect their own Hindu and Muslim interests and educational establishments (83). However, the deeper ideological shifts in neo-colonial and bourgeois aspirations persist as represented with dark humor by Trinidadian novelist Merle Hodge in *Crick Crack, Monkey*. And there was growing disillusionment in the late 1960s (independence was achieved in 1962) in terms of unemployment. Hence, the publication of the audacious "Fifteen Year Education Plan 1968–1983" met with resistance from the growing Black Power Movement.[26]

Additionally, color-based hierarchies in the Caribbean were rigidified by a colonial hierarchy, and they dominate access to education even today. Elementary education for the poorer classes, secondary and higher for the middle and upper classes whose curriculum was dominated by European classics. The Cambridge examinations set up a kind of "universal" British standard that permeated all the colonies; British entrance exams were linked with the privileges of joining the civil service and generally marking one's intellectual status. Island Scholarships in the Caribbean carried that status as well.

In India, caste hierarchies played a role similar to race and color demarcation in the Caribbean and Africa. Caste, like race and class, determined who had access to English education in India—Brahmin boys belonging to the highest caste were more privileged than boys or girls of other castes. Male/female ratios were exacerbated additionally by inequities among Hindus and Muslims in terms of educational opportunities. As recorded by the Parliamentary Committee on the Affairs of the East India Company, "Female Schools have also been successfully established; at the different Missionary Stations there were, in 1823, nearly 1,200 female children, and that number has gradually increased to 3,000." In other British colonies as well, prejudice against girls' education persisted through most of the nineteenth century. In Trinidad, as Campbell records: "Before 1870 the pattern was that there were more boys than girls in elementary schools. . . . The strong religious and social motivation behind the provision of elementary schools was not sex-specific. It might be assumed, however, that since both in Africa and England more importance was attached traditionally to the education of boys, that prejudice in favor of boys informed the thinking of local educators and parents" (87). Educating boys was believed to bring income into the family, whereas girls were more useful as domestic helpers. When secondary schools were established for girls, they could compete for what were called "college exhibitions"—before 1923 they were not allowed to compete. After that, girls regularly beat boys at these exams.

There is a key difference between the former British colonies in East and West Africa, and Caribbean colonies such as Trinidad, namely, that formal education had a much earlier start in Caribbean colonies, as also in India. And since most African cultures were oral, newly independent African nations had lower literacy rates than other colonies, and had to implement programs for primary education whereas in Trinidad and other colonies, post-independence was a time to develop secondary and higher education. Even in terms of primary education, certain factors accounting for increase in girls' schooling are delineated by Claire Robertson—population size, the relative wealth or poverty of the nation, parent's decisions, urbanization. Per capita income did not always influence parents' decisions to send girls to school. Other social and cultural factors override the issue of cost especially since several nations had free primary schooling. Especially in rural areas, girls' labor was required at home, fetching water, looking after younger siblings, cooking. Robertson notes other deterring factors such as girls having to walk long distances to go to school, irrelevant curriculum, and parental objections to coeducational classes. Ironically, coeducation schools are often better equipped and managed. But this system is frowned upon, especially among Muslim populations. However, Robertson points out that "religion does not make a large difference in the growth of girls' education . . . [She indicates] the danger of making facile generalizations on the impact of Islam on Africa that ignore local variations" (103). Often the efforts to secularize schools went along with promoting coeducation. "In general, the impact of coeducation," remarks Robertson, "on girls' enrollment is difficult to assess" (103). Further, Robertson points out "a great deal of hidden sex segregation" where girls and boys are separated in terms of the curriculum offered—typically, home economics for girls, mechanics for boys. Although there is a greater chance of "equalizing the curriculum" in this coeducational system than in separate sex schools, there are other disadvantages such as "discrimination against girls" in the classroom, and their hesitation in speaking up as inculcated by their "social conditioning."

Even when girls do enter schools, they drop out more often than boys. Robertson cites factors such as "early marriage, insufficient secondary places for middle school leavers, coeducation, cost of education, low quality of girls' schools, and the irrelevance of formal education or economic needs" (100). Above all else, girls' labor value at home "not only impedes scholastic achievement but also decreases their level of attendance at school" (100).

Robertson also traces "geographical and political factors on the growth of girls' education" especially the colonial powers' efforts in promoting or neglecting education for natives. Britain shows a better record, largely attributable to missionary efforts in southern Africa, notes Robertson, than other colonizers especially the Portuguese and Italian. Governmental ideologies in the post-independence era demonstrate higher figures in education of girls in socialist countries as opposed to "moderate" and "conservative" ones. Robertson notes the particularly problematic case of Guinea-Bissaue, which has the worst record in education despite the fact that women played such a vital role in the liberation war against the Portuguese.

Often, mothers are more responsible for sending daughters to school than fathers. Robertson notes marital instability that leads to women getting custody and being expected to provide school fees. Bostawanan/South

African Bessie Head's short story, "The Collector of Treasures," represents a female protagonist Dikeledi who after bearing three children is deserted by an irresponsible husband. She wants her children to be educated and to have more options in their lives, so she works her fingers to the bone to come up with their school fees. Significantly, the last line of the story, after Dikeledi is arrested for killing her husband in resistance to his "defiling" her life, recognizes her efforts at educating her children. Her kind neighbor Paul, described in the story as "a poem of tenderness" remarks to Dikeledi: "You don't have to worry about the children. . . . I'll take them as my own and give them all a secondary school education."[27]

Gender, Caste, Class, and Religion: Britain's Classic Divide and Rule Policy in Colonial Education

British educational policy in India was one of the key spaces that introduced not only the English classics, but also their ignominious divide and rule policies that operated by fostering divisions among previously harmonious groups with different religions, castes, and classes. Statements that appear objective, in fact mystified the emphasis on the superior race and religion of Britain over the colonies, for instance, "The great end [of education] should not have been to teach Hindoo learning, or Mohamedan learning, but useful learning" (*PP*). The British attempted to "infiltrate by keying into 'long-established practices among Hindus—for example, giving instruction at their own houses, by the stimulus of honorary marks of distinction, and in some instance by grants of pecuniary assistance.' All these would accrue 'considerable advantages' from 'a political point of view' "(*PP*, 1832, 484).

English educational policy institutionalized a broader divide and rule policy in general, particularly along religious lines. As the following extract from the Evidence Given in the Second Report of the Commons Committee (*PP*, 311) states,

> Nearly the whole of the Parsees speak English. They have invariably educated their children in English, and many of them can speak it as fluently as Europeans. The Parsees have more pride, and have taken more pains to understand English, and all our laws and institutions, than any other class of Indians, not excepting the Brahmins of Calcutta. They are by far the most intelligent class. Hindoos are also educating very fast, but they have not made that progress which the Parsees

have. The Mohamedans, generally speaking, are not so industrious, and have stronger prejudices against sending their children to school.

There was often a slippage between the lowest castes and the state of women in terms of educational opportunities. Among the few female educational spaces that existed was the Calcutta Ladies' School for Native Females. As reported in *Parliamentary Papers*, June 1825, a society of ladies united for the promotion of female education in Calcutta and its vicinity. They applied to the government for the sum of 10,000 rupees to purchase land and build a school.

Along with playing on religious loyalties and beliefs, the British bureaucratized the realities of caste, class, and gender inequalities already upheld by indigenous patriarchy. After all, it was in the interest of colonial patriarchy to collude with and maintain indigenous patriarchy rather than opposing sexual inequities.

In India, Munro, as mentioned in *PP* 1825, notes that

> reading and writing are confined almost entirely to Brahmins and the mercantile class.... To the women of Brahmins and of Hindoos in general they are unknown, because the knowledge of them is prohibited, and regarded as unbecoming of the modesty of the sex, and fit only for public dancers. But among the women of Rajbundah and some other tribes of Hindoos, who seem to have no prejudice of this kind, they are generally taught. The prohibition against women learning to read is probably, from various causes, much less attended to in some districts than in others; and as it is possible that in every district a few females may be found in the reading schools, a column has been entered for them in the form proposed to be sent to the collector. The mixed and impure castes seldom learn to read; but as a few of them do, columns are left for them in the form. (33)

The British were concerned about the negative repercussions of forced conversions and "open interference with the religious observances of our native subjects." The debate on this matter is recorded by the Parliamentary Committee on the Affairs of the East India Company:

> Do you consider that the giving to the natives systematically an enlightened education, affords the best chance of the advancement of the Christian religion in India? It is the only rational foundation. [The very minimal progress in converting natives to Christianity in Bengal is noted.] Any efforts to force such results, by open interference

with the religious observances of our native subjects might, without advancing the great cause in view, produce consequences the most injurious. Such proceedings might tend to our expulsion from the country in the midst of our career of usefulness and cast back the objects of our care into their ancient ignorance. . . . It is true that the consequences of our teaching the natives the value and extent of their power will lead to their asserting it, and to the subversion of our rule; but [when] this occurs . . . we shall retire gracefully; gratitude will succeed to resistance; and instead of our being execrated as reckless tyrants, our memory will be revered as belonging to enlightened benefactors. (*PP*, 1825)

Such sentiments are also expressed by Tambu's ironic comment in *Nervous Conditions* when she wonders why British missionaries and educators undertook self-sacrificing tasks of "brightening up diverse darknesses" in which the natives lived.

Postcolonial literary texts represent how the education of the mind was reinforced by a saving of the soul since English education was often enmeshed with propagation of missionary goals. Novels such as Trinidadian Merle Hodge's *Crick Crack, Monkey* historicize the roots of an educational system in colonial missionary structures and attitudes. Some of Tee's confusion is related humorously: "Now at school I had come to learn that Glory and The Mother Country and Up-There and Over-There [London] had all one and the same geographical location. . . . And then there was 'Land of Hope and Glory / Mother of the Free' " (30). Mrs. Hinds, their teacher, "naturally" takes it upon herself to do whatever she could "towards our redemption." Tee reports faithfully that each "day began and ended with the intoning of the sounds which we could perform without a fault while our thoughts drifted elsewhere behind our tightly-shut eyes":

> Our father (which was plain enough)
> witchartin
> heavn
> HALLE
> owedbethyname
> THY
> kingdumkum
> THY
> willbedunnunnert
> azitizinevn . . . (26–27)

Hodge accurately and humorously recreates a scene where speech, recitation by rote, is part of a collective memory for children in colonial schools. Tee and her classmates repeat words that they do not understand, they cannot question, they must memorize and repeat, without thinking and be reverential about all white values. Their education does not teach them to discriminate between, say, which aspects of "Gen Terjesus me kan mile" might be empowering, and which others that would lead directly to racist self-denial and self-hatred. For instance, at Sunday school when Tee is given "a picture and a Bible verse—pictures of children with yellow hair standing around Jesus in fields of sickly flowers" she recites what amounts to a denial of her very self:

> Till I cross the wide water, Lord
> My black sin washed from me
> Till I come to Glory Glory, Lord
> And cleansed stand beside Thee,
> White and shining stand beside Thee, Lord,
> Among Thy blessed children . . . (30)

Missionary education spans two generations in Dangarembga's *Nervous Conditions*. Tambu narrates with astute irony how her grandmother took nine-year-old Babamukuru "wearing a loin-cloth to the mission, where the wizards took him in. They set him to work in their farm by day. By night he was educated in their wizardry" (19). When Tambu herself encounters white people at the mission, she thinks back on her grandmother's description of these people as "holy," and adds with an ironic twist that "the missionaries were about God's business here in darkest Africa. They had given up the comfort and security of their own homes to come and lighten our darkness" (103).

Colonial missionaries were replaced often by native missionaries. When Tambu wins a scholarship to a nun's mission school where only a select few Africans are admitted, Nyasha is skeptical about its impact on Tambu since this education has no respect for indigenous culture which remains invisible in this world. Nyasha worries that such an experience can make one an outsider to one's own community. Natives who are assimilated into a colonial educational system and values have "an honorary space" in which they must "behave." But Nyasha insisted that "one ought not to occupy that space" (179).

Although religion was central in missionary education, the British retained a stance on neutrality about religious matters in the early 1800s.

Further, even a discouragement of missionary activity in India led to "the central contradiction of a government committed to the improvement of the people," notes Viswanathan, "while being restrained from imparting any direct instruction in the religious principles of the English nation . . . the conflict of interests between commitment to Indian education on one hand and to religious neutrality on the other rendered the communication of modern knowledge virtually impossible. . . . Because the knowledge of the West could not be imparted directly without seeming to tamper with the fabric of indigenous religions, British administrators were virtually paralyzed from moving in either direction" (37). Viswanathan argues that this "tension between increasing involvement in Indian education and enforced noninterference in religion was productively resolved through the introduction of English Literature" (38).

A careful colonial policy, in the interest of colonial self-preservation, did not wish to challenge "particularly the Muslims, from cultivating a native literature held in pious veneration—a literature that was deeply interwoven with the habits and religion of the people and comprised valuable records of their culture" (39–40). Somehow, the British had to transform the notions of Indian religious heads learned in Arabic and Sanskrit that western knowledge was necessary, and ultimately superior. As knowledge of English became essential, it was recommended (as in a letter from W. Astell, R. Campbell, etc. September 29, 1830), that "a thorough knowledge of English can only be acquired by natives through a course of study beginning early in life and continued for many years. . . . Native languages and literatures may be adequately pursued as a subordinate branch of education in an English college" (*PP*, 1832). This is still largely true. Educational policy tried not to collide with the teaching of the sacred books of Hindus and Muslims. But subtly and not so subtly it was conveyed that it was "highly advisable for natives to acquire a thorough knowledge of English; being convinced that the higher tone and better spirit of European literature can produce their full effect only on those who become familiar with them in the original languages" (*PP*, 1832). Racial superiority is evoked, and domination here works through consent rather than force—the natives would recognize the "superiority," not to mention the material advantages of learning English, and would want more rather than less of this education. English learning would inspire "intelligent natives" to undergo training as teachers and translators and they would be able to propagate and communicate "to the minds of the native community, that improved spirit which it is to be hoped they will themselves have imbibed from the influence of European ideas and sentiments ... [such] qualified natives will be highly honored by the government" (*PP*, 1832).

The ideals of an English public education were to develop leadership qualities, independent thinking and moral character. A Matthew Arnoldian balance of philosophy and literature was used commonly for English school curricula in India. Even as this western learning equipped Indians to be questioning and independent thinkers, their opportunities to work in the colonial bureaucracy were extremely restricted and at low level clerical positions which was frustrating. Such a contradiction could inspire rebellion. There is a further gender paradox in the educating of women who had to be "protected" from "foreign influences" especially as they became westernized through their English education.[28]

The secular agenda was infused subversively with religious authority in the ways in which literary texts were taught and in subtle ways of discrediting the tenets of Hinduism. "The effect modern learning had on shaking native systems of learning contributed quite literally to their sacralization of its content. And so in achieving what religious teaching aimed at all along—the destruction of the 'errors' of Hinduism—British secularism firmly and irrevocably aligned itself with Christianity."[29] The British saw no contradiction in including subtle critiques of a polytheistic religious system such as Hinduism in spelling-books. The titles of some essay topics assigned to Indian students "were worded in such a way as to predetermine the response" remarks Viswanathan, citing examples such as, "On the disadvantages of Caste, and the benefits of its abolition," "On the internal marks of Falsehood in the Hindu Shastras."[30]

A fascinating historical record of an Anglo-Indian teacher, Derozio who personified these contradictions inherent in the teaching and propagation of English is delineated in Manju Dalmia's essay, "Derozio: English Teacher."[31] Derozio had a vast influence on the upper-class and caste Hindu boys who studied under him at Hindu College, Calcutta. Controversy brewed over the questioning of Hindu religious practices and superstitions. As Indian students participated in debating societies that overtly declared the inferiority of the Hindu religion over Christianity, and English values, parents were outraged and Derozio was dismissed in 1831. Dalmia remarks, "The usefulness of English was never questioned. Its ill effects were seen to reside in the style of teaching, in particular the style of Derozio" (57). The "solution" was to stop religious discussion. Dalmia draws a further important implication from this history, namely that in the early stages of English education, there really was no social standing for this English educated class; this occurred later as law courts and government used English for their work.

Parliamentary debates on educational policy even as they discussed matters of religion, indigenous languages, and translation, often expressed trepidation that educating the natives would eventually equip them to oust their colonial rulers from India. As the following extract from the Summary of Evidence given by Eminent Persons before the Lord's Committee states: "The increasing of the sources of education and intelligence must in the end tend to drive us out of the country. It is not in human nature to suppose that when their minds are armed with intelligence they will not use it. They cannot go on with the means of intelligence, and let a handful of Europeans govern them. They ought decidedly to be enlightened, but the effect will be, that we shall lose the country" (*PP*).

Indian Social Reformers and Women's Education

British colonial educational policies were often buttressed, challenged, reformulated by indigenous social reformers whose agendas were caught between revivalism and reform. Racist colonial onslaughts instigated two distinct reactions: a revival of ancient Hinduism, the glories of the Vedic past, and on the other hand, Anglicization in speech, dress, behavior, values. Revivalism went along with nationalism and anti-imperialism as Radha Kumar points out in her important text *The History of Doing*. Reformers like Ishwarchandra Vidyasager, Rammohan Roy and others in the forefront of movements to ameliorate women's downtrodden situation were caught in this double bind between what Uma Chakravarty describes as "Anglicism and Orientalism." Radha Kumar demonstrates how "the women's education movement was 'Indianized' over the course of the century" (8). Initially, in the 1810s, the first schools for girls were started by English and American missionaries. "In 1819 the first text on women's education in an Indian language (Bengali) by an Indian, Gourmohan Vidyalamkara, was published by the Female Juvenile Society in Calcutta. By 1827 there were twelve girls' schools run by missionaries" (14). By the mid-nineteenth century, fears were expressed about the proselytizing intentions of missionary schools. In radical moves by the unorthodox Brahmo Samaj, upper-class girls were educated at home often by English or Scottish tutors. This challenged the private, inner household space that high-caste women occupied, called *andarmahals* (inner sanctum, so to speak, where women lived, like the *zenanas*).

Kumar discusses how the need for women's education was articulated by middle- and upper-class men who saw it as advantageous to have selected westernisms for their women. They tried, often contradictorily, to both reform certain aspects of "backward" Hindu practice (such as women being confined to the inner home spaces), as well as to glorify other aspects of that same "tradition." Of course, it was the women who fell through the cracks of this male rationalizing; women had to fulfill both traditional and modern roles, a double bind that still controls contemporary women, especially the educated ones. One way in which the reformers critiqued the limitations of the secluded inner world, as Kumar points out, was to condemn forms of entertainment "through popular cultural forms such as songs and recitals (*kirtans, panchals, kathakars*) . . . as low and 'obscene'. . . . Nor is it surprising that the ribald humor of popular Bengali songs, in particular, drew disfavor from the Victorians, who condemned so much of their own literary heritage as lewd" (15). Even as women's enjoyment of such material was seen as exposing them "to wantonness and vulgarity" their pleasure at such entertainment "was described as indicating their 'natural' tendency towards depravity" (15). Education would save women from their very natures even as such prejudice against popular cultural forms marginalized them "pushing their performers into seeking new avenues of employment. Traditional spaces for the expression of 'a woman's voice' were thus further curtailed" (15).

By the 1840s, the impact of Jyotirao Phule's work was significant. Kumar writes that in 1848, he "founded his first school for girls in Poona. . . . In the same year, students of Elphinstone College in Bombay opened a school for girls and started a monthly magazine for women. By 1852 Phule had opened three schools for girls, and one for 'untouchables' [the lowest caste among Hindus]" (15).

By the 1850s, Ishwarchandra Vidyasagar launched a campaign for widow-remarriage that was built on the importance of education in general. Education, as supported by nineteenth-century social reformers was so gendered that in lower primary standards a choice between "Hemming or Arithmetic," and in upper primary, "cutting out a koorta, sewing on buttons and strings, and making buttonholes; or Arithmetic" was provided (16). Such choices would hardly encourage girls to favor accounting over sewing. Educational ideology leading to awareness of oppression and working toward social change would need not only to transform female, but even more importantly, male consciousness since male privilege is a given in patriarchal societies.

Kumar draws out "different strands" in the social reformers' philosophies on female education in the 1860s—a desire toward Anglophilia as expressed by the Bombay Parsi, Framji Bomanji who wanted "the English language, English manners and English behaviour for our wives and daughters" (20). Others were opposed to such Anglo-mania—Sayyid Ahmed Khan encouraged Muslim girls to be educated at home, but cautioned against their Anglicizing. Dayanand Saraswati espoused women's education on the "secular rationalist line," apart from any religious faith, though also asserting "the theory of a golden age in ancient India (Vedic) which had accorded a special place to learned women" (20). Similarly, Lajpat Rai's *History of the Arya Samaj* glorified women's "pedestal position" in ancient India along with a paradoxical assertion of their equality with men. Kumar says, "As regards education and marriage they [men and women] held an equal position. The girls were equally entitled to receive education, and no limitations at all were set on their ambition in this direction. . . . The only difference was that, in the case of girls, their period of education expired sooner than that of boys. The minimum age of marriage for girls was sixteen, as compared with twenty-five for boys" (21).

For most social reformers, women's education enabled them to be better wives and mothers, and most female school curricula emphasized sewing, cooking, and childcare. Education was not valued in itself but for its potential to make women better mates while leaving the male social power structure intact. Even when in the face of deeply entrenched prejudice, women were educated, the content and extent of their learning was controlled. Despite their constraints, noteworthy nineteenth-century women acquired higher education, for instance, Pandita Ramabai, a Sanskrit scholar, and Anandi Joshi, the first woman medical doctor who studied in the U.S. and died at the age of thirty-five. These women's own remarkable intellectual gifts had to be supported initially by males—Ramabai's father, and Anandi's husband. Pandita Ramabai started a school for child-widows called Sharada Sadan. She trained as a teacher in England (1883), and then joined the Episcopalian Church much to the horror of the Brahmin orthodoxy that had conferred the title of "Saraswati" on her for the depth of her Sanskrit knowledge. By the 1880s and 1890s, backlashes to social reform for women had set in. Ramabai's conversion drew public outcry and "foreign" influences were condemned as interfering with Hindu religion. The hegemony of Brahminic codes was being challenged and shaken in campaigns to ameliorate women's predicament as widows, and even as productive members of society. Even male social reformers were deeply divided on questions of higher education for women since that clearly shook the sexual status quo; as Kumar writes, they believed that "the character of girls' education should be different from that of boys. . . . The education we give our girls should not unsex them," as stated in one of the Hindu tenets in Arya Dharma (29). By the turn of the century, Kumar indicates that along with these reservations went an increasing preoccupation and declaration of "Hindu" identity, and discussions about "the education of 'Hindu' girls, and not as they did before, of 'Indian' girls" (30). Indeed, the nineteenth-century social reform movement has been critiqued overall for its focus on largely upper-caste Hindu women's issues such as sati, and widow remarriage.

English Education and Female Socialization: Indigenous Values and Cultural Alienations

"This Englishness will kill you," notes Tambu's mother warning her daughter in response to Nyasha's near-fatal bulimic state in Dangarembga's *Nervous Conditions*. There are remarkable commonalities in female protagonists' conflicts of belonging within indigenous cultures when viewed through their English-educated gaze—Tee in Trinidadian Merle Hodge's novel *Crick Crack, Monkey*, Nyasha and Tambu in Dangaremba's *Nervous Conditions*, Lalita in Indian Kamala Markandaya's *Two Virgins*, and Laila in Indian Attia Hosain's *Sunlight on a Broken Column*.[32] These novels explore the conflicts arising from an English education espousing values that clash with indigenous cultures, especially with regard to gender roles. Female protagonists are caught in painful ambivalence between shame in their own culture, often denigrated by colonial schools that assert the superiority of white culture. They acquire fluency in English often at the expense of their mother tongue as in Nyasha's case who is uprooted and taken to England at a young age. She is relocated for the advantages of an English education, but ironically she is disadvantaged in her increasing alienation, linguistic and social, from her own culture and became increasingly alienated linguistically, and even bodily, from her community.

The texts noted above focus on their protagonists' adolescence when female sexuality is controlled more rigorously (under the name of protection) than in childhood. The psychological and cultural dislocations of outsiderness are experienced by the female body which becomes the site of both struggle and resistance—Tee, in her darkest moments of alienation wishes "to shrink, to disappear," and by the end of the novel, she is anxious to be physically re-located, body and mind, to England. Lalita's lure for adventure and glamour leads her physically away from her village-home, into the city and into unwanted pregnancy. She undergoes an abortion, and continues to resist her parents' desire to make her conform to a limited, albeit respectable life in the village. When her body quite literally takes flight, her parents cannot locate her. Nyasha's bulimia is an expression of her rejection literally of the food that her father forces her to eat, and metaphorically of her vomiting out the aspects of both English-ness and her Shona-ness that oppress her as a female. Young Laila, like Nyasha, is an avid reader who devours books. She believes in education, and delights in English classics as well as Persian and Arabic texts. She learns to juggle not only words in different languages but also the different value systems that these words convey. Her confrontations with patriarchal controls of her body and movement are resolved less tragically than in Dangarembga's text. Laila, unlike Nyasha, for all her intelligence and questioning of feudal ways, has a solid base within the love of the joint family, within the fabric, however troubling, of age-old custom. The ordered hierarchy of her family structure, albeit feudal, sustains Laila through bodily and mental crises of belonging. Also, unlike Nyasha, Tambu is a survivor. She has grown up in poverty and hardship along with a love for the rural landscape that one can imagine sustaining her during times of confusion and alienation at a new school where she is only one of six African girls in a sea of white faces.

Even as education equips these female protagonists to think for themselves, that very autonomy ironically separates them from their own communities. Lalita's English education in Markandaya's *Two Virgins* leads to her growing frustration with her own culture, "the ignorance" that she judges her rural parents to be steeped in. In the midst of an orthodox and circumscribed village community, an Anglo-Indian, Miss Mendoza runs the Three Kings School (once called Mission High School). The curriculum included "how to dance around a bamboo pole which Miss Mendoza said was a maypole. There was a fee to pay for these privileges whereas the state school was free" (14). Learning English goes along with other English customs like drinking tea, sitting in chairs rather than on the floor, eating with utensils rather than with fingers. The acquisition of English language education transcends the simple change from one's mother tongue to English; it leads to a change of consciousness. Markandaya problematizes how such education, fostering independent thought while situated in strict village customs, enjoins women to conform to norms that displace an intelligent woman like Lalita. Since her education makes her increasingly dissatisfied with the limitations of village life, she ventures into the city, hoping to have a glamorous life. She gives in to enjoying her sexuality but when she finds herself pregnant and has to undergo an abortion, she is disgraced in the eyes of the village. The novel ends with Lalita running away to the city. Like Nyasha, Lalita is caught between independence of mind fostered by her education and the suffocating social restrictions of being a "proper daughter."

Home and school reinforce sexist standards of masculinity and femininity in male and female socialization. As a girl is socialized to be reticent and self-sacrificing in school as at home, Leela Dube asks whether educational reform in itself would have an impact when the larger society continues its sexist standards? In her very useful essay, "Socialisation of Hindu Girls in Patrilineal India," she asks: "Can we really think of reforming the educational system or of a reformed system of formal education to bring about a more 'enlightened' relationship between the sexes as long as the larger structures which provide the context for this educational system continue to reproduce gender-based relationships of domination and subordination?" (190).[33]

Dube's essay also usefully outlines the physical deportment, and appropriate social spaces that girls are taught to occupy, many of which are broken by Lalita much before her exposure to the city. Restrictive codes such as how a girl carries herself, taking "soft steps (long strides denote masculinity), keeping knees together while sitting, standing, or sleeping is 'decent', and indicates a sense of shame and modesty. 'Don't stand like a man' is a common rebuke to make a girl aware of the demands of femininity" (177). Girls must speak softly, not laugh loudly or be argumentative. Other physical details of comportment include restrictions on girls whistling which "signifies amorous inclination . . . smiling without purpose, and glancing furtively. . . . Shyness and modesty are approved of and considered as 'natural' feminine qualities" (177). Dube also notes "a curved posture" as associated with "a dancing girl" and hence girls being restricted from "leaning against a wall or a pillar. . . . In many parts of India girls were traditionally forbidden to look into a mirror or comb their hair after sunset since these acts were associated with a prostitute getting ready for her customers" (177). The heavy controls that supposedly protect female modesty place restrictions on girls' freedom to leave the home space. "Constraints of time and space," remarks Dube, "create problems for middle-class girls in terms of choice of schools, colleges and courses—coeducation and staying out till late which certain courses demand are frowned upon—and consequently, in their choice of careers" (178).

Relocations and English Education

Educational opportunities necessitate the stepping out of a familiar geography and into a different class environment that sometimes feels like being in a different country. Young Tee, Tambu, Nyasha, are all required to relocate for the benefits of English schooling. Tee and Tambu, as "poor relatives" are raised up from economically deprived conditions into the homes of middle-class, urban relatives, and given the "gift" of an English education. That experience and its outcomes are fraught with conflict and ambivalence for the girl-child's sense of identity and belonging. Such physical journeys in order to acquire an education place particular demands on female adolescent bodies. Bodily relocations often lead to mental states of exile and non-belonging. As they gain an education, and learn to imbibe upwardly mobile class aspirations, they are rendered outsiders and must search for new spaces of belonging. And, as inspired by their new learning, they often need new intellectual spaces of belonging that may be found outside their native spaces when they migrate. But the pain of feeling cut off from their own families of origin, often un-English educated, remains. Both Hodge and Dangarembga use a first person narrative where Tee and Tambu relate their stories from their adolescent points of view. Although Markandaya uses the third person omniscient narrator, the story is seen through pre-pubescent Saroja gazing adoringly and often in confusion at her adolescent sister Lalita's burgeoning sexuality.

For lower-class Tee and Tambu, educational opportunities require a change of locale and class. They move in with middle-class relatives who can afford to send them to English schools. This physical relocation does not entail simply leaving home to go to a boarding school; the new space evokes a serious questioning of what has been left behind, especially the values of one's non-English educated parents. Tambu's move to her uncle and aunt's privileged home with modern amenities like running water inevitably changes her attitude to the deprived, rural homestead she has left behind.

Tee's development from girlhood to adolescence is traced through her English education mixed with bourgeois values of the black middle class at her Aunt Beatrice's. Tee inhabits her black body more and more uncomfortably, at times stepping outside her body, rejecting it, at times, creating a persona that is the "proper" Tee. Although she is fascinated with books, English education does not include any of her own history or geography. Chimneys and apple trees are not a part of the Trinidadian tropical landscape. Books transport Tee "into Reality and Rightness, which were to be found Abroad." She imagines "the enviable reality of real Girls and Boys who went a-sleighing and built snowmen, ate potatoes, not rice" (61).

By the end of the novel, Tee is going on a physical and mental journey taken by many colonized peoples when as though multiply located, from the physical location and vantage point of the mother country, they study their own culture. They rediscover their own history often denied by their English education, and they often return home as insiders/outsiders. They can build on the advantage of studying their culture, as insiders, but from an outside location. Hodge concurs with this reading in her interview comment that what she had in mind with Tee was "that the whole conflict would be resolved by her experience in England."[34] Tee would be able to understand her two aunts and where to place them as well as herself in these value systems. Hodge and other writers have made such journeys outside their cultures into the colonizer's space. That foreignness becomes the enabling space from within which colonized peoples look at their own history, re-evaluate it, and are able often to synthesize the best of different worlds. They can reintegrate themselves into their own culture even as they develop a healthy critique of the limitations, especially for women, of certain indigenous social norms (discussed in depth in the next chapter on "Tradition"). They recognize what is energizing and nourishing about both cultures. As outsiders in the colonizer's land, but equipped with the master's tongue and knowledge of his culture, colonized people are situated uniquely to avail of the intellectual tools of the mother country.

In the same interview in *Callalloo*, Hodge comments that she does not believe that "Tee's enlightenment happens at all within the confines of the novel." Tee is in a situation where she finds herself at the end wanting to reject her relatives. According to Hodge, "this is not a situation that perhaps, a child can resolve" (654). Hodge also adds that she wrote this novel when she was in England as a student and when she was immersed in the Negritude movement. She was one among "all these Caribbean and African people going to European countries and discovering there that all they'd been told about their own countries was a lot of hogwash, and that their own culture was valid" (654).

Rhoda Reddock's discussion of "Colonial Policy on Women's Education" in her study entitled *Women, Labour and Politics in Trinidad and*

Tobago: A History provides useful historical material within which to place Tee's postcolonial dilemmas.[35] Reddock analyses the sexual, color, and class division of educational opportunities available to women. A gendered emphasis in education was introduced with the controversial Education Code of 1935, so that girls were trained in domestic science and other housewifely tasks. In Reddock's analysis, prior to the 1930s, women were still required in agriculture, and there was not much overt differentiation in curricula for girls and boys. However, as women were gradually excluded from the agricultural sector in the post–First World War period, an emphasis on home-making assumed importance.

Education became key to assimilating the "new ex-slave society" to the norms of "a civilized community" acceptable to the colonizers. Reddock quotes from Rev. J. Sterling's justification of negro education in a report to the British government in 1835: the production of "a civilized community will depend entirely on the power over their minds." If they are not educated, "property will perish in the colonies." In Reddock's historicized discussion, she states that since "brute force could no longer be the main form of labour control, new ideological forms had to be found and popular education was one of them. . . . Colonial education was not meant to liberate the colonized. Rather, it was the means through which the values and interests of the colonizers and masters would be internalized by the colonized and perceived as their own. In Trinidad this was a much more urgent task as the pervasiveness of French and Spanish cultural symbols, languages and Roman Catholicism necessitated a strong anglicizing policy" (217–218).

Although girls received primary education, there was only one girls' secondary school by the beginning of the twentieth century.[36] The only "career" open to women was that of teaching. This option was further curbed in the Education Code's forbidding "the employment of married women as teachers," remarks Reddock, "except where the services of a suitable unmarried female teacher cannot be obtained" (Education Code, 1935, 15).

The public debate on women's higher education from the 1830s is revelatory in this study of gender inequities in higher education introduced by colonizers and continuing today. And the colonizers' gendered educational policies colluded with indigenous patriarchal traditions as evident in this 1836 comment on women's education: "We did not wish to see our young ladies and daughters become 'blue stockings', we did not ask for Creole de Staels and Mary Somervilles" (222). During this period, secondary education "was the prerogative only of the white and coloured bourgeoisie and a few of the upper middle strata" (222). Not only color prejudice, but moral norms excluded blacks from these opportunities, primarily in the stigma of "illegitimacy" that automatically excluded them from schools. By the 1850s only a few black or colored boys had the opportunity "to win 'exhibitions' or scholarships to secondary school" (222). No scholarships were available for girls, hence the working class was significantly excluded. Such exclusion and denial of educational opportunity is apparent even in contemporary times—several of the Jamaican Sistren collective's life stories in *Lionheart Gal* portray working-class mothers who, growing up in the 1950s, did not have the educational opportunities that were available a generation later to their daughters. But the stigma of bastardy, of the colonial Christian prejudice of having children outside traditional bourgeois marriage had severe repercussions on women's entire lives as represented in one of the Sistren stories in *Lionheart Gal*, "Grandma's Estate." During colonization, an unwanted pregnancy outside marriage could get an adolescent girl expelled from school, a scenario that perpetuated a cycle of female poverty and dependency.

Education and class advancement went hand in hand. An article in *The Mirror* (January 12, 1903) quoted in Reddock "bemoaned the fact that poorer colonies than Trinidad had established good colleges for girls with 'two or three well trained and cultured European lady teachers' and noted that the wealthy could send their daughters to Europe but for the 'respectable man' this was not possible" (223). Another article in *The Schoolmaster*, no.1, 1903 pleaded for women's education since wives could be more effective "helpmates" to their husbands, and could "come up to the ideal of what a cultured woman ought to be. Particularly the middle class of people would benefit" (223). In 1908, *The Teachers Journal*, as recorded by Reddock, argued for women's education on the grounds that it would improve "our domestic economy as well as our morals" (224). In contemporary times, although Tee in Hodge's *Crick Crack, Monkey* does get an education despite her lower-class roots, she had to move from her working-class Tantie's home to the middle-class bourgeois home of Aunt Beatrice in order to go to a prestigious school.

The actual content of girls' education in the early part of the century embodies what Reddock terms "the actual process of Western European 'housewifization'" (226). Sarah Morton, Canadian Missionary, writes about the subjects that the Girls Training Homes established by the Mission covered: worship with the family, gardening, sewing, writing scripture, washing, ironing. "In the daily sewing class the girls learned to cut and sew garments of many descriptions including English dresses and jackets." (Morton, 1916, quoted in Reddock, 349). The girls were also "initiated into the mysteries of English dishes ... imposing cakes were made for our brides" (226). As Morton argues, the purpose of these establishments was clear—to train women to become preachers, or proselytizers in the community, and to prepare them to marry suitably and avoid "the danger of being given to non-Christian or otherwise unsuitable men" in marriage (347).

Marriage as the primary goal and purpose of education was fostered in colonial policies and in postcolonial times with varying degrees. Joan French, in her very useful study entitled "Colonial Policy Towards Women After the 1938 Uprising: The Case of Jamaica," analyzes The Moyne Commission Report (chaired by Lord Moyne and set up after the Jamaican uprising of 1938, regarded as "the worst of the 'disturbances' in the British West Indies in the 1930s").[37] The Report, in its ideology, strategy, recommendations, is geared to be conciliatory—under the guise of promoting social welfare programs and education for dissatisfied natives. The Jamaica Federation of Women was set up which promoted social work by middle-class women, and overtly propagated monogamous marriage and family life, on the British nuclear model. It was the belief that a stable family would solve many of the social and economic problems, and women's education is only for such family welfare. Girls' education "was seen in terms of how it fitted [them] for marriage," remarks Joan French. In order to be successful companions to their husbands, women needed "cultural education" as the Moyne Report put it. This included domestic science and vocational training. Although the Moyne Report propagated a nuclear family model with the male bread-winner (also aiming to solve vast unemployment problems), encouraging the dependent wife-homemaker model for women, this hardly worked for working-class women. Even though the man as head of household hardly worked in the West Indies "where promiscuity and illegitimacy are so prevalent," notes the Moyne Report quoted by French, "and the woman so often is the supporter of the home" (12), the colonial attitude was hegemonically thrust down the throats of the colonized; in this case, as French notes, "The Moyne Commission had clearly decided that the way to address the problem was to make man the head of the family, even if only in theory" (12). Further, colonial policies could have it both ways—in terms of using these women as domestics "servicing the public and 'private' areas of ruling class life," as French remarks (11), and to give them just minimum education that they can perform these tasks to the satisfaction of their masters. This scenario continues in terms of female domestic workers for the black middle and upper classes (in Jamaica, domestics are called "helpers"—same difference!)

The issue of class enters prominently into this scenario since different standards applied to upper-class girls who had access to secondary education and they could study subjects previously reserved for boys—mathematics, Latin, physics, and chemistry. The Moyne Report made claims at fighting prejudice against women going in for professions such as nursing or teaching. For these, women need to study more than domestic science. "Complaints were made to us," notes the Moyne Report, "in evidence of the difficulty of obtaining girls with the education necessary to enable them to enter the nursing profession" (10). Over a hundred years later, this has a familiar sound in today's Affirmative Action advocates who with the best intentions often display a disturbing naiveté when they whine that minority candidates are impossible to find for certain kinds of jobs. There is hardly ever the more radical questioning as to basic inequities in educational opportunities to different classes. In secondary education, girls were not subjected to the " 'rigors' of scholarship examination until 1947," remarks Reddock, "although for boys this had begun since 1870." Ironically, even when girls took part in "exhibition scholarships," and even if they won, their options were severely circumscribed. Reddock relates the case of Elsie Padmore who won a handicraft exhibition scholarship in 1926, but "was refused entrance to every branch of handicraft she chose to pursue" (227), such as photography, book-binding. The master-craftsmen "were not keen on having girls."

As in the Caribbean, feminist recuperation of the agendas behind women's education in most of the ex-colonies reveals that "women's education was a force," as Reddock puts it, "for maintaining rather than changing the system." Groups that promoted social reform in the various colonies often allied with British liberal, even conservative politics. For instance, French points out that the Jamaica Federation of Women, founded in 1944 by Lady Molly Huggins, wife of the colonial governor, was "modelled on the Women's Institute of Great Britain [whose] motto . . . was 'For Our Homes and Our Country' " (18). As the British and Canadian Institutes, the ones in the colonies imitated a similar thrust, the most problematic one being that they defined themselves as non-political. In terms of education, they "promoted civic education and made representations to District and County Councils representing the rural housewife's point of view" (19), but they did not intervene in policy making. "In patterning itself on the

Women's Institutes," comments French, "the JFW was establishing a link with the most conservative branch of British feminism at the time" (20). They strengthened the image of the housewife, and in its efforts to bring together women of different classes and colors, they promoted, ironically enough, similar reactionary positions as earlier formulated by the Moyne Report, namely, emphasis on family, women as dependent housewives, women as willing voluntary social workers. The Jamaica Federation of Women was not concerned, as French points out, "with the issue of wage work or unionisation of women. The Civics Committee went as far as training women in mothercraft and childcare. However, JFW, by 1948 had an impressive membership of 30,000 and about 400 projects" (40).

Similar gendered agendas of colonial educational policies, namely, to educate women to be good housewives, are found in other British colonies. In India, Kumari Jayawardena, in *Feminism and Nationalism in the Third World*, remarks that "the policies of promoting women's education and the type of education provided were not intended to promote women's emancipation or independence but to reinforce patriarchy and the class system" (87). Female education in India was promoted by Indian social reformers as one way to eradicate problematic social customs. Female social reformers like Pandita Ramabai, and Ramabai Ranade actively promoted female education. Jayawardena notes that Mary Carpenter's visit to India "resulted in the establishment of a teacher's training college in 1870. By 1882 there were 2,700 educational institutions for girls with 127,000 pupils; the majority were primary schools, but there were 82 secondary schools, 15 teacher's training institutes and one college" (87). However, the vast majority of girls who attended schools lived in urban areas and belonged to middle-class families. Some women did manage to accomplish credentials even in this situation: "By 1902 there were 242 women in medical schools," notes Jayawardena, "and numbers were trained as teachers, nurses and midwives. In 1882, Cornelia Sorabjee, a Parsi was the first Indian woman to graduate in law in Oxford, though it was only after 1923 that women were allowed to practice law" (89). Jayawardena also records the names of early women doctors like Anandibai Joshi who graduated in 1886 from Women's Medical College in Philadelphia, Kadambini Ganguli, graduate of Calcutta University and Bengal's first woman doctor; Annie Jagannadhan who studied at the Edinburgh School of Medicine for women in 1888 and 1892 and worked as a house surgeon in a Bombay hospital; and Rukmabai who got a medical degree from London University in 1895 and worked in the Women's Hospital in Rajkot.

Jayawardena remarks that these women had to struggle against the weight of tradition. She cites Rukmabai's example as one who "rebelled against Indian traditionalism, in order to study medicine. She left her husband who filed a suit against her. She was bitterly criticised and even sentenced to six months imprisonment if she did not agree to live with him. A compromise was finally reached whereby she had to pay her husband a large sum of money. It was, however, decreed in accordance with Hindu Law, that Rukmabai could never marry again" (90).

A fascinating nineteenth-century life story, *Anandi Gopal*, has recently been republished. Anandi was married as a child-bride to an "eccentric pioneer" Gopalrao. His intention to educate his wife appears liberating from a modern perspective but at that time, Anandi, as a Brahmin woman, was heavily censured. She is even beaten by her mother and grandmother for reading and being "lazy" rather than doing household chores. One prejudice was that if women are educated "it will cause adultery." Anandi is caught between her husband's wishes to educate her and her social ostracization. Her exilic state is described as: "It seemed that she did not belong anywhere" (75). By age twelve, in 1877, Anandi reads English history, biography, and geography. She travels to America for medical studies—an exceptional step for a Hindu wife at that time. Even so, Anandi holds on to many traditional values such as vegetarianism. Rather than judging her inability to step out of traditional mores, "her almost impossible efforts to live within the frames set for her by her husband totally contrary to what her knowledge and her logic must have told her" (Foreword by Chitnis, ix), I regard Anandi as taking agency and forging her own identity as the first woman doctor trained in western medicine.

Education and Female Agency

If Anandi Gopal could surmount gendered stereotypes against female literacy and higher education in the nineteenth century, protagonists in contemporary postcolonial women writers' representations cope in different ways to balance English education with asserting female agency. Laila, in Attia Hosain's novel, *Sunlight on a Broken Column* makes overt and covert compromises between confronting and conforming to English education. Although orphaned, Laila is allowed to fulfill her father's wish that she receive an English education. Laila is a bookworm and the family worries that "those insect letters will eat away [her] eyes" (17). Her teacher, the British Mrs. Martin changes Laila's name to Lily. "I felt my cheeks burn," remarks Laila, "hearing the alien name she had given me" (46).

Laila is intellectually excited about the opportunities that an education can bring. However, as a female dependent, the decision of whether or not she can go to college is made by her Uncle Hamid as head of the feudal household. In a double entendre, he declares: "I have always believed that elders should not force their decisions on the young. That is why I have asked you to come here to listen to what we think is best for you" (109). Laila immediately thinks, though to herself, "What if we do not agree? What alternative was there for us?" Fortunately, Laila's uncle believes in "the education of girls," useful also since "young men want their wives to be educated enough to meet their friends and to entertain" (110), not so much for female independence or for asserting agency over their lives.

Laila's questioning and fiery spirit is balanced by self-protective instincts much like Tambu's in *Nervous Conditions*. Both have inner voices that guide them as to when to resist, and when to retreat without being totally defeated. In contrast, Nyasha's precocious courage makes her overtly confrontational. Her searing honesty lands her in bitter conflicts with her father. Once, in a fit of rage, he calls her a whore. Tambu is horrified, but she remains silent, knowing when to assert agency and when to curtail questioning. She remarks in retrospect: "If I had been more independent in my thinking then, I would have thought the matter through to a conclusion. But in those days, it was easy for me to leave tangled thoughts knotted, their loose ends hanging.... I took refuge in the image of the grateful poor female relative.... It mapped clearly the ways I could or could not go, and by keeping within those boundaries, I was able to avoid the maze of self-confrontation" (116).

Tambu is portrayed as much more assertive in her life at the homestead before she moves to middle-class Babamukuru's home to go to school. At the homestead, Tambu fights sexism about denying schooling to girls, as well as poverty, by raising her own school fees. She grows and sells mealies to the whites in town who ironically remark, "The child out to be in school, learning her tables, and keeping out of mischief.... The Governor is doing a lot for the natives in the way of education" (28). Tambu succeeds and is determined to escape a circumscribed female destiny as her mother's. But Tambu's new learning does exclude her mother who is entrenched in constant childbearing and poverty. She feels betrayed by Tambu who relates more to her educated aunt than to her mother. But, Tambu's mother challenges the silence imposed upon her because she is un-English educated: "But me, I'm not educated, am I? I'm just poor and ignorant, so you want me to keep quiet, you say I mustn't talk. Ehe! I am poor and ignorant, that's me, but I have a mouth, and it will keep on talking.... If it is meat you want that I cannot provide for you, if you are so greedy you would betray your own mother for meat, then go to your Maiguru. . . . I will survive on vegetables as we all used to do. And we have survived, so what more do you want?" (140).

For Tambu's generation, survival alone is not enough. However, their English education sadly alienates them from their un-English educated family. Not that Tambu's mother lacks wisdom; however, her indigenous knowledge is invisible in this new environment of formal schooling. Although the older generation of mothers and grandmothers lived in circumscribed worlds, they devised creative ways of asserting agency different from the book-ideas cramming their daughters' heads.

Tambu is capable of subtly resisting her uncle Babamukuru's authoritarianism, and she is more tactful than defiant Nyasha. When he decides that Tambu's parents who have been married in Shona tradition should undergo a Christian wedding as a "cleansing ceremony," Tambu is upset though she cannot disagree with him openly. After all, the Christian wedding is a hypocritical show that negates Shona tradition. So, on the morning of the wedding Tambu resists by using her body—she feigns illness, and refuses to move or speak. Her silence is strategic and she avoids going to the wedding. She remarks almost with wonder at how she can manipulate her own limbs in order to get what she wants:

> The morning of the wedding I found I could not get out of bed. I tried several times but my muscles simply refused to obey the half-hearted commands I was issuing to them. . . . I knew I could not get out of bed because I did not want to. Nyasha talked to me. . . . But I was slipping further and further away from her, until in the end I appeared to have slipped out of my body and was standing somewhere near the foot of the bed, watching her efforts to persuade me to get up and myself ignoring her. . . . Babamukuru walked into the room, without knocking and looking dangerously annoyed. The body on the bed didn't even twitch. Meanwhile the mobile, alert me, the one at the foot of the bed, smiled smugly, thinking that I had gone somewhere where he could not reach me, and I congratulated myself for being so clever. (166)

The punishment of disobeying Babamukuru is also felt bodily in the fifteen lashes that Tambu receives. But she secretly exults at her victory: "to me that punishment was the price of my newly acquired identity" (169).

Similar to Tambu's mother, working-class Tantie sends Tee to English school in Hodge's *Crick Crack, Monkey*. However, Tantie does not bargain for the depth of alienation that separates Tee from her in feeling ashamed of Tantie's country ways, her boisterousness, and smelly foods. As Tee longs to board the plane to take her to London, Tantie makes a poignant farewell speech that evokes her loss. Even as she recognizes the value of Tee's education, she is sad about the intellectual distance from Tee: " 'Well now the speech we have to make is, to wish God-bless to my chirren'—Tantie stopped and her face grew thoughtful. 'But why they must take mih chirren, what it is I do them, at-all?' " (111).

Physical and Psychological Resistance via Education: Contradictory Empowerment and Disempowerment for Female Protagonists

Models of feminist fore-mothers may inspire literary representations of exceptional women whose education both enables them to challenge unfair female roles, and disables them, at times, from surviving. Anita Desai's novel, *Clear Light of Day*, portrays a female educator Bim whose book-learning initially provides an escape from marriage, though her loneliness and isolation by the novel's end hardly make her situation enviable. As a confident school girl, she had imagined the many opportunities that can come with education. As young women, when her sister Tara cannot think of alternatives to marriage, Bim retorts, "I can think of hundreds of things to do instead. I won't marry. . . . I shall work—I shall do things. . . . I shall earn my own living . . . and be independent" (140–141). Bim is the successful, bright, ambitious student, head girl, one who excels at studies and wins honors. Although she was not quite sure where this work would lead "she seemed to realize it was a way out. A way out of what?" (130). She cannot quite define that as the adult teacher as she trains her students "to be a new kind of woman." Sadly, she confides that this "new" status has not fulfilled her: "If they knew how badly handicapped I still am, how I myself haven't been able to manage on my own" (155). Desai's grim portrayal of this unmarried and independent woman is hardly a model.[38] Bim is embittered, lonely, and isolated in middle age. Her book-learning hardly sustains her emotionally or financially. Bim's personal history certainly plays a role in this—neglected by parents less interested in their children than in spending time at the club, and her intimate closeness, almost bordering on an incestuous attachment to her brother Raja. Education, instead of giving her the options she had dreamt of, in fact, disempowers her.

English literature and a shared passion for Lord Byron seal Raja and Bim's brother-sister closeness. The seeming "universality" of Byron's words cannot hide the alienation that this poetic dream-world leads them into. It is significant also that at the end of the novel, a graying Bim, attending an Indian music concert recalls "the memory of reading, in Raja's well-thumbed copy of Eliot's *Four Quartets*, the line: 'Time the destroyer is time the preserver' " (182). Bim arrives at an uneasy reconciliation with her various histories—her somewhat uncomfortable role as an Indian middle-aged and unmarried woman living in a decaying house looking after a disabled sibling. Time the destroyer of youth will also be time the preserver of its memories. Even as the reader gets close to Bim's feelings, Desai's prose also consciously keeps the reader outside Bim's emotions, almost walking around them without touching. The reader is an objective spectator watching Bim, barely touching her pain. Bim's martyrdom is hardly in character. Her education did not equip her with alternatives to marriage. Unmarried, she becomes de facto the caretaker for her autistic brother. As a single woman, despite her education and modest financial independence, Desai portrays her situation as worse than her married sister Tara's who is a traditional wife, financially dependent on her husband but who gets to travel and has more options, ironically, than Bim does.

Similar to Desai keeping the reader outside Bim's pain, circumambulating her emotional world without entering it, Desai also portrays the 1947 historical events of partition—horrific religious riots and killings—from a distance. Bim and Raja watch the fires burning in the city at a safe distance from their home. Desai's representation of history in this novel—"independence," marked with dividing India and Pakistan as two separate nations—is troubling. Partition serves merely as a backdrop for the unfolding drama within the characters' hearts and minds which is Desai's focus. However, Desai's situating her text during the very time that history is being made on the streets, when religious violence ousted Muslims from India, and Hindus from a newly created Pakistan, and keeping the reader unengaged with that history is somewhat dissatisfying.

Desai does venture into a kind of literary historical intervention in portraying the Hindu Raja enamored of Muslim poetry, attending poetry soirees at his neighbors', the Hyder Alis, and wanting to study Islamic culture at college (much to his parents' horror). Although his literary leanings have clear political affiliations especially during that troubled time of religious conflict, Desai leaves it up to the reader's inclination to interpret Raja's poetic leanings as integrally a part of conflicts caused by the sociopolitical situation.

Similar to Raja's identification with Islamic culture outside of his Hindu household, Nyasha in *Nervous Conditions*, rather than being an obedient daughter, well-versed in Shona cultural tradition, "read a lot of books that were about real people and their sufferings: the condition in South Africa.... She read about Arabs ... about Nazis and Japanese and Hiroshima and Nagasaki.... She wanted to know many things ... the nature of life and relations before colonialism" (93). This intellectual curiosity makes her question authority and she is a misfit at home in 1960s Rhodesia having returned after several of her formative schooling years in England. Maiguru in this extract means that her children are "too Anglicized" and Nyasha tells Tambu: "I can't help having been there [England] and grown into the me that has been there. But it offends them [her parents]" (78). Nyasha has "forgotten Shona," and she is "morose and taciturn" when she returns to an almost alien home; nor can she belong in England.

Nyasha's outsiderness leads to a crisis that drives her into an internal drama with food. She becomes bulimic waging a devastating battle on her body. As her father forces her to eat, she does, and then throws up. The drama around food makes Babamukuru even more authoritarian as a telling metaphor describes him as the one who has "chewed more letters" than anyone in the family. Maiguru's inability to oppose Babamukuru's sexism is devastating for Nyasha. Maiguru's attempt to keep the peace during father-daughter conflicts comes across as abandoning Nyasha emotionally and being complicit with her husband.

Nyasha's bulimia is a physical manifestation of her severe mental depression and isolation. She manifests her grief by vomiting out literally what she has been fed, and metaphorically, what she has imbibed mentally in her English education. Her body becomes the only avenue that she can control as she is faced with painful contradictions such as opposing injustice in the world, and struggling against her father's domination. As she expels, literally, what he force-feeds her, she ejects his authority as well as the lies that her colonial education has fed her. If she survives she might be able to forge a new identity, to find a new space within which she can nurture and not hurt her body.

Nyasha, though self-aware, is unable to reconcile the empowerments she has acquired through her education with the requirements of being an obedient daughter. She belongs nowhere as she says poignantly, "I very much would like to belong, Tambu, but I find I do not.... I am me—hardly, I admit, the ideal daughter for a hallowed headmaster, a revered patriarch" (196–197). After the traumatic scene when fourteen-year-old Nyasha begs her father not to hit her, he does anyway, and she hits him back, Nyasha confides in Tambu: " 'I know,' she interrupted. 'It's not England any more and I ought to adjust. But when you've seen different things you want to be sure you're adjusting to the right thing. You can't go on all the time being whatever's necessary. You've got to have some conviction, and I'm convinced I don't want to be anyone's underdog. It's not right for anyone to be that. But once you get used to it, well, it just seems natural and you just carry on. And that's the end of you. You're trapped. They control everything you do' " (117). Nyasha describes her father sarcastically as "a bloody good kaffir, a good boy, a good munt" and has accepted that he must "grovel" before the whites. " 'I won't grovel, I won't die,' she raged" (200). The death that she fights against is as much physical, embodied in the havoc on her body, as it is sociocultural, located in the obedient-daughter-self, as it is in the colonised-grateful-kaffir that she struggles against, as it is psychic in the emotional and mental traumas of her nervous breakdown.

The key is survival—will Nyasha survive? The question hangs like a frozen stalactite at the end of the text. Sadly enough, the one way for her mental sadness to be recognized was for her to turn her grief inward and hurt her female body. Her unhappiness erupts in a hysterical scene where she lashes out against the lies fed to her by an English education. She is "beside herself with fury, [she] rampaged, shredding her history book between her teeth ('Their history. Fucking liars. Their bloody lies.'), breaking mirrors, her clay pots, anything she could lay her hands on and jabbing the fragments viciously into her flesh.... 'They've trapped us.... But I won't be trapped. I'm not a good girl. I won't be trapped.... I'm not one of them but I'm not one of you' " (201).

Maiguru's brother tries to get an appointment with a psychiatrist who "said that Nyasha could not be ill, that Africans did not suffer in the way we had described. She was making a scene. We should take her home and be firm with her" (201). There were no black psychiatrists; a kind, white one finally admits Nyasha into a clinic and her treatment begins though her "progress was still in the balance." Tambu fears that "if Nyasha who had everything would not make it, where could I expect to go?" This "everything" that Nyasha had, ironically lacked some key elements of bodily belonging and anchoring that Tambu had in her poverty-based childhood.

Nervous Conditions is the first and only African novel to date that portrays a female protagonist's struggle with bulimia—a disease associated commonly with the west and Nyasha as the westernized one succumbs to this peculiarly western ailment. It is hardly imaginable within most third world societies where there is most often not often to eat. But Nyasha's family is middle class and comfortable in terms of food. So, food as a mode of control is available to her. Nyasha has been as tragically colonized as her parents, all divorced from any indigenous healing methods that would be available within their culture. Nor would Babamukuru or Maiguru believe in traditional healing. And, even if they were to consult the wisdom of indigenous medicine, in what language would they describe Nyasha's illness, something that has no name in their language, no reality in their context? As discussed in chapter 2, indigenous healing strategies such as those aided by spirit-mediums like Nehanda might have been sustaining forces for Nyasha. She cannot step outside the colonizing walls around her body trapped in English boundaries that are more tightly clamped by her father's authoritarianism. Western medicine then, psychiatry, will intervene and try to save Nyasha's life.

The novel ends on a hopeful note—a wiser Tambu, confronted with her dear cousin's physical collapse, begins "a long and painful process" of questioning, locating, and not escaping who she is. She knows that she needs a place within her own tradition even as her education leads her to discover new worlds. The first step toward constructing this self is in the very writing of the novel: "the story I have told here," Tambu notes, "is my own story." And she is ready "to fill another volume" that will tell the tale of where she has arrived as the adult who has written *Nervous Conditions*. The latter only records "how it all began," and there is promise of more to follow.

Education and Bodily Markers: Light-Skinned Color/Class Privileges and Other Marginalities

The inter-connections between gender, class, and color prejudice are represented in Indian Eunice de Souza's "Mrs. Hermione Gonsalvez."[39] The poem's colloquial tone and humor flavor the female narrator's tale, a whining complaint about once having "looks and color," and now, sadly married to "a dark man":

> In the good old days
> I had looks and colour
> just look at my parents
> how they married me to a dark man
> on my own I wouldn't even have
> looked at him. Once we were going

somewhere for a holiday and I went on
ahead my hubby was to come later
and there were lots of fair
Maharashtrian ladies there and they
all said Mrs. Gonsalvez how fair and
beautiful you are your husband must be
so good-looking too but when Gonsalvez came
they all screamed
and ran inside their houses
thinking the devil had come.

In this poem, color is coded with religious overtones—darkness and the devil inhabit the same space; fairness is equated with beauty, goodness, and moral virtues. De Souza's characteristically ironic tone reveals the serious overtones of an arid relationship between Mr. and Mrs. Gonsalvez, one that is marked and marred by color prejudice. The colonial roots of such prejudice cannot be gainsaid, although in many ways native peoples must often fight "the enemy within," their own internalized racial inferiorities and prejudices, some home-grown, and others exacerbated by colonial encounters.

In India, as in other parts of the postcolonial world, prejudice against dark skin often blocks access to educational or economic opportunities. The complex inter-relations among class and color in the Caribbean have particular ramifications that often determine who has access to education. This is a distinctive aspect of Caribbean history that has deeply influenced and injured certain populations. The prejudice against dark skin is accompanied usually by class privileges held by a light-skinned Creole population. Class and color also have different ramifications for women and men. Further, marginalization by gender supersedes class and includes both privileged and working-class women.

"Grandma's Estate" in Sistren's *Lionheart Gal* portrays the light-skinned, privileged class, alienated from the black majority because of its status and education from working-class deprivation depicted in the other life stories. Like Nyasha in *Nervous Conditions*, caught painfully between her English-language acquired identity and her Shonaness, the narrator Ella in "Grandma's Estate" must untangle herself from the Caribbean's particular historical web of color and class as defining bodily markers of identity and belonging specifically represented in language, speech, and education.

Such contemporary expressions of class and color prejudice in the Caribbean that often determine who has access to education are rooted in the history of slavery, plantation society, colonization, and neocolonization. Edward Kamau Brathwaite asserts that this history of slavery and plantation society with its hierarchies of class and color is the commonly shared heritage of the Caribbean region. Another important historian, Elsa Goveia asserts in her book *Slave Society in the British Leeward Islands at the End of the Eighteenth Century* that since "the slave society is one of the most fundamental experiences shared by the West Indies, its understanding must be of significance for our future as well as for our past."[40] Goveia's term "slave society" usefully describes "the whole society based on slavery including masters and freedmen as well as slaves."[41] Goveia asserts that "there were general ordering principles at work, in towns as well as on the plantations, shaping the status relationships of all groups in the society" (10). The whites, though a minority, were the most powerful, the property-owning class and "the leaders in social and cultural affairs." Although there were poor whites, they mostly banded together "on racial solidarity," and one may add, superiority.

Goveia describes the "patterning of the segments of British West Indian society into a white, brown, black pyramid of superiority and inferiority" (11). Apart from the external color hierarchy, the more crucial underlying fact was that this order influenced "the internal order of the whole society" that was formulated along "distinctions of race and colour." The legacy of "slave laws" that Goveia discusses, that legitimized inequalities between the races in the eighteenth century still lingers today. Goveia notes the undocumentable types of "psychological injury" that vast numbers suffered when faced with "the myth of Negro inferiority," or with the superior position of standard English versus Creole forms. This legacy of denigrating patois lingers today, and neocolonial attitudes make this linguistic situation even more serious. In other words, although patois is spoken by the majority, its speakers are disadvantaged by their inability to speak and write standard English that remains the language of power in postcolonial society. In strange twists of racial and class boundaries, middle-class proponents of encouraging patois are accused of "romanticization," and of acting "irresponsibly" toward working-class people.

Goveia's work "provided a conceptual framework for historical reconstruction: it spelt out the four-letter word, 'race', as the determinant of social organization," remarks Lucille Mathurin, "and thereby illuminated a whole complex of attitudes and events" (9). Another detrimental heritage of slavery times is the insistence on black inferiority by "race [and] not just of social position.... This relationship of dominance of a light skinned minority over the black majority is still one of the leading aims of the West Indian social system" (10–11). Goveia points out a contradiction between "a political system" that ensures "equality" in the black population having suffrage, along with a "social system" that considers them unequal and "inferior." One can relate this analysis more particularly to women, in that having the vote, important as that is, does not automatically ensure women's equality in most social systems. Race and gender also intersect class lines. Even with blacks in a majority on those islands like Jamaica that have a small brown, and white class present, the political systems are dominated by a light-skinned upper class; in Trinidad, a large Indian population belongs color-wise to the lower rungs, and as agricultural labor, to "the lowest rung." Color codes Caribbean populations—immigrant whites from Europe, notes Goveia, would get into a middle-class level. Color, reflecting race and ethnicity influences class—the smaller the group, the wealthier, whereas the majority continue in economic difficulties. Goveia urges concerted attempts at democratization. In this struggle, culture workers play a significant role—in reviving folk songs and dances, in deploying indigenous traditions like calypso, in appreciating oral cultural forms that are often a part of the daily life of the majority of the black populations.

In an important historical study, *The Development of Creole Society in Jamaica, 1770–1820*, Edward Kamau Brathwaite defines creolization as "a way of seeing the society, not in terms of white and black, master and slave in separate nuclear units, but as contributing parts of the whole."[42] He analyses the various segments of the society, such as "The Assembly, the Judiciary, the Militia, the Church, the Press" in order to demonstrate how the entire whole functioned and was held together. These institutions upheld power hierarchies established along class and color lines which also determined who had access to English education. Social and economic hierarchies by class and color prevail among differently colored peoples.

In Brathwaite's paradigm, the "colonial [ingredient] is essential to creolism, which in itself contains the element of its own disequilibrium" (312). With the abolition of the slave trade in 1807, the white "Creole" class had to contend with changes imposed by the colonizers.[43] Such changes, far from erasing an enslaving mentality, rigidified color and class hierarchies. Even as slaves were "given" the status of human beings, the Creole white class was increasingly dependent economically on colonial powers for the production and markets for sugar. With this economic dependency, and monetary profits, they accepted other social re-adjustments to color hierarchies in their society. Brathwaite's "reference to the creole apartheid legislation of the period," notes Mathurin quoted in Brathwaite, *The Development of Creole Society*, "indicates the degree of white Jamaican's neurotic horror of being marooned on an island of blackness without a life line to Europe" (187). Brathwaite regards "interracial sexual relationships as the most significant inter-cultural creolisation, the creole mulatto" (303).

Brathwaite's and Goveia's historical discussions of color and class ramifications, and I would add, gender, are given literary representations in Rhys's only novel set in the Caribbean, *Wide Sargasso Sea*. Issues of identity and belonging are seriously debilitating and psychically traumatic for the protagonist Antoinette. As in "Grandma's Estate," personal history forms the backdrop for an exploration of a wider history of color and class prejudice, with severe repercussions on the female body. Written nearly forty years after she left her birth-place Dominica at age sixteen, Rhys remarkably portrays a Creole community's un-belonging to either European (the English and the French fought over Dominica until the British took the island in 1783) or to Afro-Caribbean culture (see Brathwaite's *Contradictory Omens*). The novel which fictionally explores the life of Bertha Mason, "the mad-woman in the attic" in Charlotte Bronte's *Jane Eyre*, is also autobiographical in the childhood sections recreating the pain and sadness of Rhys's own upbringing as a white-Creole child, bearing the privileges of the "big house," with servants, and educational opportunities as albatrosses around her neck. Antoinette is intensely lonely as a child, rejected by black friends like Tia, and forced to abort possibilities of meaningful relationships with someone whom she loved rather than with Mr. Rochester to whom she is sold in marriage.

Color and class prejudices continue to pursue Antoinette who is caught in her society's equation of whiteness with power. Her own desperate disempowerment is evident in her isolation and fear. Rhys paints a nightmarish image of the boy who follows Antoinette from school and terrifies her. He embodies a bizarre mixture of races as evident in his hair and features. Rhys evocatively uses color to describe him: "a white skin, a dull ugly white covered with freckles, his mouth was a negro's mouth and he had small eyes, like bits of green glass. . . . Worst, most horrible of all, his hair was crinkled, a negro's hair, but bright red, and his eyebrows and eyelashes were red" (48). Though silent, he frightens Antoinette. It is as if the boy's image embodies the painful creolization history that is part of Antoinette's own life. The condemnatory taunts—branding Antoinette, "crazy like [her] mother"—are spoken significantly by the black girl who walks with him. Both remain nameless, more important as symbols than as individuals in illuminating a painful history and in bringing Antoinette face-to-face with it.

Until seventeen, the convent becomes Antoinette's "inside" sanctuary and also a place of "death" as an escape from the outside forces of a prejudiced world. This "haven" cannot last, especially since as a female, once Antoinette attains womanhood, her adult sexuality must be deployed, if possible to her family's advantage. Her handsome dowry makes her a desirable marriage commodity. Her stepfather arranges to "sell" his stepdaughter to an English bidder, desirable for his color, and eager to acquire Antoinette's dowry. The fact that Antoinette is educated hardly gives her options to escape this sexist trade; in fact, as with educated Maiguru discussed earlier, education offers contradictory empowerments since Antoinette is unable to exert agency over who she is to marry, or to prevent being sold to the highest bidder.

Insiders/Outsiders: Racial Prejudice Resisted via Education

Educational opportunities and class privilege in postcolonial societies go hand-in-hand—working-class people have less access to education than middle and upper classes. Climbing the educational and class ladder are not unabated advantages since cultural alienation, and other costs of English education are experienced often in the very bodies of female protagonists. But the body is not only and always victimized in this alienating predicament; it is also used as a vehicle to resist alienation.

Educational opportunities interface with internal racial prejudice within communities whose color stereotypes, often deeply rooted in indigenous cultures, are exacerbated by the colonizers' white superiority. Can education enable the protagonist Margaret, a Masarwa, a racially oppressed group as depicted in Bessie Head's novel *Maru*, to override racial prejudice? Educated Margaret, a qualified schoolteacher, faces racial discrimination as a Masarwa, considered an outcast group by the dominant Bamangwato people in Botswana. She is treated as an outsider. In the absence of a sense of belonging within their societies, protagonists struggle to create a home within their female bodies. As they journey from alienation to nurturance of their bodies, they enter a new geography where they discover home inside their female bodies.[44]

I analyze Margaret's use of education as an avenue of resistance and complicity in this struggle to own and to feel at home within her female body. External prejudices are often internalized into the body and psyche; hence these protagonists need to undergo rituals of healing their female bodies before they discover their space in their communities. In her search for home and belonging, Margaret undergoes bodily breakdowns, physical disintegration that is followed by restitution through indigenous and western rituals of healing and reintegration into her community. Physical breakdowns then are not the end point, but those harrowing experiences become catalysts for new beginnings, new self-knowledge, and new spaces of belonging.[45]

Bessie Head, racially marginalized in her personal life, "longed to write an enduring novel," she remarks, "on the hideousness of racial prejudice." She continues, "But I also wanted the book to be so beautiful and so magical that I, as the writer, would long to read and re-read it."[46] *Maru* achieves this in the mythologized portrayal of Maru, who "listens to the gods in his heart" (8), who is "a born leader," who "set(s) the tone for a new world" by marrying Margaret to make a political point.

In *Maru*, Head is concerned with racial prejudice with a black face—black on black prejudice such as the brutal psychological realities facing a Masarwa child. Head takes a searing look at racisms that haunt nearly every nation. She probes where these prejudices come from, what nurtures them, and why they persist even among educated people, and in defiance of human advancements. All racial groups "have their monsters," remarks the narrator early in the novel: "whites at the top regard Asians as 'a low, filthy nation'; Asians 'could still smile—at least they were not Bushmen...' Then, seemingly anything can be said and done to you as your outer appearance reduces you to the status of a non-human being.... [Among Africans,] 'the worst things are said, and done to the Bushmen. Ask the scientists'" (11).

Margaret, racially marked as Masarwa can only belong on the lowest racial and class rung of that society. She resists this racial oppression marked on her body through the education given to her by English Margaret Cadmore, who adopts her at birth. For the mother who gives the adopted child her English name, this Masarwa baby is an experiment by which she wishes to prove: "environment everything, heredity nothing." She wants to create something "new and universal," a product that she tells her adopted daughter, "will help [her] people." She hopes that education will transcend race. While the adoptive mother theorizes, the child herself faces the physical consequences of racial prejudice: children spitting at her in school, of being called derogatory names. The English woman's certainty that education will transcend race ironically also smacks of racism, although of a different kind from the racist attacks that the child faces from the dominant black population.

In his provocative text, *Postmodern Geographies: The Reassertion of Space in Critical Social Theory*, Edward Soja's discussion of "the spatialization of history, the making of history entwined with the social production of space, the structuring of a historical geography," sheds light on Margaret's predicament. An external lived reality is guided by a set of social relations and "space is fundamental," notes Soja, "in any exercise of power" (18). Margaret's history is intertwined integrally with the geographical locations that she occupies—as a child, adopted and displaced from her own people, she grows up in the English Margret Cadmore's rather stiff, formal, and cold world. Next, equipped with an education, she moves to Dilepe as schoolteacher, with the authority of knowledge but despised by local administrators, and by the end, she and Maru leave the narrow prejudiced village and drive off not into the sunset but towards a place where "the sun rose new and new and new each day."

Margaret is described physically as having "lived like the mad dog of the village with tin cans tied to her tail" (9). This physical description of her body, and the recurrent image and sound of the tin cans rattling through the novel are a harsh reminder that she will always be perceived, racially, as an outcast. Margaret's resistance is located also in the female body, for instance, unlike other Masarwa owned as slaves in the text, she declares ownership of her Masarwa identity—an ethnic identification that is physically evident on her body. She declares her tribal identity by displaying it in a disarming manner when she declares forthrightly to people and much to their consternation, "I am a Masarwa." She is advised to pass as "coloured" but she says that she is "not ashamed of being a Masarwa" (22). The contradiction between her apparent racial identity and her "near perfect English accent" confuses people.

Paradoxically, Margaret's education empowers and disempowers her. As a trained schoolteacher, she can earn a living; as an educated Masarwa, and not having any contact with Masarwa people, she is totally cut off from that community. Soja's concept of "a critical theory that re-entwines the making of history with the social production of space, with the construction and configuration of human geographies" is useful in recognizing that Margaret is "making history" in her physical relocation as the first Masarwa schoolteacher in Dilepe. Further, Soja's comment that "new possibilities are being generated from this creative commingling, possibilities for a simultaneously historical and geographical materialism" (11) illuminates Margaret's unique position, despite prejudice, in earning her living unlike other Masarwa in the village who are slaves.

Pete, the principal, wants to get rid of her: "It's easy. She's a woman," he says, revealing the power and pettiness of such pseudo-educated males. But the community, however prejudiced, recognizes that Margaret is the educator of their children. The novel demonstrates that eliminating racial prejudice through education and knowledge is an uphill road with many twists and turns of gender and class. Margaret, as educated female and Masarwa challenges the educated males' racial and power structures. Knowledge and female-ness combined in Margaret raise significant questions of power. Her very presence, her educated body, is an affront to the community's status quo. Paradoxically, the same education that empowers her also renders her into an anomaly—an educated Masarwa, an oddity who is isolated from her own people and from the prejudiced dominant group. Margaret has to undertake a macabre dance between margin (as Masarwa), and belonging to the community (as teacher). Wherever she travels in this dance, she is very alone. Her education, though it challenges, cannot change overnight certain rigidly embedded gender and race prejudices.

Simultaneously and paradoxically, Margaret does not seem to live in her body. As Head writes, she "belonged nowhere" (93). Head creates for Margaret an internal sense of belonging through her paintings and her surreal art, visions that she dreams and recreates in paintings. For two days she gets into "a restless fever ... [and through] sleepless nights and foodless days," she produces thirty paintings (100). However, Head somewhat troublingly takes away even that subjectivity and agency from Margaret since Maru, the powerful chief projects his hallucinatory images into her consciousness. The images haunt her until she puts them down on paper as "a true and sensitive recorder." Maru decides that he loves Margaret, and that he must marry her (whether she loves him or not) in order to set an example against his peoples' prejudices. Though this marriage elevates Margaret socially, she has no choice about it. Head's resolution is troubling as Margaret is thrust into the socially acceptable institution of marriage as a way of belonging.

Several key events in the novel are described through bodily experience including Margaret's physical collapse when she hears that the man whom she loves, Moleka, has married another woman, Dikeledi. "No sound reached her. A few vital threads of her life had snapped behind her neck and it felt as though she were shrivelling to death, from head to toe. The pain was so intense that she had to bite on her tongue to prevent herself from crying out loud" (118). She faints until Maru comes to "rescue" her, and remarks casually, "She's not dead. . . . It's only her neck that's broken." He forces her to step out physically from her collapse: "She moved her limbs and they tingled painfully. . . . She struggled to an upright posture, but even to regain life and movement again was a joy in itself. She had been incapable of movement or thought or feeling for hours and hours and hours and a portion of her mind which was still alive felt it keenly as the past year had been the most vital and vivid of her life. She was to question that sudden breakdown, that sudden death later, but what filled her now was this slow inpouring of life again" (123).

In a fairy tale ending, Maru and Margaret leave the village, "heading straight for a home, a thousand miles away where the sun rose, new and new and new each day" (125). In marriage, Margaret does not gain autonomy and freedom, but shelter. Maru voluntarily relinquishes his hereditary role as chief; the villagers consider him "dead" since he marries a Masarwa. He leaves the village and takes on a willing separation from that narrow-minded community. Margaret and Maru leave as a couple and in their search to set up a new home in some unspecified location, Head presents a westernized cultural resolution: a married couple with autonomy of movement and no rooted belonging to a place or community.[47]

The idealized conclusion takes the text totally out of Margaret's own subjectivity. Both the senior Margaret and Maru have taken away Margaret's agency even as, paradoxically, they give her educational opportunities and marriage to a chief, unthinkable for Masarwas. She is sacrificed for "the liberation of her people." Her marriage to Maru inspires a sense of freedom in them as the narrator asserts in the utopian words at the end: "When people of the Masarwa tribe heard about Maru's marriage to one of their own, a door silently opened on the small, dark airless room in which their souls had been shut for a long time. The wind of freedom, which was blowing throughout the world for all people, turned and flowed into the room. . . . They started to run out into the sunlight, then they turned and looked at the dark, small room. They said, "We are not going back there" (126–127).

On several levels, one is critical of the older Margaret's "experimentation" on the younger Margaret. The Englishness in which the mother steeps her adopted daughter renders the child out of touch with other

Masarwa, and with her own culture. She is simultaneously uprooted and advantaged, ameliorated by this educational opportunity. The tools of her knowledge do not equip her to make a place for herself in a prejudiced society. The older Margaret's intentions, missionary-like, to "save" Margaret from ignorance and poverty raise a crucial question: Can the oppressed Masarwa be the authors of improving their own lives by themselves, or do they have to rely on well-intentioned do-gooders like Margaret Cadmore to intervene on their behalf? By the end of the novel one wonders which solution was better for Margaret—education as conceived by the English woman, or intermarriage? Is Maru's statement in marrying a Masarwa a more visible and bold statement against prejudice than Margaret's work as a female teacher? Both solutions are to be problematized within this text.

With marriage, Margaret and Maru exchange social spaces of respect and status—Maru gives up his title, honors, and elects a simpler life; Margaret's social standing is elevated since Maru is a chief. On one level, her world expands; Maru's shrinks. Both of them paradoxically embrace and reject their identities as representative of their particular ethnicities, and prejudiced worlds. Their very names evoke tradition and change—Maru is associated with rain, most welcome in that dry land. Rain brings hope for a future and is acknowledged by the Bushmen as "a supernatural personage."[48] Maru as embodiment of tradition, as hereditary chief is portrayed as "god-like." In his rejection of that role, and his drought-like act of marrying a Masarwa, his people feel dead, as if a rainless scenario has deprived them of hope for a future. Margaret's name is clearly western, given with self-perpetuating instincts by Margaret Sr. Westernism as embodied in Margaret's education does not in itself guarantee change and modernization.

Despite her education, Margaret's silence gets louder as her own individuality and agency are forced to merge with Maru's powerful will and personality. Her passivity makes her more powerless than before her marriage when the reader "heard" Margaret's voice in her paintings. This nonverbal form despite the English mother's cramming Margaret with English words and education, speaks more effectively to a member of a disadvantaged group. Margaret's inward-looking artistry sustained her emotionally, even as her external verbal role as educator of the village children sustained her financially. However, the marriage without her verbal consent takes away her agency even as, ironically, she gains social status in marrying a powerful chief.

Although Maru makes a loud political statement by marrying a Masarwa, self-consciously "liberating" a member of the oppressed group, the sexual politics of his decision are troubling.[49] Part of Maru's motivation for wanting Margaret as his wife is to take her away from his rival Moleka whom Margaret loves—an age-old contest of two men locked in a power struggle over winning a woman.

Head's use of marriage as a solution to a complicated situation of racial prejudice is problematic especially since it is an anathema in Head's artistic vision to sacrifice an individual for a larger political end. Head's particular kind of personal politics has in fact been largely misunderstood—her statement, for instance, that she is quite hopeless in dealing with revolutionary issues leads to a mistaken conclusion that she wants nothing to do with politics. In a previously published essay, I discuss what I term Head's philosophical/political vision.[50] So, although I disagree with charges that describe Head as "politically ignorant," I do find the sexual politics in *Maru* highly problematic.

Climbing In and Out of Your Color: Surviving Alienations via Ritual in Erna Brodber's *Jane and Louisa Will Soon Come Home*

Do the young Tees, Nyashas, Lalitas have knowledge of indigenous strategies of survival, ritual, obeah known to their mothers and grandmothers? Can these women's ways of knowing assist them to reconstruct their fragmented selves, divided between English and Creole English, Shona, or Urdu, between their bodily struggle to balance their new learning and their own culture's rules and behavior? Dilemmas of belonging and the use of indigenous healing strategies are portrayed in Jamaican Erna Brodber's multi-genre text, *Jane and Louisa Will Soon Come Home*. Although ritual may be used in different contexts, here, Brodber portrays how conflicts arising from English education are resisted through indigenous ritualist means. Brodber, like Head, exposes the Jamaican middle class's internal color, class, sexual prejudices, although a colonial history crucially frames and encourages these contemporary prejudices. Similar to and different from Margaret, Nellie undergoes physical and psychic breakdown, followed by a reintegration into her familial history, and social community.

Brodber's literary form, fragmentary and non-linear, strikingly mirrors Nellie's fragmented personality. The form itself of Brodber's text embodies "the spatiality of history," Soja's concept of the important component of location within history. The spatial realities of dislocations within geographic spaces, as Nellie's un-belonging given the class and color prejudice of her society, provide a framework for internal, psychic breakdowns.

As Evelyn O'Callaghan notes, Brodber, in creating Nellie, was originally writing "a case study of the dissociative personality for her social work students. The dissociative personality has been fragmented through a series of traumatic experiences and is thus unable to connect and integrate aspects of the self and the past."[51] I take O'Callaghan's analysis further and focus not only on the "personality" but, crucially, the body, to argue that Nellie's body needs to be healed. The biographical fact that since 1976 Brodber "has been a member of Twelve Tribes of Israel, a Rastafarian sect" connects to her work, particularly, healing through religion and ritual. Her fictional work draws uniquely on social history, psychology, ritual, community—a tapestry that evokes the sociopolitical reasons underlying psychic collapse, and attempts to reintegrate the body within the community.

Nellie's alienation from her body is caused by her own light-skinned middle class. Nellie is educated as a normative aspect of her privileged class, though alienated from her community, and seeking a home within her female body. Education provides a paradoxical empowerment. Contrary to a simple equation of knowledge with power, one questions whose knowledge and how this knowledge significantly disempowers her in alienating her from their community. As Michelle Cliff remarks in her essay, "If I Could Write This in Fire, I Would Write This in Fire," learning English history and geography crucially bred self-hatred among native peoples. In her words, "The red empire of geography lessons. 'The sun never sets on the British Empire and you can't trust it in the dark'. Or with the dark peoples. . . . Another geography, or was it history lesson?"[52] Knowledge as power is a commonplace concept though including gender, class, colonial relations, and postcolonial relocations within that remain challenging. For instance, colonial education's history and geography lessons are replete with gender and racial implications to the disadvantage of indigenous peoples. As a woman of a particular racial and class background, the effects of the knowledge/power paradigm are deeply and psychically troubling in the severe denials of her identity. In finding new words and English knowledge, Nellie must initially lose herself, coming dangerously close to losing her subjectivity. She is able to reconstitute herself after her body and mind have suffered breakdown, and exilic isolation from community.

Within a Caribbean historical context, one recognizes both the power and the marginalization of the light-skinned middle class from the majority, their part in a history where they were both participants and onlookers in exploitations of the majority. The controls and disciplines imposed over the very territory of Nellie's body, by her own class, are part of the ideological construction of consolidating their power. Brodber's text, self-conscious of this history, explores how personal and historical realities of class and color that one carries visibly on one's body constitute a part of educated Nellie's psyche: "Papa's grandfather and Mama's mother were the upper reaches of the world. So we were brown, intellectual, better and apart, two generations of lightening blue-blacks and gracing elementary schools with brightness. The cream of the earth, isolated, quadroon, mulatto, Anglican" (7).

Though reconnecting with her past, and accepting the spectrum of color in her ancestry are all significant, her reintegration occurs crucially in her physical body as she steps out of one *kumbla* into another. "A kumbla, as outlined in the Anancy story within the novel," notes O'Callaghan, "is a self-created protective camouflage assumed by an individual to cope with societal pressures" (80). Both the integration and the conflict in indigenous cultural history and western knowledge appear in these lines "Go eena kumbla- Brer Anancy begged his son Tucuma./-Go eena kumbla-Polonius advised" (15).[53] Brodber uses the kumbla as an indigenous ritual, as a means of healing the body. Her fictional work draws uniquely on social history, "folk psychiatry," ritual, community—a tapestry that evokes the sociopolitical reasons underlying psychic collapse, and the attempts to reintegrate the body within the community. Does Nellie have access to indigenous strategies of survival, uses of ritual, of magic and obeah that might help her to reconstruct her fragmented self, and broken tongue speaking different languages? Nellie's disintegration of body and self and her restitution and reintegration into the community is reminiscent of Wole Soyinka's theory of Yoruba tragedy.[54] Although a painfully alienating experience, Nellie's psychic breakdown is not a completely isolating battle on her body; rather, it is part of a ritualistic tradition of destruction and creation, a kind of disintegration that leads to reintegration with the community.

Nellie's struggle throughout the text is to reintegrate the fragmented parts of herself, her broken body and mind, by discovering a reconciliation to her personal familial history as it unraveled within the larger social history of slavery, rape, mixed children who are caught in between different races, colors, and classes. She is ensconced in the historical conflicts embodied in a middle-class, Creole family, conflicts that are exacerbated by the shame, denial, and sexual repression enjoined upon women of her class. Brodber presents diametrically opposed and confusing codes of female decorum—at home, strict controls on the female body encoded in fear and shame; and at school, messages of sexual freedom. The restrictions narrow Nellie's world as she faces a sunless arena of repression and sexual denial. Her alienation from her self, body, color, family, community is evoked through the recurrent image of the kumbla—a protective circle that can be both comforting and destructive. In a beautiful passage Brodber describes a kumbla: "like a beach ball. It bounces with the sea but never goes down. It is indomitable. . . . The kumbla is an egg shell. . . . It does not crack if it is hit. . . . It is a round seamless calabash that protects you without caring. Your kumbla is like a parachute . . . a helicopter, a transparent umbrella, a glassy marble, a comic strip space ship. You can see both in and out . . . like the womb and with an oxygen tent. Safe, protective time capsule. Fed simply by breathing!" (123)

Nellie adopts the dry, intellectual life as a coping mechanism against her bodily alienation. She is all brain and no body as she sits, almost disembodied at "meetings," taking minutes, involved in "progressive" causes for the masses. The death of her lover evokes a profound sadness and futility about mortality from Nellie: "We had been bodies: and what was there to show for it?" (52). Her physical expression of grief is to cry "so hard, my tears no longer held salt." But she continues to work and with a characteristic British expression remarks, "I took the minutes with a stiff upper lip" (52).

Nellie's escape into an intellectual cocoon is a kumbla where she completely denies her sexuality. Nellie can step out of her body, self-exiled by the repression encouraged by her light-skinned middle class; she can climb into her mind and function through her intellect, also because of the class privileges that have given her an education. The kumbla, paradoxically, is both safe and dangerous in terms of Nellie's escape into the temporary protectiveness of sexual repression and intellectual dryness. In this kumbla she tries, like Anancy to trick herself into a permanent facade of respectability and repression, but she does not succeed, and in fact, her psychic breakdown becomes a necessary stage of fragmenting her body so that it can be reintegrated into a community. Nellie is forced to wrap around her body the false protection of sexual repression, to deny the layers of the family's black ancestry. Nellie falls in line with her predecessors like Tia Maria who disappears from the family so that she may give her mulatto children a better chance; like Aunt Becca who aborts her child to retain her social standing and not marry below her class. Nellie, directed by this history of bodily shame, dances into her own kumbla of sexual repression, denial, and frigidity.

Both Nellie's capacity to repress and to self-heal are contained in the ritualistic framework of the kumbla. When she becomes pathological, she experiences a sense of levitation before losing consciousness: "My body lifted itself into the air and I became nothing. Light. If weighed in the balance . . . I would no doubt be found wanting. . . . Those circles I was walking, were they natural, or had I been forced to walk them? . . . I knew Baba's past. He knew mine. On this we shared a common language" (66). She is guided into consciousness by Miss Elsada's grandson Baba. Nellie registers the physical sensations of "the smell of beef soup and ginger tea," "the feel of Baba's index finger tracing the sweat around the baby hairs of my forehead," seeing his smile and hearing his words: "Welcome back you lucky creature. You too know what the resurrection is like. You have a clean slate, you can start all over again.' It had a warmth and a human-ness that was a far cry from an 'infliction' " (67).

Both Nellie's capacity to repress and her ability to self-heal are contained in the same ritualistic framework of the kumbla. Her entry, with Baba's help, into a more integrated space than was possible in her repressed state, is actualized in her verbal "lapse" into Creole—a bodily expression that invites her own body "home." She uses her voice in Creole that belongs in her personal and sociopolitical history. Brodber also evokes the importance of male figures like Baba (or Legba in Haitian voodoo), acting as intermediaries between the physical and spiritual worlds. Baba combines the wisdom of age with the innocence of a child. At first, the recognition of Baba's point, namely "that [they] singly or as a group . . . should stop hiding and talk about [themselves]" seems "quite reasonable." And in a graphically physical description, she asks, "Who told him that he could touch parts of us that we elected to leave untouched!" (62). Baba has a spiritual and physical healing touch in his "surgeon's hands."

The recovery through Baba's healing hands unfolds gradually over time: Nellie's need to have "great gushes of tears" stream out of her head, his capacity to "absorb" them. With his touch, "with just his index finger he had probed the base of my skull that day, had made me sweat and broken my fever. He could draw water from the brain" (81). She describes him as "this obeah man of an anancy." This evokes a parallel when Maru declares that Margaret's neck is "broken," and only he has the power to heal her. He is much more authoritarian to the extent of compelling Margaret to marry him than Baba's more nurturing healing of Nellie. With Baba's help, Nellie gets stronger, and after nearly six weeks she wants "to feel [her] strength, to test [her] becoming. For the longest while I had been asking Baba to take me out . . . anywhere. I needed to know myself in the world. It was not a pool of water, a placenta. . . . My path lay now through the aliens who surrounded me. . . . I was willing to learn their ways but someone had to show me, to born me. . . . Someone had to help me test my feet outside the kumbla" (70). She finds courage to venture, almost as a rite of passage, into the dance hall. "Morning had broken. I was no longer alone. Baba had settled me in with my people" (77). Nellie has drawn upon a tradition of spiritual healing, and further, has created a passage that is her own, a passage through which she experiences a rebirth. Physical breakdown then is not the end point, but the point of a new beginning.

As the list and litany of ancestors "pick their way through [her] brain" she arrives at recognition and reconciliation:

> Puppa, my father Alexander's obscure father, black, squat, with a thin bent brown woman looking adoringly at him . . . great grandfather Will. . . . White, smiling with both hands resting on the shoulders of a fidgety, thin black woman . . . scores behind them popping up, popping up. . . . It was art from any angle . . . music, shape, production, performance, colour scheme, blending of colours, a pageant. . . . I saw that if I knew all my kin . . . Obadiah, Teena, Locksley, Uroy, I could no longer remain as a stranger; that I had to know them to know what I was about . . . the black and squat, the thin and wizened, all of them. (78–80)

The chapter ends strikingly with a physical change in the narrator—with this new consciousness she is covered in perspiration, her "hair grey and those funny stripes on my behind" (81), the marks of punishment and the pain of various forms of enslavement, bodily and mental.

Although a painfully alienating experience, Nellie's breakdown leads to recovery via ritual healing, unlike Nyasha in *Nervous Conditions* who has no access to traditional Shona ritual. Brodber depicts Nellie's psychic breakdown not as a completely isolating battle on her body as Nyasha's bulimia is, but rather as part of a ritualistic tradition of destruction and creation, a kind of disintegration that leads to reintegration. For both protagonists, the analogy of food and education, feeding the body and the mind coalesce in disturbing ways—Nyasha, in her bulimic attacks, rages against "the lies, their fucking history" that had been rammed down her throat.

Nellie recalls " 'the pale one' at communion every month or so when kneeling, took from him the body and blood of our Lord, gobbling, gobbling, chanting nonsense syllables registering deep in our personal unconscious" (30).

In conclusion, cultural alienation caused by their English education renders female protagonists in several postcolonial texts into insiders/outsiders in their own families, communities, and cultures. Even as education equips them with knowledge, their western learning places them apart from their parents' generation and from indigenous ways of knowing. English education is a crucial aspect of colonial ideology and colonial weaponry inculcating western culture often to the detriment of indigenous cultures and languages. Some texts have open-ended resolutions: Tee on the brink of leaving for the mother country; Tambu, chastened by Nyasha's illness and alienation, and trying to integrate the best of different worlds. Others like Lalita may be lost to the city which beckoned her as her education contributed to her dissatisfaction with village life. The privileged class that takes education for granted suffer different alienations—Ella, Antoinette, Nellie in the Caribbean context; Bim in 1947 India with independence and partition (from Pakistan) riots; Nyasha in 1960s' pre-independent Rhodesia. These texts demonstrate how educational opportunities interface with indigenous and colonial prejudices that are based in race, class, color, and gender. Education equips Margaret to take on racial prejudice in *Maru*, as education enables Tambu to challenge the downtrodden status of being poor, black, and female that her mother had to accept.

These adolescent female protagonists demonstrate amazing bodily courage in resisting cultural alienation as they struggle to discover ways of belonging to their female bodies, at times, to repossess their bodies from exilic conditions resulting from internalized sexist and racial pressures from their own communities as well as prejudices that they encounter in English schools. Even as they experience insider/outsiderness, they challenge racial, class, and color prejudices in their societies. The texts present creative ways in which they challenge physical and psychic alienations from their bodies and communities, and ways in which they are able to reconnect—using ritual, speech, silence, illness, bulimia—with their community. Their arduous journeys bring them "home" into their female bodies and into circles of belonging.

CHAPTER 4

Cultural "Traditions" Exiling the Female Body

The ideals, ethics, and morality heaped on women since time immemorial are suffocating and killing. The adjectives used to praise us have become oppressive. Calling us loving, they have locked us in the closed room of culture . . . they have handcuffed us with modesty and chained our feet with loyalty, so that far from running, we have not been able even to walk.

Now we must refuse to be Sitas. By becoming a Sita and submitting to the fire ordeal, woman loses her identity. This fire ordeal is imposed on women today in every city, every home. . . . We can be fearless since we have no models.

—Saroj Vasaria, *Manushi*

Tradition was thus not the ground on which the status of woman was being contested. Rather the reverse was true: women in fact became the site on which tradition was debated and reformulated. What was at stake was not women but tradition. Thus it is no wonder that even reading against the grain of a discourse ostensibly about women, one learns so little about them. . . . Neither subject, nor object, but ground—such is the status of women in the discourse on sati.

—Lata Mani, "Contentious Traditions:
The Debate on *Sati* in Colonial India," in
Recasting Women: Essays in Colonial History

*P*ostcolonial women have to deal with multilayered traditions rooted in indigenous custom with overlays of colonial influence. Resisting tradition, such as "refusing to be Sitas" is an important aspect of my study. Traditions exile the body especially when, as Mani indicates, tradition itself is made more important than women. Ironically, such attitudes buttressed by indigenous and colonial impacts continue to haunt women—during pre-colonial times, as well as during nationalist struggles when women are required to carry the additional burden of being the guardians of tradition, particularly against the colonizer, and into the postcolonial era. In women writers' representations, there are attempts to challenge, even reverse such paradigms. However, within patriarchal structures, women often need to negotiate rather than reject regressive interpretations of tradition outright. Women writers represent how their female protagonists make creative compromises with traditional roles ascribed to them throughout their lives: as daughter, wife, mother (of sons versus daughters), as workers, as single, lesbian, widow, or priestess.

As with English education, women experience alienation, even exile from their bodies as they negotiate traditional norms and roles. Traditions are used often to control female sexuality, and controls of the female body are mystified as being faithful to tradition. Tradition itself is ahistoricized and regarded as fixed, timeless, and unchanging. Women must pay severe costs for confronting tradition. Both within family and outside, tradition designates female roles within patriarchal frames and parameters: woman as wife and mother is valorized; single women, lesbians, and widows face prejudice. There are different experiences of women's sexual being, some acceptable, even venerated, others unconventional and condemned. Rather than glorifying the traditionally, that is, patriarchally accepted female roles, women writers demystify them and reveal that many traditional controls of feminine body/sexuality are located within family and personal parameters that then radiate outward into larger society. Ideologies that buttress women's subordination are supported by family and perpetuated both in the private and public realms—whether it is unequal wages, or gender discriminations in the family and the workplace.

Women writers explore a variety of strategies of coping against traditional constraints: for instance, writing itself, particularly personal and autobiographical expressions; the uses of silence and speech as portrayed by Lucia, Maiguru, Tambu, and others in Zimbabwean Tsitsi Dangarembga's *Nervous Conditions*; the uses of the female body in illness, mental breakdown, "madness" in Indian Kamala Das's *My Story*, and in Dominican Jean Rhys's *Wide Sargasso Sea*; in Ampoma's "willing" sacrifice (suicide), dying in her husband's place in Ghanaian Efua Sutherland's play, *Edufa*.[1]

My analysis of tradition in the postcolonial context is enabled partly by Lata Mani's ground-breaking essay (later incorporated in her book entitled *Contentious Traditions*) quoted as an epigraph to this chapter.[2]

Although Mani's concern is specifically with how a horrific practice such as sati was debated by indigenous social reformers and colonizers in nineteenth-century India, her arguments are useful for the postcolonial context as a whole. She discusses issues such as the specifically colonial intervention into nineteenth-century notions of women and scripture; both the elevation of woman as "heroine" and her pitiable state as "victim," which end up "preclud(ing) the possibility of a complex female subjectivity" (117). Both representations make the widow "particularly susceptible to discourses of salvation, whether these are articulated by officials or the indigenous elite. It thus comes as no surprise that both offer to intercede on her behalf, to save her from 'tradition', indeed even in its name" (117). Debates on social reform in India in the nineteenth century were not about women but about "the moral challenge of colonial rule," notes Mani. "In this process women came to represent 'tradition' for all participants: whether viewed as the weak, deluded creatures who must be reformed through legislation and education, or the valiant keepers of tradition who must be protected" (118). Rather than tradition being the "ground on which the status of woman was being contested," Mani finds the reverse to be true, namely that "women in fact became the site on which tradition was debated and reformulated. What was at stake was not women but tradition" (118).

I extend Mani's discussion of nineteenth-century discourses on sati to contemporary postcolonial women's texts that represent female protagonists negotiating their expected "traditional" roles in overtly obedient and covertly defiant ways. Contrary to the mostly silent widows about whom male colonizers and male indigenous elite wrote, contemporary texts explore complex negotiations that females must undertake in order to assert their subjectivities and not ascend the funeral pyre out of respect to a tradition that kills them. Several literary texts portray the heavy costs on women's bodies when they take on traditions that have the weight of scriptural and patriarchal authority. Whatever a girl or woman's particular negotiation— speaking against, being complicit within, or resisting tradition—female protagonists experience self-exile, a sense of not belonging to themselves, and particularly not to their female bodies. They must mediate physically among the categories of belonging to their bodies, to their desired sexualities, and to traditional norms, or opting out of conforming, and thus facing serious consequences. In this chapter I explore the gaps, costs, and lags in these negotiations, as well as the parameters of exercising agency for female protagonists living within different class structures, religious beliefs, and familial bonds. As with the histories of other oppressed groups, covert rather than overt expressions of agency generate situations of possibility. It is important to discover those covert means and not to be too quick to assume powerlessness when a woman "conforms" to traditional roles. What is more significant are the many ingenious strategies of working from within institutional structures rather than defying them outright, which can have fatal consequences. This covert action is not less radical than an overthrow of the system; it is often more courageous to conform on the surface while devising resistances from within accepted institutional, such as marital frameworks.

Postcolonial women's texts offer a variety of demystifications of traditional female roles, for instance, wifehood, not as it is traditionally expected to be fulfilling and nurturing but as enslaving. Unfulfilled wifehood is expressed in physical ailment, nervous breakdown, madness as in Kamala Das's autobiography, and in several of Anita Desai's novels. Nigerian women writers like Buchi Emecheta and Flora Nwapa take a complex view of the alienating effects of polygamy on their protagonists' bodies. In the Caribbean context, informal polygamy places enormous emotional and physical strains on women, as represented in several of the Jamaican Sistren stories. Other traditionally legitimate female roles such as the proper behavior of widows and of single women lead to experiences of physical alienation from their bodies which in turn cause intense mental suffering. Literary and other cultural texts such as activist women's interventions through songs, posters, pamphlets present female resistances to these devastating forms of physical and mental alienation.

Patriarchal claims that women are the "guardians of tradition" are at root aimed at controlling female sexuality and fertility. Tradition often mystifies actual control over female sexuality. Tradition is often problematically ahistoricized, so that cultural traditions are presented in dominant ideologies as timeless and totalizing, whereas, in fact, tradition is dynamic, as well as historically and culturally specific. Female sexuality is controlled effectively through a reifying of tradition. Tradition is gendered so that the same elements of tradition, such as religious belief, education, dress codes, freedom of movement are enforced very differently on males versus females. A struggle over what is tradition is a battle over the female body— how to control it and keep it familiar within recognizable and legitimized patriarchal codes.

The costs of confronting or breaking tradition are often fatal for women and experienced physically as attacks on the body. For instance, in Buchi Emecheta's *The Bride Price*, Aku-anna dies in childbirth as "foretold" by Igbo tradition.[3] She is punished for marrying the man of her choice who is not accepted by her family (since he belongs to the outcaste *osu* group). And her family effectively ostracizes Aku-anna by refusing to accept the traditional bride-price from her husband. Similarly, in Ama Ata Aidoo's *Anowa*, the protagonist is ostracized socially because she is unable to have a child (though the text implies that her husband is sterile) and she commits suicide. Bessie Head's protagonist in the short story "Life," in her volume *The Collector of Treasures* who goes against her husband's dictates of monogamy, is murdered by him.

Female protagonists are faced with a complicated mesh of power relationships that they have internalized. As they negotiate these institutionalized prescriptions of sexual behavior, they face no-win situations: obey the dominant code and survive, even if that entails serious self-censorship; or disobey tradition, step outside the boundaries, and pay the ultimate price. Aku-anna, Anowa, and Life who defy traditional controls of their bodies, suffer fatal social marginalization that gives them no community to turn to, nowhere to escape to, no space in which they can belong. Such social exiling is so absolute that these women are often silenced in violent deaths. As a related aside, I wish to note that for many women writers of these imaginative stories, emigration is often necessary for intellectual survival.

Cultural traditions originate and are nurtured within specific historical and political frameworks. Two common tendencies in postcolonial societies must be challenged: 1) to exalt traditional culture, however oppressive, particularly for women (most common during nationalist movements which glorify "tradition" in order to counteract colonialist attitudes); and 2) to ahistoricize social customs as inexplicably a part of "human nature."

The arena of "tradition" is highly contested and mediated in postcolonial studies today. Far from being seen as unchanging emblems of a culture, traditions and their varying configurations must be historicized and gendered. Colonial intervention is only one among other events that significantly interrupted indigenous cultures and complicated whatever fragile balance of power existed between the sexes in pre-colonial times. Colonization certainly ruptured indigenous evolutions of traditions; given racist onslaughts, local peoples were pressed into a range of responses to their tradition—glorification, denigration, rejection. Women writers' stances vary partially as dictated by their own class backgrounds, levels of education, political awareness, and their search for alternatives to existing sexual inequities that are often inscribed within the most revered traditions.

The notion of the "invention of tradition," as proposed by Eric Hobsbawm and Terence Ranger, is compelling, as a means of historicizing tradition.[4] In his Introduction to *The Invention of Tradition*, Hobsbawm remarks: "Traditions which appear or claim to be old are often quite recent in origin and sometimes invented. . . . 'Invented tradition' is taken to mean a set of practices, normally governed by overtly or tacitly accepted rules and of a ritual or symbolic nature, which seek to inculcate certain values and norms of behaviour by repetition, which automatically implies continuity with the past. In fact, where possible, they normally attempt to establish continuity with a suitable historic past" (3). Even when traditions refer to a historic past, "the peculiarity of 'invented' tradition is that the continuity with it is largely factitious" (4).

Traditions change according to new political frameworks in societies; hence, as Hobsbawm points out, practices such as initiation ceremonies that took place in small communities, may not continue in the same way in larger entities such as nation-states. "However, both new political regimes and innovatory movements," he adds, "might seek to find their own equivalents for the traditional rites of passage associated with religion" (10). Any study of "invented traditions cannot be separated from the wider study of the history of society. . . . All invented traditions, so far as possible, use history as a legitimator of action and cement of group cohesion" (12).

I relate this notion of the "invention of tradition" to Benedict Anderson's idea of the nation as an "imagined community."[5] "Traditions" are invented and assume status within communities in particular spaces and times, as nations are constituted around geographic boundaries often drawn arbitrarily by colonizing powers that paid scant attention to the inhabitants' race, ethnicity, religion, and language. Both nation and tradition have imagined dimensions. Both have parameters that are challenged by historical factors—national boundaries contested by the horrors of ethnic cleansers, or age-old traditions transformed by the introduction of new technologies such as those in the reproductive arena.[6] Colonized peoples' indigenous traditions have been rigidified, or challenged and transformed through collisions with such westernized interventions in medicine, or legal systems.

In the colonies, traditional controls of female sexuality received a boost through Victorian notions of sexuality. Colonial and indigenous patriarchies colluded often and their concerns were hardly about women, but rather, as Mani points out, about preserving that sacred entity called "tradition." The colonizers often regarded themselves as "liberators" of native women from "barbaric" customs. British interventions in discourses on female sexuality did not deal with its positive aspects, such as female pleasure and desire; rather they focused on horrific customs such as widow burning. British discourses on sati, contrary to being liberating for women, created through language, that is, knowledge and evocation of religious and Brahminical authority on this custom, new controls, containments, and validations for such practices. Ironically, the British were complicitous in maintaining such cruel practices because they were more concerned with "respectful" posturing to tradition and religious authority, which, if challenged, would threaten the smooth functioning of a colonial regime.

Cultural traditions control a woman's entire life—from early socialization as a daughter, to indoctrination into a wife (polygamy or nuclear family), mother, or if less fortunate, into widowhood. Alternate family topographies such as single women, or lesbian couples with children, may have heavy, often physical costs extracted from female bodies that have dared to transgress acceptable norms of family and sexuality. Accordingly, the uses, abuses, and controls of reproductive technologies become significant areas of feminist concern. In India, for instance, among large nonliterate populations, contraceptives are imposed on women not for birth control but sterilization.[7] How little control a woman has over her body is evident in the gross abuses allowed by governmental family planning, that is, family control policies. The effects of these abuses are most evident among poor and illiterate women. The concept of education for family planning is directed almost entirely to women, as if men have no part in engendering a child. The patriarchal framework, codes of masculinity, and male privilege in matters of sexuality are left intact.

Oppressive traditions are located specifically within the arena of female sexuality. Contemporary postcolonial novels represent women as reproductive units bought and sold through traditions of dowry and brideprice. Fertility and infertility are made visible through the institution of marriage, polygamy or monogamy, in which a woman may be fulfilled or enslaved. Her body may be prostituted even within marriage, and her power or powerlessness is expressed via uses of speech, silence, nervous breakdowns, and madness. Marriage and children usually go together within the Indian context, whereas "outside" children whose "baby fathers" may have "inside children" within marriages are common within the Caribbean. Lesbianism as sexual preference falls outside all these parameters and is most often invisible for fear of violent reprisals. Varieties of singlehood are tolerated often at a cost to women's bodies: social stigma against singlehood by choice; sexual abstinence and other bodily cruelties such as starvation enjoined on widows, legitimized by patriarchally mandated religious custom. Socially legitimized cruel treatment of widows can make life unbearable, and as recently as 1987, in living memory, there was a most disturbing incident of sati in Rajasthan. The rhetoric, initiated during colonial times, namely, the widow's "willingness" to immolate herself, was replayed in postcolonial times, complete with the posturing and pseudo-religiosity of the woman who committed sati, transformed into a "goddess" by her family, and indeed the wider community including politicians. A terrible and unfair choice that faces widows is to endure as a social outcaste, and face a kind of living death, or to mount the terrifying funeral pyre. Similarly, the shameful spate of women murdered, and passed off as "suicides" or "accidents" staged as "kitchen fires" have a direct correlation to escalating demands for dowry. The actual horrific burning of a woman's body to ashes displays a macabre use of the icon of fire, that has creative and destructive potential, so important in Hindu rituals and mythology.

Fire, a potent symbol in religious ceremonies, embodies various cruelties toward women justified "traditionally" through the use of religion. Religion is evoked to mystify female sexuality, sometimes to women's advantage as in uses of obeah to resist certain forms of patriarchal control, but more often to their detriment, as, for instance, when a woman is elevated to priestess status. Although this enhances her social standing, she is considered inadequate if she is unable to bear children. Expression or denial of sexuality are controlled through a patriarchal and political interpretation of traditional religion and ritual as in Aidoo's *Anowa* whose mother prevented her from being betrothed as a priestess, and whose inability to bear children is blamed on this contravention of tradition. Anowa had "the nimble feet of one meant to dance for the gods." Anowa, if allowed to become a priestess, would belong within the traditional frameworks of ritual and religion that contain her strength and unusual creativity. Without that containment, Anowa is a "danger" to herself and to society.

I do not wish to imply, in this above discussion, that all traditions are oppressive for women. I acknowledge the empowering potential in certain myths, legends, and in other oral and expressive forms such as proverbs, folktales, dance. Traditions of female solidarity have been developed by women's groups such as Sistren in Jamaica, or Jagori in Delhi via telling life stories, creating new songs, poems, art, drama, dance as the authors of their own experience. They use the creative potential in these cultural forms to transform situations of traditional imprisonment into spaces of freedom.

Whether a folktale is empowering or disempowering for women depends upon its representation and interpretation. Female strength, for instance, can be highlighted in one reading of say, Draupadi's role in the Indian epic *The Mahabharata*. The same story can be read as Draupadi's victimization. Often, a fear of female fertility, its mystery and power, lies at the root of woman-hating proverbs and disempowering folktales. Such cultural modes express a culture's ways of controlling female life-giving potential, most commonly not by denigrating it (since it is highly valued and necessary), but ironically by venerating, even glorifying female fertility. Such idealization is one way to contain its mystery within patriarchal boundaries that tries to limit its possibilities and power.

Fulfillment and Enslavement of the Female Body in Monogamous Marriage

Cultural traditions are used to validate controls of female sexuality. Key aspects of such domination are legitimized by an evocation of ideologies of family, female roles, rules of acceptable sexual behavior such as wifehood under monogamy, polygamy—formal and informal (visiting relationships)—and motherhood. Culturally illegitimate sexual behaviors can also be described as "traditions," albeit aberrant ones such as prostitution. The negative social judgments on a woman's choice to be single, to have a lesbian relationship, or to elect other forms of female autonomy and self-definition outside of patriarchal ownership by father, husband, son can also be seen as upholding "tradition." In postcolonial regions, one discovers striking cultural commonalities in patriarchally legitimized uses of women's bodies, though there are undoubtedly significant differences in the practice of, say, traditions such as dowry in the Indian context, and brideprice in the African; or between urban polygamy as depicted in Nigerian Buchi Emecheta's *The Joys of Motherhood*, and informal sexual relationships where poor women trade sex for food, as represented in the Jamaican Sistren stories.

Marriage as the legitimate institutional framework for the expression of female fertility is regarded differently in the Caribbean than in the Indian and African contexts discussed here. In Caribbean literary and testimonial representations, marriage is more an aspiration than a reality. In "Colonial Policy Towards Women After the 1938 Uprising: The Case of Jamaica," Joan French analyzes the history of the institution of marriage as shaped, indeed, as often imposed by the colonizers on local peoples. French draws upon the Moyne Commission Report that ascribed several social ills such as single motherhood and female poverty to "the social, moral and economic evils of promiscuity," which was defined to include all non-marital relations. There was a concerted campaign to wipe out "co-habitation" and encourage monogamous marriage. French comments: "From the time of slavery black Jamaican women had made their position to marriage quite clear, rejecting it as 'too much work' and putting them too much under the control of men" (19). The colonizers were bent on enforcing the bourgeois family ideal and sexual division of labor, glorifying women's role inside the home. The ideal of the nuclear family was enforced via "Mass Weddings." French remarks that "through the Mass Marriage campaign, wedding rings were sold for 10/-. A total of 150 mass marriages were organized and this succeeded in raising very slightly the percentage of the total population who married. This was in spite of a massive public campaign . . . [that] marshalled the churches, schools, press, radio, welfare agencies, and 'national' association" (22). There was also a kind of surveillance move to "register fathers," intended "to discourage illegitimacy," which was criminalized. Further, as French points out astutely, "There was no suggestion that fatherhood involved anything but financial support—a subtle assumption of the male breadwinner/dependent housewife ideology. Married men, on the other hand, by definition could not be sued for child support as long as they remained in the nuclear home—even if they were bringing in nothing and were being supported by their wives" (21–22). In contemporary Caribbean society, marriage is not the only socially acceptable framework for procreation; there is less social stigma against single mothers than in the Indian or African context. But this does not imply that women necessarily have more autonomy over their bodies. Often, ignorance and mystification of women's bodies lead to unwanted pregnancies.

Wifehood and marriage are portrayed at times as fulfilling, and at others as enslaving. Options such as divorce, or singlehood, or homosexual partnerships are usually not validated socially and women have to negotiate social spaces in difficult ways. Marriage is not to be analyzed only within a private and domestic sphere since this institution is conditioned importantly by cultural and political factors in each society. For postcolonial women, additionally, oppressive traditional power structures were worsened with the colonizer's introduction of capitalism and cash economy that had direct bearing on gender relations within the family. As Karen Sacks puts it in *Sisters and Wives: The Past and Future of Sexual Equality*, a woman's biology becomes "an unconscious metaphor for social relations."[8]

Maria Cutrufelli echoes this analysis: "Social control over access to women, i.e. the marriage mechanism, is the very keystone of the [traditional kinship] system. The woman, as a 'producer of producers, constitutes the most powerful prospective means of production.' Controlling women thus means controlling the reproduction of the production unit. In political terms, control over access to women legitimizes social hierarchy, namely, the authority of the old over the young, of the dominant over the dominated lineages, of one caste over another."[9]

Wifehood in monogamous marriage provides an avenue of legitimized sexual expression in most postcolonial patriarchal societies. Women's texts represent a range of patriarchal colonizations of women's bodies within the marriage institution. Socially, marriage enables women to belong within cultural expectations; marriage often involves shifting authority from father to husband. While writers acknowledge the status and privilege given to wives (and mothers), they demystify the image of contented wife, and probe its enslaving aspects as in Buchi Emecheta's *The Slave Girl*.[10] Wifehood often renders women powerless in terms of economic dependency and emotional subservience. Wifehood is equated dangerously with romantic expectations of love. Wifehood equates psychological torture as in Antoinette's case in Dominican Jean Rhys's *Wide Sargasso Sea*. As wives, women may subconsciously internalize sado-masochistic roles, and become unable to emerge from situations of physical and psychological battering. Often at the root of these predicaments, lie complex webs of female socializations, and ironically, of patriarchal codes necessitating female complicity with unequal power relations in monogamous marriage. Such female socializing is buttressed by colonial education that does not challenge gender inequities within the family, often rooted in sanctimonious "respect" for "native tradition." Given these layers of female willingness to participate in a male-dominated model of marriage, women writers question whether such consent is an exercise of free will, or whether it is the only option for most women in the cultures depicted.

It is important also to recognize that women are socialized to participate in dangerous romantic notions of love and self-fulfillment through marriage. Women must subsume their identities under their husbands'; such renunciations have dangerous effects as portrayed in Indian writer Anita Desai's early novels. In *Cry, the Peacock*, Maya is married off to her father's protégé, who is so bound to rationality that he stifles Maya's emotionality. Her needs for sensitive connections with her mate and the natural world around her are ignored and put down until she spirals into a private universe of madness. Maya's isolation makes her an exile from her community and her body. This husband's male power is strengthened by his use of paradigms from Indian myths that revere suffering and self-sacrifice as part of women's fate, and that codify the notion of husband as god, and as part of her *dharma* (sacred duty). Further, Maya's identity is so fragile that it can be thwarted by the stronger males in her life. And she does not even have the language to contest such domination. She has no space to question these "ideals" of self-abnegating women presented to her as a priori truths. In such unequal power struggles, her only recourse is sadly a self-destructive battle waged on her own body and mind. She becomes increasingly isolated, not belonging to herself, or to any community. Such exilic feelings draw her into mental imbalance.[11]

Another text that portrays the self-abusive outcomes of a woman's stepping out of traditional expectations of wifely behavior is Kamala Das's autobiography, *My Story*. Das's protagonist recognizes that she enjoys bodily pleasure, even lust outside marriage. Linked with this hard-hitting recognition of the body are dangerous ideals of romantic love and the paradoxes of lust and love that nearly destroy the protagonist. Rather than being empowered, she too, like Maya retreats from the world, this time into nervous breakdown, and the unreal coping space created by medications. However, the protagonist is not a total victim—she is advised to write and express her pain. Creatively, she begins to use her personal voice ironically cleared by her breakdown to write her life story. The deeply abiding injury to her body and soul when she was raped as a child-bride of sixteen surfaces. Self-expression probes the frustrations of fulfilling wifely duties on the surface, and remaining unfulfilled emotionally and sexually.[12]

Das's persona uses writing as a means of coping with breakdown. Other protagonists use nurturing or self-destructive means to deal with oppressive marriages. Lucia, the only unmarried woman in Zimbabwean Dangarembga's *Nervous Conditions*, though criticized as "wild," even as a "witch," importantly retains autonomy over her body. The males in the family are forced grudgingly to admire her ability to fight back and assert her rights. Ironically, uneducated Lucia can speak for herself, whereas educated Maiguru is silent, even complicitous with male power in a situation when she could have defended Lucia. Maiguru remains trapped in a double bind—as an educated woman who works outside the home, she is untraditional; she is also a traditional wife who willingly "effaces" herself so that her husband's identity is not threatened. Maiguru tries to create her own variety of educated traditionalism that requires its own kind of negotiation between the woman's own agency and societal norms in 1960s Rhodesia.

A parallel questioning of how women's potential for resistance is circumscribed occurs at the end of one of the Jamaican Sistren life stories, "Grandma's Estate" in *Lionheart Gal*. Ella, after much anger and frustration at her grandmother's internalized race hatred, her inability to ascribe blame to a patriarchal system of oppression that was complicit in exploiting the bodies of female slaves, comes to an acceptance of the historical limits of possibility that faced slave and free women in the 1890s. For Ella's contemporary generation as she recognizes, unlike the historical realities for slave women, models of resistance exist—Marcus Garvey, Black Power, among others. This is not to imply that female slave resistance was never possible; they have their own limits of possibility, almost enjoined by that history.[13]

Wives who feel physically enslaved and mentally colonized within marriages often deploy bodily resistances including the use of speech and silence in Ghanaian Efua Sutherland's *Edufa*; nervous breakdown, "madness" in Kamala Das's *My Story*; as also in Dominican Jean Rhys's *Wide Sargasso Sea*. Mental breakdowns become tools for female autonomy in situations of powerlessness, often faced with unsympathetic spouses. Das's persona is told by her husband that she is going "mad," Antoinette in Rhys's novel is branded, "crazy like her mother"; and Ampoma in Sutherland's drama must pay the ultimate price of her life for her spoken oath that she would die in her husband's place. In these texts, love is fatal for the female protagonists; the use of oaths, obeah, other religious rituals plays a part in "rescuing" the woman to her detriment. There are evocative parallels between the use of obeah in the Caribbean tradition, and of "oaths" in the Ghanaian tradition. In all three texts, the protagonists belong to a privileged class: Das's persona is clearly upper class; Ampoma has a life of opulence and ease; and Antoinette's family although it has seen better days, can pay a handsome dowry that procures her an English husband.

In *Edufa*, the wife as metaphoric slave is reminiscent of Nigerian Buchi Emecheta's novelistic rendering of the actual tradition of slave-trading among Africans, and further, her gender-specific portrayal in *The Slave Girl* of a freed female slave who nonetheless continues to experience a slave-like bondage in marriage. The mediations between metaphoric and actual slavery are negotiated vividly in *The Slave Girl* where the protagonist, as a child, is sold into slavery by her brother who needs the money to further his status in the community by acquiring "titles." Ironically, when her slave-owner's son wishes to marry her, once again, there has to be a transaction where he has to purchase this wife and settle all debts so that he is clearly the new owner. And this marriage is described as her re-enslavement as wife: "Ojebeta, now thirty-five has changed masters."

Rhys and Sutherland take European canonical texts as starting points and significantly transform those master narratives in the light of a colonized history and from the colonized woman's point of view. *Edufa* is based on Euripides's *Alcestis*, a story of wifely self-sacrifice; Rhys is inspired to give human form, life, context, and history to the animal-like, dehumanized Bertha Mason, the mad woman in the attic in Charlotte Bronte's *Jane Eyre*.

In *My Story*, Das creates a self-conscious persona, a female subject of an economically privileged class who experiences particular kinds of distresses—depression, breakdown, self-destructive fantasizing—conditions that make her feel exiled both from herself, her role as wife, and from a restrictive social environment. She feels imprisoned within the status and privilege of middle-class wife and mother. The persona experiences a marginalized state, confined ironically by her class privilege. Here is also an example of a dangerous self-marginalization arising from the persona's self-victimization that is itself embedded in her female socialization and symbols that powerfully equate wifehood with suffering, that uphold ideals of subservient, self-sacrificing women from Hindu myths and epics. The deeply psychological experiences of exile and marginality in this text are influenced by the ideological belief-structures, indigenous and western. Woman's status as inferior, inscribed in Hindu scripture, continues in varying forms in contemporary times rendering them alienated from family, community, and bringing them into states of self-exile as Das's persona.

This autobiographical narrative depicts the deeply confining cultural mores that control female sexuality. In Das's text, licit sex within marriage is associated in a seeming paradox with both violence and with motherhood; illicit sex can be tender and loving but cannot allow socially sanctioned motherhood. The narrator remarks, "The women of the best Nair families never mentioned sex. It was their principal phobia. They associated it with violence and bloodshed. They had been fed on the stories of Ravana who perished due to his desire for Sita and of Kichaka, who was torn to death by Draupadi's legal husband Bhima only because he coveted her" (26).

Das's persona stays within the boundaries of social convention, as wife—initially, she has no choice since she is married off by her parents at age sixteen. She describes being raped on her wedding night: "I took off my sari which was of heavy gold tissue and sat on the bed. Then without warning he fell on me, surprising me by the extreme brutality of the attack.... The rape was unsuccessful.... Perhaps I was not normal, perhaps I am only a eunuch, I said.... Again and again throughout that unhappy night he hurt me and all the while the Kathakali drums throbbed dully against our window and the singers sang of Damayanti's plight in the jungle" (93). Das's personal experience of wifehood begins with this violent encounter of a rape sanctioned within marriage. One of her finest poems, "The Old Playhouse," also presents a wife as victimized and without personal will:

> You called me wife,
> I was taught to break saccarine into your tea and
> To offer at the right moment the vitamins. Cowering
> Beneath your monstrous ego I ate the magic loaf and
> Became a dwarf. I lost my will and reason, to all your
> Questions I mumbled incoherent replies.[14]

For the persona and other women depicted in Das's story, violent marital sex often results from the custom of child-marriage. Married when hardly out of childhood, a mere girl is confronted usually with a much older husband whose "sexual haste on the wedding-night" gives her "a rude shock." The scars of such an experience as happens to the persona are carried into adulthood (rape-nightmares) and motherhood. The resultant frustration and unhappiness within marriage—her husband is described as "the man who did not ever learn to love (her)" (95) lead to sexual fantasies, idealizing and romanticizing love, "looking for an ideal lover" (180), and self-destructive preoccupations. Illicit sex, even desire outside of marriage—the kind that is punished severely in mythical models—becomes attractive to the persona. However, her "yearning for adventure" (123) does not bring fulfillment but a sado-masochistic suffering. As an adolescent, the persona makes this distinction between husband and lover: "It would not do to marry a wicked man. Being a mistress to him meant pain in a bearably moderate dose and plenty of chances to forgive the sweet sinner" (61). The protagonist dwells on real and imagined affairs, but if these liaisons produce a child, both mother and child would be socially ostracized. Sex is legitimate within marriage since it can result in motherhood.

Das's persona is increasingly frustrated with the social rewards for a woman of her class—husband, children, in-laws, and economic security. She decides to rebel flamboyantly against the restrictions of arranged marriage and enforced monogamy: "I made up my mind to be unfaithful to him (husband), at least physically. I knew then that if love was what I had looked for in marriage, I would have to look for it outside its legal orbit. I wanted to be given an identity that was lovable" (99). She decides to step out of the double standard legitimized in Manu's Laws: "Though destitute of virtue, or seeking pleasure (elsewhere), or devoid of good qualities, a husband must be constantly worshipped as a god by a faithful wife."[15] Although her unfaithfulness is not totally constructive for herself, this is not to validate Manu's strictures. *My Story* explores the dangerous and limited options available to this persona—she must remain within the boundaries of respectable though unhappy marriage, or she must step out of the codes of faithful wife, take lovers, or leave her husband. Sadly, in the text, she does not find any socially legitimized space to express her passionate and sexual being.

Further, the persona's deliberate uses, real or imaginary, of her female sexuality as ways to gain control over her life, do not alleviate her sense of non-identity within her marriage. She cannot emerge out of the marriage prison. She rejects divorce even when one of her lovers, Carlo wishes to marry her. Her children are the "chains" that bind her within a bad marriage: "We can probably have a love affair, I said, remembering the peace of my nights and the faces of my little sons closed in sleep. I am not the divorcing kind" (127).

The persona's decision to remain within the prison-house of a failed marriage is sado-masochistic. However, even this response is part of ideological conditioning and female socialization that encourage remaining within marriage, however miserable or violent. Note the common saying with which parents send their daughters as brides to their husband's homes: "we are sending out your bridal palanquin; let only your corpse return to this house." Such norms are internalized so dangerously that they have a hold on conscious and subconscious levels.

Though she feels imprisoned, Das's persona remains within the societal classification as wife. Further, she remains complicit in her suffering; any resistance to it, through writing, through affairs does not change her actual social situation. Her suffering is elevated and legitimized dangerously within a mythological framework of extremely low expectations as a wife within marriage. The subconscious hold of socialization patterns inculcated through the popular mythological stories of figures like the ever-suffering Sita as virtuous wife, the all-sacrificing Savitri who rescues her husband from death is played out in the persona's conscious acceptance of suffering as the fate of wifehood and motherhood. Further support for such acceptance is embedded in popular cultural productions and in religious ritual. The dominant message is that of suffering as purifying, even inevitable for a woman. Concurrently, visions of happiness, of romance are devastatingly within the realms of the unreal, the unreachable, the fantastic. The struggle in Das's story is between romantic notions of love that merge with lust, and desire experienced differently by males and females. The persona fantasizes about escaping from restrictive social conventions of marriage while remaining within the confines of the institution.

Sexuality and spirituality are mystified through powerful mythological tales of Rama, of Krishna, where god and lover are merged. Marriage provides a strict boundary within which woman's sexuality, which is judged in the scriptures as boundless, is controlled. The female body cannot legitimately experience pleasure outside the marital framework; sexuality is equated with duty. Woman's fertility, her ability to bear a child are both revered and feared. In the very mythologizing of female power, embodied in her sexuality, lies a deeply oppressive paradox. Male power and male sexuality are legitimate, for instance in the worship of the Shiva *lingam*; female sexuality, mystified as female power must be controlled and bounded through social custom, primarily within marriage. Even goddesses were tamed, their power restrained when they were married to strong male gods.

A useful analysis of how female power, beneficent and malevolent is mythologized in the figure of Kali is presented by Madhu Kishwar, Joanna Liddle, and Rama Joshi. The myth provides a rationale for the control of female power through a male, and through marriage:

> The concept of marriage, involving male control of female sexuality, is important for understanding how the mother goddess [in pre-Aryan India] was incorporated into the patriarchal Brahmin religion.... The story of Kali—India's matriarchal myth—is that she was created to save the gods from their more powerful enemies, but having done so, she continued on a rampage of uncontrollable killing, which could only be stopped by her husband Shiva lying down in front of her. In her malevolent aspect she receives blood sacrifice. As Lakshmi she is benevolent, bestower of wealth, progeny and happiness, and passively devoted to her husband. In this aspect she never receives blood sacrifice. The goddess is Lakshmi when she is under the control of the male god.... As Susan Wadley suggests,

it is marriage and the dominance of the male that transforms the goddess's dangerous power into benevolence.[16]

Ironically enough, the dimension in Hindu mythology that recognizes the spiritual in the physical, often regarding the body as the vehicle to reach spiritual heights (as in Yoga) has dangerous social connotations for women—when sexuality and spirituality merge, women are socialized to mystify sexuality, sometimes by elevating it to a spiritual realm, leaving behind the realms of the physical, of desire, of pleasure.

The highly sexualized discourse in *My Story* is so self-absorbed, often navel-gazing as to be problematically sensationalized and voyeuristic. Nearly 40,000 copies were sold within the first year of its publication. Sexual fantasies of lovers, flamboyant displays of lust by an upper-caste female persona, displays of a pleasure-seeking heroine tend to detract from the actual pain and anguish of wifehood and motherhood. *My Story*'s tone verges on the sensationalized value of a "proper" high-caste woman displaying her sexual desires and fantasies in public—a theme that had guaranteed shock value. "Every middle-class bed," reads a blurb to the text "is a cross on which the woman is crucified." Das's prose often does not transcend that shock value. The text delights in displaying lust and desire. The persona who calls herself a "nymphomaniac" (186) hardly gains personal autonomy by flaunting social custom. The self-indulgent fantasies are often ends in themselves, disempowering, self-pitying, masochistic, all situated within a privileged life-style with servants, doctors, and enough food to eat. Perhaps the most useful aspect of Das's story is a hard-hitting realization that the body is ultimately inescapable, that the route to self-awareness is through the body and not through its denial.

Emecheta's *The Slave Girl*, which won her the Jock Campbell Prize, depicts the female condition of slavery, both literal and metaphoric. The actual buying and selling of girls as slaves is as much part of the fictional fabric as the depictions of enslaved wifehood and motherhood. Ojebeta, the protagonist is socialized to believe that throughout her life a female needs a man to belong to for her own identity. When only a child, she is orphaned. Her ambitious brother wants to acquire a traditional title, and he gets the necessary funds by selling off his sister as a slave. He negotiates a good price for his voiceless, though "strong, well-fed, and healthy sister" (67), sold as an animal. She has no say over this transaction that will determine her destiny. Her brother's rationalization is striking: "After all, you are only a daughter" (79).

The Desired Marital Status Under Disempowering Traditions of Dowry and Bride-Price

Traditions that inscribe woman-as-property—dowry in India, bride-price in African societies—were reinforced and became more dangerous for women within a capitalist wage economy introduced by the colonizer. The external transaction of social customs like dowry and bride-price takes place within a dialectic relationship between patriarchy and capitalism, reproduction and production. The female body, or rather, woman as reproductive unit is bought and sold through these culturally legitimized ways of controlling women. The exchange value of women's bodies often ensures the perpetuation or increase of family wealth. "The introduction of cash as a dominant means of exchange," notes Christine Obbo, "was responsible for changes in marriage arrangements as well as personal relationships."[17] There is a direct relationship, as Maria Mies argues in *Patriarchy and Accumulation on a World Scale*, "between women's oppression and exploitation, and the paradigms of never-ending accumulation and 'growth', between capitalist patriarchy and the exploitation and subordination of colonies."[18] The task of socialist-feminists, as Michele Barrett suggests, is to explore "the relations between . . . domestic production, the household, and historical changes in the mode of production and systems of appropriation and exploitation."[19]

Why is it that even among the educated classes in India, and particularly among them, the incidence of dowry murder is higher than among the uneducated? As discussed in chapter 3, education leads to contradictory forms of empowerment for women. Often, equipped with their new learning, women are alienated from their communities, and they must try harder, at times, than uneducated women, to find spaces of belonging. Contradictorily, then, educated women may be more susceptible to the pressures of tradition than uneducated ones. Personal stories of female battering are recounted in texts such as Agnes Flavia's *My Story . . . Our Story of Rebuilding Broken Lives*.[20]

Culturally sanctioned traditions such as dowry often are represented uncritically in Indian Anita Desai's or Kamala Markandaya's novels. Other traditions that uphold the ingrained low status of women, or that reinforce ideals of female self-sacrifice and silent suffering, are endorsed rather than challenged in their literary representations. At best, writers attempt to "revise" or rework images of women from Indian epics, such as a modern day Sita, or Draupadi; at the worst, they present female oppression as simply a part of Indian culture, and in exalting tradition, even in its retrogressive aspects, they validate female oppression. In discussing violence against women's bodies, often culturally enshrined and scripturally sanctioned, activist materials by women's groups from India openly condemn violence, discuss modes of resistance, and share feminist strategies for social change.[21] Also, the expressive arts such as dance, contemporary choreography, re-envision the role of traditional female figures such as Sita and Draupadi.

Activist mobilizing against dowry murders is found in non-literary forms of expression such as letters, sometimes by the survivors of dowry-related violence, sometimes by the mothers of the victims; essays in feminist journals such as *Manushi*; and testimonials of successful social humiliation strategies used against dowry murderers. These materials based on personal testimony are more useful for an analysis of dowry than are imaginative cultural forms such as the novel written by Indian women writers. The use of letters and testimonies allows us to expand beyond traditional literary forms as sources of social critique. Consider, for instance, the rousing words in the letter by Saroj Vasaria, quoted at the beginning of this chapter, about how women today must "refuse to be Sitas."

In India, escalation of dowry-related murders, and attempts by women's groups to use traditional methods of social humiliation and shaming of perpetrators, especially in the face of blatant failures of the legal system, underline the low status of women. At independence in India in 1947, women legally secured several important rights such as the vote. However, it was not only the British who displayed contradictory attitudes to women's liberation; Indian national leaders were as entrenched in patriarchal structures. Women who resisted were judged as unpatriotic, and influenced by western education. While native male politicians supported women's suffrage (partly to undermine British power and to demonstrate Indian progressiveness), they "opposed the principles [of sexual equality] in marriage and inheritance," note Kishwar et al., "which threatened their own privileges as men in the family" (36). Women's inheritance rights were perceived as dangerous since they might lead to women's refusal to marry.

Hence, many laws in India today, such as the 1961 Prohibition of Dowry Act, are merely "paper tigers." The Report of the Committee on the Status of Women pointed out that the Dowry Prohibition Act was completely ineffective. The Report buys into the myth that dowry is given "voluntarily" (which disturbingly echoes the British invention of such problematic categories as "willing" and "unwilling" satis), and its recommendation that no more than 20 percent of parental income be used for dowry does not challenge the sexist underpinnings of this tradition. As Madhu Kishwar remarks in her excellent essay in *Manushi: A Journal of Women and Society*, "Dowry—To Ensure Her Happiness or to Disinherit Her?": "The concept of dowry is based on the idea that a girl is a burden, therefore a man must be bribed to take her off her parents' hands.... [Dowry perpetuates] the mentality of viewing woman as a worthless object."[22]

Why dowry murders have steadily increased over the past ten years is a complicated question that must be explored within the cultural politics of women's status in Indian society. Hindu scriptures demonstrate an ambivalent attitude in both the exaltation and denigration of women. The Laws of Manu, in particular, which prescribe sexual codes of behavior, are full of double standards, favoring Brahmins over other castes, and males over females. In fact, women are often equated with the lowest caste called *sudras* (renamed by Gandhi as "Harijans," children of God): "Both women and *sudras*," according to Manu, are "life-long slaves from birth to death, with slavery inborn in them."

This gender-based power hierarchy has an economic base within tradition, according to which a female from birth is regarded as *paraya dhan*, literally, "another's wealth." A girl-child cannot claim to own this wealth of her body; she must be separated from her parental home and function as a reproductive unit for another family when she is married, along with a dowry. This traditional concept of "wealth" is exacerbated dangerously by materialistic greed and consumerism encouraged by advanced capitalism.

Similarly, a girl-child in traditional African cultures is prepared from her earliest age to believe that she will fulfill her role not in her parental home, but elsewhere. "She is aware that somehow she is on her way out," comments Lauretta Ngcobo in her essay, "African Motherhood": "It is significant that in some of the Bantu languages," notes Ngcobo, "the word marriage is synonymous with journey."[23] Ngcobo regards the girl-child as "an outsider who is being prepared for the central role that she will play at her in-laws ... a place where [she] will finally belong. But ... disillusionment awaits [her]. This is double jeopardy, for [she] will never really belong anywhere" (142–143). As female, the exilic state of not belonging within the parental or marital home often translates as an exile from the female body itself. In the very struggle to find a space to survive with some dignity, women have to negotiate both their participation in and their resistance to patriarchal domination. This is a shifting, even at times a contradictory process of colluding and resisting, and at times even resisting via colluding.

In India, along with scriptural authority confirming woman-as-slave/ property, powerful images of ideal womanhood are part of a collective consciousness, represented and reinforced in mythological stories. As "god," a husband can commit no wrong (the Hindu pantheon is a lively, anthropomorphic array of male deities who commit errors, but get away with them); a woman is enjoined to take any kind of abuse from him uncritically. While the epics reinforce scriptural definitions of woman as inferior, they have a stronger hold than religious tracts on the popular imagination in their evocative power as stories. Further, although the epics are full of examples of irresponsible behavior on the part of fathers and husbands (Draupadi was gambled away by her five husbands), it is always the woman who must suffer. Her only recourse is her virtue, and often the gods descend to the human world to protect a virtuous wife, as Krishna does to defend Draupadi's honor. Although Draupadi argues her case most effectively, speaking in her own voice in a male court, none of the men intercede on her behalf. Her dishonoring proceeds as she is disrobed publicly. She is the scapegoat used to humiliate her husbands who cannot protect her. As the never-ending saree spins out yards and yards, it becomes clear that a higher power is at work.[24]

Models such as Sita undergoing a trial by fire in *The Ramayana* in order to prove that even after her abduction by Ravana (through no fault of her own) she is chaste, play a prominent part in female socialization, and are invoked and validated effectively in contemporary mass media. The violent subjugation of women, ranging from rape to verbal/physical abuse in commercial Indian cinema, is perversely and disturbingly popular. Hindu tradition exalts suffering, even death for a husband's welfare. Such values are so ingrained in female socialization that, internalized, they render women alien to their own bodies. In such exilic conditions, women take on physical abstinence and self-flagellation as violent acts on their own bodies, which they hardly own; they watch the violence as outsiders to their own skin and bone. Such alienation also creates physical and mental space for bodily cruelties imposed on women, often in their most fatal form, in dowry-related murders. Even when women face threats to their very lives from cruel and greedy in-laws (who prepare to kill a wife so as to get a new bride and a new dowry), they cannot escape. No doubt there are social reasons for women staying in dangerous marriages, such as the stigma of divorce and the refusal of parents to take their daughters back into their home. However, their already alienated condition, their sense of not belonging to their own bodies, as a result of their internalization of models of suffering and self-sacrifice, plays conscious and subconscious roles in keeping women in situations fraught with risk to their very lives.

Apart from cultural and religious factors at the base of the dowry tradition, there are significant economic and political factors to consider. "The significance of dowry is not primarily economic but political," notes Kishwar in the same essay, "in the sense that it defines a power relation between the man and the woman. . . . Dowry as practiced in India is a war declared by men against women, using women as pawns" (11). Kishwar prefers personal, sexual bodily politics to the economistic arguments that are given for dowry abuses, namely modern demands for material goods like refrigerators and cars. It is not as if "dowry makes a poor man into a rich one," notes Kishwar. "In fact, the richer a man is, the larger the dowry he expects. . . The dowry is an acknowledgement of his status, not a determinant of it." This argument explains why there are more dowry murders among the wealthy than among the lower classes. A more insidious capitalist patriarchy has taken the place of a feudal one.

As with social class, so also with education: the more educated a man is, the greater the dowry he expects (regarded as repayment for his educational expenses). Such a man does not have, as one might expect, a higher consciousness that would encourage his rejecting this tradition. Education rather than challenging sexist codes in society, ironically, can strengthen them. A woman's education is often viewed as an additional commodity to be sold along with her body. Education seldom prevents her from being perceived as incomplete without marriage. But recently, "Pledges in Response to Manushi's Call for Boycotting Dowry Marriages" have encouraged women to denounce dowry publicly.

Many cases of dowry murders reported in *Manushi* show that when women attempt to take refuge in their parents' home, they are encouraged most often to return to their husbands, and often to imminent death. "Most parents would rather see their daughters dead," notes Kishwar, "than have her get a divorce and return permanently to the parental home. Dowry is supposed to act as a bribe to the son-in-law to keep the daughter . . . that is why parents are ever ready to meet with continuing demands made by the husband's family, provided he keeps her in his house" (5). The parting advice to a daughter as she leaves her parent's home at marriage has a macabre ring to it considering the large numbers of dowry murders: "We are sending your *doli* [bridal palanquin] today. Let only you *arthi* [corpse] come out of that house."

The complicity of women in their own oppression is striking and tragic. Mothers-in-law in patriarchy, who attain "male" privilege with age and as mothers of sons, often participate in these horrific acts. Mothers of victims often ignore their daughters' pleas for help. After the horrible truth of their daughters' murder sinks in, some mothers have organized campaigns through letters and testimonies as reprinted in *In Search of Answers*. In this latter text, Manini Das, in "Women Against Dowry," narrates the story of Tarvinder Kaur, twenty-four, who died of burns; however, Premlata was saved because her family withdrew her from marriage when their advance dowry (*sagan*) was met with further demands. The family staged a public humiliation protest to shame the groom-to-be and his family. Das commends the "anti-dowry tone" of this protest especially since "usually the girl's family dare protest only when the girl has died, and it is the murder, not the dowry in itself that is condemned" (223).

Historically, female domination was necessary, note Kishwar et al., to maintain the upper-caste Brahmins' "economic and social supremacy," and such "deterioration of women's status "had a material basis in the maintenance of property within the caste" (65). Property passed down the male line; daughters could not inherit immovable property such as land. They could inherit only movable property such as clothes and utensils, which are hardly comparable to a son's share of land, or a house, or a shop. "The goods given in dowry are not income-generating forms of property," comments Kishwar. Rather they reinforce women's sphere within the household and their financial dependence. Dowry, contrary to scriptural claims that it is provided for the daughter's happiness, in fact, increases her dependency. Few parents would spend as much as they do on dowry to help a daughter live independently without marriage.

Dowry murders, when first exposed as murders (and not suicides) in the 1970s, became significant rallying points for women activists. A wide variety of activist efforts have proliferated over the past twenty-five years—street theater, posters, songs, testimonies—to the extent that there is even a self-critique about the effectiveness of these cultural modes. Madhushree Dutta, a multidimensional writer, director, activist, notes that "Any play about *sati* or dowry is not [necessarily] women's theatre."[25] However, before this kind of important self-reflection and criticism, many laudable anti-dowry cultural modes were used—for instance, the street theater performances of *Nari Itihas ki Talash Me* (In Search of Women's History), are structured around key actions by women's groups, organized around issues such as anti-price rise, anti-rape, anti-sati, and anti-dowry. "Atrocities will increase if we do not speak up" is the overall agenda in this cultural militancy.[26]

Another anti-dowry dramatization is presented by the Nari Samta Manch of Pune, in which a target of dowry murder, Manjushree, survives and discusses her fate: "Could I have spoken out when I was alive? / Did I have independent thoughts to speak out? / Who would have supported me if I had spoken? . . . Today there are loud speeches / Lamenting my death; / Today processions of protest are / being taken out on my behalf." Manjushree analyzes who is to be blamed and ascribes it to the family and to "this society, this culture that has psychologically handicapped us since our very birth. . . . [It has] taught us to glorify the concept that a woman should always be dependent on a male." She ends by addressing the audience directly and placing responsibility on them: "Aren't you all keeping your eyes open? Aren't you listening to what I am saying? I am eagerly and anxiously awaiting your reply. I—Manjushree."[27]

In both traditions of dowry and bride-price, a woman is commodified although there is a supposed higher respect for women in the African bride-price tradition. As Lauretta Ngcobo remarks in her essay, "African Motherhood—Myth and Reality": "Marriage amongst Africans is mainly an institution for the control of procreation. . . . The basis of marriage among Africans implies the transfer of a woman's fertility to the husband's family group. There is a high premium placed on children and the continuity of each lineage. To facilitate this transfer of fertility, a dowry must be paid; not to buy the wife as missionaries have wrongly understood. The dowry not only gives exclusive sexual rights to the man, but essentially it is a means of social control over the children that the woman might bear in marriage" (141–142). It is important to note that Ngcobo uses the word "dowry," not "bride-price," in her discussion. She links this tradition usefully to the ownership of children: if dowry is not paid, the children belong to the wife's people. If dowry is paid, then the children belong to the father and even if he dies, the widow is often married to the husband's brother or another relative "in order to keep the children within the family, biologically and socially" (142). The custom has intricate variations in rituals and regulations among different African groups, as discussed in Maria Cutrufelli's *Women of Africa*. Cutrufelli also discusses the changes in the tradition accompanying political changes, especially when "the transfer of cattle [among the Ngoni] has increasingly been replaced by cash transfer and accordingly the woman has increasingly become a commodity" (50). Cutrufelli adds, "Thus the dowry or bridewealth, which originally sanctioned the marriage alliance . . . has, after the introduction of the money market, degenerated into 'womanwealth'. And, like any other price, it depends on the fluctuation of business, demand, supply, and speculation" (50).

Literary representations of this tradition demonstrate its hold on women's well-being. Contrary to the representations of bride-price by prominent male African writers like Wole Soyinka and Chinua Achebe, women writers like Buchi Emecheta portray the severe physical repercussions that fall upon the female protagonist's body for breaking this tradition.[28] In Emecheta's *The Bride-Price*, when Aku-anna suddenly loses her father, she has to return home to rural Ibuza, where one of her aunts is quick to voice the community's thoughts on her destiny: "They will marry her off very quickly in order to get enough money to pay Nna-nndo's [her brother's] school fees" (38). Aku-nna's schooling in Lagos will enable her uncle, who now takes her father's place, to demand a higher bride-price for her. Since education significantly raises the amount a father can ask for his daughter's head, this is often the sole reason to send girls to school. A similar situation faces Tambu in *Nervous Conditions*, which begins with this striking line, "I was not sorry when my brother died." His death, after all, enables Tambu to go to school. Her father, the lazy Jeremiah, savors the idea, sanctioned by tradition, of getting a higher bride-price for his educated daughter. That is her only worth as a female, not the fact of her labor in the household—raising younger siblings, cooking, fetching water, and performing other female tasks along with her mother.

While *The Bride-Price* ends tragically, Ghanaian Efua Sutherland's drama, *The Marriage of Anansewa* presents a comic rendition of this tradition. Sutherland draws upon the traditional Ananse figure, a trickster who acts as an intermediary to resolve a complicated issue.[29] The daughter's supposed "sacrifice" (drawing upon a universal archetype, as seen also in the western tragic mode when Iphigenia is sacrificed in order to win propitious winds for Agamemnon's battleships) does not end in her physical death; she only feigns death to help her father's scheme. Father Ananse decides to sell his human possession Anansewa, as is legitimized socially. Strapped financially, he hits upon a scheme to use his daughter's physical beauty captured in a photograph to secure not one, but four suitors. Ananse's openly materialistic motives are mocked—his craving for western-style luxuries such as refrigerators, comfortable chairs, invitations to state functions and embassy parties.

The drama opens with Ananse addressing his prized possession, Anansewa: "My daughter, it isn't well with the home, therefore sit down and open up the machine I bought for your training, and let the tips of your fingers give some service from the training for which I'm paying. I have very urgent letters to write" (2). Obvious sexual connotations mark this father's demanding "some service" by "open(ing) up the machine." The expenses that he has incurred in educating his daughter must be repaid by her very body that will be bartered in marriage to the highest bidder. Her body becomes the vehicle for his economic gain as well as for Anansewa's continuing her education. Even before the actual marriage, Ananse can extort gifts and money in return for promises to hold his daughter for a particular suitor.

Ironically, Anansewa is physically the executor of the transaction as she types her father's dictated words to the four chiefs: "All is well with the object of your interest. I look forward to the time when it will come out of my custody into your hands" (8). This "object" commodifies herself as she uses her very hands to seal the transaction from father to husband, as custodian and benign jailer. She believes naively that she is promised to only one of the four chiefs. When she discovers the truth, it is too late for her to extricate her body physically from the intricate web that her father, the spider-man, has woven around her. On stage, the web-screens as significant props are moved around and placed behind each character as s/he is caught in Ananse's web. "Do what it is necessary to do," commands her father, that is, play dead. Ananse will play God the Father and as she feigns death, he will deceive her suitors, and at the right time he will "see to it that she returns to life." Anansewa feigns death as each suitor enters the room and her father loudly laments the loss of "his one and only possession." When the last of the four chiefs enters, the father proclaims "the power of amazing love" and restores his daughter to life. (This plot is reminiscent of Hermione's "statue" coming to life in Shakespeare's *The Winter's Tale*.)

Anansewa's body, whether she belongs to father or husband, is objectified. Is it possible for women to step out of such commodification, perhaps, even in play, to assume the trickster's role themselves? In the Caribbean context, Sistren's play, *Muffet Inna All a Wi*, portrays a female Ananse who plays the trickster role to help and forewarn women against the violence of men in their communities.[30] In a radical revision of a male tradition, Sistren recreate an Anancy who is in solidarity with female efforts to ameliorate their situation socially and economically. The play enacts the violence that working-class women, living on the edge, face in their daily lives, in their homes and communities. As the play unfolds, the female protagonist learns to cope with her well-founded fears of male violence—robbery, rape—and learns to fight back. The drama uses songs effectively as rallying points of feminist awareness and solidarity.

Prostitution: Within and Outside Marriage

Whatever the complex emotional, psychological, financial reasons leading to prostitution, women writers generally represent this "tradition" unmoralistically. After all, it is one type of exchange value where a woman gets paid for sexual services. The boundaries between women prostituted on the streets, or within marriages are often blurred as represented by women writers. In Ghanaian Ama Ata Aidoo's short story, "Two Sisters," in *No Sweetness Here*, both Connie and Mercy, the former, respectably married and the latter, a single, independent woman who seeks rich lovers, are commodified sexually. Mercy who works as a secretary has fantasies of acquiring material wealth by getting a rich man. The other women in her profession do the same. Conservative Connie is horrified when she discovers that her sister is having an affair with a wealthy politician, one who has "many wives and girl-friends." Her husband James remarks cynically: "Since every other girl she knows has ruined herself prosperously, why shouldn't she? . . . I am sure you [Connie] are the only person who thought it was a disaster to have a sister who was the girl-friend of a big man" (98–100).

As a traditional wife, Connie's choice of monogamy and her tolerance of her husband's infidelities is hardly represented as the ideal. In fact, in the Akan folktale tradition of the "dilemma tale," Aidoo provides no single answer, often leaving her endings open-ended, or suggesting alternate conclusions by making the reader a participant in solving a particular dilemma facing her characters. In the oral tradition, the story-teller presents two or more sides in the resolution of a societal problem and leaves it up to the live audience to discuss, debate, and come up with one or more resolutions. Hence, interpreting "Two Sisters" as a dilemma tale, one finds that Connie's complicity within her abusive marriage is as problematic as Mercy's greed about acquiring "big men" and decadently climbing the social ladder. When Connie is pregnant with their second child, she recalls James's abusive remark, even though he regretted it later, during her first pregnancy: "After the third month or so [of Connie's pregnancy] the sight of her tummy the last thing before he slept always gave him nightmares" (97).

Mercy's claim over her own body, her decision to be commodified as one of the rich men's girlfriends is complicated in terms of what this autonomy means. Sexual fulfillment, material prosperity, and social status? When Mensar-Arthur is jailed after the coup, Mercy takes up with the new leader, Captain Ashley. Aidoo reveals the double standards in both monogamy and polygamy for men versus women: Connie is monogamous though she cannot change her husband's polygamous behavior, and Mercy settles for a modernized polygamy, not as a second or third wife within a traditional structure, but as one of several girlfriends of rich men. This new, crassly materialistic polygamy allows only casual sex without any responsibility as in traditional polygamy where one man has to take care of several socially accepted wives.

Urban prostitution as a means of economic survival for women also features in Aidoo's short story, "In the Cutting of a Drink," in *No Sweetness Here*, where the refrain goes: "any kind of work is work." Mansa has left her village and is "lost" in the city where her brother goes to find her. When he discovers her with a painted mouth "like a raw wound," drinking, and clearly trading her body for money, he is speechless. Through the representations of Mansa and Mercy, Aidoo raises the socio-economic and cultural factors that are part of women's decision to prostitute their bodies. These women select prostitution as a conscious choice and are not victims. Aidoo also questions the norms that sexual fulfillment and pleasure may be experienced outside marriage. When women courageously exercise such agency, they have to pay at times with their lives.

Another woman who takes such autonomy over her own body is Life in Botswanan Bessie Head's short story of that title. She traverses the opposite journey from Mansa who leaves her village and lives in the city. Life decides, after living in Johannesburg, surviving as "singer, beauty queen, advertising model, and prostitute," to return to her village "home." Those were her options in the city—all emphasizing sexualizing and objectifying her body, often traded for money. Though the villagers, as is their custom, welcome her back, they wonder how she has so much money. They soon recognize her trade and interestingly "what caused a stir of amazement was that Life was the first and only woman in the village to make a business out of selling herself. The men were paying her for her services" (39). The *cash* value of sex (part of the money economy introduced through capitalist wage relations, and defining human interactions) was something new to the village. What attracts Life to Lesego also comes out of her city experience: "He was the nearest thing she had seen for a long time to the Johannesburg gangsters she had associated with—the same small, economical gestures, the same power and control ... he took his dominance and success for granted ... she saw in him the power and maleness of the gangsters; he saw the freshness and surprise of an entirely new kind of woman" (41–42). When Life agrees to marry him, she remarks: "All my old ways are over' she said. 'I have now become a woman.'" She rejects her former life-style, and her former self, and now, entering marriage, "become[s] a woman" (42).

However, she cannot sustain the "deadly dullness" of daily village life. The narrator describes in physical terms what happens to her psychically: "Something seemed to strike her a terrible blow behind the head. She instantly succumbed to the blow and rapidly began to fall apart ... she had nothing inside herself [this new kind of woman] to cope with this way of life that had finally caught up with her" (43). The language here indicates that somehow it is woman's destiny to lead "this way of life"—as respectable wife, following a routine, and surviving the monotony. Since Life cannot endure this kind of survival that had become "like death to her," she takes up her old ways again, and enjoys her body with various men. True to her husband's threat that if she ever went with any man again he would kill her, he does. Life could not belong to the circumscribed world of monogamous wife whose body is owned by only one man. Lesego punishes her "failure" as a traditional wife by murdering her with a kitchen knife.

Life pays the ultimate price for enjoying her sexuality outside marriage. In contrast, Dikeledi, in Head's short story "The Collector of Treasures" is punished for the opposite "crime"—of withholding sexual service to an abusive "husband" who had deserted her with three children and who returns demanding sex. For women, the public and private are not as dichotomous as for men who desert their wives publicly, yet privately demand sex. For women the public and private come together within their very bodies that bear children: Dikeledi, abandoned by Garesego, suffers neglect and starvation publicly. She deals with this pain privately by a denial of her sexuality, especially when Garesego demands sex. Such an act would be tantamount to prostituting herself for Garesego, and she would rather kill him than accept his "defilement of her life that had become holy to her" during the years that she had struggled alone. For him to enter her body physically is an evil penetration that she will not allow. She kills him, and contrary to the punishment of five years in jail given to Lesego for "a crime of passion" (as put by the judicial system), Dikeledi is imprisoned for life.

Widowhood, Divorce, and Other Non-Traditional Single Women

Representations in postcolonial literary texts of strong, independent single women who are content with their untraditional decision not to marry are rare. Most often they are unhappy and bitter as Bim in Indian Anita Desai's *Clear Light of Day*. One exception is unmarried Lucia in Dangarembga's *Nervous Conditions*. Lucia is a striking contrast to all the married women in the text who are oppressed in different ways—Maiguru, educated and subservient to her husband, and at the opposite end, Tambu's mother, uneducated and poor whose lazy husband is hardly a good provider. Though unmarried, Lucia conceives a child. The family patriarchy gathers to discuss this situation and to determine the father's identity. Traditionally, the "dare" can only be attended by men who gather to discuss a woman's fate, except for the eldest woman who has honorary patriarchal status and can join the discussion. When Maiguru as the patriarch Babamukuru's wife is invited to express her opinion, she chooses silence, endorsing her complicity with the patriarchy. Finally, Lucia herself intervenes, bursts in upon the somber meeting and exposes the men's hypocrisy. She claims Jeremiah, Tambu's father as accountable for her pregnancy. Lucia is described in the text as "wild" and unruly, even a witch ungoverned by social rules. The men fear her since she takes control of her body and enjoys her sexuality. Such freedom is regarded as unwomanly, since Lucia takes lovers outside of patriarchally sanctioned marriage. Such bodily autonomy is regarded as Lucia's acting "like a man."

As a single woman, Lucia does not belong within a patriarchal framework. But she is hardly exiled, ostracized, or unhappy. Rather, unlike the married women in the text, she astutely manipulates the patriarchy to her benefit. She can use her own voice, speak on her own behalf better than the educated Maiguru can. Even if she disapproves of Babamukuru, she is savvy enough to use his position and power to get herself a job. When the idealistic Nyasha is critical of how Lucia grovels before Baba, Lucia retaliates with some home-truths that Nyasha cannot recognize, namely, that if Lucia can attain her goals, namely, to get a job through Babamukuru's influence, and to attend school, then it is fine to "grovel" to Babamukuru. By feeding his ego and pride, Lucia is able to advance herself. She uses her female agency from within patriarchal structures to her own benefit. She rejects male domination in a marital frame, and creates an autonomous life as a single woman and mother.

In most tradition-bound cultures studied here, single women face prejudice, and at times, outright ostracization from community. Since marriage is upheld as the institutional framework within which women fulfill their biological destiny, singlehood by choice is considered anomalous, and pitiable. Exilic psychological states result when women are widowed, divorced, or suffer other forms of aloneness resulting from desertion and abandonment without material support. In these exilic states, women are forced outside a familial and communal circle of belonging. Recent cases that have received media attention thanks to feminist interventions include the sati of Roop Kanwar, and a poor Muslim woman, Shahbano's divorce battle. These are only two of the better-known cases of predicaments that face many women.[31]

Widowhood has a particular history in the Indian context. The eradication of sati has a long history though one might expect this to be a simple matter of banning a cruel practice. However, the matter was not so simple entangled within a web of religious code, low status of women, the power brokering among the colonizers, religious authorities, and indigenous reformers in the nineteenth century. Key events of that history illuminate some of the reasons behind the disturbing resurgence of sati in contemporary times (as recent as 1987 and 1989). The British colonial discourse on sati was framed problematically in discussing the traditional versus modern, religious versus secular. The radical elimination of sati itself was obfuscated. The fact of women being burnt to death ironically took secondary place after other theoretical arguments such as authentic or inauthentic tradition, "willing" or "unwilling" satis.

From 1750 on, when the British established themselves in India, they were aware of the practice of sati, though it was not until 1829 that sati was legally prohibited. The British never intervened to make radical changes in women's issues when such changes threatened, as they inevitably did, the patriarchal and spiritual domination of Brahmins. "In 1772, Warren Hastings, Governor of Bengal had decreed the religious texts of the Brahmins," comment Kishwar et al., "as the sole authority on Hindu law" (57), particularly with regard to marriage, and inheritance laws which have direct effects on women. Ironically, in cases where one expects colonizers to use "reason" (hegemonically preserved as the white race's claim to be "civilized"), they display racism and sexism in their policy of "non-interference" in religious matters.

Among the complex reasons behind a woman's sacrificing her life on her husband's funeral pyre are the extremely harsh, even inhumane austerities enforced upon widows: eating minimal food for survival and not for enjoyment, wearing only coarse clothing, no ornaments, and generally dedicating oneself to the service of children and the extended family. A widow's presence is considered inauspicious, hence she cannot participate in any joyous community events such as weddings and births. Her world shrinks, and she is treated as a pariah and an unfortunate outsider. Without proper physical nourishment and denial of sexual needs, she is encouraged to live a life of complete self-abnegation—rather than accepting this choice of being a living corpse, the fearful funeral flames might beckon her into self-immolation.

The horror of eighteen-year-old Roop Kanwar in Rajasthan committing sati on September 4, 1987 was followed by a rally on September 16 attended by 300,000 people who publicly "endorsed" this event. Although sati is prohibited, the government did not intervene in this "religious matter," their attitude sadly was no different from that of the colonizers' non-interference in religious matters. A massive outcry from women's groups all over the country resulted in an anti-sati demonstration that was counteracted with sati-supporters who were defending their "religious freedom."[32] The root problem of reducing widows to a death-in-life condition, un-belonging to family and community needs to be addressed. Contemporary extra-literary materials such as documentary films provide useful insights—for instance, in *From Burning Embers* made by Mediastorm in Delhi, Uma Chakravarty remarks that traditionalists have made dangerous uses of certain words and concepts such as *agni* (fire). This word is used to give an air of antiquity and authority to tradition. The film itself severely critiques the participation of priests and community onlookers who viewed the macabre spectacle of Roop Kanwar mounting the funeral pyre. The film questions: Who lit the fire? Not Roop Kanwar. She was murdered as a woman, and it is important to contest the claims that her act has made her a *devi* (goddess), or *sati ma* (mother). Her life was taken not by her free will. Priests glorify the act with dangerous mystification as this ordinary woman suddenly becomes a goddess. Contemporary boosts to this "tradition" are manifested in peculiar materialist forms such as the building of sati temples.

From a colonizer's perspective on history, today, revisions of histories from the colonized peoples' viewpoint are revelatory especially in discourses on sati. The British styled themselves as liberators of women from an oppressive tradition like sati, as protecting them from their own sexist men. As Lata Mani argues in her ground-breaking work on sati, the actual law prohibiting sati in 1829 "was the culmination of a debate during which

8,134 instances of *sati* had been recorded, mainly, though not exclusively among upper caste Hindus" (88).[33] Colonial rule, in its "modernizing" efforts, supposedly re-evaluated "traditions," introduced a capitalist "modern" economy, and made progress "at least at the level of ideas about 'women's rights.'" Mani's analysis takes a searing look at both Indian reformers like Rammohan Roy and colonial officials whose discourses colluded in asserting colonial ideologies. She argues that

> tradition is reconstituted under colonial rule, and in different ways, women and brahmanic scripture become interlocking grounds for this rearticulation. Women become emblematic of tradition. . . . [Given] this intimate connection between women and tradition . . . these debates are in some sense not primarily about women but about what constitutes authentic cultural tradition. Brahmanic scriptures are increasingly seen to be the locus of this authenticity. . . . The horror of the burning of women is, as we shall see, a distinctly minor theme. Second, this privileging of brahmanic scripture and the equation of tradition with scripture is, I suggest, an effect of a 'colonial discourse' on India. By colonial discourse I mean a mode of understanding Indian society that emerged alongside colonial rule and over time was shared to a greater or lesser extent by officials, missionaries and indigenous elite. (90)

The colonizers always had power over their choice of native-informants. The British manipulated such information in their insistence that "brahmanic and islamic scriptures were prescriptive texts, containing rules of social behaviour. . . . Further, they could institutionalize their assumptions as Warren Hastings did in 1772, by making these texts the basis of personal law" (91). Such personal law derived from religious texts had enormously negative ramifications for women.

The overlaps and dissonances among "the official and indigenous discourses on *sati*" reveal that women were merely the ground on which "tradition" was discussed; and death for women themselves remained "marginal" in discussions about their right to live or die. The British insistence on "systematic and unambiguous modes of governance, of law" led them to ignore the often paradoxical, even contradictory statements in scriptures. The need to regularize their power was behind their obsession with the barbaric nature of certain customs. Such discourses increased the controls on natives, in this case, they fatally controlled women's destiny.

Similar to Foucault's discussion of how discourses on sexuality increased social controls over women's bodies, the colonial discourse on sati ironically strengthened its practice. One devastating linguistic conundrum set up by the British is noteworthy especially in its continued deployment by neo-colonial leaders in contemporary India. This was the distinction between "voluntary" and "involuntary" satis in the 1813 legislation. Mani quotes from magistrates' records: "the widow voluntarily sacrificed herself," "ascended the pyre of her own free will," she burnt "in conformity with the Shaster" (94). Significantly, the widow's voices are absent. They are contained and mystified in what Mani terms "these overdetermined colonial representations of them" (97). Mani acknowledges that "the mental states of widows were complex and inconsistent" (97); however, the voluntary-involuntary division forces the discourse into a simplistic distinction, and the practice itself is attacked, *only when it is forced.* The defining factors of force are many especially when widows had to face a life worse than death. The division of "legal" and "illegal" satis also provided criteria "for an *officially sanctioned sati*" (emphasis added, 100). The widow is represented as a passive victim, not a subject with agency. Again, a simplistic dichotomy divided widows into what Mani describes as "either pathetic or heroic victims. . . . Superslave or superhuman, women in this discourse remain eternal victims" (97).

The British claim that they were acting in accordance with Hindu religion and this made the abolition of sati difficult. Their devastating equation of religion with scripture rendered the debate into an arcane and academic one rather than one that involves the burning of a woman's physical body. Mani points out that "although scriptural authority was claimed . . . a careful reading of the Parliamentary Papers suggests that such authority was dubious" (100). Further, the scriptures included several different texts such as *Srutis*, *Dharmashastras*, and *Smritis*, written at different times and with various commentaries. So, the British could select particular interpreters of the scriptures, and effectively manipulate sati's religious base, supposedly uncontested by Hindus, both perpetrators and victims. Colonial officials often dictated the terms of how pundits should respond to their inquiries about sati, for instance, they "were instructed to respond with 'a reply in conformity with the scriptures'" (98). Mani notes that "the working of colonial power is nowhere more visible than in this process" (98). (A similar bias is apparent in colonial educational policy, as Gauri Viswanathan has argued, when students were asked to respond to such leading topics as "On the Disadvantage of the Caste System.")

Before it was abolished, officials were content with a "'scripturally authentic' sati, and official presence was required at each sati" (102). Mani argues: "So much for official arguments that *sati* was 'horrid' and its toleration merely strategic! In addition, whatever the official claims to religious non-interference, the process by which knowledge of sati was produced was specifically 'colonial' and its vigilant enforcement thoroughly interventionist" (102).

Mani points out that although officials were aware of the material reasons behind sati, they preferred to focus on the religious side; after all, religious reasons could mystify material realities. The British, to the detriment of Indian women equated "scripture, law and tradition, and the representation of women as tradition produced a specific matrix of constraints within which the question of sati was debated" (91). The British styled themselves as the ones who preserved the "true" traditions by enabling natives to interpret their own scriptures. They "saw themselves as resurrecting an ancient tradition that had been interrupted by the corruption of preceding centuries, but was this in fact the case? Were brahmanic scriptures the basis of law in pre-colonial India?" (114). Brahminic scriptures were privileged and rigidly distinguished from Muslim texts, and the seeds of a deadly division between Hindu law and Muslim law were sown, laws that would virulently raise their monstrous heads and be deployed ironically in religious riots during the partition of India and Pakistan, and later during the Babri Masjid debacle and nationwide riots in 1999, and into the genocide of Muslims spearheaded by the Hindu fundamentalist political party (the Bharatiya Janata Party) in Gujarat in 2002.

Colonial discourse was supported ironically enough by indigenous reformers like Rammohan Roy who opposed sati but also used scripture and the issue of the widow's will to determine if a sati is voluntary or "suicide and female murder," notes Roy, "the most heinous of crimes" (104). Roy's male point of view constructed and constrained by his own time was often contradictory. For him, remarks Mani, "sati exemplifies women's strength of mind and character . . . heroism and resolve" (106), as well as "the opposite claim: the vulnerability of women." Mani sums up astutely: "I am not 'accusing' Rammohan of 'approving' of sati. Rather, I suggest that, even for the staunchest abolitionist, the idea of sati continues to provoke ambivalence. The ambivalence is enabled by the construction of woman as either supreme being or victim. It would not have been as credible given a more complex notion of female subjectivity" (106). At both extremes, as "heroine" or as "victim" "the possibility of a complex female subjectivity [was] precluded" (117). Such representations of the widow "make her particularly susceptible to discourses of salvation, whether these are articulated by colonial officials or by the indigenous elite. It thus comes as no surprise that both offer to intercede on her behalf, to save her from 'tradition', indeed even in its name" (117).[34]

On the other side of such "liberal" discourses on sati that presented ambivalence, the conservative stance on sati is valorized unambiguously. The orthodox faction argued that "the East India Company's criminalizing of sati was based on an erroneous reading of the scriptures." The problem as Mani locates it, lies in both conservatives and liberals debating the sati issue "within the framework of scripture" rather than arguing for its eradication on the simple fact that "sati was cruel to women" (110). Further, both colonial officials and indigenous male elite privileged scripture over custom, and in scriptures, they valorized the more ancient texts. Supporting their stance here was "the belief," remarks Mani, "that Hindu society had fallen from a prior Golden Age" (111). So, both Bentick and Roy could praise "ascetic widowhood" wherein widows "could be true both to the laws of government and to 'the purest precepts of religion'" (112). Mani questions whether in pre-colonial India brahminic scriptures were the basis for constructing Hindu law. Mani follows D. D. Kosambi in arguing against this precept; Kosambi is critical of "the British 'brahmanising' tendency" which ironically granted the brahmin pundits much more authority than their previous roles as interpreters (not the sole authorities, nor the only voices) of religious texts.

When colonial officials and indigenous reformers argue on the basis of restoring to Indians their "authentic" traditions, they view tradition dangerously as timeless and transhistorical. Such analysis can also equate tradition, as Mani points out, with religion and culture, and all these spheres are regarded "as distinct from material life." The consequences of such stances as Mani argues are that sati is analyzed "in purely 'cultural' terms that empty it of both history and politics. Secondly, this notion of culture effectively erases the agency of those involved in such practices" (117). Mani argues persuasively that "women are not subjects in this discourse" (117). She concludes that nineteenth-century debates on women, whether about sati, or education, or other matters "were not merely about women, but also instances in which the moral challenge of colonial rule was confronted and negotiated. In this process women came to represent 'tradition' for all participants" (118).

Contradictory Empowerments of Widowhood in *Phaniyamma*

A fascinating portrait of the continuing cruelties enjoined on widows who live on after their husband's deaths is represented in a text by M. K. Indra, and a powerful film, *Phaniyamma*, by Prema Karanth based on a nineteenth-century true story from India.[35] This film reveals how female sexuality is simultaneously denied and elevated to a spiritual plane. *Phaniyamma* is the story of a child widow who hardly understands the abstinences suddenly forced upon her. Her long, luxurious hair, a mark of her sexuality, is cut off in a dramatic scene, and she is allowed to subsist on the most meager, un-arousing foods. As she herself matures into a woman, maintaining the restrictions placed upon her as a widow, and then observes a sexual encounter, she is repulsed by the very expression of sexuality that she has had to deny even before she could ever experience, not to mention, enjoy it. Phaniyamma is an exceptional woman and she becomes a respected elder who helps other women, especially during difficult childbirths. Phaniyamma is often the only one who with her incredibly small and gifted hands can deliver a child, often saving the lives of mother and child in rural areas with minimal medical assistance. Phaniyamma lives to the age of 112, and the film asserts what I regard as contradictory empowerments that she uses through her extremely harsh life—for instance, Phaniyamma is supportive of a young woman who when suddenly widowed refuses to have her hair cut. She recognizes the injustices of such practices forced upon women by patriarchal authority justified through scripture. Phaniyamma's story is narrated orally to a sympathetic female relative, Banashankari, and is written down by Banashankari's daughter, Indi "who had heard Phaniyamma's story from (her) mother, and had actually seen Ancheyatthe (herself)." The story is thrice removed from Phani, and is a complicated negotiation through the interstices of Phani's own enforced silence almost throughout the text.

I evoke parallels between *Phaniyamma* set in colonial India and *Nervous Conditions*, set in colonial Rhodesia, each text dealing with its culture's particular "traditions" of female sexuality as celebrated, feared, controlled, even mythologized. In *Phaniyamma*, traditional, Brahminical authority rules the rural world; even as the coming of the twentieth century is noted (bicycles, roads, hospitals, schools), the lives of Phani and her community seem totally untouched by colonialism. *Phaniyamma* deals with an illiterate, uneducated protagonist; as a contrast, *Nervous Conditions* explores how colonial education strengthens Nyasha mentally to fight unfair sexism (as enforced mainly by her father), though the same education also alienates and marginalizes her from her own language and culture. Phani and Nyasha resist their oppressions through strategic choices of speech, silence, of bodily denials, and starvation. In *Nervous Conditions* (1988), the disease has a name, bulimia; in *Phaniyamma* (set in the 1850s), forced denials of food are part of the condition of widowhood along with denials of female sexuality. The effects of the resistances in the two texts are vastly different—Phani grows from her silent acceptance of widow's garb as a child, to gaining a paradoxical power within the community. Her abstinences, though troubling from our feminist perspective, elevate her to a highly respected position in the community. Nyasha on the other hand, moves from her open, verbal defiance of her father's patriarchal authority to the fatal silence and withdrawal of an anorexic person. Her life hangs in the balance by the end of the text; Phani lives to be 112.

The protagonists experience outsiderness from their female bodies, each contextualized within their cultures and refracted by colonial prisms. Paradoxically, their marginalities in fact open up spaces for resistance. Phani, as a well-respected widow, supports another widow's decision not to shave her head, and undertake unfair austerities; Nyasha as the defiant daughter, refusing to be force-fed by her father, embodies a contradictory empowerment that serves as an example of resistance to the narrator Tambu.

Divorce As a Form of Widowhood: Muslim Women and the Shahbano Case

Mani's epilogue discusses the contemporary ramifications of colonial discourse on sati, namely, how scripture framed the nineteenth-century discussion on how women were neither subject nor object but the ground on which debates about tradition unfolded. In recent times, Mani cites a landmark decision by India's Supreme Court granting lifelong maintenance to a divorced Muslim woman Shahbano. Shahbano's husband had insisted that according to Muslim personal law he did not need to support her beyond three months after the divorce. The Supreme Court's decision aroused nationwide debate and controversy, remarks Mani, "on the question of religious personal law and the desirability or otherwise of a uniform civil code. The Shahbano case dramatizes the working of the woman-tradition-law-scripture nexus, now complicated by a political environment that is blatantly communal" (119). Mani traces how the Shahbano case raises many of the same issues as the debates on sati. Unfortunately, the notion that woman is the repository of tradition is still held commonly though challenged by contemporary feminists. And whereas nineteenth-century widows did not speak in their own voices, Shahbano did. Even her own voice does not simply make her a speaking subject with free will and agency; in the multiplicity of legal, religious, governmental discourses surrounding the Shahbano case, her own subjectivity is fractured and constructed by each group for its own arguments. Although Shahbano took legal action against her husband, she later retracted when under fire that she was betraying the Muslim faith itself. As Mani demonstrates, arguments from both Muslim and Hindu fundamentalists were problematic in terms of hostility to the issue of gender, and certainly favoring *religious* authority over female well-being. Muslim fundamentalists contended that an attack on Muslim personal law was an attack on the Muslim religion and community. And "disingenuous Hindu fundamentalists," notes Mani, "are lamenting the fate of Muslim women and demanding that they be brought 'into the twentieth century.' (The echoes of colonial rhetoric here are too obvious to labour)" (120). In India, the struggle for a civil, secular code of law continues, though it appears remote especially in the escalating communalism engulfing the nation after Babri Masjid's destruction that led to nationwide riots in 1992–1993.

The Shahbano case had the positive effect of seeking "reforms in specific aspects of personal law" (120). In India, the history of colonial laws is so important because it continues to frame our contemporary lives. A colonial "tradition" that privileged scripture still controls contemporary lives. So, a discussion of women's status often begins "with unqualified references to *Manu Smritis* and the scriptures."

Shahbano is divorced and abandoned after forty years of marriage, a fate similar in material terms to that of losing her husband to death. Shahbano fights for maintenance rights. In their excellent essay, "Shahbano," Zakia Pathak and Rajeswari Sunder Rajan note that after ten years of struggle, the Supreme Court grants Shahbano "Rs. 179.20 (approximately $14) per month from her husband.... The judgement created a furor unequaled, according to one journal, since 'the great upheaval of 1857'" (278).[36] Pathak's and Rajan's discussion of the contemporary relationship between "state or secular law to personal or religious law" is guided by a useful historical situating of colonial legislative acts that intervened in matters relating to family "such as marriage, divorce, maintenance, succession to property, inheritance, and custody and guardianship of children, as well as adoption. [These] came to be known as 'personal laws' and would vary from one religious community to another" (258). The British also empowered the courts to take local custom and usages into account and often passed legislation that was "less liberal than religious laws, as in the case of Muslim women and property inheritance. It was largely due to this conflict that the Shariat Law was passed in 1937. The Shariat Law provides that Muslims in India will be governed by Muslim religious laws in matters relating to the family" (258).

The furor of response around the Shahbano case spurred the government of India to salvage its secular image and to work towards a uniform civil code. Different from the sati materials where the widows' voices are silent, Shahbano speaks in her own voice. However, Pathak and Rajan analyze how such subaltern voices even as they resist "the family's ideology of protection and the law's ideology of evolution" are contained within powerful patriarchal constructions of the very institutions that supposedly protect women—family and law.

Pathak and Rajan trace several "discursive displacements" as they put it, where "the Muslim woman, as subject, is either absent or fragmented in the various legal, religious, sexual, and political texts that develop into a discourse supposedly about her" (260). While these critics keep the seventy-three-year-old Shahbano at the forefront of their analysis, this case has far-reaching legal, religious, and gender implications. Religious discourse argues to preserve Muslim Personal Law however regressive that may be for women; reformers and activists take up "the liberal discourse of secularism and constitutional rights"; parliamentary debates typically walk the fine political line between placating religious and secular factions. Ironically, all these factions claiming to "protect" the Muslim woman, in effect use protection "as a camouflage for power politics.... Where, in all these discursive displacements, is Shahbano the woman?" (260).[37] Hindu fundamentalists use this situation to judge Muslims as backward, and claim "to save Muslim women from Muslim men." Muslim fundamentalists regard this situation as an attack on their religion and personal laws. The government tried regressively to reconcile both sides. Progressive feminist stands are extremely complicated when dealing with a minority community. As Madhu Kishwar puts it in her article, "Pro Women or Anti Muslim? The Shahbano Controversy": "[A] minority community's reactions have a logic of their own and cannot be lightly dismissed, especially if the minority has been a disadvantaged community.... The most important task is to prevent the Hindu communalists from using what is essentially a women's rights issue for the purpose of stirring up communal hatred against the Muslims and other minorities."[38]

Pathak and Rajan even as they note Shahbano's "gendered subaltern subjectivity," probe the avenues of resistance available to her, not through interviews which are translated and sensationalized by media hype, but through "the actions she initiated in the law courts" (266). Although Pathak and Rajan discuss how gender and class intersect with religion in the Shahbano case, they never lose sight of the fact that each "discursive displacement" (from religion to gender, or from gender to class) renders it more and more difficult to "construct that unified and freely choosing individual who is the normative male subject of Western bourgeois liberalism.... To live with what she cannot control, the female subaltern subject here responds with a discontinuous and apparently contradictory subjectivity" (268).

Hence when Shahbano won her ten-year-long struggle and was faced with the furor of having betrayed her religion and community, she had to denounce the Supreme Court judgment and retreat into the "safety" of belonging within, rather than challenging the confines of Muslim personal law. She feels ostracized by her very community that accuses her of betrayal. Such communal "procedures of exclusion" to use a phrase of Foucault's, effectively impose exilic conditions on a woman like Shahbano, and convert her courageous act into an affront to "tradition" and religious authority. Even within Shahbano's shifting positions, Pathak and Rajan find resistance. Shahbano as a destitute and abandoned wife who takes action against her husband "is envisaged as a potential threat to the public peace. It would seem that ironically it is only when a woman threatens the public realm as an excluded figure, as criminal, prostitute, or vagrant, that she fulfills her (anti-) social role" (271).

Pathak and Rajan close with quotations from "feminist and reformist groups" who came together despite ideological differences around the fundamental issue of "the dismally low status of women [as] a reality for all sections of women regardless of caste or community [and] the necessity for affording minimum legal protection to all women" (271). Various women's organizations from all over India joined in efforts to demand a uniform civil code.

Pathak and Rajan assert "a certain cautious optimism" in the light of events following Shahbano: "The first two legal verdicts under the new act have gone in favor of divorced women. In January 1988, Rekha Dixit, a woman magistrate in the Lucknow court, ordered Shafat Ahmed to pay his divorced wife Fahmida Sardar Rs. 30,000 as 'reasonable and fair provision' plus Rs. 3,000 as *iddat* (maintenance) and Rs. 52,000 as *mehr* (dower).... In making these generous settlements, Rekha Dixit was interpreting liberally the statutory provision regarding 'reasonable and fair provision' as laid down in the act."[39] Somehow through all the legal and religious debates Pathak and Rajan succeed in keeping Shahbano "within the concerns of a feminist project—to ensure that the crisis initiated by her does not move away from the issue of destitute women—that the question we posed at the beginning, 'Where is Shahbano the woman?' finds its tentative answer" (275).

Lesbian Invisibilities

In postcolonial societies, lesbians are mostly invisible for fear of violence. Or, they maintain lesbian partnerships under a mystified appearance of "sisterhood." The mystified reality that most lesbians have to embrace in postcolonial societies is that they are "single" and "asexual" since the only socially acceptable sexuality is within heterosexual marriage. There are courageous lesbian women who have "come out," often at great risks to their personal safety. However, the majority have their voices shrouded for fear of physical reprisals by patriarchal authority exerted by fathers, brothers, and sometimes, even mothers who find such homosexual life to be, at best, unacceptable, and at worst, "perverted" or "sinful."

While issues of "coming out," of "breaking silence" have a lot of currency in western societies (not to discount the pain and courage that this process entails even in the west), third world women often rely on more covert means to resist an obdurate patriarchy and age-old prejudice. They may work from within the system to preserve a façade of hetero-normativity whereas their life-styles are the opposite. This certainly places huge emotional and psychological strains on women and there are cases of nervous breakdown and other mental illnesses given this unhealthy scenario of lies and secrecy.

There are various efforts in third world contexts, despite the harshness of patriarchal pressures, to offer support to lesbians and gays. There are women's groups that have monthly meetings, and some have newsletters where women may write personal stories, ask questions, seek advice, even seek partners. Notable among these is *Bombay Dost*, *Arambh* (New Delhi), *Khush Khayal* (Toronto), *Shakti Khabar* (UK). Of course, such avenues of support for South Asian gays and lesbians are more common in the west than in the third world. A magazine like *Trikone*, published from San Jose, California, has chapters in various cities in the U.S., such as, Sangat (Chicago), and SALGA (South Asian Lesbian and Gay Association, New York).

On the Indian scene, Giti Thadani, scholar/activist, usefully documents how the ancient Indian scriptures, namely the Vedas, demonstrate same-sex love, especially in depictions of paired goddesses and gods. Thadani's study of same-sex iconography is path-breaking. She is also the founder of a Delhi-based lesbian activist group, Sakhi. It is unfortunate to note that according to Thadani, "Sakhi has never been invited to any feminist event" (*Trikone*, April 1994, 5). Thadani remarks that there are divisions between feminists and lesbians on the Indian scene. Sadly, even the word "feminist" is sometimes dismissed for fear that it evokes lesbianism. "Sakhi" tries to debunk several such "myths" such as "there are no lesbians in India," or that "Indians are tolerant by nature. Hence, there is no need for either a lesbian identity or a debate about it." Contrary to this myth, Thadani points out that "there have been known incidents of lesbians being killed, beaten, drugged, given electric shocks, exorcised, rejected, and punished in various forms. Further, the old British law on sexuality has been used as an instrument of coercion, often by fathers, to break up lesbian relationships."

Another common "myth" is that "lesbianism is a decadent elitist Western phenomenon and the privilege of only a few upper class Westernized women." As Thadani points out, there are more visible lesbian movements and groups in the west, but this does not mean that lesbians do not exist in India. Further, just as there are reinterpretations of political or literary theories for particular contexts, similarly, lesbianism in third world regions has its own definitions and reasons for visibility or invisibility. "No attempt is made," notes Thadani, "in looking at the reason for the construction of lesbian invisibility or researching into lesbian histories and languages" (6). A noteworthy contribution to research and knowledge in this area is Ruth Vanita and Saleem Kidwai's edited volume, *Same-Sex Love in India: Readings from Literature and History*.[40] This text includes rich documents from ancient, medieval, and modern India that represent same-sex connections, and re-definitions of "friendship" in the Indian context. The book is usefully inclusive of Sanskrit (Hindu), as well as Urdu (Muslim) traditions, and regionally diverse to encompass the subcontinent.

In the spirit of providing testimonials and personal narratives, a polemical piece signed, "Sakhi Bhavana" appeared in *Bombay Dost*. The article challenges several prejudices not only in heterosexual society against gays and lesbians, but even sexism within the gay community. The writers, signed as "Sakhi" also confront the "sexophobia and homophobia" of the feminist movement that does not challenge the norms of compulsory heterosexuality. "The silence on women's sexuality and the exiling of pleasure from women's sexuality in the context of continuing objectification of women for male pleasure and procreation has made it very difficult for any meaningful reclamation of our bodies and sexualities." In an effort to move out of "individual and social isolation," this group, "Sakhi" in Delhi has made "a commitment to work against our invisibility . . . wishing to break out of our isolation. Let us break the official silence and communicate with each other. Dialogue is the first sign of our mutual lesbian recognition" (8).

The inaugural issue of *Bombay Dost* sets out "The Charter" which makes some important points: "To provide a platform for people interested in an alternate sexuality and all its implications" and also lists such worthy goals as promoting community, encouraging self-confidence and self-esteem, providing counseling and information, to network with organizations that support this alternate sexuality, "whether in the Indian subcontinent or abroad." It is important to note also that the last third of the magazine is in Hindi.

In March 1995, a group of lesbian women in Bombay decided to form an organization called Stree Sangam (Women's Collective). The first issue of *Scripts*, their newsletter, presents a playful, popular sound: "the indigenously produced Bombay dykes, edited, supposedly 'written' mostly 'lifted' occasional newsletter." This issue includes an excerpt from Audre Lorde's "The Master's Tools Will Never Dismantle the Master's House." The back cover of *Scripts* lists "Who We Are and What We Do": Active networking with lesbian and bisexual women in Bombay, as well as in other parts of India and beyond. The first national gathering of women who love women was held in June 1996 and the second in May 1998; and a National workshop on Strategies to Advance Lesbian and Gay Rights in India in November 1997. A Lesbian Issues workshop and a Special Meeting of Lesbian and Bisexual Women was included at the Sixth National Conference of Women's Movements in India at Ranchi in December 1997.

An invitation to the Second National Gathering of Women who Love Women, in May 1998 is striking in its title as well as some notes such as "The venue of the Gathering is confidential. . . . Since confidentiality and safety are very important to some women who would attend, *please be cautious whom you tell about this Gathering.* We want to make this a safe space for all women who attend" (original emphasis).

What is striking to me in researching this section is that the prejudice against lesbian sexuality in third world societies often results in seeking support from an international venue. For instance, there are international gay and lesbian conferences where representatives from third world societies are invited and speak out. This is not to deny the dismal and much-needed lack of support to lesbian life-styles on the local level, and in daily life. Even magazines like *Trikone*, though published in California, reach audiences in the third world, and *Bombay Dost* has readers in London, Kerala, New Jersey.

One of the major issues that is discussed in magazines and at conferences is the problem of invisibility, isolation, and the need for community. Within the third world context, the importance of family and sadly, even of family pressure leads to "living a lie" syndrome when gays and lesbians give in to heterosexual marriage in order "to please the parents." Several testimonials, often under pseudonyms note the pain and conflicts involved in such a scenario. In *Bombay Dost*'s inaugural issue, under "Outreach," there is an impassioned appeal that "let us be visible to one another and get to know each other. Let us build a support network through mutual trust and commitment. This would empower us to assert our existence and our right to live in peace and dignity. Let us declare: "WE ARE O.K. . . . At this stage, we are definitely not talking of 'coming out.' All we want you to do is to write to us at *Bombay Dost*. . . . Let us and others know that YOU EXIST" (7).

In getting support from lesbians and gays in the west, Urvashi Vaid's name, executive director of the National Gay and Lesbian Task Force in the U.S., is almost iconic. As a lesbian, woman of color, and an Indian-American, Urvashi brings the issues of race, sexuality, nationality, and class to the forefront. She was chosen Woman of the Year (1990) by *Advocate Magazine* (National Gay and Lesbian Newsmagazine, USA, December 18, 1990). As the Editorial in *Bombay Dost* remarks: "Her presence alone does a great deal for us here in India" (*Bombay Dost*, 1,1, 1991). Vaid is the author of a seminal book entitled, *Virtual Equality: The Mainstreaming of Gay and Lesbian Liberation* on gay and lesbian issues.[41]

The first Asian Lesbian Conference was held in Bangkok, Thailand in December 1991 and was attended by fifty lesbians from all over the world. As reported by *Bombay Dost* (1992), "The 3-day conference contained presentations of country reports in plenary sessions. There were workshops on: Prioritising Issues, Politics of Lesbianism, The Lesbian Family, Lesbianism in History, Networking, among other issues. The realities of ostracism by society, the pain of having to lead double lives, problems of coming out to the family were common to all despite some cultural differences." Also noted were the prejudices by Asian feminists against lesbianism that is put down as a western fad. The conference ended with the formation of Asian Lesbians Outside Asia (ALOA) which would retain links to the Asian Lesbian Network (ALN).

Postcolonial societies have a long way to go in terms of accepting lesbians and their sexual choices, to be partners, and to have families. There is intense pressure on Indian women to have traditional heterosexual marriages, motherhood is usually acceptable only within the marital framework. In the Caribbean, however, children outside marriage are more accepted than in the Indian context. But accepting lesbians remains an uphill battle. In African societies, some of the harshest prejudices are reserved for gays and lesbians whose sexual behavior is judged as aberrant, sinful, perverted, and who face very harsh social stigma. Thus, sadly, invisibility becomes a modus operandi in terms of living one's daily life. What may appear as a simple matter of one's private and intimate life in most western cultures, often comes in for communal and public censure in African and other postcolonial societies.

Given the relatively more open environment for lesbians to create artistic work in the west, diasporic representations by women of South Asian origin are noteworthy, especially in film and video. London-based filmmaker Pratibha Parmar represents lesbian issues in her film entitled, *Khush*. U.S.-based and second-generation South Asian American filmmaker, Nisha Ganatra depicts a lesbian relationship in her feature film, *Chutney Popcorn*, as well as her short film, *Junky-Punky Girlz*. Canada-based Trinidadian-Indo-Canadian writer and filmmaker Shani Mootoo explores lesbian identity in her experimental video, *Wild Woman in the Woods*.

Mystifications of Female Sexuality: A Dangerous "Tradition"

Patriarchal and political interpretations of traditional religion and ritual often control the expression and withholding of female sexuality. Religion is used to mystify female sexuality sometimes to the advantage but more often to the detriment of women. In this arena of mystification, controls of female sexuality in terms of women's fertility and infertility are crucial.

In India, powerful mystifications of female sexuality are ingrained through mythological tales, popular cinema, and religious ideology. Especially in the vastly popular commercial Hindi cinema, incidents of rape and other forms of physical violence against women are portrayed uncritically, and feed dangerously into conscious and subconscious social sanction. Such predictable violences, such as rape, battering, and other forms of sexual and verbal abuse are depicted and popularized in formula films. The message is clear: safety lies in the legitimate expression of female sexuality within marriage, the protection of a husband, and obeying patriarchal authority. Women's groups and magazines produce critical reviews of such films where the heroine is usually taken by surprise when she becomes pregnant outside marriage. Nothing in her socialization or education prepares her for this and conception seems to be magical with a woman exerting no will of her own.

Women's groups work against such mystification, even mythifying of the female body are combated by women's groups through educational materials such as Kali for Women Press's published versions of *Our Bodies, Our Selves* in Indian languages such as Hindi and Gujarati, portraying visually both male and female reproductive anatomies. Such work militates against a socially legitimized ignorance that furthers women's subjugated status. Unfortunately, educational systems encourage a dangerous repression of bodily knowledge, and hence support romantic delusions about male-female relationships. The actual facts of sexual intercourse, conception, and pregnancy remain mystified, and dangerous misinformation is picked up in an ad hoc manner.

Other popular culture expressions of traditionally sanctioned dimensions of female sexuality are depicted in Indian classical dance where the female *shakti* (strength) is expressed with a simultaneous physical and spiritual dimension where the devotee longs to be united with lover and god. The simultaneity of these representations, of intricate uniting and separating of the physical and the spiritual are challenging for feminist analysis. Within the confines of classical dance forms, the female body yearns for the male lover and there is also a transcendental, spiritual longing for unity with one of the deities represented in the song—Shiva, Vishnu, Krishna. Female passion is expressed freely though within the strict discipline of the dance form. No doubt, the content of the poems and songs used in classical dance forms such as Bharata Natyam are within the parameters of cultural sanction—marriage, wifehood, motherhood. Some songs also describe the wanton woman, the mistress, and the unfaithful husband. As in the Greek pantheon, mythological tales describing the gods' foibles and dalliances abound—Krishna can spend the night with another woman, and return to a heartbroken, angry, satirical Radha, who will in the course of the dance express her feelings, work them out, so to speak, and then accept Krishna into her space once again. The wrong doer and the wrong doing are contained within the overarching victory of tradition—of husband and wife, and of marriage vows. The message is clearly that the woman must learn to accept her husband as lord with all his foibles, including his affairs.

A de-coding of the ordinary tales of ordinary women, as the stories in *Lionheart Gal* portray, enables both the story-teller and the audience/reader to "release the power contained in images and create a basis for political action." Many of the stories discuss, often with bitterness, the complicity, ironically enough, of mothers keeping their adolescent daughters ignorant about their female bodies. The mystifications of "let no boy trouble you" hardly prepare teenage girls for the facts of the life. Or, as the narrator in "Rock Stone A River Bottom No Know Sun Hot" is told when she first gets her period: "Yuh turn big woman now. Dis a yuh period. If yuh have *anyting* fi do wid a man, yuh wi get pregnant" (emphasis added, 69). The narrator herself admits that she knows "notten bout pregnant." Several stories poignantly depict the surprise, shock, and sense of betrayal by one's female body. Caribbean women writers reveal the violence inherent in traditions, for instance, socially and culturally legitimized sexual violence within the so-called "private" sphere. The stories, based on personal testimony, explore situations of physical battering, as well as more subtle aspects of irresponsibility when men impregnate women and abandon them to bear the total financial and psychological responsibility of bringing up children. Moreover, many of the working-class women note their complete ignorance during adolescence about their female bodies. A theme which recurs almost like a sad refrain is: "me know notten bout pregnant." Such ignorance itself leads to a kind of powerlessness about any control over their own sexuality. Often, the resulting event of pregnancy itself touches violent boundaries. As Ford-Smith states in the Introduction: "The first word in male power is violence and the last word in female leverage is sexuality."

However, there is a remarkable lack of sentimentality in the women's reporting of their personally painful experiences. In fact, in their own lives, they insist on a demystification of female sexuality, and open discussions of these issues with their daughters. Here one finds a positive re-channeling of history rather than a hopeless repetitiousness of the mothers' destinies being repeated on their daughters. In the life story "Me Own Two Hand," the narrator remarks, "Me try me best fi siddung and talk to her [daughter] and show her di difficulty of pregnancy and relationships wid men. Ah show her di part dat can be good too. . . . It no mek no sense fi have sex as no secret" (174). As the narrator in another story puts it, a mother must "mek sure she and di daughter can reason good" (78).

An ironic situation recurs like a refrain—mothers deliberately keep their daughters ignorant about the facts of sexuality, and then are enraged when the daughters discover to their surprise that they are pregnant. The stories certainly critique the mothers' mystifications about sexuality though they also historicize the mothers' generations and their socializations that did not allow them to talk openly about sexuality. "Rock Stone A River Bottom" begins with the depiction of an intimate closeness between mother and daughter. The mother advises the daughter/narrator: "Be independent. Depend upon yuh own income" (66); along with a mystification about sex: " 'Member seh man a green lizard. Man is a ting weh change. Di instant when dem see one next woman, dem no waan bodder wid yuh" (65). When the daughter unfortunately does become pregnant by "a black man! Wid rolly-polly black pepper head," Mama loses all self-control and wants nothing to do with "dat deh pickney" since "di faada not even have lickle colour" (72). Toward the end of the story the narrator remarks about her mother: "She feel dat by telling me 'man a green lizard' she would prevent a situation, but she mek it worse. Madda fi really siddung and talk to dem daughter inna certain ways of life. Yuh as a madda fi mek a daughter know weh she go face inna life. No just mek she go out deh just go drop pon it" (77).

The narrator places this "personal" issue in a broader sociopolitical framework—color-discrimination in Caribbean society which her mother faced and which convinced her that "Di colour a yuh skin a di colour a yuh mind" (69). The daughter reasons this out: "Mama did really waan lickle teachment for she did backward. Inna Mama time if yuh no white, yuh couldn't go a high school and so all dem tings mussy mek her believe di colour of yuh skin haffi do wid yuh ability" (77). The narrator's words of warning echo from the depths of her own personal experience: "Being a madda meself so young, me never enjoy it.... Yuh can have a bwoyfriend, but yuh no must get pregnant before yuh ready. A fi safeguard yuhself gainst pregnancy. No matter what nice tings a man a go tell yuh seh fi have sex, remember a YUH a go get pregnant" (78).

In the story, "Criss Miss," Prudence is brought up by Goddy and Papa T—her own mother is dead and her father, an alcoholic, remains a distant presence: "See yuh father passing deh!" Prudence was so proper at school that everyone called her "criss miss." Goddy was very strict and taught Prudence nothing about men, so when Prudence falls in love with Colin, she gets into trouble: "I didn't know anything about sex and what could really happen. Colin taught me many things about men and he opened my eyes to the world outside, but when it came to having babies I was really blank. I didn't know that sex caused pregnancy. I just can't tell you where I thought babies came from. I was dumb and ignorant (135).

Goddy's response when she finds out is to condemn Prudence: "Look how yuh try with di girl and look how di girl bring down disgrace pon yuh. What a shame!" (134). Prudence's own hopes of becoming a nurse were dashed—she was 16 when she became pregnant: "I had to put aside my desire for a profession in order to find bread for my child and myself. Having to bring up a child alone with no maintenance was a big responsibility" (138). The story goes on to describe Prudence's desperation financially and for a home—circumstances which lead her to Ralston who turns out to be a violent man. Three weeks after her second child is born, she recalls a painful experience—here personal testimony plays the role of consciousness-raising for other women readers/listeners: "I don't want to talk about it, but I want people to know what young girls meet ... he wanted to have sex with me. When I refused he beat me. He threw me against the boards of the bed and I bruised my spine" (141).

The stories also critique, more rigorously, an educational system that perpetuates ignorance about sexuality for the daughters as it did for their mothers. Within family structures, it seems to be more the mother's responsibility than anyone else's to educate their daughters about the facts of male and female bodies. However, most often, the mothers hide behind mystifications rather than facts. In "Me Own Two Hand" the narrator's mother refuses to allow her to get an education because she is a girl: "Me nah spend no more money pon gal pickney. Gal pickney just a go tek man inna grass head" (165)—a sexist argument that restricts female roles to that of bearing children and not for education that may open up other choices. "Mama never help me," remarks the narrator and along with a sad condemnation of the mother goes a sadness at the mother's own uncritical internalization of sexist stereotypes that prevent her from enabling her daughter to get an education, and to aspire to a better destiny.

Empowering Traditions:
Using Voice, Writing the Body

> "Words the weapon to crucify."
> —Eunice de Souza, "Autobiographical," in *Fix*

In representations of male violence, physical and psychic, women writers use language as a coping mechanism. In Sistren's use of "patwah," African rituals in their dramas, figures like Ni from the oral tradition, many empowering cultural elements are used. During independence struggles and after, cultural productions—song, rhythm, testimony—invoke the ancestors' strength and enable communities to confront new struggles in an ongoing process of decolonizing. The testimonies in *Lionheart Gal* draw upon the power in "the tale-telling tradition" which has always been the "places where the most subversive elements," notes Ford-Smith, "of our history can be safely lodged." She continues:

> These tales encode what is overtly threatening to the powerful into covert images of resistance so that they can live on in times when overt struggles are impossible or build courage in moments when it is. To create such tales is a collective process accomplished within a community bound by a particular historical purpose. The tales and the process of making them suggest the possibility of a unity between the aesthetic imagination and the social and political process. They suggest an altering or re-defining of the parameters of political process and change. (Introduction, *Lionheart Gal*)

This "altering or re-defining of political process and change" begins from within the women's own lives.

In representations of male violence, physical and psychic, women writers use language as a coping mechanism. As with de Souza's "words, the weapon to crucify," so with Bessie Head's autobiographical novel *A Question of Power* that uses the power of language to record the female protagonist's Elizabeth's nervous breakdown, hallucinations, and torment caused by male and female nightmarish figures.[42] The writing itself is one important mode of survival for Elizabeth.

In conclusion, traditions inform and control women's lives from birth to death. Traditions are used to control female sexuality, and to justify such domination. When women confront traditions, they often have to negotiate and work within the boundaries of patriarchal structures such as marriage. Stepping outside of tradition often results in severe reprisals on the female body that may be exiled and ostracized in different ways from a larger community. Women do resist the restrictions enjoined and justified by tradition—some triumph over harsh conditions in unique though sad ways, as the widow Phaniyamma who lived to be over a hundred; others like Ampoma, lose their lives; and still others like Lucia manage to manipulate a traditional patriarch like Babamukuru to acquire employment, and even schooling as an adult. Women writers represent the many overt and subtle ways in which traditions control female bodies. They also depict protagonists who courageously resist these controls, and whether they win or lose, survive or die, their very resistances offer models for social change.

CHAPTER 5

Motherhood Demystified

Esi: Ei, *everyone should come and listen to this [She walks round in all attitudes indicating surprise.] I have not heard anything like this before.... Human beings deciding when they must have children? Meanwhile, where is God?... yet only a woman who is barren will tell her neighbours such a tale.... Why did you not tell us that you and your wife are gods and you can create your own children when you want them?*
—Ama Ata Aidoo, The Dilemma of a Ghost

Forgive me, mother,
that I left you
a life-long widow
old, alone.

> *It was kill or die*
> *and you got me anyway ...*
> *In dreams*
> *I hack you.*

—Eunice de Souza, *Fix*

Control of female sexuality is legitimized, even effectively mystified under the name of "tradition." Motherhood is a key tradition venerated and glorified often outside of its realistic parameters in terms of mothers' actual struggles of feeding and rearing children. Women writers contest such mystification, especially the equation of womanhood with motherhood. In many traditional societies, a woman's sole purpose is to bear children; motherhood is her sole and only identity. As a mother, her outsiderness to patriarchal power is slightly ameliorated especially if she bears sons who will preserve male authority. In most traditional societies, infertility is considered a woman's worst fate because her entire identity relies on bearing a child. If she cannot, she has no self at all, and is often seen as not worthy of living. She is considered a failure by her culture, and worse, since this failure is internalized, she believes it herself. It is as if she is doubly exiled from her body—once as a woman, an outsider to patriarchal power, and next as an infertile woman who cannot fulfill her biological destiny. This chapter contests some of these problematic "natural" and essentialized assumptions of mothering imposed on female bodies.

Rather than glorify motherhood as a personal matter, I analyze it as an institution that is socially, even economically constructed. Mothering is located within specific historic times and spaces, within a dialectic relationship between patriarchy and capitalism, between reproduction and production. Woman's biological functions and their participation in the socio-economic sphere of material production are assessed first, as autonomous categories, and later, as integrally and dialectically related. The task before us, as Michele Barrett remarks, is "to identify the operations of gender relations as and where they may be distinct from or connected with the processes of production and reproduction."[1] I do not wish to reduce the issue of gender to an analysis merely of women's participation in and exclusion from the operation of capital. Rather, patriarchy and capitalism as systems collude in order to perpetuate women's subordinate social positions. As discussed in previous chapters, it is important to recognize the social arrangements of gender, and female socialization into womanhood and motherhood as constructed within the complex layers of indigenous cultures, colonial ideologies of domesticity, Victorian mores and Christianity, and contemporary societies where motherhood enters a new, twenty-first century dimension, namely, its attainment by technological means.

The status and respect that women as mothers enjoyed in pre-colonial cultures shifted with the constraints of colonial gender and economic relations. Colonialism brought new female ideals through the notion of "good wives and mothers" within the home. The separation of private and public increasingly rendered motherhood into a private activity within a nuclear family. Within monogamous, nuclear families, communal responsibilities recede which adds more difficulties for single mothers who may be deserted or abandoned. Often the total responsibility for child-raising falls on mothers which heightens the social, economic, political factors that enable or hinder mothering. Often, female isolation of mothers suits a capitalist economy where the binary division of public/private, male/female, master/servant serves to keep women and lower classes in subordinate positions. In pre-colonial times, power-sharing between the sexes prevented such rigid dichotomies—there was more blurring among these arenas, and such gray areas enabled women to acquire and retain social authority, even political power.[2]

Postcolonial women writers while acknowledging the significant role of mothers, challenge the romanticization of motherhood as motherland, mother earth, woman as earth-goddess possessing mysterious powers of fertility. Women writers' demystification of such notions reveals certain negative, even violent experiences of motherhood. For instance, a single line by poet Noemia de Souza describes her sister as "a servile figure leashed with children." Women writers explore the realistic problems of, say, the expectation of ceaseless childbearing. As M'ma Asana in Ghanaian Aidoo's short story, "Certain Winds from the South" puts it, "Pregnancy and birth and death and pain; and death again" (81).[3] In this story, women are abandoned by their men lured away from their native village to the south, supposedly to earn a living. In such traditional settings, males have more options in terms of leaving than females who must stay behind. The shadow of colonialism also falls heavily on this tale, when M'ma Asana recalls that her husband had left her when enlisted by the British during the Second World War. "He could not take me along with him," she tells Hawa. "You see, he said, since we were under the Anglis-people's rule and they were fighting with the German-people" (82). Aidoo recreates M'ma's memories in a unique narrative form that reflects the orality and call-and-response evocations of a heard story with a live audience: "Ask me, my child, for that was exactly what I asked him, what has all that got to do with you and me?" (84). Now, a similar fate visits Hawa though in the form of postcolonial economic ruin such that even in remote rural areas, money is necessary, and men like Hawa's husband, finding no work, are enjoined to move into urban areas. M'ma Asana consoles her weeping daughter, a ten-day-old mother, by relating her own story: "Hawa, you have a lot of strength. . . . [You were] three days [old] and suddenly [in response to the news that her husband had been killed in the war] like a rivulet that is hit by an early harmattan, my breasts went dry" (55). Just as she and Hawa survived, so will Hawa and her newborn son. Like mother, like daughter, a difficult destiny repeats and yet the women continue with dignity and manage to live, to overcome aloneness, and to rear strong children.

In another Aidoo tale, "A Gift from Somewhere," Mami Fanti endures the awful tragedy of infant mortality three times, and prepares to face the next: "Now all I must do is to try and prepare myself for another pregnancy, for it seems this is the reason why I was created . . . to be pregnant for nine of the twelve months of every year. . . . Or is there a way out of it? And where does this road lie?. . . It is the pattern set for my life" (80–81). After steering the story in one direction, the narrator surprises the reader-audience with this statement-question that recreates a heard orality so characteristic of Aidoo's short stories: "But do you know, this child did not die" (81). As her son grows and goes to school, the mother fondly describes him as "a scholar," and since she "had never heard of any scholar doing it [following the taboos that she believes prevented this child's death], my son is not going to be the first to do it" (83).

An analysis of women's procreative abilities is part of a broader canvas of creativity that is located within culturally specific contexts. Further, the conjunctions and tensions between procreation and creation, between mothering as a creative and/or limiting reality are culturally distinct. Often, women's artistic expression in writing, song, dance, oral story-telling are supported by their procreative, mothering functions as acknowledged in Nigerian Buchi Emecheta's dedication of her novel *Second Class Citizen* to "my dear children, Florence, Sylvester, Jake, Christy and Alice, without whose sweet background noises this book would not have been written."[4] "The notion that this is remotely possible," remarks Alice Walker in an essay entitled "A Writer Because of, Not In Spite of Her Children," "causes a rethinking of traditional Western ideas about how art is produced. Our culture separates the duties of raising children from those of creative work."[5] As Walker points out, postcolonial women writers challenge certain western concepts of creative output such as Virginia Woolf's "room of one's own."[6]

Postcolonial women writers do recognize motherhood as a significant part of cultural tradition, a role that is personally sustaining, and that carries enormous social status and prestige. A different aspect of mothering is also commonly revealed, that is, mothering as m-othering, when the experience of being a mother, or of not being one (infertility, or by choice) is alienating and destructive to a woman's psychic state. Failure to be a biological mother exiles the woman from her body. She is regarded as a failure, not a complete woman; infertility is considered unfortunate, sometimes even a curse. Such views persist even among educated classes in postcolonial societies. Such othering leads to experiences of outsiderness and alienation, exiling the infertile woman, often unfairly branded as such by a community that finds evidence of fertility only in pregnancy and childbearing. Male impotence or sterility is hardly discussed, and if revealed at all, leads to suicide as Amarajeme's in Flora Nwapa's *Idu*, and Kofi's in Aidoo's *Anowa*.[7]

Patriarchal ideology, in supervaluing motherhood, paradoxically contains and controls women. Female lives are governed by anticipation and attainment of motherhood. Even as women writers recognize the respect that motherhood has in traditional societies, they unravel the concrete, daily hardships of mothering within specific sociocultural and economic systems. They reveal the interconnections between female sexuality and motherhood, between biological procreation and sociocultural systems that nurture or repel mothering. Additionally, economic factors play a role in women's fulfilling her role as mother—for instance, the harsh realities that make Paulina's mothering of her son Isaac in Bessie Head's *When Rain Clouds Gather* so tragic are located within economic struggles that force Paulina to send her eleven-year-old child to a remote cattle-post where a disastrous drought claims his life.[8] A different economic reality is represented in Jamaican Lorna Goodison's "My Last Poem": "I gave my son/to a kind woman to keep/and walked down through the valley/on my scarred feet,/across the river/and into the guilty town/in search of bread/but they had closed the bakery down,/so I returned and said child/there was no bread/I'll write you my last poem instead."[9]

Female sexuality has many expressions, only one of which is mothering. Motherhood is one concrete manifestation of fertility, and related roles of childbearing, and child-rearing are performed often entirely by women. Women writers evoke the troubling internalization of patriarchal values where sons are valued over daughters who may suffer prejudice, malnourishment, neglect, or abandonment. Women also compete over sons in polygamous households and make allegations of witchcraft that turn women against one another. Womanhood equated with motherhood, results in conflictual, even tragic situations for women who are not mothers because of infertility, or by choice. Often, even as mothers, they experience the practice of mothering as m-othering and alienating. Madness, psychological breakdown, suicide are some of the violent manifestations of m-othering as represented in texts such as the Ghanaian writer Aidoo's play, *Anowa*, the Jamaican Sistren's *Lionheart Gal*, and the Indian Kamala Das's *My Story*.

Womanhood as Motherhood—Joys and Sorrows

Lorna Goodison's poem "For My Mother (May I Inherit Half her Strength)," celebrates her mother's strength even as she laments how her father, "whom all women loved," the man with the always smile "hurt his bride."[10] Weeks after her mother buries him, "dry-eyed," the pain, love, and loss bubble up "and she cried," realizing that "she did not have to be brave, just this once."

Demystification of the one-dimensional definition of womanhood as motherhood is represented strikingly in Nigerian Buchi Emecheta's *The Joys of Motherhood*, exemplary in its representation of the joys that are experienced paradoxically as the sorrows of motherhood.[11] The protagonist Nnu Ego is socialized most effectively to believe that motherhood is her sole identity as a woman. After bearing several children, and even as she struggles to raise them, she belittles herself in this admission that she does not know "how to be anything but a mother." Nnu Ego's experiences reveal the violent implications in the social notion of womanhood equated with motherhood. A woman is nothing, a non-human if she is not a mother. Incessant childbearing is also a form of violence which consumes Nnu Ego's bodily strength. It is as if she is exiled from her own body which did not belong to her; it is consumed in bearing nine children, feeding them, and dying prematurely at forty.

Nnu Ego faces tremendous pressure to continue to bear children even though they cannot be fed and clothed adequately. She works herself to the bone to feed them—back-breaking work like chopping firewood for sale when her husband Nnaife was enlisted by the British during the Second World War. Nnu Ego is caught in the double standard enforced by tradition, namely that "money and children don't go together . . . if you wanted children, you had to forget money, and be content to be poor" (80).

Although Nnu Ego's social self is totally identified as mother, her ambivalence about motherhood is expressed in her personal ruminations. However, her thoughts do not find social support and hence there is no change evident in the novel. Importantly, her physical strength is exhausted bearing nine children and battling poverty. "'God, when will you create a woman who will be fulfilled in herself, a full human being, not anybody's appendage?' she prays desperately." Nnu Ego realizes that "her love and duty for her children were like her chain of slavery" (186), and she despairs that she "will never be free." In life, she has to struggle to feed her children; even in death, "if anything should go wrong, if a young wife does not conceive or there is a famine, my dead spirit will be blamed" (187). She admits that she is "'a prisoner of her own flesh and blood. . . . The men make it look as if we must aspire for children or die. That's why when I lost my first son I wanted to die, because I failed to live up to the standard expected of me by the males in my life, my father and my husband—and now I have to include my sons" (187).

Although Nnu Ego recognizes her bondage, and the fact that she has accepted the ideological baggage that says she is not a complete woman unless she is a mother, she cannot take action to change this prejudicial belief. What can she do in the midst of grinding poverty and when childbearing does not cease, when she has no way of controlling her own sexuality? Although initially, she wants desperately to be a mother, and hence choses this role, even feels fulfilled by it, the ceaseless childbearing almost takes her body out of her control—she becomes a childbearing body. Womanhood and motherhood become inextricably and dangerously merged in her one body almost to the extent that her identity as mother overwhelms her womanhood, and ultimately claims her life. She is described as "the mother of clever children," "a full woman with children," though the words of Noemia de Sousa seem more appropriate for Nnu Ego as a woman "leashed with children." Nnu Ego's ambivalence about motherhood is expressed in her refusal, after her death, to assist women to conceive when they pray at her gravesite.

The Violences of M-othering

Social Violence of Infertility

In most traditional societies, women who do not become mothers almost automatically carry (though this is not logical since it could well be that their male partners are sterile though they may not be impotent) the stigma of infertility. This severe social and psychological prejudice exiles the woman further from her body that has failed to provide the visible physical marks of pregnancy and child-birth. I interpret this social censure as a form of violence on women's bodies, minds, and psyches. Women writers, even as they poignantly render the sorrows of motherless women, also demystify infertility. They depict how the onus of not having a child falls squarely on a female protagonist, and not on her husband. She is quickly condemned as infertile according to local custom, and not medical facts. In Emecheta's *The Joys of Motherhood*, Nnu Ego is branded wrongly as barren by her first husband who returns her to her father, as is Ira in Markandaya's *Nectar in a Sieve*.[12] Both judgments, harsh and bitter in terms of the woman's own self-esteem and her standing in her community are proven false in the women's subsequent ability to bear a child. However, no social censure falls on those impatient first husbands.

In *Anowa,* Aidoo explores the related aspects of female sexuality, motherhood, and social ostracization because of childlessness. Anowa is condemned as a witch who "ate up" her husband's manhood. It hardly matters in that traditional society of the 1870s (the time-period when the drama is set) that it was Kofi Ako, Anowa's husband, whose participation in the slave trade made him sterile. If Kofi's slave trade wealth brings such poetic justice on his head, the irony is inescapable that the bodily marks of this punishment are borne on Anowa's female body. Physically, as he "expands," and is dressed in rich clothing and jewelry, Anowa becomes more and more emaciated and chooses to wear rags. Her innate sense of justice cannot condone Kofi's getting rich on slave trading.

Aidoo dramatizes the implicit violence in the many culturally legitimized ways of controlling women's bodies and minds, such as Anowa's own mother who instructs her daughter: "A good woman does not have a brain or a mouth"; or Anowa's husband who tells her: "After all we all know you are *a* woman and I am *the* man. . . . You should have been born a man" (emphasis added, 30). Anowa's suicide by drowning, her unanswered poignant question, "why didn't anyone teach me how to be a woman?" tragically reveal that her inability to have children, even though the drama reveals that her husband Kofi is sterile, brands her as a non-woman. Anowa is rendered an outsider without any emotional support. Childlessness renders her into an outcast, an other in that village community. Further, her own devastating internalization of this cultural construction of herself as "a failed woman" hastens her decline and eventual suicide. This is particularly poignant and tragic because Anowa is an exceptional person, and ahead of her time in terms of wanting to work side-by-side with her husband. The community, in the condemnatory voice of the choral figures, disapproves of her being more intelligent, even more courageous than him. Sadly, there is no space for a woman like her within a traditional framework where women must be wives and mothers. The fact that Aidoo selects this nineteenth-century legend (related by her mother "in the form of a song") for dramatic rendition in contemporary times is revelatory. Certainly, much has changed for exceptional women like Anowa; however, as Adioo's autobiographical remarks indicate, educated and professional women face prejudice and sexism in 1970s Ghana: "They had always told me I wrote like a man. . . drove like a man . . . . Since doing anything like a man implies that you are doing whatever it is impressively, it should be submitted that not only aptitude and skill, but also expertise, professionalism, diligence, perfection, talent, genius—are all masculine. [She wrote this in response to one student's remark that her English was absolutely masculine.]"[13]

In the drama, when Anowa confronts Kofi about his manhood, this public humiliation drives him to suicide. He shoots himself, and Anowa drowns herself, appropriate choices for their value systems, namely Kofi's materialism and Anowa's connection to the natural world. The final condemnation, as stated by the Chorus is placed on Anowa—she drove Kofi to death. It hardly matters that he, as a weak "cassava man" as he is called in the drama, and indeed sterile too, led Anowa to such ostracization that she is driven to suicide. He is not blamed for his sterility which is hardly made public in this society; however, there is no acknowledgment of an exceptional women like Anowa. Anowa's fate is reminiscent of Sita's in the Indian epic *The Ramayana*. Sita, Rama's pure and virtuous wife is absconded by the demon Ravana to Lanka, hence her chastity is questioned. In one among different versions of this epic, Sita, upon her return, is required to prove her purity by walking through fire. She appeals to mother earth who opens a furrow in the ground where she welcomes her innocent daughter.

Single Mothers

Single mothering is hardly a matter of choice in the traditional societies represented by postcolonial women writers. This is markedly different from the choices before a very small percentage of urbanized, educated, and privileged women who might chose to bear children through contemporary technological means. Rather, in most postcolonial literary representations, women become single mothers because of abandonment, desertion, or neglect and abuse. There is of course a further irony for married women with husbands who for all practical purposes, and like single mothers, bear total emotional and at times even financial responsibility for child-rearing.

The pressures on single mothers are uniquely different in varying cultural contexts. How society values their women, and cares for children is hardly congruent with the level of privilege or development as evident in advanced capitalist states such as the U.S. that has extremely inadequate childcare facilities that are affordable even to middle-class, leave aside poor women. In more interdependent, communally based societies, women still face grave social censure if they are single mothers because of divorce. In Aidoo's short story, "No Sweetness Here," a bitter custody battle ensues when Kwesi's mother decides to divorce her abusive husband. She runs a tremendous risk in terms of losing her only son to the father's family. And as she feared, the elders make that decision sanctioned by patriarchy. However, Kwesi is suddenly and prematurely taken away from life itself when he does not survive a snake-bite.

The mother in "No Sweetness Here" had endured abuse not only from "a selfish and bullying" husband, but also "contempt and insults from his [other two] wives." Women's complicity in supporting patriarchal authority is revealed in the advice that Maami Ama receives from her own mother, a response to Maami's complaint about her husband mistreating her: "In marriage, a woman must sometimes be a fool" (61). This echoes Badua's remark in *Anowa*, "A good woman does not have a brain or a mouth." But Maami decides to fight back: "I have been a fool for far too long a time" (61). Sadly, she is all alone in this battle—her relatives do not take her "seriously. They feel [she is] only a discontented woman" (61). Maami's grief in losing the legal battle when the elders decide that she must give up her son to his father is nothing compared to the final loss in Kwesi's sudden and premature death by snake-bite. " 'And he was his mother's only child. She has no one now. We do not understand it. Life is not sweet!' Thus ran the verdict" (71). For Kwesi's father, the devastating loss of his son is a kind of poetic justice for his greed and acquisitiveness during the divorce proceedings, and for abusing Maami during their marriage. He is so sure that the elders will validate their shared patriarchal authority and that he will win yet another battle over Maami. But, winning Kwesi has only brought dust and ashes. Materialistic gains are shattered since no negotiation can bring him back to life. The story's final image is of Maami "kneeling, and like one drowning who catches at a straw . . . clutching Kwesi's books and school uniform to her breast" (74). The setting sun at the end of the story takes the reader back to the previous day when Kwesi's beauty (described as almost "indecent" since it is so striking in a male child) made the sunset seem like sunrise "for the care-worn village woman" (63). The play of light and darkness, of life and death, youth and old age resonate as the story ends and Maami needs to find the strength to face another sunrise.

In Bessie Head's novel, *When Rain Clouds Gather*, Paulina carries enormous emotional pressure as a single mother. Paulina is different from "most women" in her village community, and has refused to take on "casual lovers." She wanted a man who would love her and be faithful to her, a desire that seems incredible in that society where most men had several women. So, when Makahaya walks into her life, it seems no less than a "miracle." He is totally different from "Batswana men [who] no longer cared . . . it was a country of fatherless children. . . . Every protection for women was breaking down and being replaced by nothing" (119). Makhaya is a humane and caring person who eases Paulina's intense efforts as a single mother. The narrator describes this as a physical struggle to "hold herself together with her backbone. And there was something so deeply wrong in the way a woman had to live, holding herself together with her backbone, because no matter to which side a woman might turn, there was this trap of loneliness. Most women had come to take it for granted, entertaining themselves with casual lovers. Most women with fatherless children thought nothing of sending a small boy [like Paulina's son Isaac] out to a lonely cattle post to herd cattle to add to the family income" (119). Even when Paulina's daughter tells her that Isaac has complained of feeling cold at the cattle-post, and hence she is knitting him a cap, Paulina holds back from expressing her sorrow and desperation because "all those hot tears might melt the iron rod that was her backbone" (121).

The joy of motherhood turns darkly into the sorrow of loss when Isaac, unknown to his family, already ill with tuberculosis, dies all alone. He was enjoined to perform the kind of work way ahead of his youth, at a remote cattle-ranch during one of the worst droughts in the land. When news of mass deaths of cattle and people dying off like cattle reaches Paulina's village, she sets out with Makhaya to look for her son. Tragedy strikes brutally—all they find is "a heap of clean, white bones lying on the floor. They lay in a curled, cramped position with the bones of the hands curved inward. The white ants and maggots had vied with each other to clear all the flesh off the little boy" (162). Makhaya is aghast at "this terrible sight, confused and angry that there was only this dead, unanswering silence in his heart" (162). He enters the hut alone and prevents Paulina from witnessing the cruel fate that the little boy met.

This horrible sight shocks Makahaya out of his own complacency into recognizing that he loves Paulina, and that he wants to share his life with her, to ease her burdens. He realizes that he needs her and that he cannot be self-sufficient even though he was so afraid of trusting another person in that deep and intimate way after his bruising experiences as a black man in South Africa, and then as a refugee on the run in Botswana.

One of the causes behind Isaac's premature death is the general poverty of rural households. As Barbara B. Brown notes in her essay "Women in Botswana,"

> Most Batswana today are part of a 'peasantariat', people who can neither survive by farming alone nor by wage labor but by combining

both. . . . Arable agricultural production, and women's central role in it—has lost its important place in community life. However, the women's loss has not been entirely to the gain of their men. Control over the means of production has shifted away from the household, away from both the male and female members of the peasantariat. The mines, factories and large ranches are under the control of a small number of foreign and national capitalists. The separation of workers from control of key resources for development is characteristic of Botswana's economic transformation.[14]

Brown also notes that in Botswana, "marriage and family relations have changed, and the value of women's labor has declined relative to that of men." Along with the "changing political economy," women's dependence on men has increased. "Marriage patterns have altered dramatically over the last seventy years," remarks Brown, "chiefly due to labor migration but also due to the spread of Christianity and the commoditization of the economy. Today, not all women marry, though almost all bear children" (260). In accordance with Tswana customs, "marriage is a gradual process with distinct stages during which the couple and their families are increasingly joined together" (260). So, until marriage, a child is the responsibility of the woman's family. Increasingly, with the constraints of modern economy, fathers may be away for extended periods as migrant laborers, often to South Africa. Thus, the woman's burdens in child-raising are increased. In Botswana, as in other so-called "front-line states," local economies were made dependent on beckoning South African mines that exploited migrant labor. So, along with capitalism that enters Botswana as it does other British colonies, this society, in Brown's words "became distorted by and dependent on migrant labor. Migration became a necessity to insure the economic survival of the family, even while it weakened the family" (266) which could hardly function as a unit. And young single women are doubly tied—without extended family support, they need childcare in order to get a wage job.

Brown notes that a single mother past age thirty is not likely to marry; she establishes her own household. "The existence of households headed by single mothers who never married represents a major change in family structure in Botswana. Today, 12 percent of all households are headed by such women. (A further 14 percent of households are headed by widows)" (261). As Brown puts it, "Women are more on their own than ever before, due to the shift in marriage patterns and to the fragmentation of society"

(264). A small minority that have education and wage employment enjoy a new kind of independence, but the majority are "economically vulnerable, dependent either on their own meagre earnings or on their family ties to men who have greater access to cattle and jobs" (264). Almost all of Bessie Head's short stories based on testimonies and village gossip that Head collected depict the breakdown of family life in Bamangwato county in Botswana. "All the background was given to me," notes Head, "by women who rear(ed) illegitimate children on their own."[15] Men who father children refuse to take responsibility and commonly abandon the woman and the child. However, Head's stories also represent good men like Paul, described as "a poem of tenderness" in "The Collector of Treasures."

Economic changes have redefined social relations and family obligations as Barbara Brown points out: "The rural family, under its male head, is no longer the key unit of production. People now work for cash wages that they earn as individuals while geographically separate from their families. This process of individualization increases the vulnerability of women. In the past, many redistributive mechanisms existed. The extended family was expected to help those in need. . . . These changes have resulted principally from the commoditization of the economy. Cash from wage employment and cattle sales have grown" (262). In this new market economy, money determines human relations more than in previous subsistence systems that are, of necessity, more humanly interdependent. "The penetration of capitalist relations of production has altered old forms of cooperation and exchange," remarks Barbara Brown. "Goods formerly exchanged on the basis of kinship or need are now bought and sold for cash" (263).

A different kind of violence is evident in keeping women deliberately ignorant of the facts of male and female sexuality, or giving false and mystified information, hence pregnancy and conception take them, as in the Jamaican life stories in *Lionheart Gal*, completely by surprise.[16] Often, these working-class women have no financial or emotional support for this major life-change. The violence of ignorance that brought them into pregnancy often continues in the violence in their having to resort to sex in order to feed themselves and their children. Adolescent women hear mystified notions of male sexuality such as: "man a green lizard," that is meant to instill fear rather than impart essential biological facts. Many of the stories discuss, often with bitterness, the complicity, even direct responsibility, ironically enough, of mothers keeping their adolescent daughters ignorant about their female bodies. The mothers, however, are within the purview of an accepted cultural tradition of repression. But their deliberate withholding of knowledge about physical biology is tantamount to disaster in terms of their daughters' future lives—education, employment, and financial burden. The mystification of "let no boy trouble you" hardly prepares teenage girls for the facts of life. Many of the Sistren story-tellers record how they have tried to change this repeated destiny when as mothers themselves, they do not deprive their girl-children of crucial biological facts.

Such mystification of the facts of male and female sexuality is rife in other traditional cultures. "Mamas never mentioned menses" is one of the lines in Eunice de Souza's poem, "Sweet Sixteen." The poetic persona wonders if she could get pregnant by simply dancing with a man. The response from the speaker, "I, sixteen, assured her, you could," fills the adolescent with false information and false dread—even touching a man might make her pregnant.

Sistren stories also demonstrate the failure of an educational system that does not teach the facts of sexuality to its female and male populations. In discussions with Sistren members, I learnt about their first drama, *Bellywoman Bangarang*.[17] The play deals with the theme of teenage pregnancy and effectively demystifies female roles such as the nurturing mother, mother/daughter relationships, and privatized notions of motherhood. One of the characters, Didi wants to create a different kind of life than the struggles she saw her own mother undergo: "Mi no waan do like mi madda, das all mi know. Mi nah inna no struggle fi find food fi give no baby.... Den if yuh no have baby, yuh no woman?" to which Patsy replies, "Yes" (21). As in other Sistren plays, the stories are drawn from working-class women's own testimonies, through elaborate strategies of re-memorying painful aspects of their own past, and by sharing those experiences through oral conversation, song, dance, gesture, they take a first step toward a healing process. One woman's memory triggers a similar one for others in the group, and through intense workshop participation and dramatic role-playing, improvisational group-work, the raw material is derived. Later, this is shaped into an artistic structure that interweaves dialogue, song, gesture, and mime. The language, in recreating working-class women's spoken patwah, retains the intimacy and authenticity of their experiences.

In *Bellywoman Bangarang*, the pregnant girls in the fifteen-year-old range have been through physical and emotional violence—one is thrown out of the house by her godmother, another, seven months pregnant, goes into labor as the result of a fight. Toward the end of the drama, Marie gives birth helped by the three mothers, and Didi thinks back to her own mother who loved her, and who also caused all her problems: "When yuh finish drink eye water fi breakfast, lunch and dinner, yuh eyes dry like cane trash and clear like river water. Mama bring me come. Is she me did know as di one dat feed mi, clothe mi, love mi. It did seem like she cause all mi problems. Tru mi couldn't go a school, and she overwork me inna di yard. Mi run away from her to town, to mi fadda. Inna di tenement yard tings get worse. . . . Now mi child is born. Him come offa my navel string, but him belong to all a we. And his labour just begin" (51–52).

The women all join in the song, "Madda, di great stone got to move/ Madda, di great stone got to move/ Madda, di great stone/ Di stone of Babylon/ Madda, di great stone got to move." Along with the struggle of these teenage mothers whose lives change drastically once they have a child, the drama also includes the problems faced by overworked nurses and a generally inadequate health service. The pregnant women bond with the nurses' struggles and offer their support. The women also hold each other through this trying time when they face this major life-change all alone—and they are themselves not fully adults. They share the little that they have such as baby clothes. When the nurse informs them that they are being discharged and that "the way out is, go down the corridor and turn left . . ." Marie responds, "Thank yuh, nurse. We know our way from here." The chorus enters and a song about the multiple meanings of "we know our way from here," concludes the play: "We have conquered frustration/ We have conquered tribulation/ Through all our ups and down/ We've learned our lessons well . . . We know our way from here./ Join hands together/ Helping one another/ Working together/ On our way from here" (53–54). The play script includes a "discography" with musical notation for the fifteen songs, set to different folk rhythms such as calypso, reggae, and kumina and songs "adapted from the repertoire of Jamaican ring games."[18]

As represented in *Bellywoman Bangarang* and in *Lionheart Gal*, the burden of mothering, financial and psychological is borne almost solely by women. For the most part, the "baby-fathers," as the patois phrase puts it, are absent. Women put up with violent and destructive men often only to get food for their children. They undertake enforced migrations to cities also to earn money for children.

Whether women manage reasonably well or disastrously as single mothers reveals a lot about their society, cultural attitudes to women, and economic state support. As unmarried and pregnant, women face social prejudice and often cannot attend school. This is an example of social violence that actively prevents women from being independent. Uneducated, or undereducated, they remain dependent on men. This scenario perpetuates poverty and keeps women downtrodden.

Women writers give new meanings to "the personal is political" cliche. "Private battering" and forced impregnation after which the men irresponsibly leave the women to bear the total financial and psychological burden of bringing up children, such as expressed in many of the *Lionheart Gal* stories are social and political matters of the greatest urgency. How are these children to be supported financially? What is the father's responsibility? These stories reveal that sexual violence within the so-called "private" sphere is socially and culturally legitimized.

In the fifteen stories, based on oral testimony/interview, many of the working-class women note their complete ignorance during adolescence about their female bodies. A theme which recurs almost like a sad refrain is, "me know notten bout pregnant." Such ignorance itself leads to a kind of powerlessness about any control over their own sexuality. Often, the resulting event of motherhood itself touches violent boundaries. "The first word," remarks Ford-Smith in her Introduction, "in male power is violence and the last word in female leverage is sexuality." Women tolerate such physical and psychological abuse in order to provide the barest necessities to their children. The amount and kinds of violence that women endure and tolerate are markers of women's status in that society. When battering for instance is not only tolerated but expected and abetted, that indicates the low respect women have in that culture.

However, there is a remarkable lack of sentimentality in the women's reporting of their personally painful experiences. In fact, in their own lives, they insist on a demystification of female sexuality, and open discussions of these issues with their daughters. Such change expresses a positive re-channeling of history—not a hopeless repetitiousness of the mothers' destinies being repeated on their daughters.

Sistren stories document women's incredible struggles to feed and clothe their children as single mothers. Often the pressures are so intense that children are abandoned, as documented in Erna Brodber's sociological study entitled *Abandonment of Children in Jamaica*. Brodber analyzes and "comment[s] on the alleged increase of abandonment of children in Jamaica."[19] The study explores some reasons behind mothers abandoning children, and the role and responsibility of government agencies dealing with this problem. Although Brodber gathers data on the reasons behind such drastic decisions as leaving a newly born child "in the elements," which includes a busy footpath, someone's car, a doorstep, or public hospitals, there is minimal discussion of male responsibility. Men who father children must be held as accountable as the women for child abandonment. Out of 208 women interviewed, "92 were in visiting unions, 92 in common-law unions and only 8 were married" (11). Clearly, monogamous marriage is not a cultural norm despite even draconian measures enforced by colonial practices such as mass marriages (study by Joan French discussed in chapter 4). Often, rural women come into urban Kingston, " 'lie in' at Jubilee Hospital," give a false address to the hospital, abandon the child, and return "innocently home to the rural areas" (14). One important factor that Brodber's study investigates is the type of support the mother has during pregnancy which would make it likely or unlikely for her to take the decision to abandon a child that she has just given birth to. In hospitals, "nursemaids who formerly helped mothers with their luggage were sometimes literally 'left holding the bundle'. After lunch mothers usually rest unsupervised. Security officers rarely question a person leaving and even more rarely those leaving in taxis. These circumstances provide opportunities for those who need it to leave the institutions without their babies" (23).

In cases where the "baby-father" is unemployed, or emotionally unsolicitous about the mother, abandonment usually follows. Often, a pregnant daughter, contrary to the stereotypical image of the caring and nurturing mother who will accept the daughter at any cost, is thrown out of the house by her own mother. There are complicated moral and financial reasons behind such harsh behavior recorded in Sistren's life stories. There is no social structure that will accept a child, as in several African cultures where the child belongs not only to the parents but to the extended kin-group, and the responsibility for rearing a child is shared more communally than individually. However, in Jamaica, "rights over a child are vested not in a lineage group but in the natural parents who, with migration to urban areas, can shed even the informal sanctions of the kin group" (23). A child belongs only to the biological parents, and even more "as purely personal biological functions of the mother's body," comments Brodber. So, the child is branded to a "social non-existence" (23).

Abandonment of Children in Jamaica focuses only on women as is a common strategy in most governmental policies that have to do with family planning or children. A similar scenario prevailed at one of the sessions of the Fourth National Conference of Women's Movements in India in Calicut. At the session entitled "National Development and Planning," a female government employee described how most contraceptive programs are geared to women who are regarded as solely responsible if they become pregnant. There was no attempt to educate the male counterparts in the whole process of conception.[20] In the Jamaican context, Brodber notes the need to socialize men and women in terms of parenting responsibilities, and to go to the root of the problem of abandonment rather than dealing with it, as the state does, only in crisis mode, and only after an unwanted child is born. This socializing should be part of the responsibility of schools and parents. In the Sistren stories, single mothers try to educate their children, not abandoning them as several of them had been, in the emotional if not physical sense in terms of being kept deliberately ignorant about the facts of sexuality, and being taken by surprise at their pregnancy.

Brodber's study is sensitive to "the social-psychological circumstances of the abandoners" with the goal of "eradicating" this social problem, which is a drain on government resources. "It costs the State at least [Jamaican] $7 per week to maintain one of its wards. The maintenance of 134 children for 18 years means nearly J$1 million of taxpayers' money" (6). Not to deny the economic drain of this situation, I would argue that there are deeper, more scarring psychological effects especially on the abandoned children who may face neglect and abuse, and who as adults often repeat their parents' irresponsible behavior. "The act of abandonment," remarks Brodber, "has nuisance as well as economic value for the general public" (6). The irony of this situation is that economically, these children often get better care in terms of housing, schooling, and food than Jamaican children with struggling single mothers. Economic deprivation is often the sole reason for abandonment which presents extremely difficult and unfair choices before the single mother—loving a child but not being able to provide for its bare necessities, or giving up the child so that the state can care for its physical needs. There is no simple solution, moral or financial.

Brodber's study also includes children who are "neglected, ill-treated, assaulted [who] may, like those abandoned fall within the general category called by the officials of the machinery 'in need of care and protection'" (25). In this category there are more boys than girls who are "uncontrollable." A curious cultural prejudice in this Caribbean context is that more boys than girls are abandoned, and there are more custody disputes seeking rights over female rather than male children. Brodber remarks that this indicates "a cultural reluctance to care for male children" (47).

The exact opposite is true in India where more female than male children are abandoned, given up for adoption, malnourished, and mistreated as inferior beings. Such social prejudice, enshrined culturally, even in scripture in the Indian context entails forms of violence in terms of mothering and the destiny of girl children. One of the worst forms of violence is in the abuse of amniocentesis used not to detect medical problems but to abort female fetuses. Women's groups and activists have mounted serious campaigns against these sex-selective abortions.

The "tradition" of sacrificing females for any number of reasons goes back to the Greek tragedy of *Agamemnon* that has at its root the unfair and violent sacrifice of Agamemnon's daughter Iphigenia in order to propitiate the gods and get favorable winds for the ships. In Bessie Head's story, "Looking for a Rain God" in *The Collector of Treasures*, two young girls are murdered in order to "make rain." The story relates the harshness of surviving a drought and how the adults' nerves are stretched to breaking point: "It was the women who finally broke down under the strain of waiting for rain. It was really the two women who caused the death of the little girls. . . . After it was all over and the bodies of the two little girls had been spread across the land, the rain did not fall" (59). The narrator is deeply sympathetic to what is described as "the subtle story of strain and starvation and breakdown" which was "inadmissible evidence at court" when the family is arrested for "ritual murder." It was against the law "and must be stamped out with the death penalty." The other villagers, even as they are struck with horror at the killing of the girls, "admit in their hearts that only a hair's breadth had saved them from sharing a fate similar to that of the Mokgobja family. They could have killed something to make the rain fall" (60). Characteristically, Head's philosophical vision even as it explores the horror of ritual murder, also situates it within the extremely strenuous scenario of drought, starvation, physical and mental collapse of bodies and moral values.

Hurt Children

The phenomenon of hurt, neglected, abused children enables a demystification of the romanticized, nurturing, all-providing mother. Jamaican Olive Senior's short story, "Bright Thursdays," depicts the poignant plight of the child Laura who craves recognition and love from her white father, Mr. Bertram "of high estate."[21] He abandons Myrtle, the black mother after indulging in sex and making her pregnant. Although Laura is born with dark skin, she has straight long hair, and "white features" which make her mother fantasize about the social possibilities the daughter will have in that class-color ridden society. "She grooms her daughter for the role she felt she would play in life," and Myrtle regards the white blood as "a gift" in the child's heritage. Such internalization of class-color privilege is sadly not uncommon, especially since Myrtle has two sons as well that she raises as a single parent. Economic hardships and hopes of a privileged life of opportunities that the white half of Laura's heritage may provide are poignant factors that make a mother like Myrtle want to give away her daughter. So, she approaches Miss Christie, Laura's white grandmother who feels some responsibility for her son's irresponsible action. Myrtle's "grooming Laura for a golden future" only makes the child alienated from others, "supremely conscious of being different from the children around her, and she soon became withdrawn and lacking in spontaneity" (41).

Miss Christie agrees to take Laura in and "was busy planning the child's future" which included the imbibing of middle-class values, decent clothes, correct speech, "erasing her country accent, teaching her table manners, getting her to take a complete bath every day—a fact which was so novel to the child who came from a place where everyone bathed in a bath pan once a week since the water had to be carried on their heads one mile uphill from the spring" (43–44). Quite a change for Laura who herself as a child has no say in her destiny. She is like a blank, silent space to be written upon, first by an ambitious mother who wants to climb the social ladder through her daughter's parentage, and next, by a white grandmother who trains her like an animal but does not show her any affection. "She wandered from room to room and said nothing all day, for now her lips were sealed from shyness. To her newly sensitised ears, her words came out flat and unmusical and she would . . . silently beg pardon for being there" (46–47). Sadly, Laura feels abandoned by both biological parents—the non-existent father, and her mother who decides that living with the white folks means "a new life . . . [and] opportunity." Laura must not let her mother down: "Chile, swallow yu tongue before yu talk lest yu say the wrong thing," her mother says, implying also that Laura's working-class, patios accent will be frowned upon in that white world.

When the absent father comes from his new home in New Jersey with his wife, Laura is filled with hope and trepidation: "How does one behave with a father? Laura thought. She had no experience of this. There were so few fathers among all the people she knew" (50). Sadly, her father did not see her or talk to her; she consoled herself that his "indifference was merely part of a play" and that he would claim her. But with stark cruelty, he tells his mother to "stop fussing so much about the bloody little bastard" (53). These words cut Laura more deeply than a physical blow and she "heard no more, for after one long moment when her heart somersaulted once there was no time for hearing anything else for her feet of their own volition had set off at a run down the road and by the time she got to the school gates she had made herself an orphan and there were no more clouds" (53). The narrator's striking use of the word "orphan" resonates accurately with Laura's plight as a child truly abandoned by both parents, a father who refuses to acknowledge her as his daughter, and a mother who wants her to be someone else by climbing the class ladder. As an "orphan," she is not only parentless, but additionally exiled from her own mixed heritage, belonging to neither and forced to become an outsider.

"Bright Thursdays" is critical certainly of the father's irresponsible behavior, but also demystifies the motherness that is blinded by class aspirations for her daughter. Myrtle abandons Laura in a manner of speaking. Although, in the Caribbean context, non-nuclear family structures are more the rule than the exception, this situation is different—the child is abandoned. Merle Hodge remarks in an interview about "Caribbean family forms," "Almost all of us are socialized—even those who had a mother and a father as I did—in a family framework which has nothing to do with the traditional nuclear family. . . . Children are shared by a network of households, which makes nonsense of this business about nuclear family—that you belong to two people alone, and these are the only people who can discipline you."[22] Hodge's analysis is also somewhat idealized given the harsh realities described in Brodber's interviews with women who feel so isolated that they chose to abandon their child.

In her essay, "The Shadow of the Whip: A Comment on Male-Female Relations in the Caribbean," Hodge presents a darker view of the violence in Caribbean society that often comes down on children.[23] "Drastic brutality—physical and verbal—upon children is an accepted part of child rearing in the Caribbean." Hodge traces the roots of such a scenario historically: "Caribbean society was born out of brutality, destructiveness, rape; the rape of the Amerindian peoples, the assault on Africa, the forced uprooting and enslavement of the African; the gun, the whip, the authority of force" (113). Hodge comments that Caribbean society "has never adequately come to terms [with] the legacy of violence and disruption."

Exilic Breakdowns, M-othering, and State-Sponsored Violence

A different parameter of violent m-othering is represented in state-sponsored violence that interrupts Elizabeth's mothering in Bessie Head's autobiographical novel, *A Question of Power*. How, when, and through what trajectories female protagonists sustain motherhood are conditioned by their socialization, how they are constituted by particular sociocultural norms, education, and economic privilege or hardship. In this section, I explore two texts, vastly separated geographically, and in style and tone, but in both autobiographical fictions the experience of mothering is interwoven with the protagonists' nervous breakdowns—South African/ Botswanan Head's most autobiographical novel, *A Question of Power*, and Indian Kamala Das's text *My Story*.[24] In both texts, the woman's exilic condition in patriarchal culture deepens in terms of her double exile as mother in situations that are profoundly alienating. Elizabeth is a walking volcano whose m-othering role is inscribed on her broken body and mind. Her breakdown is located concretely in terms of how it is instigated from the outside, from external, artificial, state-sponsored hierarchizations by race, education, gender, class in apartheid South Africa. Similar gender and class hierarchies prevail in Das's text. A dialectic interplay between the forces inside and outside women's consciousness reveals the very social ground of race, sex, and class realities, such as Head's and Das's specific contexts on which mothering or m-othering stands.

Head's personal history expressed in an autobiographical piece in *Ms. Magazine* starts like this: "I was born on the sixth of July, 1937, in the Pietermaritzburg Mental Hospital, in South Africa. The reason for my peculiar birthplace was that my mother was white, and she had acquired me from a black man. She was judged insane, and committed to the mental hospital while pregnant. Her name was Bessie Emery and I consider it the only honor South African officials ever did me—naming me after this unknown, lovely, and unpredictable woman."[25] State-sponsored violence, and state dictates in terms of even the possibility of practicing motherhood or not is demonstrated vividly in Head's case. Her mother is not allowed to raise her child since she is judged "insane" by a medical establishment that capitulates to the racist rules of the apartheid regime. The child is shunted from one foster home to another, and never wholly accepted since she was "colored"; the mother commits suicide when her daughter is six. Young Bessie grew up as an "outsider," on the margins of both color spectrums. Her mother's sad history unfairly brands the daughter. As Adetokunbo Pearse comments, Head "depicts childhood experiences as central to the mental makeup of the adult . . . but the emphasis is on society, the situation of the parents in it, and how these become instrumental in the social instability, as well as the mental imbalance of the protagonist later on in life."[26]

As a child, Head is stigmatized because her mother was branded "insane." As Pearse remarks, "there is no clear indication that the woman was actually mad" (82). This is used by those establishment authority figures who terrify Elizabeth about her own "inherited," and hence "inescapable" impending doom, as when the missionary school Principal, "a gaunt, incredibly cruel woman" remarks casually to the child: "We have a full docket on you. You must be very careful. Your mother was insane. If you're not careful you'll get insane just like your mother. Your mother was a white woman. They had to lock her up, as she was having a child by the stable boy, who was a native" (16).

The question of sanity and insanity is determined by the apartheid state and its racist Immorality Act of 1957 which prevented sexual relations between whites and blacks. Whatever the real condition of Head's sad mother, the stigma of being named insane by the state powers is enough to propel her daughter into emotional trauma. She is a half-caste, rejected by both families. Her illegal status from the time of her birth seems to pursue her into adulthood when Head herself leaves South Africa on an exit-permit which meant that she could never return until the recent repeal of all apartheid laws and the return of political exiles. Sadly, Head did not live to experience the exhilaration of Mandela's assumption of leadership in South Africa.

In 1964, Head relocated outside the geographical boundaries of what she described as "the unholiest place on earth," and moved to neighboring Botswana. Elizabeth, like Head, goes to Botswana in search of peace, away from the "permanent nervous tension" (19) experienced by people in South Africa. Head regarded herself, like "innumerable people of [her] generation scattered throughout the world as refugees." In the same autobiographical piece, she notes that "the Botswana government turned out to have an extremely hostile policy toward South African refugees. In 1966 they put us on a police roll, and from then to this day I have been reporting to the police every week" (73). Head faced incredible emotional and psychological strains of not belonging anywhere; she called herself "a stateless person," one who "never (had) a country, not in South Africa or in Botswana" or anywhere else.

Self-exiled Head, through the experience of her own difficult life recreated in *A Question of Power* illuminates the social and racial roots of psychological collapse. The concrete realities of Head's geographical (as exile) and linguistic (as non-Setswana speaker in Botswana) marginalizations took a severe toll as evident in her difficult life and early death at age forty-eight. Kamala Das's *My Story* illuminates the traumas of a female subject who experiences forms of personal exile from her body, similar to and different from Head's. Das's persona is part of an economically privileged class. Like Elizabeth, she undergoes depression, breakdown, self-destructive fantasizing. She feels imprisoned within the status and privilege of middle-class wife and mother. Both writers explore their female protagonists' conditions of marginality—in Head's novel, these marginalities are determined along racial, national, and linguistic lines. Elizabeth is doomed to be an outsider by color, language, and nationality; Das is confined by class privilege, by self-victimization embedded in her female socialization that dangerously equates wifehood with suffering, that upholds ideals of subservient, self-sacrificing women from Hindu myths and epics.

Motherhood as Choice: Technological Mothering, Options and Abuses

Modern medicine is both a boon and a dubious blessing as represented in Aidoo's short story, "The Message" in *No Sweetness Here*. Aidoo's rootedness in Akan oral traditions and folk forms serves her creativity in experimenting insightfully with, and in mixing literary forms of prose, poetry, and drama in her short stories. As in drama, characters appear in Aidoo's stories fully formed, at times without names, at times playing the role of communal, choral commentators, at other times, engaged in a lively discussion of some dilemma facing society. "The Message" opens with a striking medley of voices discussing, dialoguing, repeating, and trying to figure out exactly what has been conveyed to Maami Amfoa in "this ten-gram [telegram] thing":

> "Look here my sister, it should not be said but they say they opened her up."
> "They opened her up?"
> "Yes, opened her up."
> "And the baby removed?"
> "Yes, the baby removed."
> "I say . . ."
> "They do not say, my sister."
> "Have you heard it?"
> "What?"
> "This and this and that . . ."
> "A-a-ah! that is it . . ." (38)

Aidoo does not name these communal voices; their identities are conveyed in their anxious voices as they introduce the story before we meet Maami Amfoa. The suspense is built almost to the end of the tale when we are relieved to learn that Maami's only grand-daughter has survived giving birth to twins by caesarean section.

In contemporary times, medicine intervenes to give women choices, and also control their bodies. The contradictions of increasing a woman's autonomy over her body go along with the abuses of certain technologies such as the uses of amniocintesis to abort female fetuses in India. Women's activist groups attempt to foster greater knowledge about women's bodies—for instance, *Manushi* reports on women's health issues in India as does *Sistren Magazine* in Jamaica. Versions of the Boston Collective's *Our Bodies, Our Selves* have been issued recently in local languages such as Hindi and Gujarati and are used widely by Indian women's activist groups. These are extremely important and worthwhile tasks in promoting a feminist consciousness of one's body, even though the culturally ingrained shame around women's bodies and bodily functions is evident in the fact that drawings of genital areas are discreetly covered with an extra sheet of paper. One has to undress the text, so to speak, and look inside! Nonetheless, this is way ahead of mystification and ignorance that unfairly and unscientifically blame women entirely for bearing female children. These Indianized versions of *Our Bodies, Our Selves* include more than physical facts about human biology. The texts include issues of women's inequality, the burdens of child rearing, the inequities of income, the fact that girl-children are deliberately underfed and regarding women's desire as less important than men's. The texts also question if a woman's sole worth lies in her ability to bear children, preferably sons. Readers are educated about infertility problems that commonly blame women. The texts encourage women to demystify the facts of fertility, and to take responsibility through educating themselves about their bodies as well as their male partners' physiologies. Women are made aware of a most significant fact, namely that infertility could well be their male partner's problem.

My Body is Mine, published by an activist women's self-help training program is dedicated "to women health activists for 'self-help' to enter their lives and their work."[27] The Program included "Gender Sensitisation; Body Politics and Beyond; Fertility Awareness and Sexuality" among other issues that attempt to place the body "in its rightful place in the personal and political framework," note Sabala and Kranti who ran the training program. The goal throughout is to educate, inform, and give women the crucial tools of knowledge about the processes of their own female bodies, to challenge stereotypes such as menstruation as polluting, or the causes of infertility as solely a woman's burden, and the male role in creating male or female children. The text begins with the eighteen women participants sharing their own life stories which form the bases for the training sessions that follow. New knowledge takes root in that soil of personal testimony and lived experience, and is then passed on to other women health activists. In their evaluation, several participants note the self-confidence that they gained, how they are able to take these new tools to their own villages, train other health workers, advise and practice herbal remedies, teach fertility awareness, and disseminate the knowledge that has empowered them.

The text documents women's inadequate access to health care systems, and nutritional deficiencies that make women prone to infections like malaria and tuberculosis. The text records the hypocrisy of the Indian government "bent on population control even while cutting back on public health expenditure. . . . The declining sex ratio favoring males speaks of the precarious life situation of women and girl children in most of India. Under the New Economic Policy (NEP) of the nineties, privatization of health care and curtailment of essential social supports threatens the health of women even more" (42).

The "myth of population explosion" is discussed. State systems use this to control the lives and bodies of poor women. Such attitudes are also buttressed "by economic forces in the countries of the North" that blame over-population "for destruction of the planet without ever questioning their own over-consumption and degradation of the earth's resources" (47). Foreign aid is tied to family planning targets. "Family planning," that is, covert and overt incentives for sterilization, are replacing any other available health care for women. Drug companies and market forces control the availability of contraceptives which hardly give autonomy to poor women who are not knowledgeable to make choices, and hence fall prey to state and planners' decisions. A song contests the state's propaganda, namely that with fewer children, the problem of poverty will disappear:

> Will poverty really go
> If we stop having kids?
> We've neither shelter,
> nor cloth to cover our bodies . . .
> For aches and pains and sickness,
> there's no hospital for us.

There's nothing to feed
the child on hip or in the belly.
There's nothing for the old woman
who slaved all her life . . .
Only poor people will disappear
poverty won't go away . . .
In family planning's name
our lives are made a misery
With Mala-D and Depo,
Copper-T and laparoscopy.
New technologies
make our bodies into laboratories. (48)

Male fertility hardly comes under discussion in state programs, even though there are safer and easier birth control methods for men than for women since most drug-based contraceptions are invasive and have hormonal and other side-effects. Given the abuses of forced male sterilizations during the emergency period in India (1975–1977 under Indira Gandhi) there remains a hands-off policy regarding male fertility. Ninety-nine percent of all family planning propaganda is aimed at women.

"Shouting Loudly, 'It's a Boy'"

"When a baby is born people shout very loudly, 'It's a boy,' or they say in a dead voice, 'It's a girl.' "[28] This saying by village women indicates the prejudice and death-like unwelcome given to a girl-child from the moment of birth. A most useful study entitled, *A Lesser Child: Girl Child in India*, published locally by the Research Center for Women's Studies at Bombay's SNDT Women's University documents the multi-dimensional issues and prejudices confronting a girl-child in India—discriminatory treatment from early childhood years, socialization and gender roles that inscribe a culture of inequality, differences in male/female access to education, exploited child-labor, and new technological invasions into the sphere of reproduction and ethical questions regarding sex-selective abortions.[29] Such research is geared to scholars and activists, to policy makers and non-governmental organizations (NGOs) with the agenda of working toward strategies of change. The varied documentation includes national reports, newspaper articles, and scholarly materials. As noted in *A Lesser Child*, there are advocacy efforts such as a Delhi-based lawyer who is fighting for a better life for children born to prostitutes—to give them schooling (55), or the "Foster Parent Scheme: Sponsor a Girl," a voluntary program supported by the Education Directorate in Maharashtra that also focuses on educating girls—"30 lakh children [20 lakh girls] in the age group of six to 14 do not go to school" (64).

In India, prejudices against girl children are played out differently at different historical times—what female infanticide did to the adverse male-female ratio in the nineteenth century is today replaced by mal- and under-nourished females. "India has the dubious distinction," notes Nikhat Kazmi, "of having the lowest sex ratio in the world (933 females per 1000 males) . . . 4% of all the child workers are girls as compared to 2.1% boys. An increase of 20% in the cases of rape was registered throughout the country since 1983–85."[30] Kazmi notes the irony of celebrating the "Year of the Girl Child" in the face of realties such as six-year-old Chutki, a travelling street performer, or sixteen-year-old Rohangir who was "bartered for Rs. 40, a lungi, and a towel, merely due to an acute water shortage in the district," or cases of young girls sold into prostitution, raped, and kept in "cages" like animals. Out of "12 million girls born every year," notes Shailaja Bajpai, "1.5 million die before their first birthday, another 850,000 before their fifth and only 9 million will be alive at 15."[31] In *Studies on Women and Population*, Malini Karkal and Divya Pandey remark:

> Food items are identified as having status or prestige. If supplies of them are scarce, such items are either never eaten by women or reserved for men. . . . A survey in India by the National Commission on the Status of Women found that women in 48.5% of the households ate after men. Special foods for women are often called 'left-overs' and husband's 'left-overs' are appropriate for the wife alone. . . . Another practice which influences food intake of individuals is the ritual 'fasting' on certain days. It will be observed that the practice of 'fasting' is more common with women than with men. . . . Female fasts are more varied, numerous and austere than those of men. . . . Appadurai points out that a new bride and apprentice cook in an orthodox house, may eat last and alone, but as a mother of a son she may be privileged to eat with her mother-in-law or other senior female members.[32]

Sons valued over daughters is a custom mired in Indian tradition even when the reasons are no longer viable, for instance, sons providing economic support to parents in their old age. This is belied often enough because it is no longer true that only daughters leave their parental home on marriage; sons leave for education, and economic opportunities. While sons do have this freedom, there is no guarantee that they will support their aged parents. The crass abuse of technology is abetted by doctors, clinics, advertisers, and an entire sociocultural fabric that legitimizes killing females. Questions of medical ethics, of doctor-patient confidentiality remain. And banning a practice hardly ensures its eradication from society since it can go underground, and people can always avail of the test in a neighboring state. However, legislation is an important, public statement against a social prejudice that targets females. Changing such deeply ingrained attitudes that favor males over females requires education at various levels, formal, informal, and popular.

Indian women's activist groups such as Saheli, Jagori, the Forum Against Sex Determination and Sex Pre-Selection Techniques have campaigned against the abuses of amniocentesis through the use of pamphlets, essays, workshop discussions, and documentary films. The Forum Against Sex Determination argues in their pamphlet that amniocentesis leading to female feticide solely on the basis of sex is a human rights issue. Such misuse of science and technology involves "women's direct oppression." The Forum states further that even when women themselves agree to abort a female fetus, that is part of their general low status in society. "Denied an independent existence and identity, women both submit to and internalize the very male dominated values which act against them." The struggle against amniocentesis then is part of a much broader spectrum of changing these values and encouraging women's independence.

The Forum's study realistically assesses the alarming rate at which these technologies are being used. Educating women and men is certainly important, and is a long-term goal. More urgently, the Forum campaigns to "awaken public opinion against the practice [and] to pressure the government of India to ban all sex determination and pre-selection techniques and for halting related research activities." The Forum urges linking up various activist groups and disseminating information through media and other institutions at a national level. Seminars, debates, and workshops would build accurate knowledge about these procedures rather than their usual mystifications which only leaves them in male control. The Forum urges that regional groups against the abuse of these technologies should collect data and expose misdemeanours by clinics and doctors performing these tests for the specific reason of selective abortions of female foetus. Street plays, slide shows, poster exhibitions would build awareness, and bring pressure against the perpetrators. As the Forum states: "A wider campaign against the advertisement of these techniques or the clinics performing them, in the newspapers and other media must be launched. Defacing of the advertisements, pasting the posters demanding ban on these techniques by the side of these advertisements, and the widespread wall writing should form part of such a campaign." The Forum also campaigns for legislation that would ban "techniques for sex-determination and pre-selection." They were successful in Maharashtra as noted earlier.

These matters of women's health that involve life and death issues require widespread education. Even as one advocates educational campaigns, one recognizes an irony in that it is often people with college degrees who participate in the abuses of this technology as much as the uneducated. Being educated, being a thinking, literate person does not necessarily equip women to challenge patriarchal controls of female bodies. Further, educated women often have an additional disadvantage in that their educated status places them somewhat outside the other uneducated members of their families. They often over-compensate their "traditional" roles so as to belong to their family and social environment. The fact that their education does not serve them in challenging the status quo within the household is also part of how historically, educational policies and institutions are part of the multiplicity of means, along with legal, judicial systems by which sexuality is regulated in patriarchal societies.

A television serial entitled, *Anuradha*, in the Gujarati language, dramatizes this issue subtly and successfully. The script, by progressive women activists Madhushree Dutta and others, presents various issues of female identity—Anuradha as daughter, then wife, and mother-to-be—in an elaborate twelve-part series. This TV serial provides an excellent popular educational forum viewed by a wide audience. It was presented first in the state of Gujarat in western India, particularly since the statistics for amniocintesis are very high in that region. "The penchant for adopting the latest technology and at the same time holding on to archaic value systems are seemingly contradictory traits," remarks Nachiketa Desai, "but they account for the widespread practice of female foeticide in Gujarat. . . . At least 10,000 cases of female foeticide are reported from Ahmedabad alone every year. The figure is a conservative estimate arrived at by the Forum Against Sex Determination and Sex Pre-Selection."[33] Desai also notes the growing numbers of clinics offering this service, and the wide publicity by signboards and advertisements in vernacular dialects." In Gujarat, this business boomed "after neighbouring Maharashtra enacted a legislation earlier this year regulating the use of medical techniques of pre-natal diagnosis so as to prevent their misuse for sex-determination" (5). The major lobbying "against the evil" and "creating public awareness" is undertaken by women's groups such as "Sahiyar" in Baroda. While legislation is important, activists agree that "mass awareness on the subject [is needed] to make the law effective." Proponents of sex-selection insidiously argue that this is a matter of "choice" for women and couples, and that doctors are simply meeting the "demands" from their customers.

> Dr. Neema Acharya, a member of the state's Family Planning Council charges that the social activists are mixing up social issues with medical issues. . . . [She] disagrees that sex-determination tests leading to female foeticide would drastically change the male-female ratio in the state. But historical evidence does suggest that the number of women per thousand men did go down to as low as 750/1000 in Central Gujarat during 1850–60 when the practice of female infanticide was widespread among the Patidars. Female infanticide was so common among the Jadejas of Kutch and Saurashtra region during the early 19th century that in 1805, Col. Alexander Walker, who was on a diplomatic mission to the region, could find only five Jadeja families who had saved their daughters from death. (5)

As Desai concludes, today, the law's sanctioning of sex-selective abortions is a new, socially-sanctioned form of killing females cleanly and quietly through scientific technology.

When I discussed the success of *Anuradha* with Madhusree Dutta, she said that their aim as writers and activists was to create a dramatic show where the audience would be involved with the characters' lives and struggles during several episodes before the controversial amniocintesis issue was introduced. On one of my research trips to India, I viewed the series on video, and was struck by its subtle artistry that accomplished the goal of educating people about the abuses of technology, while demonstrating that women themselves, like Anuradha, despite heavy familial and societal pressure, can exercise autonomy over decisions about their bodies.[34]

Since this is a dramatic and fictional rendition of a serious social problem, its artistry involves the audience emotionally without direct confrontation. After all, the characters, even as they resemble one's neighbors and friends, remain within a fictional realm. The skilful script uses literary qualities to probe and provoke guilt from the guilty parties. As in Shakespeare's Hamlet, where the hero hopes "to catch the conscience of the king" through the play-within-the-play, so, also in Anuradha, the feminist-activist writers aim to stir those guilty viewers in their audience into recognizing the unethical use of technology to oppress Anuradha. Let me recapitulate the plot and its resolution.

Anuradha has a good relationship with her husband who is initially likeable and sympathetic. This changes when during her pregnancy, he tricks her into taking the amniocintesis test telling her that it is *only* for health reasons, whereas he wants to know the baby's sex. When the test shows that Anuradha is carrying a female child, the husband is adamant about aborting the fetus. Anuradha is distraught. She struggles against an almost united front of family and friends who all support the abortion. Anuradha wants this female child. In one of her most poignant discussions with a close female friend, Anuradha wonders if she or her female friend would have been born at all if this test had been available to their mothers. A devastating insight into willed self-annihilation, not female infanticide, but female feticide. As Anuradha struggles on her own, a women's activist group offers support. She is flabbergasted to discover the biological fact that male sperm determine the fetus' sex. Anuradha's recognition of this fact is almost epiphanic. She realizes that such knowledge is mystified deliberately in order to make women unfairly carry the entire blame for bearing a girl. They are enjoined to deal with guilt and shame for something that is not their fault at all.

Anuradha resolves to preserve this female child at the risk of losing her husband and home. Where will she go? As a wife who might be thrown out by her husband, she will not have any respectable space to belong to in her community and will experience a form of exile. The last episode shows Anuradha writing in her journal, addressing her dead mother. She connects with a female legacy stretching over three generations—her mother, herself, and her unborn daughter. Anuradha expresses her need to know herself, to accept her own femaleness as well as that of the unborn girl-child. In this acceptance and search for self-knowledge, Anuradha arrives at a courageous resolution—however difficult for her personally, even at the cost of being exiled from her husband and home, and facing social censure, she will carry this child to term.

It Never Ends: Grandmothers Mothering

Grandmothers raising grand children, at times willingly, at others, out of necessity are represented in literary texts. Most are strong and wise, holding some threads of a family together, but not all are romanticized. In Head's short story, "The Wind and a Boy" in *The Collector of Treasures*, Friedman is brought up by his grandmother Sejosenye. Her unmarried daughter who lived in town had become pregnant as a result of "some casual mating she had indulged in" (70). She was keen to maintain her urban life-style and her job as typist, hence Freidman was handed over to Sejosenye "and that was that." The neglect and abnegation of the mother's responsibility are conveyed subtly at this point in the story because, after all, Friedman finds more love from his grandmother than he might have even with two parents. He is depicted as "a beautiful creature ... tall, spindly-legged, graceful gazelle with large, grave eyes. There was an odd, musical lilt to his speech ... he could turn his hands to anything and made the best wire cars with their wheels of shoe polish tins.... For his age he was a boy who knew his own mind" (70). Friedman's "beauty" is reminiscent of Kwesi's beauty in Aidoo's short story, "No Sweetness Here." Both boys have gruesome and premature deaths where their beauty is obliterated, Friedman's by a road accident when his bicycle is hit by a truck-driver and his body is smashed beyond recognition: "The boy's pretty face was a smear all along the road and he only had a torso left" (74). Kwesi is killed by snake-bite as if to avenge the unfair divorce court ruling that he must leave his mother and live with his father.

In Head's story, the mother's neglect of her son from the time of his birth is critiqued because she had sent him to her mother, and sadly, she had provided the money for the bicycle on which he lost his life. The bicycle was to help him to run errands for his grandmother. The mother (who remains nameless) earns the kind of wages that enable her to afford this modern means of transport. But, how could anyone have foreseen that on those new roads, new drivers do not take the responsibility that goes along with such modernization: "The driver of the truck had neither brakes on his car nor a driving license. He belonged to the new, rich civil-servant class whose salaries had become fantastically high since independence. They had to have cars in keeping with their new status; they had to have any car, as long as it was a car; they were in such a hurry about everything that they couldn't be bothered to take driving lessons. And thus progress, development, and a pre-occupation with status and living-standards first announced themselves to the village. It looked like being an ugly story with many decapitated bodies on the main road" (74). The shock of losing her beloved grandson was so severe that Sejosenye loses her wits. In hospital, she "sang and laughed and talked to herself all the time" and died two weeks after Friedman.

The grandmother figure, Ma, in Trinidadian Merle Hodge's novel *Crick Crack, Monkey* plays a central role in Tee's childhood and the bedrock of her future identity. Tee shares her holidays in Ma's enchanted countryside home, described as magical and lyrical. Above all, Ma believes that Tee has the spirit of Ma's great grandmother—a straight-backed and resolute woman who refused to answer to the name given to her by the slave-masters, and who insisted on holding on to her "true-true name." Ma wants Tee to have this name. Although Ma tells this name to Tantie who does not "bother to remember it," one hopes that the spirit of this ancestor that Ma believed is in Tee will sustain the young girl through the many conflicts and struggles that she must face in her postcolonial and neocolonial society.[35]

The grandmother in Anita Desai's novel *Fire on the Mountain*, Nanda Kaul is reluctant to take on the responsibility for her great-granddaughter, Raka who is sent to the remote house at Acrignano in Kasauli since her own mother has suffered a nervous breakdown.[36] As in Desai's *Clear Light of Day*, parental figures are aloof and shadowy. They neglect their children who cope in different ways with this peculiar form of abandonment by parents who are present and yet absent. In *Fire on the Mountain*, Raka learns to be so self-possessed and independent that she appears to have almost no emotional needs, at least not expressed openly. Since Nanda Kaul wishes to withdraw from family obligations, she regards Raka as "an intruder, an outsider, a mosquito flown up from the plains to tease and worry" (40). Nanda Kaul had hoped to live a "pared, reduced and radiantly single life" (31). But Raka enters her world and as they embrace "there was a sound of bones colliding" (40). The two are a curious match for each other since they are both loners though with a difference: "If Nanda Kaul was a recluse out of vengeance for a long life of duty and obligation, her great-grand-daughter was a recluse by nature, by instinct. She had not arrived at this condition by a long route of rejection and sacrifice—she was born to it, simply" (48). As G. S. Balarama Gupta points out, Nanda Kaul "resents Raka but she cannot disown her."[37] Her desire to escape from her past, from the pain and loss of having a husband who carried on a life-long affair with another woman, eludes her. Now, she craves peace and total solitude, but Raka's independent nature warms Nanda Kaul into a closeness of telling the child about her life. Sadly, Nanda makes up a life that she had not had. "She had lied to Raka, lied about everything. Her father had never been to Tibet. . . . Nor had her husband loved and cherished her and kept her like a queen. . . . And her children—the children were all alien to her nature. She neither understood nor loved them. She did not live here alone by choice—she lived here alone because that was what she was forced to do, reduced to doing" (145). The poignancy of this heart-confession only in the narrator's voice, reported as Nanda's thoughts, not verbalized to any human soul are followed by Raka's cataclysmic words: "Look, Nani, I have set the forest on fire" (145). As the novel's last line states, "black smoke spiralled up over the mountain," as though these shattered lives of failed mothering and grand-mothering, of neglected and abused children will be engulfed and destroyed. All ashes and embers.

Aidoo's collection of stories, *No Sweetness Here* ends with "Other Versions" that evokes a mother-son bond across the geographies that black people have traversed. The narrator Kofi travels from his home in Ghana to the United States as a student and comes face-to-face with the history of slavery and forced dispersal of blacks in the diaspora. While at home, Kofi could not verbally express the emotional closeness that he feels with his mother, especially in his authoritarian father's presence. Only when he is thousands of miles away from home does he connect indirectly with his mother, and through her with other black peoples in the diaspora. The indirect conduit is provided by the older African American women whom he runs into—one is a kitchen-helper, and the other whom he sees on the subway seems to bring his mother's face before his very eyes. Through his mother, who has guided him throughout his life, Kofi connects his destiny with that of the shared destiny of black peoples in Africa and elsewhere. The mother who had given him life now guides him into a future where he is aware of a wider history.

Conclusion

This study establishes a field of literary study on postcolonial women writers and gives serious scholarly attention to postcolonial women writers such as Ama Ata Aidoo, Bessie Head, Erna Brodber, Eunice de Souza among others. They are pioneers in this field, and serve as models for younger writers such as Tsitsi Dangarembga, Lorna Goodison, and Merle Hodge among others.

Politics of the Female Body makes an important scholarly contribution in analyzing postcolonial women writers' representations of female exile from the body and community, and resistance via speech and silence, and the outcome that may be fatal or positive such as reintegration into the community. At times, outsiderness or ostracization may be experienced as a kind of "death," for instance, in Ama Ata Aidoo's drama, *Anowa* when the protagonist's marginalization is severe and isolating. Or in Tsitsi Dangarembga's *Nervous Conditions*, when Nyasha becomes bulimic and her life hangs in the balance by the end of the novel. Widows in the Indian context, subject to cruel treatment and malnourishment live on the margins, though widows like Phaniyamma resist and gain authority in the community.

This book explored the different avenues through which the female body is socialized in postcolonial societies—the significance of the English language and educational systems interfacing with indigenous tradition and custom often resulting in complex psychological and economic repercussions for female protagonists. Educated women have to juggle family and work, and at times, they decide to "efface" themselves as Maiguru does in *Nervous Conditions*, in order not to threaten her husband's ego. Education presents choices and challenges and is not always empowering in a straightforward way. There are trade-offs, especially in cultures where patriarchal systems remain intact as do power relations outside the home. If male privilege and authority are reconfigured only through the goodwill of exceptional men (such as Paul, described as "a poem of tenderness" in Bessie

Head's story, "The Collector of Treasures") then this is hardly the only way to bring about social change.

However, I assert the particular usefulness of the literary and aesthetic as evocative avenues for imagining social change in women's lives. To the extent that a materialist-feminist approach to the study of literary texts enables a participation in a historical process of social change, this book also addresses women's movements in postcolonial societies. An analysis of female sexuality in terms of socialization and cultural tradition from the imaginative viewpoint of postcolonial women writers, and the broad recognition that art is contiguously a part of development and change, enhances a greater incorporation of such materials within postcolonial women's movements than exists at present. Feminist activists and scholars can also participate together in working toward these goals. Women's groups such as the Lawyers' Collective in India that link activists with lawyers can intervene in legislation and challenge age-old social customs or oppressive religious law. The struggle for a Uniform Civil Code in Indian society has involved diverse supporters including feminist lawyers and members of women's organizations. Similarly, discriminatory laws governing sexual behavior of gays and lesbians have been resisted by women's groups in Trinidad and other parts of the Caribbean.

This study makes an important contribution by engaging issues of female sexuality in domestic and public space, and challenging silences about sexuality in most postcolonial societies. Women's struggles for autonomy over their bodies often need to contend with state-sponsored violence. For instance, the Immorality Laws in apartheid South Africa had judged Bessie Head's white mother "insane" since she had become pregnant by a black man, and she was not allowed to raise her colored daughter.

A key connecting factor in this study is the use of English by colonized writers, often a political, even emotional choice. Writers recognize strategic benefits of using a world language and addressing audiences beyond their native lands. But sadly, at times, English supplants writers' fluency in their indigenous languages. They do speak other languages such as different English patwahs in the Caribbean; African languages such as Igbo or Shona; Indian languages such as Tamil or Punjabi, some smattering of street Hindi (considered the national language, though this is debatable) and the Hindi of popular Bollywood cinema.

The comparative scope of this study aims to strengthen solidarity among women with common struggles across national lines. Increasingly, transnational border crossings are part of our world. Even when nationalism was useful as a rallying cry in anti-colonial struggles, it was a vexed concept that could slide into fundamentalist notions of inclusion and exclusion and virulent racism that leads to genocidal "ethnic cleansings" as in Rwanda, or the former Yugoslavia.

Containments and spilling over of ethnicities, castes, linguistic groups, religious affiliations are rife under the rubric of fighting for a "nation." Maps are not neutral blueprints; they participate in the constituting of ethnic and national communities. Colonial histories created new geographies where maps were redrawn and often, new national boundaries were imposed; such re-drawings on paper often ignored ethnic and religious conflicts. Different ideologies lie behind drawing maps—when the colonizers entered so-called "blank spaces," often decimated native populations, they "invented" and named these spaces as it suited their economic and political interests. Such maps do not mirror the reality of local peoples' ethnic and linguistic boundaries. Maps must be read as texts, deconstructed as much in terms of what they reveal as what they hide. Who draws maps and to what ends are crucial considerations. Geography importantly inscribes contemporary history.[1]

Homi Bhabha's linking of "nation and narration" argues for "the impossible unity of the nation as a symbolic force."[2] Just as narratives contain multiple meanings, nations need to transcend unitary definitions of identity and ethnicity. Rather, ambivalence and crossing rigid boundaries are necessary in resisting normative definitions of a nation and its culture. Nationalist discourses may be powerful but Bhabha usefully notes "the particular ambivalence that haunts the idea of the nation" (1). I would extend the spatial limits of national boundaries by bringing in Bhabha's notion of "cultural temporality of the nation." Cultures evolve in time and historical forces that led to national boundaries being drawn may be challenged. I agree with Bhabha that the nation "as a system of cultural signification, as the representation of social life rather than the discipline of social polity, emphasizes this instability of knowledge" (4).

The realities of migration seen in the light of a colonial history embody the journeying of postcolonial women writers as exiles and expatriates with new, multiply hyphenated identities. These predicaments necessitate a type of tightrope walking where even as we travel with relative ease (direct flights on supersonic jets), we cannot with as much ease step out of our skins, assume identities, and kaleidoscopes of colors as we step off the ladder into the humid air and tropical smells of Bombay, or into the brisk coolness of jetway corridors and white-washed efficiency of Heathrow, or Kennedy.

Several postcolonial diasporic writers such as Jhumpa Lahiri (Indian-American), or Michelle Cliff (Jamaican-American), and scholars such as Arjun Appadurai, Chandra Mohanty imaginatively challenge the linearity of time and the specificity of space by juxtaposing their here and now, with their past histories and geographies.[3] "The present epoch," as noted usefully by Foucault, "will perhaps be above all the epoch of space. We are in the epoch of simultaneity: we are in the epoch of juxtaposition, the epoch of the near and far, of the side-by-side, of the dispersed. We are at a moment, I believe, when our experience of the world is less that of a long life developing through time than that of a network that connects points and intersects with its own skein."[4]

In our time, displacement of large numbers of people who move locations for labor and economic benefit, or to escape political persecution, or for intellectual sustenance is common.[5] Among writers and scholars, global and cosmopolitan labels are increasingly common, for instance, writers like Salman Rushdie, Amitav Ghosh, and Kamau Brathwaite. Migration and transmigration place Saladin Chamcha, the protagonist of Rushdie's novel, *The Satanic Verses* in those spaces of falling in limbo between London and Bombay, where he must embody being the man "with a thousand voices and one." Or Amitav Ghosh's novels that traverse the globe, encompassing with as much skill and passion, India, as Burma and Cambodia, Egypt and Calcutta. Not all intellectuals and writers relocate to western regions. Some migrate internally such as Cameroonian postcolonial theorist, Achille Mbembe, now residing in post-apartheid South Africa, even as at an earlier time, Bessie Head left apartheid South Africa and migrated to neighboring Botswana.

Increasingly, as diasporic communities get established and make homes in metropolitan areas such as people from Ghana or South Africa in Britain, people from India and the Caribbean in the United States and Canada, the field of postcolonial literature includes diasporic writers who may divide their time between native and metropolitan spaces. Traveling writers and traveling theorists are a common phenomenon today. There are several noteworthy writers of Asian, African, or Caribbean origin now living in the United States, Britain, and other regions of the north. Most of them have hyphenated identities such as Pulitzer prize-winning Indian-American writer, Jhumpa Lahiri, and others such as Antiguan-American Jamaica Kincaid.

Although this is a literary, academic study, my methodology included more than an academic audience. My critique of certain trends in postcolonial theory and the role of the postcolonial critic is perhaps the most academic part of the discussion, necessitated by my own position in academia, and by a rising tide of institutionalizing postcolonial theory over postcolonial literature. A broad, rigorous critique of the production and dissemination of the literature and theory is crucial, namely, who is producing this knowledge, who is benefiting, to whom one is accountable, who one's audience is, and where one's constituency lies. These issues have significant repercussions on cultural productions and women's issues in postcolonial societies.

The postcolonial critic faces paradoxes in facing challenges in his/her personal identity (whether the critic is from postcolonial areas or from the west), and his/her professional space within the academy. Biddy Martin's questions, raised in another context are appropriate here: "What assumptions about institutions and the workings of power within them are embedded in our efforts to take up and/or resist identities? What assumptions about institutions and the workings of power within them underlie any definition of a particular field or position as marginal?"[6]

Is postcolonial literature one more addition to the line of "minority" fields in U.S. universities? The very positionality of the postcolonial critic is contradictory—often marginal in terms of ethnicity, race, the teaching of non-canonical texts, and simultaneously occupying significant intellectual spaces created by institutional desire to promote postcoloniality, "cultural diversity," and "third worldism." This contradiction is also a productive dialectic in terms of institutional power dynamics—postcolonialism becomes more "desirable," somehow less immediately threatening than African-American and ethnic studies, engagements with race politics in this society. After all, postcolonial theory along with other minority discourses partakes in a macabre dance on a marginality spectrum. And can the participants avoid falling through the cracks of this dance between marginal and un-marginal (not really the center), as dictated by institutional power, desire, domination, an erotics of postcoloniality, which decide when, and for how long a certain field will be promoted (hirings, research support, etc.)? How can we not be a part of producing what David Hwang has called "Orientalia for the intelligentsia"?[7]

When the production and dissemination of knowledge about postcolonial societies happens to a large scale in the first world, by a heterogeneity of voices, one recognizes links among the production of postcoloniality itself, the visibility of postcolonial discourse, and new complicities on the part of critics in global systems of domination. One finds new forms of colonization, new ways of acquiring territories, that is, brains, which are partly responsible for intellectually impoverished conditions in the third world. A socially responsible postcolonial critic is aware of this complicitous position, and undertakes a progressive critique of this scenario. Postcolonial critics need to make a more concerted effort to genuinely "share" information across geographic boundaries. The geopolitics of sharing and withholding information in the context of what Walter Ong calls "the technologizing of the word" is tacitly acknowledged, but seldom confronted.[8]

A postcolonial critic's attempts to use progressive critical practices can be helped or hindered by his/her academic and institutional location. As Rosuara Sanchez asks, can one "in fact ever represent a counter project while being funded, housed and incorporated within the system?"[9] Are postcolonial critics even as they sound oppositional (to dominant discourses, texts), simultaneously complicit with institutional power? Is it possible to be otherwise and yet be heard, or must one then be silenced? Our attempts at resisting, even negotiating institutional power structures bring us up against what Barbara Harlow has termed "the politics of containment."[10]

In the United States's academic marketplace, desirous of theory, the postcolonial critic's generally marginal position in terms of the writers that s/he deals with is centered by the use of a fashionable discourse. This has serious implications for the development of postcolonial literary tradition. Theoretical domination rests solidly on economic power and privilege, and raises issues of agency and of access—who gets to learn a certain theoretical language, in what spaces that talk is produced, consumed, and rewarded, and who the audience is. Theory has become an essential category for graduate students to master since the market demands this. But the consumption of theory as a commodity, and hegemonic tendencies that favor certain western theories as essential for employment is problematic. I do not wish to convey an anti-theoretical position, but simply to question the uses of theory, which ones get privileged and rewarded in the academic system.

The types of theory that one practices address some audiences, and leave out others; theory is centered, and often the writers themselves about whom the theory may be talking are marginalized. There are significant imbalances here. By and large, cultural production comes from the "third word," though critical work is vastly produced and consumed in the first.

The producers are consumed and then reproduced in theoretical work without having access to this material. And even when third world cultural producers get to read what their creative work has inspired, the inaccessibility of theoretical language often renders those very producers marginal in a discourse that is supposedly about them!

In conclusion, postcolonial women writers analyzed in this book make their own unique contributions through their evocative portrayals of the exile and struggle to recuperate the female body, and these very representations enable literary readers and progressive people to imagine a just future for postcolonial societies.

NOTES

Preface

Kamala Das, "An Introduction," in Kamala Das, *The Old Playhouse and Other Poems* (New Delhi: Orient Longman Ltd., 1973), 26.

1. "Autonomous" indicates that these groups are not affiliated to any political party, although they are, of course, involved in political, even militant action. See Veena Poonacha, "Gendered Step: Review of Two Decades of Women's Movement and Women's Studies," in *Economic and Political Weekly*, 29, 13 (1994), 725–728. See Vibhuti Patel, "Emergence and Proliferation of the Autonomous Women's Organisations in India" (Bombay: Research Centre for Women's Studies, SNDT Women's University, 1986, repr. 1990). Patel usefully documents the multifaceted activist work undertaken by groups which have grown between 1975 and 1985. These groups are different fundamentally from an earlier tradition of middle-class women's organizations in post-independence India that dealt with sociocultural activities without challenging the status quo. Now, pressure from these "agitational" groups, as they are called, that organize campaigns against dowry, rape, family violence, and prostitution, have led to "setting up of special legal cells for women's problems, family courts to deal with dowry harassment and violence in the family." Patel also traces women's issues over the 1960s and 1970s—anti-price, and student movements—that led to many of these groups' births.

    I am deeply indebted to Vibhuti Patel for her generosity and support in facilitating my research in Bombay.

2. In fact, one incident is imprinted indelibly in my mind: an academic-sounding presenter (and since this style was familiar to me, and was also in English which is my strongest language, I was getting engaged in the presenter's talk) was interrupted by the audience, and told point blank that she was giving too many "details," and was wasting the group's time! Quite an honest and forthright statement, which would be refreshing as we sit politely through many irrelevant "details" at MLA sessions!

3. I discuss widowhood in more detail in chapter 4.

4. I include third world peoples themselves, inhabiting native spaces and metropolitan areas where they may reside as expatriates or exiles. I also include progressive peoples of other races and nationalities who are in solidarity with issues of social change in third world societies.
5. Ama Ata Aidoo, Untitled, in Philomena Mariani, ed. *Critical Fictions: The Politics of Imaginative Writing* (Seattle: Bay Press, 1991), 149–153.
6. Neil Lazarus, *Resistance in Postcolonial African Fiction* (New Haven and London: Yale University Press, 1990), 1. See also, essays by Ella Shohat, "Notes on the 'Post-Colonial,' " and Anne McClintock's "The Angel of Progress: Pitfalls of the Term 'Post-Colonialism,' " in *Social Text*, 31/32 (1992), 84–113, for astute discussions of the drawbacks of the term "postcolonial." McClintock points out that "the almost ritualist ubiquity of 'post-' words in current culture . . . signals . . . a widespread, spochal crisis in the idea of linear, historical 'progress' " (85). Shohat is concerned about the "ahistorical and universalizing deployments [of the term postcolonial] and its potentially depoliticizing implications" (99). Though both writers provide useful critiques of the term, and provide cautionary remarks on the limits of using the term "postcolonial" in different contexts and historical periods, I want to use it with qualification. I agree with both Shohat and McClintock as to the dangers of academic fashions when certain fields are institutionalized, valorized, and often at the expense of others that may be more confrontational and uncomfortable. For instance, I would be cautious of the contexts, as Shohat valuably points out, when hybridity in the postcolonial field is promoted over the more dismal realities of race politics, say in African American and ethnic studies.
7. On a recent visit to my home in Bombay, I was struck by the visible flaunting of the Indian government's "new economic policy" of welcoming multinational corporations with open arms—Coca Cola, Barbies, disposable diapers. I recalled with some sadness and nostalgia how in the 1970s as an undergraduate at St. Xavier's College in Bombay, I had taken great pride in supporting a campaign to keep Coke out of India. Now, the "wealth" of consumer items that satisfy middle-class taste would be daunting to any campaign against them. For instance, Kellogg's sells a variety of "Rice Crispies" cereal re-named "Basmati Flakes" with ringing Indian idiom and cultural evocation! Plus, Kellogg's, unlike local manufacturers, can afford expensive advertising campaigns such as offering free stainless steel bowls and spoons with the purchase of certain sized cereal boxes.

A useful documentary video entitled, "Lifting the Veil" by Sonali Bose deals with the negative impacts of the "new liberalization policies" of the Indian government that really benefit the wealthiest class, and who embrace the "trickle down Reagonomics" that hardly ever reach the vast majority of the poor and destitute. Liberalization policies have their supporters and detractors even on the Indian scene, for instance, those who argue that competition encourages quality control, and who often present a simple-minded view of "progress" and development. Hence, to NOT support globalization is seen as retrograde, as supporting old-fashioned ideologies that are not in step with the late twentieth and early twenty-first centuries.

One stark example of cultural imperialism is the presence of cable television in third world societies—MTV Asia, BBC Asia, along with a variety of U.S.

sitcoms and shows such as *Baywatch* and *MASH* broadcast daily. CNN news permeates people's living rooms and provides news about not only the outside world but often about what may be occurring in our own backyards. The important issue about self-representation raised by Edward Said in his interview "In the Shadow of the West" is important in terms of this power of the media that projects news about ourselves as produced by outside powers that have access to electronic media.

8. Edward Said, *Orientalism* (New York: Vintage, 1978), Introduction. See also Said's *Culture and Imperialism* (New York: Knopf, 1993).
9. Ngugi wa Thiong'o, prominent Kenyan writer has written in essays and novels about the punitive measures that native speakers of Gikuyu suffered in colonial English-only schools during the 1940s and 1950s.
10. The words Zoroastrian and Parsi are used interchangeably. Zoroastrian refers to the followers of Zoroaster, the prophet (also called Zarathusthtra) who lived in ancient Persia around the fifth century BC; Parsi refers to the region called Parse in Iran from which the Parsis migrated to India.
11. Lloyd W. Brown, *Women Writers of Black Africa* (Westport, Conn. and London: Greenwood Press, 1982); Carole Boyce Davies and Anne Adams, eds. *Ngambika: Studies of Women in African Literature* (New Jersey: Africa World Press, 1986); Selwyn Cudjoe, ed. *Caribbean Women Writers* (Amherst: University of Massachusetts Press, 1990). There are also a few single author studies such as Vincent Odamtten, *The Art of Ama Ata Aidoo* (Gainesville: University Press of Florida, 1994); Cecil Abrahams, ed. *The Tragic Life: Bessie Head and Literature in Southern Africa* (New Jersey: Africa World Press, 1990). See also my essay on Bessie Head in Jay Parini, ed. *World Writers in English* (New York: Scribers, 2004), 157–176.

Another useful scholarly avenue for studies of postcolonial literature and theory is special issues of journals such as *Research in African Literature*, 21, 1 (Spring 1990), Special Issue on Critical Theory and African Literature; *South Atlantic Quarterly*, 87, 1 (Winter 1988), Special Issue on Third World Literary and Cultural Criticism; *Kunapipi* 11, 1 (1989), Special Issue on Post-Colonial Criticism. See also a useful text, Henry Schwarz and Sangeeta Ray, eds. *A Companion to Postcolonial Studies* (Oxford: Blackwell, 2000).
12. The efforts of women's groups in India to counter such prejudice is noteworthy. During one of my research trips to India, I had the opportunity to witness Stree Mukti Sangathana's (a women's activist group based in Bombay) street theater production called *Mulgi Zali Ho*, translated as "A Girl is Born." Through dramatic dialogue, song, gesture, the play explores the social, even scriptural legitimizing of prejudice against girls. The play strongly condemns such unfairness and suggests alternative visions that family and community members can uphold about their female members. I am grateful to Vibhuti Patel for informing me about this production held in Borivli, Bombay.
13. India became independent in 1947, most African and Caribbean nations in the 1960s.
14. See the useful two-volume compilation of K. Lalitha and Susie Tharu, eds. *Women Writing in India: 600 B.C. to the Present* (New York: Feminist Press,

1990). Feminist Press has also published two volumes of *Women Writing Africa* (New York: Feminist Press, 2003).
15. Gayatri Chakravorty Spivak, translated and introduced, *Imaginary Maps: Three Stories by Mahasweta Devi* (New York and London: Routledge, 1995). All quotations are from this edition. See also Gayatri Chakravorty Spivak and Sarah Harasym, eds. *The Postcolonial Critic: Interviews, Strategies, Dialogues* (New York and London: Routledge, 1990); Gayatri Chakravorty Spivak, *Death of a Discipline* (Calcutta and New Delhi: Seagull Books, 2004).
16. Salman Rushdie, *Imaginary Homelands: Essays and Criticism, 1981–1991* (London: Granta Books in association with Penguin, 1991).
17. A beautiful literary example of sharing is found in Bessie Head's text, *Serowe: The Village of the Rain Wind* (London: Heinemann, 1981). Here, Head as griot (that is, oral historian) interviewed local people and gathered useful material about the community in the spirit of "giving something back," as she remarks, of the people and place that had become her home after years of being stateless and in exile from South Africa.
18. Achola O. Pala, "Definitions of Women and Development: An African Perspective," in Filomena C. Steady, ed. *The Black Woman Cross-Culturally* (Cambridge, MA: Schenkman Publishing Company, Inc., 1981), 209–214.
19. Ama Ata Aidoo, *Changes* (New York: Feminist Press, 1991).
20. Barbara Harlow, Guest-Ed. and Introduction in *Critical Exchange*, 22 (Spring 1987), Introduction, i–iv, 85–86.
21. My research into local publications by women's activist groups is more extensive for India than for Africa and the Caribbean since I wanted to balance the mostly middle-class English-language Indian writers with activist publications dealing with lower class and caste women's issues. My project also seriously acknowledges the links between artistic and activist energies—writing poems, creating art works as posters, or publishing a pamphlet on rape are all important avenues in working toward common goals of a just society.

Some of the many local publications by women's groups that I have found useful for my theoretical and practical analyses into various aspects of women's oppression in this book are: *Moving On . . . But Not Quite There*, by The Forum Against the Oppression of Women, Bombay, 1990; *Saheli: The First Four Years*, Delhi, n.d.; Stree Shakti Sangathana's *We Were Making History: Life Stories of Women in the Telangana People's Struggle* (New Delhi: Kali for Women, 1989); *Hamara Sharir, Hamari Baat*, Delhi, 1985. The last text is a Hindi version of *Our Bodies, Our Selves* which has also been translated into Gujarati and other Indian languages.

Cultural products such as street theater (some recorded on video) are significant for my project. I am grateful to Madhushree Dutta for sharing a copy of *Nari Itihas ki Khoj Mei* (Women in Search of Our History). There are published street theater booklets: Jyoti Mhapsekar, *Mulgi Zali Ho* (A Girl is Born) (Bombay: Laxmi Printing Press, 1985, repr. 1988). This play, originally in Marathi, and translated into Hindi in 1986, has had over a thousand productions.

I consult local research publications from the Research Centre for Women's Studies (RCWS) of the SNDT Women's University, Bombay, such as Maithreyi

Krishnaraj, ed. *Evolving New Methodologies in Research for Women's Studies* (Bombay: Research Centre for Women's Studies, 1988).
22. See Arjun Appadurai, *Modernity at Large: Cultural Dimensions of Globalization* (Minneapolis and London: University of Minnesota Press, 1996). Also, M. Jaqui Alexander and Chandra Mohanty, eds. *Feminist Genealogies, Colonial Legacies, Democratic Futures* (New York and London: Routledge, 1997).
23. Vacha is housed in Sonal's own apartment where one room is set aside, as a quiet space for reading and reflection. Such space is a precious commodity in communally shared family spaces in India. During research visits back home, I have spent many fulfilling hours in Vacha's library which is a most useful resource used by scholars and activists. I deeply appreciate Sonal's own commitment and effort in running this very important library. Another research collection is found in the "Akshara" library in Bombay.
24. Tsitsi Dangarembga, *Nervous Conditions* (London: The Women's Press, 1988, republished Seattle: The Seal Press, 1989). I use the Women's Press edition for all quotations.
25. Tsitsi Dangarembga, "This Time, Next Year . . ." *The Women's Review of Books*, 8, 10–11 (July 1991), 43–44. All quotations taken from this essay.
26. Dangarembga has received much critical attention. See A. E. Wiley and J. Treiber, eds. *Emerging Perspectives on Tsitsi Dangarembga: Negotiating the Postcolonial* (New Jersey: Africa World Press, 2002).
27. Kumkum Sangari and Sudesh Vaid, eds. *Recasting Women: Essays in Colonial History* (New Delhi: Kali for Women, 1989, reprinted by Rutgers University Press, 1990, 1997); Nandita Gandhi and Nandita Shah, *The Issues at Stake: Theory and Practice in the Contemporary Women's Movement in India* (New Delhi: Kali for Women, 1991); Radha Kumar, *The History of Doing: Illustrated Account of Movements for Women's Rights and Feminism in India, 1800–1990* (New Delhi: Kali for Women, 1993).

CHAPTER 1 *Theorizing a Politics of the Female Body*

1. Francoise Lionnet, *Postcolonial Representations: Women, Literature, Identity* (Ithaca, New York: Cornell University Press, 1995).
2. Ama Ata Aidoo, *Anowa* (London: Longman, 1970). Anita Desai, *Clear Light of Day* (New York and London: Penguin, 1980).
3. Chandra Mohanty, *Feminism without Borders: Decolonizing Theory, Practicing Solidarity* (Durham and London: Duke University Press, 2003), 8.
4. Maithreyi Krishnaraj, "Advances in Feminist Scholarship" (Bombay: Research Center for Women's Studies, SNDT Women's University, 1987), 12.
5. Amilcar Cabral, *Return to the Source: Selected Speeches of Amilcar Cabral*, edited by Africa Information Service (New York and London: Monthly Review Press, 1973), 9.
6. Harlow, "Introduction," in *Critical Exchange*, 85.
7. African universities suffer from what is described sadly as a "book famine." This raises serious questions about the production and dissemination of knowledge and cultural productions. As a contrast, in India, since the 1990s there has been an

explosion of book production. Publishing houses such as Oxford and Longmans have branches in India and produce affordable paperbacks by Indian writers. This is very different from the 1960s when I was in college in Bombay when most literary and scholarly texts in literature were imported and hence prohibitively expensive.

8. Alexander and Mohanty, eds. *Feminist Genealogies*, 28–29.
9. Chandra Mohanty, Ann Russo, Lourdes Torres, eds. *Third World Women and the Politics of Feminism* (Indiana: Indiana University Press, 1991), Introduction, 1–47. See also Rajeswari Sunder Rajan, *Real and Imagined Women: Gender, Culture, and Postcolonialism* (New York: Routledge, 1993) and Rajeswari Sunder Rajan, *Signposts: Gender Issues in Post-Independence India* (New Brunswick, New Jersey, and London: Rutgers University Press, 2001).
10. Edward Soja, *Postmodern Geographies: The Reassertion of Space in Critical Social Theory* (London and New York: Verso, 1989).
11. M. M. Bakhtin, *Speech Genres, and Other Late Essays*, trans. Vern W. McGee, eds. Caryl Emerson and Michael Holquist (Austin: University of Texas Press, 1986). I am extremely grateful to Professor Esha De of UCLA for suggesting that the work of Mikahil Bakhtin would augment my argument. De's comments have also been most instrumental to my thinking of resistance and agency in this chapter.
12. Madhu Kishwar, Rama Joshi and Joanna Liddle, eds. *In Search of Answers: Indian Women's Voices from Manushi* (London: Zed Press, 1984), 206–207. I undertake a more extensive discussion of this "cultural tradition" of dowry in chapter 4.
13. Esha De and Sonita Sarkar, eds. *Trans-Status Subjects: Marking Time and Territories* (Durham and London: Duke University Press, 2002). See Introduction, 1–27. All quotations are from the Introduction.
14. Some useful texts that deal with female sexuality include Perveen Adams ed. *m/f*, "The Woman in Question" (Cambridge, MA: MIT Press, 1990); Luce Irigary, "Women's Exile," in *Ideology and Consciousness*, 1 (1977), 62–76; Shari Benstock, ed. *Feminist Issues in Literary Scholarship* (Indiana: Indiana University Press, 1987); Pat Caplan, ed. *The Cultural Construction of Sexuality* (London and New York: Tavistock Publications, 1987); Ann Rosalind Jones, "Writing the Body: Toward an Understanding of L'Ecriture feminine," in Judith Newton and Deborah Rosenfelt, eds. *Feminist Criticism and Social Change* (New York: Methuen, 1985), 86–101; Elaine Marks and Isabelle de Courtivron, eds. *New French Feminisms* (Amherst: University of Massachusetts Press, 1980); Sandra Gilbert and Susan Gubar, "Sexual Linguistics: Gender, Language, Sexuality," in *New Literary History*, 16, 3 (Summer 1985), 515–544; Donna Haraway, "A Manifesto for Cyborgs: Science, Technology, and Socialist Feminism in the 1980s," in *Socialist Review*, 15, 2 (March–April 1985), 65–107; Domna C. Stanton, ed. *Discourses of Sexuality: From Aristotle to AIDS* (Ann Arbor: The University of Michigan Press, 1992); Ann Laura Stoler, *Race and the Education of Desire: Foucault's History of Sexuality and the Colonial Order of Things* (Durham and London: Duke University Press, 1995); Uma Narayan, *Dislocating Cultures: Identities, Traditions, and Third world Feminism* (New York and London: Routledge, 1997); Keya Ganguly, *States of Exception: Everyday Life and Postcolonial Identity* (Minneapolis and London: University of

Minnesota Press, 2001); Mrinalini Sinha, *Colonial Masculinity* (New York: St. Martin's Press, 1995); Robert J. C. Young, *Colonial Desire: Hybridity in Theory, Culture and Race* (London and New York: Routledge, 1995); Sangeeta Ray, *Engendering India: Woman and Nation in Colonial and Postcolonial Narratives* (Durham and London: Duke University Press, 2000).

15. Eve Kosofsky Sedgwick, *Between Men* (New York: Columbia University Press, 1985).
16. Eve Kosofsky Sedgwick, *Touching Feeling: Affect, Pedagogy, Performativity* (Durham and London: Duke University Press, 2003), 2.
17. Chinua Achebe, *Hopes and Impediments: Selected Essays (1965–1987)* (London: Heinemann, 1988); Wole Soyinka, *Art, Dialogue and Outrage: Essays on Literature and Culture* (Ibadan: New Horn Press, 1988); Ngugi wa Thiong'o, *Decolonizing the Mind: The Politics of Language in African Literature* (London: Heinemann, 1986).
18. Erna Brodber, "Yards in the City of Kingston." Typescript of Working Paper no. 9, Institute of Social and Economic Research, University of the West Indies, Jamaica, 1975, 75.
19. See a text that I co-edited with Shirley Garner, Veve Clark, and Margaret Higonnet entitled *Antifeminism in the Academy* (New York and London: Routledge, 1996). The volume of essays deals with the intellectual harassment of feminists that is related to and different from sexual harassment in the academy. Intellectual harassment involves attacking and belittling the scholarly work of women who identify as feminists or who are identified from the outside as feminists. They face varieties of harassment from students, colleagues, administrators, and publishers.
20. Ama Ata Aidoo, "To Be an African Woman—An Overview and a Detail," in Kirsten Holt Petersen and Per Wastberg, eds. *Criticism and Ideology: Second African Writers' Conference, Stockholm, 1986* (Uppsala, Sweden: Scandinavian Institute of African Studies, 1988), 155–171, 180–185. Quote on 183.
21. Quoted in Petersen and Wastberg, eds. *Criticism and Ideology*, 175.
22. Brown, *Women Writers in Black Africa*, 3.
23. Emmanuel Ngara, *Art and Ideology in the African Novel* (London: Heinemann, 1985).
24. Oladele Taiwo, *Female Novelists of Modern Africa* (London: St. Martin's Press, 1984).
25. I have discussed Dangarembga's own disillusionment with her attempts to publish her text in her native Zimbabwe in my Preface.
26. Bessie Head, *The Collector of Treasures* (London: Heinemann, 1977), title story, 87–103.
27. Bessie Head, Autobiographical Essay, *Ms. Magazine*, November 1975, 72–75. See also Gillian S. Eilersen, *Bessie Head: Thunder Behind Her Ears: Her Life and Writing* (London: Heinemann, 1995).
28. Bessie Head, *A Bewitched Crossroad: An Historical Saga of Africa* (New York: Paragon, 1986).
29. Craig MacKenzie, "Short Fiction in the Making: The Case of Bessie Head," in *English in Africa*, 16, 1 (May 1989), 17–37.

30. Sistren with Honor Ford-Smith, *Lionheart Gal: Lifestories of Jamaican Women* (Toronto: Sister Vision Press, 1987).
31. Edward Kamau Brathwaite, *History of the Voice: Development of Nation Language in the Anglophone Caribbean Poetry* (London: New Beacon Books, 1984).
32. Gauri Viswanathan, "Currying Favor: The Politics of British Educational and Cultural Policy in India, 1813–1854," in *Social Text*, 19–20 (Fall 1988), 85–104.
33. Sangari and Vaid, eds. *Recasting Women*, Introduction.
34. Eunice de Souza, "The Language We Use," in *Journal of Commonwealth Literature*, 144–148.
35. Aidoo, "To Be an African Woman," 155–171. See also Ama Ata Aidoo, *Our Sister Killjoy, or Reflections from a Black-Eyed Squint* (New York: NOK Publishers International, 1979).
36. Chinua Achebe, "The African Writer and the English Language," in *Morning Yet on Creation Day* (New York: Anchor Books, 1976), 74–84.
37. Since 2002, Ngugi is the director of the International Center for Writing and Translation (ICWT) at the University of California, Irvine. In this capacity, he has organized many intellectual debates on marginalized languages and the importance of translation. He also challenges the usual one-way process of lesser-known languages always translated into the global language of English. Rather, he wishes to promote work in indigenous languages, even using translation to link marginalized languages to one another (for instance, translations of Yoruba writers from Nigeria into Swahili that is read in Kenya and other parts of Africa, or Hindi to Mandarin) and not always rely on English as the link language.

    A series of excellent seminars entitled "From Here to There: Languages in Conversation," hosted by the ICWT has brought together speakers of native Hawaiian, Maori from New Zealand, Icelandic, and Indonesian. Among many memorable events, "The Maori Shakespeare" stands out. Merimeri Penfold, a Maori poet and translator read her Maori translations of Shakespeare's sonnets and discussed how she wanted to face the challenge of finding out if her mother tongue Maori would withstand the test of translating Shakespeare's English. She was very satisfied with the results and thereby provided her own Maori community with Shakespeare's work in their own language. Another event, "Island Voices," brought together writers from different ends of the Pacific Islands—Kamau Brathwaite from Barbados, Eva Siegel from Samoa, and Witi Ihimeara from Maori New Zealand.
38. Some noteworthy critiques of *The Tempest* are Retamar's essay, "Caliban," in *The Massachusetts Review*, 15, 1–2 (Winter–Spring 1974), 7–72 which embraces Caliban rather than Ariel as a more worthy model for native peoples with histories of domination. See also, Rob Nixon's "Caribbean and African Appropriations of *The Tempest*," in *Critical Inquiry*, 13 (Spring 1987), 557–578; D. O. Mannoni, *Prospero and Caliban: The Psychology of Colonization* (New York: Praeger, 1956, repr. 1964).
39. See Edward Kamau Brathwaite, *Contradictory Omens: Cultural Diversity and Integration in the Caribbean* (Mona, Jamaica: Savacou Publications, 1974, repr. 1985) for a fine discussion of racial and color spectrums and hierarchies as part of Caribbean history and culture. See also Rex Nettleford, *Caribbean Cultural Identity: The Case of Jamaica* (Los Angeles: UCLA, 1979).

40. Marlene Nourbese Philip, *She Tries Her Tongue, Her Silence Softly Breaks* (Charlottetown: Ragweed Press, 1989). See also by Philip, *Frontiers: Essays and Writings on Racism and Culture* (Ontario: The Mercury Press, 1992).
41. For instance, the twenty-year gap between the publication of Achebe's novel, *A Man of the People* and *Anthills of the Savannah*, was interpreted in the western press as "Achebe's silence," notwithstanding the fact that he had worked in his native Igbo language during that period.
42. Rosemary Bray, "Nefertiti's New Clothes," in *Voice Literary Supplement* (June 1982), 13–14.
43. Mikhail Bakhtin, "Discourse on the Novel," in Michael Holquist, ed., Caryl Emerson and Michael Holquist, trans. *The Dialogic Imagination: Four Essays* (Austin: University of Texas Press, 1981).
44. Pam Morris, ed. *The Bakhtin Reader: Selected Writings of Bakhtin, Medvedev, Voloshinov* (London, New York: Edward Arnold: 1994).
45. Mikhail Bakhtin, *Rabelais and His World*, trans. Helene Tswalsky (Bloomington: Indiana University Press, 1984).
46. Morris, *The Bakhtin Reader*, 21.
47. Among numerous useful theoretical studies on this subject, see Lenore Hoffmann and Margo Culley, eds. *Women's Personal Narratives: Essays in Criticism and Pedagogy* (New York: Modern Language Association, 1985); Margo Culley, ed. *American Women's Autobiography: Fea(s)ts of Memory* (Madison: University of Wisconsin Press, 1992); Bella Brodzki and Celeste Schenck, eds. *Life/Lines: Theorizing Women's Autobiography* (Ithaca and London: Cornell University Press, 1988); Kathleen Ashley, Leigh Gilmore, and Gerald Peters, eds. *Autobiography & Postmodernism* (Amherst: University of Massachusetts Press, 1994).
48. Introduction, Sistren and Honor Ford-Smith, *Lionheart Gal*, 17.
49. Honor Ford-Smith, "Sistren: Jamaican Women's Theater," in D. Kahn and D. Neumaier, eds. *Cultures in Contention* (Seattle: The Real Comet Press, 1985), 85–91. See also Honor Ford-Smith, "Sistren: Exploring Women's Problems through Drama," in *Jamaica Journal*, 19, 1 (February–April, 1986), 2–12; Joan French, "Organizing Women through Drama in Rural Jamaica," in *FAO Magazine*, "Idea and Action," 138, 4 (1985).
50. Bray, "Nefertiti's New Clothes," 13–14.
51. Cosmo Pieterse and Dennis Duerden, eds. *African Writers Talking: A Collection of Radio Interviews* (New York: Africana Publishing Corporation, 1972), 19–27.
52. Arjun Appadurai, "Disjuncture and Difference in the Global Cultural Economy," in Appadurai, *Modernity at Large*. Previously published in *Public Culture*, 2, 2 (Spring 1990), 1–24.
53. Gloria Anzaldua, *Borderlands, La Frontera: The New Mestiza* (San Francisco: Spinsters Press, 1987), Preface.
54. Soja, *Postmodern Geographies*, 18.
55. Michel Foucault, "Of Other Spaces," in *Diacritics*, 16 (1986), trans. Jay Miskowiec, 22–27.
56. Gauri Viswanathan, *Masks of Conquest: Literary Study and British Rule in India* (New York: Columbia University Press, 1989). I will discuss this issue further in chapter 3.

57. Michelle Cliff, "If I Could Write This in Fire, I would Write This in Fire," in Rick Simonson and Scott Walker, eds. *Multicultural Literacy* (Saint Paul: Graywolf Press, 1988), 72.
58. Louise Kennedy, "A Writer Retraces her Steps: Jamaica Kincaid Finds Herself in Her Words," in *The Boston Globe*, November 7, 1990, 89.
59. Mohanty et al., eds. *Third World Women and the Politics of Feminism*, Introduction. See also Laura E. Donaldson, *Decolonizing Feminisms: Race, Gender and Empire-Building* (Chapel Hill, North Carolina: University of North Carolina Press, 1992).
60. Robin Morgan, ed. *Sisterhood is Global: The International Women's Movement Anthology* (New York: Archer/Doubleday, 1984).
61. Bina Agarwal, "Positioning the Western Feminist Agenda: A Comment," in *The Indian Journal of Gender Studies*, 1: 2 (July–December 1994), 249–255. See also Kamla Bhasin and Nighat S. Khan, *Some Questions on Feminism and its Relevance in South Asia* (New Delhi: Kali for Women, 1986, repr. 1994); Kamla Bhasin and Nighat S. Khan, *The Quota Question: Women and Electoral Needs* (Bombay: Akshara Publications, 1991).
62. Roy's personal involvement in the anti-Narmada project, and her celebrity status that brought global attention to this matter are recorded in a documentary entitled DAM/AGE. The film also records Roy's own battle with the Indian Supreme Court over her protests.
63. Vibhuti Patel, "Women's Liberation in India," in *New Left Review*, 153 (September/October 1985), 75–86.
64. Maithreyi Krishnaraj, "A Discussion Paper for ICSSR—Regional Workshop on Women's Studies, May 29–30, 1987, Pune" (Bombay: Research Center, SNDT Women's University, 1987), 1–16. See also, Maithreyi Krishnaraj, ed. *Feminism: Indian Debates 1990* (Bombay: Research Centre, SNDT Women's University, 1990); also see Krishnaraj, ed. *Evolving New Methodologies in Research on Women's Studies*.
65. Filomena Steady, "African Feminism: A Worldwide Perspective," in Rosalyn Terborg-Penn, Sharon Harley, and Andrea B. Rushing, eds. *Women in Africa and the African Diaspora* (Washington D.C.: Three Continents Press, 1987), 3–24. See also Stanley M. James and Abena P. A. Busia, eds. *Theorizing Black Feminisms: The Visionary Pragmatism of Black Women* (London and New York: Routledge, 1993).
66. Oyeronke Oyewumi, *The Invention of Women: Making African Sense of Western Gender Discourses* (Minneapolis and London: University of Minnesota Press, 1997). See also Nfah-Abbenyi and Juliana Makachi, *Gender in African Women's Writing: Identity, Sexuality, and Difference* (Bloomington: Indiana University Press, 1997).
67. Hazel Carby, "White Woman Listen! Black Feminism and the Boundaries of Sisterhood," in *The Empire Strikes Back: Race and Racism in 70s Britain* (London: Hutchinson, 1982), 212–235.
68. Valerie Amos and Pratibha Parmar, "Challenging Imperial Feminism," in *Feminist Review*, 17 (Autumn 1984), 3–20.
69. Niara Sudarkasa, " 'The Status of Women' in Indigenous African Societies," in Terborg-Penn et al., eds. *Women in Africa and the African Diaspora*, 25–42.

70. Olive Senior, "Letter from the Lesser World," in *Talking of Trees* (Kingston: Calabash, 1985), 47–48.
71. Davies and Graves, eds. *Ngambika*, 1–24.
72. Quoted in Alan Sheridan, *Michel Foucault: The Will to Truth* (New York: Tavistock Publications, 1980), 217.
73. Jana Sawicki, *Disciplining Foucault: Feminism, Power, and the Body* (New York and London: Routledge, 1991).
74. Michel Foucault, *The History of Sexuality, Volume I: An Introduction*, trans. Robert Hurley (New York: Vintage Books, 1980).
75. Irene Diamond and Lee Quinby, eds. *Feminism and Foucault: Reflections on Resistance* (Boston: Northeastern University Press, 1988), Introduction.
76. Quoted in R. Radhakrishnan, *Diasporic Mediations* (Minneapolis and London: University of Minnesota Press, 1996), 37.
77. Helen Tiffin, "Postcolonialism, Post-Modernism and the Rehabilitation of Post-colonial History," in *The Journal of Commonwealth Literature*, 23, 1 (1988), 169–181.
78. This is similar to the theoretical challenges to the category of "race" although racism is very much alive, and similar also to the challenges to the category of "woman" although sexism is all around us.
79. R. Radhakrishnan, "Toward an Effective Intellectual: Foucault or Gramsci?" in his text, *Diasporic Mediations*, 27–61.
80. See my Afterword to Ama Ata Aidoo's collection of stories, *No Sweetness Here*, reissued in 1995 by Feminist Press in New York.
81. Frederic Jameson, "Third World Literature in an Era of Multinational Capitalism," in *Social Text*, 15 (Fall 1986), 65–88, quote on 65. The necessity to take issue with this particular essay is distressing especially since I respect and admire Jameson's many significant contributions to literary criticism over the past several years, and I consider him a political ally.
82. Aijaz Ahmad, "Jameson's Rhetoric of Otherness and the 'National Allegory,'" in *Social Text*, 17 (Fall 1987), 3–27. See also Aijaz Ahmad, *In Theory: Classes, Nations, Literatures* (London: Verso, 1992).
83. Chandra T. Mohanty, "Under Western Eyes: Feminist Scholarship and Colonial Discourses," in *Boundary 2*, 12, 3 (Spring/Fall 1984), 333–358.
84. Wole Soyinka, "The Critic and Society: Barthes, Leftocracy, and Other Mythologies," in Soyinka, *Art, Dialogue and Outrage*, 146–178.

CHAPTER 2   *Indigenous Third World Female Traditions of Resistance*

1. Apart from Frantz Fanon, Amilcar Cabral, Homi Bhabha, Gayatri Spivak, literary writers who engage with colonial history in their essays and interviews include Ngugi wa Thiong'o, Wole Soyinka, Ama Ata Aidoo, Kamau Brathwaite, Merle Hodge, and Eunice de Souza.
2. Alexander and Mohanty, eds. *Feminist Genealogies*, xli.
3. See Mohanty et al., eds. *Third World Women and the Politics of Feminism*; Mohanty, *Feminism without Borders*; Schenck and Benstock, eds. *Life/Lines*; Michele Barrett, *Women's Oppression Today: Problems in Marxist-Feminist*

Analysis (London: Verso, 1980); Amrita Basu, *Two Faces of Protest: Contrasting Modes of Women's Activism in India* (Berkeley: University of California Press, 1992); Ilina Sen, *A Space Within the Struggle: Women's Participation in Peoples' Movements* (New Delhi: Kali for Women, 1990).

4. Kumari Jayawardena, "Women and Myths of Colonialism," The Bunting Institute Colloquium, Radcliffe College, January 13, 1988, typescript, 1–20.
5. Much of this history is corrected by feminist historiographers like Elsa Goveia, Lucille Mathurin Mair, among others, in the Caribbean; Margaret Strobel, Stephanie Urdang, Christine Qunta, among others, in Africa; historians and interdisciplinary culture studies scholars like Kumkum Sangari, Sudesh Vaid, Joanna Liddle, and Rama Joshi, among others, in India.
6. Uma Chakravarti and Kum Kum Roy, "Breaking Out of Invisibility: Rewriting the History of Women in Ancient India," in S. Jay Kleinberg, ed. *Retrieving Women's History: Changing Perceptions of the Role of Women in Politics and Society* (Oxford [England], New York, Berg, Paris: Unesco Press, 1988), 319–337.
7. Romila Thapar, "Traditions Versus Misconceptions." Interview with Madhu Kishwar and Ruth Vanita in *Manushi*, 42, 3 (1987), 2–14.
8. *The Ramayana* continues to inspire contemporary artists as in Indian-American playwright Shishir Kurup's 2004 play entitled *As Vishnu Dreams*. Although Kurup's script remains fairly close to the classical version, the use of theatrical elements such as Balinese puppets add a spectacular dimension to the story. However, Kurup does not take his revisions far enough, especially in the representation of Sita. A plot twist at the very end when Sita claims Ravana as her father does not really do much to reinterpret the traditional roles of good and evil although Kurup tries to reverse the roles by humanizing the demons and Ravana, while making Rama monstrous and blood-thirsty rather than the ideal and fair ruler.
9. Foucault, *The History of Sexuality*, 94.
10. Frantz Fanon, *The Wretched of the Earth*, trans. by Constance Farrington (New York: Grove Press, 1961, repr. 1977), 57.
11. Kumari Jayawardena, *Feminism and Nationalism in the Third World* (London: Zed Books, 1986), Introduction.
12. Lucille Mathurin, *The Rebel Woman in the British West Indies During Slavery* (Kingston: The Institute of Jamaica, 1975). All quotations are taken from this text. See also, Mathurin, "Women Field Workers in Jamaica during Slavery," The 1986 Elsa Goveia Memorial Lecture (Mona: University of West Indies, 1986); Barbara Bush, *Slave Women in Caribbean Society 1650–1838* (London and Bloomington: Heinemann and Indiana University Press, 1990); Marcia Wright, *Strategies of Slaves & Women: Life-Stories from East/Central Africa* (London: James Currey, New York: Lillian Barber, 1993).
13. Bryan Edwards, "The History of the West Indies," in Richard Price, ed. *Maroon Societies: Rebel Slave Communities in the Americas* (Baltimore and London: Johns Hopkins University Press, 1973, repr. 1979), 230–248. See also Mavis Campbell, *The Maroons of Jamaica, 1655–1776: A History of Resistance, Collaboration, and Betrayal* (Trenton, New Jersey: Africa World Press, 1990).

14. Elsa Goveia, *Slave Society in the British Leeward Islands at the Ed of the Eighteenth Century* (New Haven: Yale University Press, 1965).
15. Orlando Patterson, *The Sociology of Slavery: An Analysis of the Origins, Development, and Structure of Negro Slave Society in Jamaica* (London: MacGibbon & Kee, 1967). See also other texts on Caribbean history: Pat Ellis, ed. *Women of the Caribbean* (London: Zed Press, 1986); James Millette, *Society and Politics in Colonial Trinidad* (London: Zed Press, 1970, repr. 1985); Campbell, *The Maroons of Jamaica*; Bush, *Slave Women in Caribbean Society*.
16. Christine Qunta, ed. *Women in Southern Africa* (London: Allison & Busby, 1987); David Lan, *Guns and Rain: Guerillas and Spirit Mediums in Zimbabwe* (London: J. Currey; Berkeley, University of California Press, 1985); T. O. Ranger, *Revolt in Southern Rhodesia 1896–7: A Study in African Resistance* (London: Heinemann, 1967).
17. Lorna Goodison, *I Am Becoming My Mother* (London and Port-of-Spain: New Beacon Books, 1986), 44–45.
18. Ranger, *Revolt in Southern Rhodesia*, xvii–xviii.
19. See also, Irene Staunton, *Mothers of the Revolution: The War Experiences of Thirty Zimbabwean Women* (Bloomington: Indiana University Press, 1990) for fascinating oral history documentation of women's participation in the liberation struggle, continuing in a tradition inspired by figures like Nehanda.
20. Bennetta Jules-Rosette, "Privilege Without Power: Women in African Cults and Churches," in Terborg-Penn et al., *Women in Africa and the African Diaspora*, 99–119.
21. Barrett, *Women's Oppression Today*, 9.
22. Judith Van Allen, "'Aba Riots' or Igbo 'Women's War'? Ideology, Stratification, and the Invisibility of Women," in Nancy J. Hafkin and Edna G. Bay, eds. *Women in Africa: Studies in Social and Economic Change* (Stanford: Stanford University Press, 1976), 59–85, quotation on 69.
23. Talwar Oldenburg, "Lifestyle as Resistance: The Case of the Courtesans of Lucknow, India," in *Feminist Studies*, 16, 2, (Summer 1990), 259–288.
24. Buchi Emecheta, *The Joys of Motherhood* (New York: G. Braziller, 1979).
25. Sangari and Vaid, eds. *Recasting Women*, Introduction.
26. Kumari Jayawardena, "Women, Social Reform and Nationalism in India," in Jayawardena, *Feminism and Nationalism in the Third World*. Subsequent information is taken from this source.
27. S. J. Joshi, trans. from Marathi by Asha Damle, *Anandi Gopal* (Calcutta: Stree, 1992). This text is the biographical/novelistic recreation of Anandi's life by the well-known Marathi male writer, S. J. Joshi. He relied on correspondence between Anandi and her husband, and the people they knew. English readers are now indebted to the translated (and abridged) version of Anandi's life presented by a female writer, Asha Damle whose text has significant feminist evocations in the representation of Anandi's life.
28. Jayawardena, Bunting Institute Colloquium, typescript, 1.
29. Madhu Kishwar, "Gandhi on Women," in *Economic and Political Weekly*, 20, 40 (October 5, 1985), 1691–1702.
30. Sangari and Vaid, eds. *Recasting Women*, Introduction.

31. Jayawardena, Bunting Institute Colloquium, typescript, 13.
32. Feminism and anti-feminism are linked also in the United States. See a text that I co-edited with Clark et al., *Antifeminism in the Academy*.
33. Fanon, *The Wretched of the Earth*. Fanon, a native of Martinique when it was a French colony, was trained in the French language and intellectual tradition. He was drafted at age nineteen for the French colonial war in Algeria. From 1944, Algeria became his adopted home. Trained as a psycho-therapist, Fanon's practice became radicalized when he had to treat torture victims during the Algerian liberation struggle. The seeds of his concept of colonialism as inherently violent as expressed in *The Wretched of the Earth* were sown. The text itself was written in an incredibly short ten-week span toward the end of Fanon's short life. He died of leukemia at the age of thirty-six.

    Gandhi, trained as a lawyer in Britain, had the historic opportunity on his way back to India, to intervene in a social protest against Pass Laws in South Africa. The seeds of a non-violent action strategy were sown, and this was practiced in various struggles during the Indian nationalist movement in the early part of the twentieth century. The impact of Gandhi's non-violent ideology was felt during the 1960's Civil Rights Movement in the United States, and in Port-of-Spain, Trinidad, among the Indians who went there as indentured laborers.
34. The correspondences and dissonances of national liberation and women's liberation are discussed in a most useful volume of essays: Andrew Parker, Mary Russo, Doris Sommer, and Patricia Yaeger, eds. *Nationalisms and Sexualities* (New York and London: Routledge, 1992). The essays range across vast geographies—Iran, India, Singapore, Argentina, India, etc. See my essay, "Indian Nationalism, Gandhian 'Satyagraha' and Representations of Female Sexuality," 395–406 in this volume. I am grateful to the editors, especially Andrew Parker and Mary Russo, for their suggestions. I use some parts of my essay for the discussion here.
35. The disturbing rise of Hindu fundamentalism led by the Bharatiya Janata Party in India spearheaded the Babri Masjid destruction. The fundamentalists' inflammatory claim (unsupported by any historical evidence) that the site where this ancient 500-year-old mosque stood is the very site where the Hindu god Rama was born led to the destruction of the mosque and to widespread riots all over the country. In Bombay, 60,000 Muslims were "expelled" from their homes. The horrific wave of "ethnic cleansing" rendered citizens into refugees with no recourse to state protection of their rights.
36. It is a testament to the ordinary majority of people in India that the BJP was stunned into a resounding defeat in the 2004 national elections. The genocide in Gujarat played a role in their defeat. The news also sent shock-waves to a worldwide business community with investments in India. Globalization and liberalization of India's economic policies over the last several years is controversial in its "trickle-down" benefits that most often do not reach the poorest segments of society.
37. Frantz Fanon, *Studies in a Dying Colonialism*, trans. By H. Chevalier (London: Earthscan Publications, 1959, repr. 1989). All textual quotations are from this edition.
38. B. Marie Perinbam, "The Parrot and the Phoenix: Frantz Fanon's View of the West Indian and Algerian Woman," in *Savacou*, 13, (1977), 7–13.

39. See Homi Bhabha's discussion on Fanon in *The Location of Culture* (London and New York: Routledge, 1994). Bhabha undertakes a psychoanalytic discussion of racial stereotypes as presented by Fanon.
40. Malek Alloula, *The Colonial Harem*, trans. by Myrna and Wald Godzich (Minneapolis: University of Minnesota Press, 1986).
41. Jayawardena, Bunting Institute Colloquium, typescript, 16.
42. Joan V. Bondurant, *Conquest of Violence: The Gandhian Philosophy of Conflict* (Princeton: Princeton University Press, 1958, repr. 1988), 7.
43. Partha Chatterjee, *Nationalist Thought and the Colonial World: A Derivative Discourse?* (Zed Press: United Nations Library, 1986), 151.
44. Mohandas Karamchand Gandhi, *The Story of My Experiments with Truth* (New York: Dover Publications, 1983).
45. Bondurant, *Conquest of Violence*, 18.
46. Sudhir Kakar, "Gandhi and Women," in *Intimate Relations: Exploring Indian Sexuality* (Chicago: The University of Chicago Press, 1988), 85–128. All references to Kakar are taken from this chapter.
47. In chapter 3, I discuss the struggles around sexuality and food as they are played out on the site of Nyasha's female body in Tsitsi Dangarembga's novel *Nervous Conditions*.
48. Pat Caplan, "Celibacy as a Solution? Mahatma Gandhi and *Brahmacharya*," in Caplan, ed. *The Cultural Construction of Sexuality*, 271–295.
49. Gandhi, *Collected Works*, 15 (Ahmedabad: Navjivan Trust, 1982), 291. Speech at a women's meeting, Bombay, May 8, 1919.
50. *Harijan*, December 2, 1931; also in *Collected Works*, 70, 381.
51. *Young India*, June 11, 1925; also in *Collected Works*, 27, 219–220.
52. Quoted in Jayawardena, *Feminism and Nationalism*, 95.
53. John Stuart Mill's "The Subjection of Women," in John M. Robson, ed. *Collected Works of John Stuart Mill*, 21 (Toronto: University of Toronto Press, 1984), 261–340 (written in 1860 after the death of his wife Harriet Taylor to whom he attributed many of his ideas) argued, for example, that education and changes in the law would ensure equality between the sexes though each would continue to retain its own "separate sphere." Mill's views echo those of Gandhi and other nineteenth-century Indian social reformers such as Dayananda Saraswati and Sarojini Naidu, whose campaigns for women's education and suffrage were related integrally to the doctrine of "separate spheres."
54. Despite the Prohibition of Dowry Act (1961), this "tradition" continues with gruesome abuses in recent years. Short news items like the following are common: "Woman burnt to death. A case of suicide has been registered. The police are enquiring into the matter." A growing number of incidents document how after marriage, a husband's family, dissatisfied with the amount of dowry brought by the wife, decide to murder her. A "kitchen fire" is staged and the murder is passed off as suicide. The husband is then "free" to remarry and acquire more dowry. Women's groups have mobilized non-violent demonstrations and insisted that these cases be brought to trial as murders. For more information, see Kishwar et al., eds. *In Search of Answers*. See also, Gandhi and Shah, *The Issues at Stake*, especially chapter 3, "Violence Becomes a Political Issue," 36–101.

55. A tradition different from middle-class women's participation in government is that of militancy among working-class women. See Gail Omvedt, *We Will Smash This Prison: Indian Women in Struggle* (London: Zed Books, 1980).
56. Suresht Renjen Bald, "From Satyartha Prakash to *Manushi*: An Overview of the Women's Movement in India." University of Michigan, Working Paper no. 23, April 1983, 18 pages.
57. *Young India*, May 21, 1931; also in *Collected Works*, 46, 189.
58. The autonomous (non-governmental) women's movement in India today includes various women's groups from all over the country, urban and rural, and covers multifaceted issues. The movement, in general, is activist in orientation. At The Fourth National Conference of Women's Movements in India, held in Calicut, Kerala (December 27–31, 1990), some 200 different women's groups were represented. There were nearly 1,800 women present from all over India, and ten different languages were represented. Urban-based groups like The Forum Against the Oppressions of Women; Bombay Union of Journalists (Women and Media Committee) deal with issues of rape, inheritance laws, pornographic publications. These groups publish consciousness-raising pamphlets as and when appropriate. Sabala Mahila Sangh (resettlement "bastis," that is, communities in and outside Delhi), Chingari, Sewa (Ahmedabad), Sahiyar: A Women's Organisation (Vadodara), Sarvadana Sangam: Tamil Nadu Women's Movement (Tiruvannamalai), Sasvika (Ajmer), Stree Jagruti Samiti (Bangalore) were some of the women's groups represented at the conference. The women's movement also encompasses feminist presses like Kali for Women (Delhi) that has published very significant texts like Sangari and Vaid, *Recasting Women*; Bina Agarwal, ed. *Structures of Patriarchy;* Gandhi and Shah, *The Issues at Stake*, among others. Feminist magazines like *Manushi: A Journal of Women and Society* (In English and Hindi) and *Stree Sangarsh* (English) provide a forum for written expression and sharing of activist strategies.
59. Kishwar et al., eds. *In Search of Answers*; Katherine Mayo, *Mother India* (London: Jonathan Cape, 1927).
60. Mary Daly, *Beyond God the Father: Toward a Philosophy of Women's Liberation* (Boston: Beacon Press, 1973).

CHAPTER 3   **English Education Socializing the Female Body**

Olive Senior, Talking of Trees (Kingston: Herald Ltd., 1985). See also Olive Senior, *Discerner of Hearts and Other Stories* (Ontario: McClelland & Stewart, Inc., 1995); Olive Senior, *Gardening in the Tropics* (Ontario: McClelland & Stewart, Inc., 1994); Paulo Freire, *The Pedagogy of the Oppressed* (New York: Continuum International Publishing Group, 2000).

1. Chiekh Hamidou Kane, *Ambiguous Adventure* (New York: Walker, 1963).
2. Homi Bhabha, "Of Mimicry and Men: The Ambivalence of Colonial Discourse," in Frederick Cooper and Ann Laura Stoler, eds. *Tensions of Empire: Colonial Cultures in a Bourgeois World* (Berkeley: University of California Press, 1997), 152–160. See also Bhabha, *The Location of Culture*.
3. Philip, *She Tries Her Tongue, Her Silence Softly Breaks*, 11.
4. Jug Suraiya, "The Chips Are Down for Post-modern Hindi," in *The Times of India*, June 19, 1990.

5. In India, "vernacular" students undergo a high school education in one of many indigenous languages such as Hindi, Urdu, Marathi. However, when they begin any four-year degree program at university, they are expected to make an almost overnight shift to having all studies conducted in English. When I started going to St. Xavier's College in Bombay, I encountered this disparity, and recognized what a tremendous advantage I had had in having attended English-medium high school. At St. Xavier's College, we volunteered and conducted English classes to bring vernacular students to the level of those who had attended English-medium schools prior to entering college.
6. Claire Robertson, "Women's Education and Class Formation in Africa, 1950–1980," in Claire Robertson and Iris Berger, eds. *Women and Class in Africa* (New York and London: Africana Publishing, 1986), 92–113. See also A. A. Saakane, *The Colonial Legacy in Caribbean Literature* (New Jersey: Africa World Press, 1987); George J. Sefa Dei, *Schooling and Education in Africa: The Case of Ghana* (New Jersey: Africa World Press, 2004); H. E. Newsum, *Class, Language, and Education* (New Jersey: Africa World Press, 1990).
7. A. Babs Fafunwa, "African Education in Perspective," in A. Babs Fafunwa and J. U. Aisiku, eds. *Education in Africa: A Comparative Survey* (London: George Allen & Unwin, 1982), 9–27.
8. Chinua Achebe, *Things Fall Apart* (London: Heinemann, 1958).
9. French colonial educational policies were markedly different from the British. The French propagated "assimilation" in all aspects, and rather than adapting any learning to the local needs and contexts of Africans, they openly thrust their superior values and culture on the natives. "Determined efforts were made," notes Fafunwa "to make colonial education a close replica of the educational system in France" (22).
10. A. Asiedu-Akrofi, "Education in Ghana," outlines the history of the Phelps-Stokes Commission which "was sponsored by the Foreign Missions Conference of North America to investigate the educational work being done in Africa and to find out how the needs of Africans were being met. The Commission was financed by the Phelps-Stokes Fund, established in 1911 for the education of negroes, Their report, published in 1922, was an epoch-making document. It was the first report that stressed sociological factors in building African curricula." In Fafunwa and Aisiku, eds. *Education in Africa*, 114.
11. Helen Kitchen, ed. *The Educated African* (New York: Praeger, 1962), 135.
12. A parallel can be evoked here with the situation of vernacular-medium students in India who come to college with inadequate English language skills. Of course, the South African situation during apartheid (eliminated since Nelson Mandela's election as president in 1994) systematically maintained the lower status of black people not only in education, but in all aspects of life. Apartheid brutality in terms of imbalances in educational opportunities for blacks, and education reform has a long history in South Africa, including the legendary courage of the Soweto student protests against Bantu education, leading to the Soweto killings of innocent children (shot in the back by police). Part of this history includes the arrest and liquidation of political activists and education reformers such as Steve Biko (killed while in prison), and the unrecorded histories of many brave men and women who often fought

machine guns and "hippos" (tanks) only with stones, and the fire in their hearts.
13. For further details on the unfolding of western-style education in Nigeria, see Onyerisara Ukeje and J. U. Aisiku, "Education in Nigeria," in Fafunwa and Aisiku, eds. *Education in Africa*.
14. C. S. Lakshmi, "Walking Erect with an Unfaltering Gaze: The Educated Woman in Modern Tamil Literature," in Karuna Chanana, ed. *Socialisation, Education And Women: Explorations In Gender Identity* (Hyderabad: Orient Longman Limited, 1988), 273–281, quote on 274. See also T. K. Pillai and K. Rajeswari, *Readings in Women's Education* (Kodaikanal: Mother Theresa Women's University, n.d.).
15. Merle Hodge, *Crick Crack, Monkey* (London: Heinemann, 1970).
16. Bessie Head, *Maru* (London: Heinemann, 1971); Erna Brodber, *Jane and Louisa Will Soon Come Home* (London and Port of Spain: New Beacon Books, 1980). See also Brodber's study *Perceptions of Caribbean Women: Towards a Documentation of Stereotypes* with an introduction by Merle Hodge (Institute of Social and Economic Research, University of the West Indies, Cave Hill, Barbados, 1982). In the Women in the Caribbean Project Vol. 4. General Editor Joycelin Massiah.
17. Ama Ata Aidoo, *No Sweetness Here* (London: Longman, 1970), 1–7. Most of Aidoo's work (like that of her Ghanaian compatriot Efua Sutherland) had been out of print for several years which exemplifies the complex conditions of publishing and distribution that can render a writer visible or invisible. A most welcome re-issuing of *No Sweetness Here* (with an Afterword by myself) is published by Feminist Press in 1995.
18. Meenakshi Mukherjee, "Dancing Dogs and Bears," in *Manushi*, 4 (1979–1980), 63–65.
19. Gauri Viswanathan, "English in a Literate Society," in Rajeswari Sunder Rajan, ed. *The Lie of the Land: English Literary Studies in India* (Delhi, Oxford, New York: Oxford University Press, 1993), 29–41.
20. Head, *The Collector of Treasures*, 76–80.
21. My historical discussion here relies on research into selected British Parliamentary Papers, especially the Parliamentary Committee on the Affairs of the East India Company; A. N. Basu, ed. *Indian Education in Parliamentary Papers, Part I* (Bombay and Calcutta: Asia Publishing House, 1952). I also draw upon Gauri Viswanathan's study, *Masks of Conquest* and Rajeswari Sunder Rajan's edited collection, *The Lie of the Land*. Viswanathan's use of Gramsci's formulation is most useful, namely, that domination in linguistic and educational curricula works most effectively not through force but through consent of the dominated.
22. Rajan evokes "the subversive possibilities of our students' (mis) appropriation of the English 'book', in line with Homi Bhabha's theorization of colonial mimicry" (7). Rajan's own exploration is useful in her contextualizing the study of English in three broad categories: "history, language, politics."
23. See also other useful studies such as Svati Joshi, ed. *Rethinking English: The Cultural Politics of Literature, Language and Pedagogy in India* (New Delhi: Trianka, 1991); D. J. Palmer, *The Rise of English Studies: An Account of the Study of English Language and Literature from its Origins to the Making of the Oxford English School* (London: Oxford University Press, 1965). Also worth noting is a

chapter entitled "The Rise of English" in Terry Eagleton's *Literary Theory: An Introduction* (Minneapolis: University of Minnesota Press, 1983).
24. Achebe, *Things Fall Apart*. See also, Hafkin and Bay, eds. *Women in Africa*; Robertson and Berger, eds. *Women and Class in Africa*.
25. Carl C. Campbell, *Colony & Nation: A Short History of Education in Trinidad and Tobagao 1834–1986* (Kingston, Jamaica: Ian Randle Publishers, 1992). See also Hubert Devonish, *Language and Liberation: Creole Language Politics in the Caribbean* (London: Karia Press, 1986).
26. Similar agitations reverberate in other colonies caught under the post-independence sense of betrayal of the dreams of a new nation. Protests around educational policies as one among other social issues that need reform, most often caught statically in colonial models, are common. Examples can be cited from state-border disputes that are linguistically instigated in India; Ngugi's call for the abolition of the English Department to be replaced by Department of Languages and Literatures at the University of Nairobi; South African black peoples' struggles against Bantu education, and social protests that led to the horrors of the Soweto killings.
27. Head, *The Collector of Treasures*, 103.
28. The topic of English education in India in the nineteenth century went along with the role of social reformers who wanted to demonstrate their acceptance of modernity by allowing women to be educated, albeit, as appropriately gendered for women. Women as educated wives and mothers rather than as career women were favored. Sacrifice for the family still remained their dominant role. See texts by Kumar, *The History of Doing* and Shah and Gandhi, *The Issues at Stake*, for more discussions on this topic.
29. Viswanathan, *Masks of Conquest*, 64.
30. Viswanathan, "Currying Favor," in *Social Text*, 19–20 (Fall 1988), 85–104. Quote on 102.
31. Manju Dalmia, "Derozio: English Teacher," in Rajan, ed. *The Lie of the Land*, 42–62.
32. Attia Hosain, *Sunlight on a Broken Column* (London: Penguin Books, 1961); Kamala Markandaya, *Two Virgins: A Novel* (New York: John Day Co., 1973).
33. Leela Dube, "Socialisation of Hindu Girls in Patrilineal India," Leela Dube and Rajni Palriwala, eds. *Structures and Strategies: Women, Work and Family* (New Delhi, Newbury Park, California: Sage Publications, 1990).
34. Interview with Merle Hodge, "We Are All Activists: An Interview with Merle Hodge," *Callaloo*, 41 (Fall 1989) by Kathleen M. Balutansky, *Callaloo*, 41 (Fall 1989), 651–662.
35. Rhoda Reddock, *Women, Labour and Politics in Trinidad and Tobago: A History* (London, Atlantic Highlands, New Jersey: Zed Books, 1994).
36. The statistics provided by Reddock are useful: "It was not until later in the 1920s however, that any other secondary girls schools were affiliated to the Queens Royal College (QRC). These were the Canadian Presbyterian Naparima Girls College in the south and the Anglican St. Hilary's Girls College in the north. . . . These schools started with very low enrollments of for example 77 for the former and 92 for the latter in 1925 at a time when QRC had an enrollment of 239, St. Mary's of 408, Naparima's of 107 and St. Joseph's Convent of 401" (222). See

also Ruby King and Mike Morrissey, *Images in Print: Bias and Prejudice in Caribbean Textbooks* (Mona, Jamaica: UWI, Institute of Social and Economic Research, 1988).

37. Joan French, "Colonial Policy Towards Women After the 1938 Uprising: The Case of Jamaica," The Hague: Institute of Social Studies, Working Paper 7, 37.
38. Although Bim's situation is grim at the end, her representation as an educated, independent, unmarried woman marks an important change from Desai's earlier novels, such as *Cry, the Peacock* (Delhi: Orient Paperbacks, 1980, repr. 1983) which I will discuss in chapter 4.
39. Eunice de Souza, "Mrs. Hermione Gonsalvez," in *Fix* (Bombay: Newground, 1979).
40. Goveia, *Slave Society in the British Leeward Islands at the End of the Eighteenth Century*, 10.
41. There is some dispute as to whether this can be called "a total social system." Orlando Patterson in his *Sociology of Slavery* regards Jamaica like most plantocracies "as a collection of autonomous plantations, each a self-contained community with its internal mechanisms of power than as a total social system." Also discussed in *Savacou*, 1, 1, n.d., Introduction.
42. Edward Kamau Brathwaite, *The Development of Creole Society in Jamaica, 1770–1820* (Oxford: Clarendon Press, 1971), 307. The word "Creole" technically refers to different racial mixtures. In the Caribbean, Creole refers not only to the more obvious black-white mixtures that result in mulatto, quadroon, octoroon, but also to a "white Creole" category. This incorporates, for instance, mixtures of English and French blood. One of the racist strikes against Antoinette in *Wide Sargasso Sea* (New York: Norton, 1966) is that her "pure-blooded" English husband views her "critically [as] creole of pure English descent she may be, but they are not English or European either" (67).
43. This is a particular designation used in the Caribbean—white Creole. The combination of whiteness with Creoleness, that is, of mixed race opens up a spectrum of color possibilities within the white race. For instance, "white" as in "English" when mixed with white as in French, or Spanish, and admixtures thereof would be designated as Creole. Another colloquial expression for a very light-skinned yet African featured person is described as "red."
44. In Head's own painful search for home and country, she finds sympathetic echoes within a history of the Bamangwato people. In two texts—*A Bewitched Crossroad* and *Serowe*—Head, as griot, undertakes a history of Botswana using archival material, as well as interviews and personal testimony.
45. I draw upon Wole Soyinka's theory of Yoruba tragedy as discussed in his essay, "The Fourth Stage," in Soyinka's *Myth, Literature and the African World* (Cambridge: Cambridge University Press, 1976, repr. 1990). See my text, *Wole Soyinka and Modern Tragedy: A Study of Dramatic Theory and Practice* (Westport and London: Greenwood Press, 1986) for a fuller discussion of "The Fourth Stage."
46. Bessie Head, "Social and Political Pressures that Shape Literatures in South Africa," in *World Literature Written in English*, 18, 1 (1979), 20–26.
47. I am grateful to my colleague Thomas Cassirer at the University of Massachusetts, Amherst, for this insight into *Maru*.

48. Isaac Shapera, *The Khoisan Peoples of South Africa* (London: Humanities Press, 1930), 178–179.
49. Maru's act is similar to that of Gopalrao's marriage to the child-bride Anandi in *Anandi Gopal*. Gopalrao, like Maru is defying social custom by this act in order to fulfill his own agenda. He initially wanted to marry a widow in defiance of social custom but when that plan did not work, he turned to a child-bride who would have literally no say in this decision.
50. See Ketu H. Katrak, "From Paulina to Dikeledi: The Philosophical and Political Vision of Bessie Head's Protagonists," in *Ba Shiru* 12: 2 (1987), 26–35.
51. Evelyn O'Callaghan, "Erna Brodber," in Daryl C. Dance, ed. *Fifty Caribbean Writers: A Bio-Bibliographical Critical Sourcebook* (New York, Westport, London: Greenwood Press, 1986), 71–82, quote on 75.
52. Cliff, "If I Could Write this in Fire, I Would Write This in Fire," 72.
53. The evocation of Polonius from Shakespeare's *Hamlet* brings to mind a different kind of kumbla. The obsequies Polonius's sneaky act of voyeurism as he hides behind the curtains to observe Hamlet and Ophelia leads to his death. This kumbla is not a safe hiding-place for him. He is punished for his do-gooding intrusiveness. In my book *Wole Soyinka and Modern Tragedy*, I discuss the different philosophical and cosmological meanings of death in Shakespearean and Yoruba tragedy.
54. Katrak, *Wole Soyinka and Modern Tragedy*.

CHAPTER 4 *Cultural "Traditions" Exiling the Female Body*

1. Kamala Das, *My Story* (New Delhi: Sterling Paperbacks, 1977); Rhys, *Wide Sargasso Sea*; Efua Sutherland, *Edufa* (London: Longman Drumbeat, 1967).
2. Lata Mani, "Contentious Traditions: The Debate on Sati in Colonial India," in Sangari and Vaid, eds. *Recasting Women*, 88–126. I use this essay for all subsequent quotations. See also Mani's expanded study of sati in her book of the same title as her essay noted above (Berkeley: University of California Press, 1998).
3. Buchi Emecheta, *The Bride Price* (New York: G. Braziller, 1976).
4. Eric Hobsbawm and Terence Ranger, *The Invention of Tradition* (Cambridge and New York: Cambridge University Press, 1983, repr. 1992).
5. Benedict Andersen, *Imagined Communities: Reflections on the Origin and Spread of Nationalism* (London: Verso, 1983).
6. I discuss some uses and abuses of reproductive technologies in chapter 5.
7. In chapter 5 I discuss the abuses of technology in manipulating female sexuality and motherhood. Indian women's activist groups, especially Saheli in Delhi, mobilized against the dumping of Norplant on poor rural women. With no follow-up care, as required for contraceptives like Norplant, many women suffered extremely serious health risks.

    Another technological problem that has been taken up by women's groups and scholars is using amniocentesis not for health reasons but for sex-selective abortions of female fetuses. Ironically, this medical advance disenfranchises women who must struggle against yet another way to reinforce sons over daughters.
8. Karen Sacks, *Sisters and Wives: The Past and Future of Sexual Equality* (Urbana: University of Illinois Press, 1982).

9. Maria Cutrufelli, *Women of Africa: Roots of Oppression* (London: Zed Books, 1983), 41.
10. Buchi Emecheta, *The Slave Girl* (New York: G. Braziller, 1977).
11. See Josna Rege's text, *Colonial Karma* (Palgrave, Macmillan, 2004) for a useful discussion of Anita Desai's work.
12. More on this issue is discussed in chapter 5.
13. See chapter 2 for my discussion of female resistances to slavery in the Caribbean.
14. Kamala Das, "The Old Playhouse," in *The Old Playhouse and Other Poems* (Madras: Orient Longman, 1973), 1.
15. *The Laws of Manu*, trans. Wendy Doniger (London: Penguin, 1991), 55.
16. Kishwar et al., eds. *In Search of Answers*, 54–55.
17. Christine Obbo, *African Women: Their Struggle for Economic Independence* (London: Zed Press, 1980), 33.
18. Maria Mies, *Patriarchy and Accumulation on a World Scale* (London: Zed Press, 1986), 145.
19. Barrett, *Women's Oppression Today*, 10.
20. Agnes Flavia, *My Story . . . Our Story of Rebuilding Broken Lives* (Bombay: Majlish, 1990).
21. Activist materials include local publications such as a pamphlet on rape published by The Lawyers' Collective in Bombay, and anti-dowry materials in the form of testimonies and letters published in feminist magazines such as *Manushi*. See also *The "Ignoble Servility" of Pati Parmeswar—Towards Equality for Women*, The Lawyer's Collective, December 1988; Nandita Hakar, *Demystification of Law for Women* (New Delhi: Lancaster Press, 1986).
22. Madhu Kishwar, "Dowry—To Ensure her Happiness or to Disinherit her?" in *Manushi* (May/June 1986). See also Mala Sen, *Death by Fire: Sati, Dowry Death and Female Infanticide in Modern India* (New Jersey: Rutgers University Press, 2001).
23. Lauretta Ngcobo, "African Motherhood—Myth and Reality," in Petersen and Wastberg, eds. *Criticism and Ideology*, 140–149.
24. In India, the vastly popular TV serial of *The Mahabharata* used to bring the country to a standstill on Sunday mornings. Before the scene of Draupadi's disrobing was to take place, there were bidding competitions among textile mills and saree manufacturers to get this contract—something equivalent to buying an ad slot on U.S. TV during the Motion Picture Academy Awards, or the Super Bowl.
25. "Review Essay on Expression: Women's Cultural Festival," *The Independent* (Bombay), May 29, 1990, 7.
26. *Exploring Selfhood—Women and Theatre* (Bombay: SNDT Women's University, n.d.).
27. Text of this piece is quoted in Vibhuti Patel, "Emergence and Proliferation of the Autonomous Women's Organizations in India."
28. See especially the bride-price transaction scene in Achebe's novel, *Things Fall Apart;* and Soyinka's drama *The Lion and the Jewel* in Wole Soyinka, *Collected Plays, 2* (London and New York: Oxford University Press, 1974) where the modern, educated Lakunle objects to paying the bride-price for Sidi and loses her (for other reasons as well) to the traditionalist Baroka.

29. Efua Sutherland, *The Marriage of Anansewa* (London: Longman Drumbeat, 1975).
30. "Muffet Inna All a Wi" is one of Sistren's co-written plays. Information gathered through conversations with Sistren members in Jamaica.
31. At the Fourth National Conference of Women's Movements in India in Calicut, a session that was meant to deal with lesbian sexuality and that was deliberately termed somewhat innocuously as, "single women," turned out to be a heart-rending session attended by widows recounting their harsh lives. Some had also effectively resisted unfair and cruel treatment legitimized by religious authority.
32. Special Issue on sati, in *Seminar*. A Symposium on Widow Immolation and its Social Context (February 1988). See especially essays by Romila Thapar, Sudesh Vaid, and Kumkum Sangari.
33. See also, Lata Mani's book, *Contentious Traditions*.
34. See Betty Potash, ed. *Widows in African Societies: Choices and Constraints* (Stanford: Stanford University Press, 1986).
35. Prema Karanth, *Phaniyamma*, trans. T. Niranjana (New Delhi: Kali for Women, 1989).
36. Zakia Pathak and Rajeswari Sunder Rajan, "Shahbano," in Judith Butler and Joan W. Scott, eds. *Feminists Theorize the Political* (New York and London: Routledge, 1992), 257–279.
37. Pathak and Rajan borrow the phrase "discursive displacements" from Gayatri Chakravorty Spivak's "Subaltern Studies: Deconstructing Historiography," in Ranajit Guha, ed. *Subaltern Studies IV: Writings on South Asian History and Society* (Delhi: Oxford University Press, 1985), 330–363.
38. Madhu Kishwar, "Pro Women or Anti Muslim? The Shahbano Controversy," *Manushi*, 32 (1986) 4–13, quote on 5.
39. Minu Jain, "Curious Role Reversal," *The Sunday Observer* (January 24, 1988).
40. Ruth Vanita and Saleem Kidwai, eds. *Same-Sex Love in India: Readings from Literature and History* (London: Palgrave, 2000; New Delhi: Macmillan India, 2001). See also Ruth Vanita, ed. *Queering India: Same Sex Love and Eroticism in Indian Culture and Society* (New York and London: Routledge, 2002).
41. Urvashi Vaid, *Virtual Equality: The Mainstreaming of Gay and Lesbian Liberation* (New York and London: Anchor Doubleday, 1995).
42. Bessie Head, *A Question of Power* (London: Heinemann, 1974, repr. 1979). I use the 1979 edition.

CHAPTER 5 *Motherhood Demystified*

Ama Ata Aidoo, *The Dilemma of a Ghost* (London: Longman, 1965), 48–49.
Eunice de Souza, *Fix* (Bombay: Newground, 1979).

1. Barrett, *Women's Oppression Today*, 9.
2. See Kamene Okonjo's essay, "The Dual-Sex Political System in Operation: IgboWomen and Community Politics in Midwestern Nigeria," in Hafkin and Bay, eds. *Women in Africa*, 45–58. See also Ifi Amadiume, *Male Daughters, Female Husbands: Gender and Sex in an African Society* (London: Zed Books, 1987); Obioma Nnaemeka, ed. *The Politics of (M)othering: Womanhood, Identity, and*

Resistance in African Literature (New York and London: Routledge, 1997); Susheila Nasta, ed. *Motherlands: Black Women's Writing from Africa, the Caribbean, and South Asia* (New Jersey: Rutgers University Press, 1992).
3. Aidoo, *No Sweetness Here*. All quotations are taken from the edition published in 1970 by Longman in London.
4. Buchi Emecheta, *Second Class Citizen* (New York: George Braziller, 1975).
5. Alice Walker, "A Writer Because of, Not In Spite of, Her Children," *Ms. Magazine* (January 1976), 40, 106.
6. In a useful essay entitled, "The Hand that Rocks the Cradle Writes the Book," Ursula Le Guin challenges "the books-or-babies myth" that is thrust upon women artists in western cultures. "While writing, the French feminist Helene Cixous calls it, writing in milk, in mother's milk. I like that image, because, even among feminists, the woman writer has been more often considered in her sexuality as a lover than in her sexuality as pregnant-bearing-nursing-caring-for-children." *The New York Times Book Review*, January 22, 1989, 1.
7. Flora Nwapa, *Idu* (London: Heinemann, 1976).
8. Bessie Head, *When Rain Clouds Gather* (London: Heinemann, 1987, 1968). All references are to the 1987 edition.
9. Goodison, *I Am Becoming My Mother*, 7.
10. Goodison, *I Am Becoming My Mother*, 47.
11. Emecheta, *The Joys of Motherhood*. All quotations are taken from the 1979 edition.
12. Kamala Markandaya, *Nectar in a Sieve* (New York: Signet, New American Library, 1982, original 1954 The John Day Co. Publishers).
13. Ama Ata Aidoo, "To Be A Woman," in Morgan, ed. *Sisterhood is Global*, 258–265, quote on 259.
14. Barbara B. Brown, "Women in Botswana," in Jane L. Parpart, ed. *Women and Development in Africa: Comparative Perspectives* (New York and London: University Press of America, 1989), 257–278. Quote on 259.
15. MacKenzie, "Short Fiction in the Making," 17.
16. A similar situation is recorded for "under-18 mothers common among poor" in India. There is high infant mortality among these young mothers, or extremely low birth weights. Although these poor women may be married (and before the legal age of 18 as stipulated by law), they are as ignorant as the Sistren women confess to being with regard to the facts of male and female biology, conception, and pregnancy. *The Hindustan Times*, October 28, 1987.
17. "Bellywoman Bangarang: The Music," typescript, courtesy of Honor Ford-Smith of the Sistren group.
18. "Kumina: an Afro-Jamaican religious cult. The traditional ensemble consists of two types of single-headed drums, the 'kbandu' (basic rhythm) and the smaller 'playing cast' (lead drum). The drummers, seated astride the drums, play using hand technique, and also a 'heeling' technique to alter the pitch of the drumhead (kbandu). Often a separate player, using 'catta sticks', plays on the body of the drum behind the drummer. Other percussion instruments, shakers, scrapers and metal triangles may also be used" ("Bellywoman Bangarang: The Music," typescript, 14, 16). There are useful notes about other traditional rhythms—Igbo, Revival, Rastafarian, Shango—with origins in African and other Caribbean regions

and adapted to a Jamaican setting. See also Edward Kamau Brathwaite, "Kumina: The Spirit of African Survival in Jamaica," in *Jamaica Journal*, 42 (September 1978); and Maureen Warner Lewis, *The Nkuyu: Spirit Messengers of the Kumina* (Mona, Jamaica: Savacou Publications, 1977).
19. Erna Brodber, *Abandonment of Children in Jamaica* (Institute of the West Indies, Mona, Jamaica, Institute of Social and Economic Research, 1974), 1. All other Brodber references are to this text.
20. I was present at this session, and like much else at this Autonomous Women's Movements Conference, I was struck by the courage and resiliency of the activist participants. At this session in particular, the female government officer who was taking a pro-planning policy stance, namely, defending the government's programs that are all directed only to women, was challenged from the floor. Counter arguments were presented, and a much more productive discussion followed in terms of activists' findings of how government programs are interested in fulfilling quotas (targeting certain numbers for sterilization in particular regions), in providing poor follow-up care, and not caring if women lose their lives to a contraception such as Norplant that requires follow-up care. Further, issues of male education and responsibility in producing children are hardly ever a part of "family planning" programs.
21. Olive Senior, "Bright Thursdays," in Olive Senior, *Summer Lightning and Other Stories* (Trinidad and Jamaica: Longman Caribbean Ltd., 1986), 36–53.
22. Balutansky, "We Are All Activists: An Interview with Merle Hodge," *Callaloo*, 655.
23. Merle Hodge, "The Shadow of the Whip: A Comment on Male-Female Relations in the Caribbean," in Orde Coombs, ed. *Is Massa Day Dead? Black Moods in the Caribbean* (New York: Anchor Books, 1974), 111–118.
24. Head, *A Question of Power* (1974); Das, *My Story* (1976). All textual quotations are taken from these editions.
25. Bessie Head, "Witchcraft", *Ms. Magazine* (May 1975), 72–73.
26. Adetokunbo Pearse, "Apartheid and Madness: Bessie Head's *A Question of Power*," in *Kunapipi*, 5, 2 (1983), 81.
27. Sabala and Kranti, *My Body is Mine*, ed. Mira Sadgopal (Pune: Satpahik Mudran, 1995). Also useful for discussions of fertility and sexuality within an activist framework are local publications by The Forum Against the Oppression of Women, Bombay-based woman's activist group; Kamaxi C. Swatija, *We and Our Fertility* (Bombay: Research Centre for Women's Studies, SNDT, 1990). See also, a documentary film called *Something Like a War* by Deepa Dhanraj available through Mediastorm in New Delhi.
28. Quoted in Patricia Jeffrey, Roger Jeffrey, and Andres Lyon, eds. *Labour Pains and Labour Power: Women and Childbearing in India* (London and New Jersey: Zed Books; Delhi: Manohar, 1989), 140.
29. Research Staff, *A Lesser Child: Girl Child in India* (Bombay: Research Centre for Women's Studies [RCWS], SNDT Women's University, 1990, repr. 1991), 71. See also, *Designing Family Research: A Model. Focus on Girl Child* (Bombay: RCWS, SNDT Women's University, 1990).
30. Nikhat Kazmi, "The Plight of the Girl Child," in *The Times of India*, March 9, 1990.

31. Shailaja Bajpai, "The Lesser Sex," in *The Indian Express*, October 28, 1990.
32. Malini Karkal and Divya Pandey, *Studies on Women and Population* (Bombay: Himalaya Publishing House, 1989), 35.
33. Nachiketa Desai, "Born to Die," in *The Indian Post*, October 7, 1988, 5.
34. I am grateful to Madhusree Dutta for telling me about *Anuradha*, and for letting me view her videotape copy of the serial.
35. See also Mildred Hill-Lubin's "The Grandmother in African and African-American Literature," in Davies and Graves, *Ngambika*, 257–270.
36. Anita Desai, *Fire on the Mountain* (New York: Penguin, 1981).
37. G. S. Balarama Gupta, "Anita Desai," in Ramesh K. Srivastava, ed. *Perspectives on Anita Desai* (Ghaziabad: Vimal Prakashan, 1984), 184–188.

Conclusion

1. See Denis Wood, *The Power of Maps* (New York and London: The Guilford Press, 1992); Doreen Massey, *Space, Place, and Gender* (Minneapolis: University of Minnesota Press, 1994); Alison Blunt and Gillian Rose, eds. *Writing Women and Space: Colonial and Postcolonial Geographies* (New York and London: The Guilford Press, 1994).
2. Homi Bhabha, ed. *Nation and Narration* (London and New York: Routledge, 1990). This is a most useful volume including essays by Simon During, Ernest Renan, James Snead, and Bhabha's much-cited essay, "DissemiNation: Time, Narrative, and the Margins of the Modern Nation."
3. Diaspora studies have become increasingly important especially in the field of South Asian writers in English many of whom have won prestigious literary prizes such as the Pulitzer Prize by Jhumpa Lahiri for her text, *The Interpreter of Maladies* (Boston and New York: Houghton Mifflin Co., 1999). Prominent writers in this field include Amitav Ghosh, Michael Ondaatje, Rohinton Mistry, Meena Alexander, Pankaj Mishra, among others. Critical studies of this field are also on the rise—texts such as Rajini Srikanth, *The Idea of America: South Asian American Literature* (Philadelphia: Temple University Press, 2004); Sunaina Maira, *Desis in the House: Indian American Youth Culture in New York City* (Philadelphia: Temple University Press, 2002); Uma Narayan, *Dislocating Cultures: Identities, Traditions, and Third World Feminism* (New York and London: Routledge, 1997); Keya Ganguly, *States of Exception: Everyday Life & Postcolonial Identity* (Minneapolis and London: University of Minnesota Press, 2001); May Joseph, *Nomadic Identities: The Performance of Citizenship* (Minneapolis and London: University of Minnesota Press, 1999), among others. See also *Diaspora and Immigration*, Special Issue ed. V. Y. Mudimbe with Sabina Engel. *The South Atlantic Quarterly*, 98, 1 and 2 (Winter/Spring, 1999); Arif Dirlik, *Postmodernity's Histories: The Past as Legacy and Project* (New York: Rowman and Littlefield Publishers Inc., 2000); Linda McDowell, *Gender, Identity and Place: Understanding Feminist Geographies* (Minneapolis: University of Minnesota Press, 1999); Mary Louise Pratt, *Imperial Eyes: Travel Writing and Transculturation* (New York: Routledge, 1992). Various journals have devoted special issues to postcolonial theory—*South Atlantic Quarterly*; *Inscriptions*;

Social Text, College Literature. Other perhaps less high profile journals that have been steadily providing space over the years for critical discussions of African and "commonwealth" writers include *African Literature Today; World Literature Written in English; The Journal of Commonwealth Literature; Research in African Literatures*.

4. Michel Foucault, *Power/Knowledge: Selected Interviews and Other Writings, 1972–1977*, ed. Colin Gordon (New York: Pantheon, 1972, repr. 1980), 63–77.
5. Frederic Jameson and Masao Miyoshi, eds. *The Cultures of Globalization* (Durham and London: Duke University Press, 1998); Pheng Cheah and Bruce Robbins, eds. *Cosmopolitics: Thinking and Feeling beyond the Nation* (Minneapolis and London: University of Minnesota Press, 1998).
6. Quoted in Teresa de Lauretis, ed. *Feminist Studies, Critical Studies* (Bloomington: Indiana UP, 1986).
7. Comment made by David Henry Hwang at a Multicultural Drama Conference at the University of Massachusetts, Amherst in February 1990.
8. Walter Ong, *Orality and Literacy: The Technologizing of the Word* (London and New York: Methuen, 1982).
9. Rosaura Sanchez, *Chicano Discourses: Socio-Historical Perspectives* (Rowley, MA: Newbury Publishers, 1983), 10.
10. Barbara Harlow, *Barred: Women, Writing, and Political Detention* (Hanover and London: Wesleyan University Press, Published by the University Press of New England, 1992).

INDEX

Aba Riots, 71
abuse. *See* violence
Accompong, 64
Achebe, Chinua, 16, 22, 28–29, 50, 53, 94, 106, 181
activists, xx, 6, 33
Advocate Magazine, 201
Affirmative Action, 129
Africa: bride-price, 174–183; education, 95; English language form, 93, 96; English-language women writers, xviii; fertility in—context, 164; languages, 245; lesbians, 202; linguistic and cultural repression, 27–29; oral story-telling traditions, 32; postcolonial commonalities and differences, xvi; racialized colonial practices, 2, 3; slavery, 229
African literature, xvi
Afrikaans, 96
Agarwal, Bina, 42
Ahmed, Aijaz, 54
Ahmed, Shafat, 197–198
Ahmedabad, x
Aidoo, Ama Ata, 244; dilemma-tale, 183–184; female resistance traditions, 57; infertility, theme of, 11, 160; internalized oppressions, xxii; motherhood demystified, 211–212, 232–233, 241, 243; naming, xii, xiii; reevaluation of women writers, 47, 53; relocation of female body, 3, 7, 16–20, 100–101; use of English language, 25, 27, 28; use of religion, 163; use of short story, 30, 37–38

Air Asiatic, ix
Airlift, 96
Ajmer, x
Akan, 57, 64, 65
Alcestis (Euripides), 169
Alexander, M. Jacqui, 7, 56
Algeria, 80, 81–82
Alloula, Malek, 82–83
ALN. *See* Asian Lesbian Network
ALOA. *See* Asian Lesbians Outside Asia
Alternate Media, xxiv
Ambiguous Adventure (Kane), 92
American Express, 73
Amerindians, 29, 229
Amherst, Massachusetts, ix
amniocentesis, xi
Amos, Valerie, 46
Anandi, 76
Anandi Gopal, 76, 131
Anderson, Benedict, 161
Anglophilia, 120
Anowa (Aidoo), 3, 37, 57, 160, 163, 244
Anuradha, 238–239
Anzaldua, Gloria, 38

Aoko, Gaudencia, 69
apartheid, 3, 20–24, 40, 96, 142, 245, 247
Appadurai, Arjun, 38, 247
Arabic, 116
Arambh, 198
Armah, Ayi Kwei, 19
Arnold, Matthew, 117
arranged marriage. *See* marriage, arranged
Art, Dialogue and Outrage: Essays on Literature and Culture (Soyinka), 16
Art and Ideology in the African Novel (Ngara), 18–19
Ashanti, 57, 62, 64–66
Asian Lesbian Conference, 201
Asian Lesbian Network (ALN), 202
Asian Lesbians Outside Asia (ALOA), 202
Astell, W., 116
Austen, Jane, xv, 31

Babri Masjid destruction, 80, 191
Bakhtin, Mikhail, 6, 9, 30–33
Bala, Sashi, 10
Bald, Suresht Renjen, 89
Bamangwato, 20, 99
Bangalore, x
Bangkok, Thailand, 201
Bantu Education Act, 96
Banyima-Horne, Naana, 47
Barbados, 25
Baroda, x, 239
Barrett, Michele, xxii, 69, 174, 210
BBC, 20
Beautiful Ones Are Not Yet Born, The (Armah), 19
Beckett, Samuel, 104
Bengal, 130, 187
Bengali, xvi
Bennett, Louise, 25
Bentick, 192
Between Men (Sedgwick), 14
Bewitched Crossroad, A (Head), 20
Bhabha, Homi, 93, 246
bhajans, xiv, xxiv
Bharati, 97

Bharatiya Janata Party (BJP), 80
birth control, 235
BJP. *See* Bharatiya Janata Party
Black Fire, 67
Black Power Movement, 109
Blyton, Enid, xvi
Bombanji, Framji, 120
Bombay, India, ix, x, xiv, 8, 25–26, 72, 77, 119, 130, 200, 246
Bombay Dost, 198–201
Boston Collectives, 233
Botswana, 20–24, 99, 143, 231, 247
bourgeois nations, xii
Boyce Davies, Carol, 47, 48
Brahmin, 110, 112–113, 120, 162, 172, 176, 179, 187–191, 193
Braithwaite, Edward Kamau, 25, 36, 37, 140–142, 247
breastfeeding, 62
bride-price, 174–183
Bride Price, The (Emecheta), 159–160, 181
British colonialism, xii, xiii, 55; commonalities and differences, xvi, xxv; disempowerments, 73–77; education and, 92–155; English-language women writers and, xviii; pre-colonial traditions of women's strength, 69–73; racialized colonial practices, 2, 3, 60
British East India Company, 107, 113, 192
British Parliamentary Papers, 105–106, 113
Brodber, Erna, 16, 99, 149–155, 229, 244
Bronte, Charlotte, 31, 142, 169
Bronte, Emily, 31
Brown, Lloyd, 18, 47
bulimia, 3, 9, 99, 122, 136–137, 154–155, 194
Burma, 247
Bush, George W., xiii
Bushmen, 144, 148
Butalia, Urvashi, xxvi
Byron, Lord, 135

Cabral, Amilcar, 5
Calcutta, India, xvi, 77, 112, 113, 117, 118, 247
Calcutta Ladies' School for Native Females, 113
Calcutta University, 130
Calicut, Kerala, ix
Callalloo, 125
Cama, Bhikaji, 77
Cambodia, 247
Cambridge examinations, 109
Cameroon, 247
Campbell, Carl, 108–110
Campbell Prize, Jock, 173
Campbell, R., 116
Caplan, Pat, 85–86
Captain, Perin, 77
Carby, Hazel, xxiii, 46
Caribbean: color codes, 141; education, 95, 109–110; English language form, 93; English-language women writers, xviii; female resistance, 61–62, 65–67; fertility in—context, 164–165; languages, 245; lesbians, 202, 245; linguistic and cultural repression, 27–29; nuclear family structure, 229; obeah, 168; oral story-telling traditions, 32, 34; polygamy, 159; postcolonial commonalities and differences, xvi; racialized colonial practices, 2, 3, 65; religious teachings, 108
Caribs, 29
Carnatic music, xiv
Carpenter, Mary, 130
caste policies in education, 110, 112–118
Chadha, Satyrani, 10
Chakravarti, Uma, 58–59, 118, 188
Changes (Aidoo), xxii
Chatterjee, Partha, 83–84
child-bride. *See* marriage, child
children, hurt, 227–229
Chimurenga, 68
Chingari, Sewa, x
Chipko movement, 43
Chittagong Armoury raid, 77

Chivanda, Mr., 68
Christian ideals, 78, 107, 113, 117, 210
Church of England, 108
Chutney Popcorn, 202
class and education, 112–118, 138–143
Clear Light of Day (Desai), 3, 134, 186, 242
Cliff, Michelle, 40, 150, 247
Collector of Treasures (Head), 20–24, 103, 160, 241
Colonial Harem (Alloula), 82
color, 138–143, 149–155
communalism, xxiv
Contentious Traditions (Mani), 157
contraceptives, 162
Contradictory Omens (Braithwaite), 142
Cott, Nancy, 86
Court, Franklin, 105
Creole, 25, 35
Creole-English, 29, 93
creolization, 141
Crick Crack, Monkey (Hodge), 99, 109, 114, 121, 127, 133
critical practices, 4–6, 20–24
Cry, the Peacock (Desai), 166–167
Cubah (female slave), 63
Cudgoe (freedom fighter), 64
Cudjoe (Maroon leader), 66
cultural alienation, 2, 92–155
cultural imperialism, xii, xxiii, 30
cultural tradition, xvii, 2, 11, 46, 156–208
Cutufelli, Maria, 166, 180

Dalmia, Manju, 117
Daly, Mary, 90–91
dam projects, 43
Dangarembga, Tsitsi, xxv–xxvi, 1, 19–20, 99, 115, 121–124, 157, 167, 186, 244
Darwin, Charles, 88
Das, Bina, 77
Das, Manini, 179
Das Gupta, Kamala, 25, 77, 157, 159, 167–173, 230, 232
daughter, role of, xi, xvii

De, Esha, 12–13
Decolonising the Mind: The Politics of Language in African Literature (Ngugi), 16, 29
decolonizing strategies, xiii, xviii, xxv
deforestation, 43
Deleuze, Gilles, 52
Delhi. *See* New Delhi
Derozio, Henry Louis Vivian, 117
Desai, Anita, 3, 6, 134–135, 159, 166, 174, 186, 242
Desai, Nachiketa, 238–239
de Souza, Eunice, 3, 26–27, 138–139, 207, 244
de Souza, Noemia, 211
Development of Creole Society in Jamaica, The (Braithwaite), 141–142
Devi, Sarala, 77
dialect, 36
dialogism, 30
Diamond, Irene, 49
dilemma-tale, 183
Disciplining Foucault: Feminism, Power, and the Body (Sawicki), 48
discrimination against women, 25, 44
displacement, xx
divorce, 165, 178, 187, 194–198
Dixit, Rekha, 197–198
domesticity. *See* stay-at-home women
Downpression Get A Blow, 34
dowry, 10, 11, 14, 84, 163, 174–183
dowry murder, xvii, 5, 43, 44, 89, 175–179
Draupadi, 87, 164, 174–177
Dube, Leela, 123
Dubois, W.E.B., 52
Dutch, 36
Dutt, Kalpana, 77
Dutta, Madhushree, 179, 238–239

economic dependencies, xii, 45–46
Edinburgh School of Medicine, 130
Educated African, The (Kitchen), 96
education: choices and challenges, 244; colonial, xvi, 2; English, xvii, xviii, 15, 92–155; flag independencies in, 8; socialization and, 10; stay-at-home women and, 73–77
Education Code, 126
Edufa (Sutherland), 157, 168–169
Edwards, Bryan, 64–65, 67
Egypt, 247
Eliot, George, xv
Eliot, T. S., xv, 135
Elphinstone College, 119
Emecheta, Buchi, 17–18, 30–31, 57, 73, 159, 164, 166, 168, 173, 181, 212
Emery, Bessie, 230
English language, x, xiv; educational policies and, 92, 104–112; form, 93, 96; link language for communication, xvi; resistance and, 3, 7, 25–38; stay-at-home women and, 73–77; women writers, xviii
English Teacher, The (Narayan), 105
Episcopalian Church, 120
ethnic cleansings, 246
ethnicity and race, 41
Euripides, 169
exile, xx, 2, 158, 160, 231

Fafunwa, A. Babs, 94–96
family planning, xi, 234–235
Fanon, Frantz, 56, 79, 60, 80–82
female agency and education, 131–134
female body: cultural traditions and, xvii, 156–208; English education and, xvii, 92–155; focus on, xi; motherhood demystified, 209–243; mystified, xvi; processes, 62; theorizing a politics of, 1–55; traditions of resistance, 56–91; women's literary texts and, xvi
female feticide, xi, 84, 233
female infanticide, 84, 90
Female Juvenile Society, 118
Female Novelists of Modern Africa (Taiwo), 19
feminism, xv, 16–18, 41–48, 56
Feminism and Foucault: Reflections on Resistance (Diamond and Quinby), 49

Feminism and Nationalism in the Third World (Jayawardena), 61, 130
Feminism without Borders: Decolonizing Theory, Practising Solidarity (Mohanty), 41–42
Feminist Genealogies (Mohanty and Alexander), 7, 56
fertility, 162, 172, 203, 209–243
Fifteen Year Plan, 109
fire, as religious symbol, 163
Fire on the Mountain (Desai), 242
First World War, 126
flag independence, xii, 8, 56
Flavia, Agnes, 174
folk-dance form, xxiv
Ford-Smith, Honor, 25, 33–36, 67, 204, 207
Forum Against Sex Determination, 237
Forum Against the Oppression of Women, x, 16
Foucault, Michael, 39, 48–53, 60, 98, 190, 197, 247
Four Quartets (Eliot), 135
Freire, Paulo, 102
French, 26, 29, 36, 108, 126
French, Joan, 128, 164–165
From Burning Embers, 188

gana, xxiv
Ganatra, Nisha, 202
Gandhi, Indira, 235
Gandhi, Mohandas, xv, 52, 56, 79, 80, 83–91
Gandhi, Nandita, xx, xxvi, 4, 44
Ganguli, Kadambini, 130
garba, xxiv
gender policies in education, 93, 112–118
genocide, 80, 191
geography, xx, 7–8, 39, 246
Ghana, 74, 95, 96, 168, 243
Ghosh, Amitav, 247
Gilroy, Paul, xiii
Gita, 84
global devastation, xix
Goodison, Lorna, 67, 244

Gopalrao, 76, 131
Gordimer, Nadine, xxiii
Goveia, Elsa, 65, 81, 140–142
Gramsci, Antonio, 52–53
grandmothers mothering, 240–243
Greek, 39, 104
Guadaloupe, 4
Guinea-Bissaue, 111
Gujarati, x, xiv, xxiv, 26, 80, 191, 203, 233, 238
Gupta, G. S. Balarama, 242

Hamam, xiv
Hamlet, 238
Harlow, Barbara, xxii, xxiii, 5, 82
Harris, Governor Lord, 108
Hastings, Warren, 187, 189
Head, Bessie, 244; critical/activist work, 16, 18; critical practice derived from literary text, 20–24; educated women, 102–103; female autonomy over body, 184–185; grandmothers, 241; male-female relationships, 244–245; migration, 3, 247; monogamy, theme of, 160; oral traditions, 7; power of language, 207; racial prejudice, 99, 143–144, 146, 149; state-sponsored violence, 229–232; stay-at-home mothers, 74; theme of education, 112; use of short story, 30
Heinemann, xxvi
herstories, recuperation of, 56–69; colonial disempowerments, 73–77; Indian women and Gandhian satyagraha, 83–88; Indian women's movements, 89–91; national and women's liberation, 77–81; precolonial traditions of women's strength, 69–73; women's resistances, 81–83
Hindu: abolition of sati, 190; conflicts with Muslims, 65, 80–81, 109–110; education, 121; exaltation of suffering, 177; language, x, xiv, 26, 203, 233, 245; female well-being and Hindu fundamentalism, 195–196;

Hindu (*continued*)
 religious line, 65; sacred writings, xvii, 78, 116, 169, 176, 192; tenants of, 117; traditions, 83, 199, 232; use of fire, 163
Hindu College, 117
Hinglish/Hindlish, 93
History of Doing: Indian Women's Movement, The (Kumar), xxvi, 118
History of Sexuality (Foucault), 48–49
History of the Arya Samaj (Rai), 120
History of the Voice (Braithwaite), 36
Hobsbawm, Eric, 161
Hodge, Merle, 244; Caribbean family forms, 229; educational systems, 99, 114–115, 121, 124–125, 127, 133; grandmothers mothering, 242; ideological shifts in aspirations, 109; resistances against sexual inequities, 3
Hopes and Impediments (Achebe), 16
Hosain, Attia, 121, 131
Huggins, Molly, 129
human geographies, 8
Hwang, David, 248

Ibuza, 30
Idu (Nwapa), 212
Igbo, 50, 57, 70–72, 160, 245
Imaginary Maps (Mahasweta), xix–xxiii
Immorality Act, 231, 245
imperialism, 46
India: activists groups in, 6, 33; caste hierarchies, 110; contraceptives, 162; devaluation of currency, xiii; dowry, 174–183; education, 95, 104, 107–108; English, 3, 93; English-language women writers, xviii; English literature, 25; female authority, 71; female roles, xvii, 10–11; fertility in—context, 164; languages, 245; linguistic and cultural repression, 27–29; male-female contact, xv; male sterilization, 235; male vs. female children, 235–236; migration, 247; oral story-telling traditions, 32; partition, 191; postcolonial commonalities and differences, xvi; racialized colonial practices, 2, 3; street theater, 33; traditions of resistance, 83–88; warrior queens, 60; women's education. 118–121; women's health, reporting on, 233; women's movements, 43, 76, 79, 89–91, 118–121; Zoroastrian community, xiv
Indra, M. K., 193
infertility, xvii, 10–11, 162, 203, 209–243
In Search of Answers: Indian Women's Voices from Manushi, 10, 179
International Monetary Fund, xiii
Invention of Tradition (Hobsbawm), 161
Invention of Women: Making African Sense of Western Gender Discourses, The (Oyewumi), 45
inyemedi, 70
Iran, xiv
Ireland, 104
Island Scholarships, 110
Issues at Stake: Indian Women's Movement, The (Gandhi, N., and Shah), xxvi, 44
Italian, 111
Ivory coast, 69

Jagannadhan, Annie, 130
Jagori, 163, 237
Jamaica, 63–67, 93, 141–142, 233
Jamaica Federation of Women (JFW), 128–130
Jamaican School of Drama, 34
Jameson, Fredric, 54
Jamshedpur, x
Jane and Louisa will Soon Come Home (Brodber), 99, 149–155
Jane Eyre, 142, 169
Jayawardena, Kumari, 4, 56–57, 61, 75–78, 83, 90, 130–131
Jehan, Nur, 61
Jehangir, Emperor, 61
JFW. *See* Jamaica Federation of Women
Joshi, Rama, 90, 120, 130, 172
Joyce, James, 104

Joys of Motherhood, The (Emecheta), 73, 164
Jules-Rosette, Bennetta, 69
Junky-Punky Girlz, 202

Kagubi, 68
Kakar, Sudhir, 85–86
Kali for Women Press, xxvi, 203
Kane, Chiekh Hamidou, 92
Kannada, x
Kanvar, Roop, 28, 187–188
kanyadan, 11
Karanth, Prema, 193
Karkal, Malani, 236
Karnataka, x
Kaur, Tarvinder, 179
Kazmi, Nikhat, 236
Keats, John, xiv
Kenya, 25, 69, 95–96
Kerala, x, 201
Khan, Sayyid Ahmed, 120
Khush, 202
Khush Khayal, 198
Kidwai, Saleem, 199
Kikuyu Independent Schools Association, 96
Kincaid, Jamaica, 40, 247
King, Martin Luther, 52
Kinglish, 39, 93
Kishwar, Madhu, 77, 86, 89–91, 172, 175–179, 196
Kitchen, Helen, 96
kitchen fire, xvii, 163
Kofi (freedom fighter), 64
Kosambi, D. D., 192
Kranti, 233
Krishna, Lord, 87
Krishnaraj, Maithreyi, 4–5, 43–44
Kumar, Radha, xxvi, 42, 118–121
Kuper, Dr., 67

Lagos, 30, 181
Lahiri, Jhumpa, 247
Lakshmi, C. S., 97
Lakshmibai, 61
Lalou, Marie, 69

Lamming, George, 21, 22
Lan, David, 66
language, 1–4; as a defining element, x; as resistance, 25–38; choice of, and politics of location, 38–41; critical practice derived from literary text, 20–24; critical practices, 4–6; feminisms for third world, 41–48; politics of female body, 8–20; postcolonial theory and social responsibility, 53–55; sexuality, body and feminists "disciplining" Foucault, 48–53; written and oral forms, 6–8. *See also specific language*
Lapland, 17
Latin, 39, 104
Laws of Manu, The, xvii
Lawyer's Collective, The, 5, 25, 245
Lazarus, Neil, xii
Lefebre, Henri, 39
lesbianism, xi, 2, 10–11, 157, 162, 165, 198–202, 245
Leslie, Molara Ogundipe, 47
Lesser Child: Girl Child in India, A, 235
liberation, national and women's, 77–81
liberation war, 68
Liddle, Joanna, 90, 172
Lie of the Land, The (Rajan), 104
Life (Head), 184–185
lifestory, 34
linguistic violence, 27
Lionheart Gal: Lifestories of Jamaican Women (Ford-Smith), 21, 25, 33–35, 67, 99, 127, 139, 168, 204–207
Lionnet, Françoise, 1, 4
literary form, 6–8, 25–38
Lobengula, King, 68
location, xx, 7–8, 38–41, 100–104
London, England, xx, 96, 201
London University, 130
Lorde, Audre, 200
Los Angeles, California, ix
Lushington, Charles, 106

MacKenzie, Craig, 20
Mackenzie, Holt, 107

Mahabharata, 84, 164
Maharashtra, 238
Mahasweta Devi, xix–xxiii
Mai Chaza, 69
Mair, Lucille Mathurin, 4
Makerere College, 96
Malayalam, x
malnourishment, xi
Manch, Nari Samta, 180
Mandela, Nelson, 231
Mani, Lata, 156–158, 161, 188–192, 194–195
Manly, Michael, 34
Manushi, 5, 175–178, 233
Mapaulos, 69
Marathi, 26
Markandaya, Kamala, 121–124, 174
Maroons, 64–68
marriage: arranged, 46, 170–171; child, 75–76, 79, 90, 131, 167; monogamous, 164–173; primary purpose of education, 128
Marriage of Anansewa (Sutherland), 181
Martin, Biddy, 248
Maru (Head), 99, 143–144, 155
Masarwa, 99, 143–149
Mashonaland, 68
Masjid, Babri, 195
Masks of Conquest (Viswanathan), 39, 104
Mass Weddings, 165
Mathura, 25, 43
Mathurin, Lucille, 61–66, 140, 142
Mayo, Katherine, 90–91
Mazumdar, 78
Mbembe, Achille, 247
Mboya, Tom, 96
McLintock, Annie, xii
Mediastorm, 189
Menon, Ritu, xxvi
menstruation, 62
mental breakdown, 154, 157, 167–168, 230, 232
Mies, Maria, 174
migration, 2, 10, 246–247. *See also* relocation

militancy. *See* violence
Mill, John Stuart, 88
Milton, John, 29
Mirror, The, 127
mobility, 12–13, 78
Mohamedans, 113
Mohanty, Chandra, 4, 7, 8, 41–42, 55, 56, 247
Mondoro, 67
Mootoo, Shani, 202
Morgan, Robin, 42
Morton, Sarah, 127
motherhood: as choice, 232–235; child's gender, 235–240; demystified, 209–213; glorification of, xvi, 157; grandmothers mothering, 240–243; pressures of, 2; role of, xi, xvii, 73–77, 164; state-sponsored violence, 229–232; violences of, 215–229; womanhood as, 213–215
Mother India (Mayo), 90
Moyne Commission Report, 128–130, 165
Ms. Magazine, 230
Muffet Inna All a Wi, 182
Mukherjee, Meenakshi, 101
Mulenga, Alice Lenshina, 69
Munro, Thomas, 106, 113
Muslims, 65, 80–81, 109–111, 116, 120, 187, 191, 195–196, 199
Mwari, 67
My Body is Mine, 233
My Story (Das), 157, 167–173, 230, 232
My Story...Our Story of Rebuilding Broken Lives (Flavia), 174
mythology, 56, 60, 87, 172

Naidu, Sarojini, 77
Nairobi, 96
naming, power of, xii, 16, 71
Nana Yah, 67
Nanny (Maroon leader), 66–67
Narayan, R. K., 105
Nari Itihas Ki Khoj Mei (Women in Search of Their History), 6, 179
Narmada River, 43

natak, xxiv
National Conference of Women's Movements in India, ix, xxiv, 200
National Gathering of Women who Love Women, 200–201
National Gay and Lesbian Task Force, 201
nation language, 36
Ndebele, 68
Nehanda, 57, 66–67, 69, 91
Nehru, xv, 83
NEP. *See* New Economic Policy
Nervous Conditions (Dangarembga): bulimia, 3, 9, 99, 122, 136–137, 154–155, 194; educational systems, 99, 114–115, 132, 139; female victimization, 8; language, 1; mental breakdown in, 154, 167–168, 244; physical and psychological resistance via education, 136–138; publishing of, xxv–xxvi, 20; self-worth, 181; single woman, 186; traditions of female sexuality, 121, 193–194; use of silence and speech, 157
New Delhi, India, x, xiii, 163, 188, 200
New Economic Policy (NEP), 234
New Jersey, 201
New York, New York, ix, xiii
Ngara, Emmanuel, 18–19
Ngcobo, Lauretta, 17, 176, 180
Ngoni, 180
Ngugi wa Thiong'o, 16, 25, 28–29, 30, 65
Ni, 57, 66–68, 91
Nigeria, xvi, xxiii, xxvi, 6, 70, 75, 93, 95, 96
Nkomo, Joshua, 69
Nobel Prize in Literature, xxiii, 3, 6
No Sweetness Here (Aidoo), 100–100, 183–184, 232, 243
Nwapa, Flora, xxvi, 18, 47, 57, 159, 212
Nyerere, Julius, 95–96

oaths, 168
Obbo, Christine, 174
obeah, 168

O'Callaghan, Evelyn, 150
Odaka, Julia, xxv
Ode to the West Wind, The (Shelley), 105
Ogu Umunwanyi, 71
Oheama, 57
Oldenburg, Talwar, 71–72
oral story-telling traditions, 6–8, 21, 30–37, 48, 59
Orientalism (Said), xii, xxiii, 83
Our Bodies, Our Selves, 203, 233
Oxford, 130
Oyewumi, Oyeronke, 45

Pakistan, 80, 135, 191
Pala, Achola, xxi
Pandey, Divya, 236
Parliamentary Committee on the Affairs of the East India Company, 110
Parmar, Pratibha, 46, 202
Parsees, 112
Parsi. *See* Zoroastrian
partition, 80, 135, 155, 191
Patel, Vibhuti, x, xx–xxi, 4, 43
Pathak, Zakia, 195–198
pativrata, 10
Patkar, Medha, 43
patois. *See* patwah
patriarchy, 2, 48, 55, 74, 79
Patriarchy and Accumulation on a World Scale (Mies), 174
Patterson, Orlando, 66
patwah, 3, 25, 30, 34–35, 93, 207, 245
Pearse, Adetokunbo, 230–231
Perinbam, Marie, 82
Phaniyamma (Karanth), 193–194
Phelps-Stokes Commission, 95
Philadelphia, Pennsylvania, 130
Philip, Marlene Nourbese, 30, 39, 93
Phule, Jyotirao, 119
pidgin, 3, 25, 30, 93
placetime, 13
politics of female body, xviii
Pollard (native commissioner), 68
polygamy, 14, 73, 159
Port Royal, 63

Portuguese, 29, 111
postcolonialism, xiii, xiv–xxiv, 53–55
Postmodern Geographies: The Reassertion of Space in Critical Social Theory (Soja), 145
power relations, 57–58, 60
Premlata, 179
Prohibition of Dowry Act, 175
proletarian nations, xii
property inheritance, 79
prostitution, 71–72, 183–186
Punjabi, x, 245
Puranic techniques, 50
Pushkin, Alexander, 29

Quaco (freedom fighter), 64
Queenlish, 93
Question of Power, A (Head), 207, 230–231
Quinby, Lee
Qunta, Christine, 66, 68

Rabelais and His World (Bakhtin), 32
race and education, 95, 143–149
race and ethnicity, 41, 99
Race and the Education of Desire (Stoler), 49
racial superiority, 2
Radhakrishnan, R., 51–53
Rai, Lajpat, 120
Rajan, Rajeswari Sunder, 104–106, 195–198
Rajasthan, x, 163, 188
Rajbundah, 113
Rajkot, 130
Ramabai, Pandita, 76, 120, 130
Ramayana, The, 58, 177
Ranade, Ramabai, 75, 77, 130
Ranchi, 200
Ranger, Terence, 66–69, 161
Rani of Jhansi, 57, 87, 91
Rao, Raja, 50
rape, xi, 25, 43, 169–173, 229
Rashtriya Swayamsewak Sangh (RSS), 80
Rastafarian, 150

Razia, Sultana, 61
Rebel Woman in the British West Indies during Slavery, The (Mathurin), 61, 65
Recasting Women: Essays in Colonial History (Sangari and Vaid), xxvi, 26, 74
Reddock, Rhoda, 125–127, 129
religion: balance with secular education, 104; central to community, 67–69; deployment of, 108; divisions, 65, 80–81; fundamentalism, xxiv; mystification of female sexuality and, 163; ideological base, 60; policies in education, 112–118
relocation, xx, 2, 10, 100–104, 124–131
reproductive abilities, as form of resistance, 56
Research Center for Women's Studies, 235
resistance: language and, 1–55; strategies, xxv; traditions of, 56–91; via education, 134–138, 143–149
Revolt in Southern Rhodesia (Ranger), 68
Rhodes, Cecil, 68
Rhodesia, 67, 168, 193
Rhys, Jean, 99, 142–143, 157, 166, 168–169
Robertson, Claire, 93–93, 107, 110–111
Roy, Arundhati, 43
Roy, Kum Kum, 58–59
Roy, Rammohan, 75, 118, 189, 191–192
Royal Reader, The, 37
RSS. *See* Rashtriya Swayamsewak Sangh
Rukmabai, 130–131
Rushdie, Salman, xv, xx, 247
Ruskin, John, xv, 86, 88
Russian, 29
Rwanda, 246

Sabla Mahila Sangh, x, 233
Sacks, Karen, 165
Sadan, Sharada, 120
Saheli, 4, 16, 237

Said, Edward, xii, xxiii, 52, 83
SALGA, 199
Same-Sex Love in India (Vanita and Kidwai), 199
Sanchez, Rosuara, 249
Sangari, Kumkum, xxvi, 26, 74–75, 78–79
Sangat, 199
San Jose, California, 199, 201
Sanskrit, 76, 116, 120, 199
Saraswati, Dayanand, 120
Sardar, Fahmida, 198
Sarkar, Sonita, 12–13
Sasvika, x
Satanic Verses, The (Rushdie), 247
sati, 5, 28, 75, 79, 90, 158, 163, 187–190
satyagraha, 77, 83–88, 90
Savitri, 87
Sawicki, Jana, 48
Schoolmaster, The, 127
Schuler, Monica, 65
Scotland, 104
Scripts, 200
Second Class Citizen (Emecheta), 212
Second World War, 109
Sedgwick, Eve, 14–15
Senior, Olive, 16, 47, 227
Serowe: Village of the Rain Wind (Head), 21
Setswana, 231
sexist inequalities, xv, 8–9, 55, 94
Sex Pre-Selection Techniques, 237
sexual harassment, xii
sexuality, xi, 13–14, 202–207, 48–53. *See also* female body
sexual promiscuity, xv
Shah, Nandita, xxvi, 44
Shahbano, 187, 194–198
Shakespeare, William, 29, 105, 182, 239
Shakti Khabar, 198
Shelley, Perry Bysshe, 105
She Tries Her Tongue, Her Silence Softly Breaks (Philip), 30
Shohat, Ella, xii
Shona, 1, 66, 67, 136, 154, 245

Shukla, Sonal, xx, xxiv
silence, as form of resistance, 56
single mothers, 217–227
single women, xvii, 101, 157, 159, 162, 165, 186–192
Sisterhood is Global: The International Women's Movement Anthology (Morgan), 42
Sisters and Wives: The Past and Future of Sexual Equality (Sacks), 165
Sistren (publication), 5, 21, 33–34, 99, 127, 139, 159, 164, 168, 182, 233
Sistren (women's group) 4, 6, 25, 36, 67, 163, 207
Sita, 87, 174–175, 177
sitting on a man, 57, 70
Slave Girl, The (Emecheta), 166, 168–169, 173
slavery, 61–65, 81, 229
Slave Society in the British Leeward Islands (Goveia), 81, 140
SNDT University, 16, 235
social change, x–xi, xxiii
social custom, xvii
socialization and politics of body, 9–10, 92–155
social reformers, 61, 75–79, 88, 118–121
social responsibility, postcolonial theory and, 53–55
Soja, Edward, 8, 13, 38, 145–146, 149
song, xxiv
Sorabjee, Cornelia, 130
South Africa, xxiii, 3, 4, 17, 20–24, 40, 96, 136, 230–231, 245, 247
South Asian Lesbian and Gay Association. *See* SALGA
Soweto, 96
Soyinka, Wole, xxiii, 6, 16, 22, 55, 151, 181
space, 39, 101
Spanish, 29, 36, 108, 126
Sparrow, Lord, 36–37
Speech Genres and Other Late Essays (Bakhtin), 9
Spenser, Edmund, 29

spirit mediums, 57, 66–69
Spivak, Gayatri Chakravorty, xix–xxiii, 4, 49–51
Stalinism, 51
stay-at-home women, 73–77, 79, 210
Steady, Filomena, 45
sterilization, 162
Sterling, J., 126
St. Joseph's College, ix
St. Lucia, xxiii
Stoler, Ann Laura
Story of my Experiments with Truth (Gandhi, M.), 83
storytelling, 20–24
Stree Jagruti Samiti, x
Stree Sangam, 200
street theater, xxiii, 6–7, 25, 33, 43, 179
Studies in a Dying Colonialism, 81
Studies on Women and Population (Karkal and Pandey), 236
Stuttgart Congress of the Second Communist International, 77
Sudarkasa, Niara, 47
Sunlight on a Broken Column (Hosain), 121, 131
Sutherland, Efua, 18, 157, 168–169, 181
swaraj, 90
Sweet Sugar Rage, 36

Taban Lo Liyong, 17
Taiwo, Oladele, 19
Tamil, x, 245
Tamil Nadu, x
Tana Press, xxvi
Tanganyika, 96
Tanzania, 96
taxation, 56, 70, 72
Teachers Journal, The, 127
technological mothering, 232–235
Telugu, x
Tempest (Shakespeare), 29
Tennyson, Alfred, xv
Thadani, Giti, 199
Thapar, Romila, 59
Things Fall Apart (Achebe), 94, 106
third world, feminisms for, 41–48

Third World Women and the Politics of Feminism (Mohanty et al.), 41
Tiffin, Helen, 50–51
Tlali, Miriam, 17
Tokyo, Japan, xiii
Tolstoy, Leo, 29
Touching, Feeling: Affect, Pedagogy Performativity (Sedgwick), 15
Trans-Status Subjects (De and Sarkar), 12
Trikone, 199, 201
Trinidad, xvi, xviii, xx, 29, 108–110, 126–127, 141, 242, 245
truth-force movement. *See* satyagraha
Turner, Victor, 2
Two Virgins (Markandaya), 121–122

Uganda, 96
umuada, 70
unemployment, 94
Uniform Civil Code, 245
United States, 4, 96, 199, 243
University College, 96
University of California, Los Angeles, xvi
University of Nairobi, 25
urbanization, 73
Urdu, 199

Vacha, xxiv
Vaid, Sudesh, xxvi, 26, 74–75, 78–79
Vaid, Urvashi, 201
Vajradanti, xiv
Valmiki, 59
Van Allen, Judith, 70–71
Vanita, Ruth, 199
Vasaria, Saroj, 175
Vedas, 199
vernacs. *See* vernacular-medium schools
vernacular-medium schools, 26, 93, 101
Victorian ideals, 78, 86, 88, 93, 119, 210
Vidyalamkara, Gourmohan, 118
Vidyasagar, Ishwarchandra, 75, 118–119
violence, xi, 44–45; abuse, xvii, 23–24, 90; against lesbians, 2; as form of resistance, 56, 62, 66, 77;

beyond physical, 80–81; liberating form of, 82; of motherhood, 215–229; state-sponsored, 229–232
Virtual Equality (Vaid, Urvashi), 201
Visa, 73
Viswanathan, Gauri, 25, 39, 102, 104, 107, 116–117, 190
Vivekananda, Swami, 75
Vividh Bharati Hindi, xiv
voice, as form of resistance, 56, 63, 157, 207–208
Vyas, Neena, 10

Waddadar, Preeti, 77
Wadley, Susan, 172
Walcott, Derek, xxiii
Wales, 104
Walker, Alice, 212
warrior women, 57, 60–61
Washington, D.C., xiii
Wide Sargasso Sea (Rhys), 99, 142–143, 157, 166, 168
Widow Remarriage Act, 79
widows: conditions, 10–11, 76–77, 244; contradictory empowerments of, 193–194; cultural traditions, xi, 157, 159, 162, 186–192; immolation, 5; prejudice toward, xvii; remarriage, 76, 119
wife, role of, xi, xvii, 73–77, 86, 157, 162, 166
Wild Woman in the Woods, 202
Williams, Eric, 109
Winter's Tale, The (Shakespeare), 182

womanhood as motherhood, 213–215
Women, Labour and Politics in Trinidad and Tobago: A History (Reddock), 125–126
Women in Search of Their History. See *Nari Itihas Ki Khoj Mei*
Women of Africa (Cutrufelli), 180
Women's Collective. See Stree Sangam
women's health, xi
Women's Hospital, 130
Women's Institute of Great Britain, 129–130
Women's Medical College, 130
Women's Press, The, xxv–xxvi
Women's Review of Books, The, xxv
women's war, 71
Women Writers in Black Africa (Brown), 18
Woolf, Virginia, 19, 212
Wordsworth, William, xiv, 31
working women vs. nonworking women, xxi
Wretched of the Earth, The (Fanon), 80
written literature, 6–8, 157, 207–208

Yards in the City of Kingston (Brodber), 16
Yoruba, 70
Yugoslavia, 246

Zambia, 69
Zanzibar, 96
Zimbabwe, xviii, xxv–xxvi, 67
Zoroastrian, xiv

About the Author

KETU H. KATRAK, born in Mumbai, India, is professor in the department of Asian American studies, and affiliated with the departments of English and comparative literature at the University of California, Irvine. Katrak's leadership as chair of Asian American studies (1996–2004) led the unit to establish a B.A. degree, and to achieve department status. Prior to her appointment at UCI, Katrak was professor for ten years in the department of English at the University of Massachusetts, Amherst. As a scholar, Katrak specializes in Asian American and diasporic literature; postcolonial literature and women writers from Africa, India, the Caribbean; and feminist theory. Katrak's publications include a book on the Nigerian Nobel Laureate, Wole Soyinka, entitled *Wole Soyinka and Modern Tragedy: A Study of Dramatic Theory and Practice*. She has published widely on African women writers (afterword to Ama Ata Aidoo's *No Sweetness Here*; essay on Bessie Head in *World Writers in English*), and on postcolonial women and feminism in journals such as *College Literature, Journal of Commonwealth Literature,* and *Modern Fiction Studies* among others. Katrak is the recipient of the Bunting Institute Fellowship, the University of California Humanities Research Institute Fellowship, and a Fulbright Research Award.